Worcester County Maryland Orphans Court Proceedings Volume 2 1800-1816

David V. Heise

Courtesy of the Maryland State Archives
Worcester County Register of Wills
(Orphan Court Proceedings)
MSA C2033

HERITAGE BOOKS
2011

HERITAGE BOOKS
AN IMPRINT OF HERITAGE BOOKS, INC.

Books, CDs, and more—Worldwide

For our listing of thousands of titles see our website at
www.HeritageBooks.com

Published 2011 by
HERITAGE BOOKS, INC.
Publishing Division
100 Railroad Ave. #104
Westminster, Maryland 21157

Copyright © 2000 David V. Heise

Other Heritage Books by the author:

Somerset County, Maryland Orphans Court Proceedings
Volume 1: 1777–1792 and 1811–1823
Volume 2: 1823–1838
Volume 3: 1838–1852

Worcester County, Maryland Orphans Court Proceedings
Volume 1: 1777–1800
Volume 2: 1800–1816
Volume 3: MH23, 1816–1832

All rights reserved. No part of this book may be reproduced or transmitted in any form or by any means, electronic or mechanical, including photocopying, recording or by any information storage and retrieval system without written permission from the author, except for the inclusion of brief quotations in a review.

International Standard Book Numbers
Paperbound: 978-1-58549-570-2
Clothbound: 978-0-7884-8853-5

INTRODUCTION

Volume 2 of the Worcester County, MD, Orphans Court Proceedings covers 1800-1816. I had hoped to go through 1825, but it was becoming too large. The clerks in Worcester Co. recorded much more information than their counterparts in Somerset Co.

The proceedings settle into a predictable pattern by 1800, each session starting with guardian bonds, followed by apprenticeships, valuations, distributions, indentures & Court orders, with various other matters thrown in from time to time. The creeping laziness of the late 1700's disappears, with full names being given instead of initials &, by 1804, the father's name returns to guardian bonds in most cases. The best source for information becomes the indentures, which give the birth date.

Book 10, 1805, is a collection of papers related to the estate of Col. Zadok Purnell. Possibly these were put together during the litigation mentioned in the account. This is the only book that departs from the pattern mentioned above.

As in Vol. 1, original spelling has been retained. When needed, clarification is given. While I have included an index of those who are identified as slaves or free Negroes, those doing Black genealogy should check the General Index, as I am sure some were not so identified. Be sure to look up every listing for those you are researching, as many implied marriages can be found by following the records over time.

Every attempt has been made to make these abstracts accurate, but as always, be sure to check the original records. I trust this volume will be a great help to all doing research in this part of Maryland.

TABLE OF CONTENTS

BOOK 7, JBR-3, 1800-1802.................1

BOOK 8, JBR-9, 1802-1804...............40

BOOK 9, 1804-1805......................85

BOOK 10, 1805.........................118

BOOK 11, MH-7, 1806-1809..............121

BOOK 12, MH-15, 1809-1811.............197

BOOK 13, MH-17, 1812-1816.............252

GENERAL INDEX.........................343

INDEX TO SLAVES.......................406

INDEX TO FREE NEGROES.................409

INDEX TO INDIANS......................412

BOOK 7, JBR 3, 1800 - 1802

MICROFILM: CR 46,718-3

MSA No.: CM 1123-7

Worcester County Orphans Court Proceedings, JBR-3, 1800 - 1802

F. 1   Tues., Aug. 12, 1800   John Postly, Esquire, Justice

Zadok Sturgis, Esq., Sheriff   James B. Robins, Register

John Postly, Josiah Mitchell, William Corbin appointed Justices

Ben Ogle   Alexander C. Hanson, Chanc.

F. 2   Oct. 14, 1800   John Postly, William Corbin present

Guardian bonds;

F. 3
Orphan; Samuel Howard
Guardian; Martha Howard [couldn't write]
Sureties; Isaac Dashiell, Stephen Howard [neither could write]

F. 4
Orphan; John Howard
Guardian; Martha Howard
Sureties; Isaac Dashiell, Stephen Howard

F. 5
Orphan; Charlotte Howard
Guardian; Martha Howard
Sureties; John Dashiell [signed Isaac], Stephen Howard

F. 6
Orphan; Robert Wright
Guardian; Attlanta Wright
Sureties; Selby Parker, Zadok Sturgis

F. 7
Orphan; Nancy Wright
Guardian; Attalanta Wright
Sureties; Selby Parker, Zadok Sturgis

F. 8
Orphan; John Wright
Guardian; Attalanta Wright
Sureties; Zadok Sturgis, Selby Parker

Orphan; Isaac Layfield
Guardian; Joseph Houston
Sureties; Anderson Patterson, Samuel Nicholson

F. 9
Orphan; Thomas Benson [also Benston]
Guardian; Michael Cluff
Sureties; William Corbin, Sewell Turpin

F. 10
Orphan; Henry White
Guardian; George Hayward
Sureties; Joseph Kellam, Alexander McAllen

F. 11   Orphan; Nehemiah Stockley Robins
         Guardian; Capt. Thomas R. Handy
         Sureties; Capt. George Hayward, James Handy (of Wm.)

F. 12   Orphan; Daniel Gore Robins
         Guardian; Thomas Handy
         Sureties; George Hayward, James Handy (of Wm.)

         Apprentice; Lemuel Henderson (of Bishop), 15
         Bound to; Joseph Bishop
         Trade; carpenter & joiner
F. 13   Sureties; Samuel Stevenson, William Cropper

F. 14   Bond from John Postly, to secure property of Caleb Powell
         taken under an attachment: sureties; Hillary Pitts, Zadok Sturgis

F. 15   Property of Caleb Powell, exe. of Milby Powell, applied to
         discharge claim against him by Catherine Powell, exex. &
guardian to deceased's children; claims include debts to Zed.
Bradford, Wm. Burbidge, Jesse Holloway, John Walter, Jesse Timmons,
         Benj. Jarman; also mentions Watson Collins; Catherine is
F. 16   widow of Milby

Charles Hammond & Belitha Burbage to view estate of John & Joshua
         Prideaux (of John), in care of John Bowen, guardian: sworn
F. 17   before Esme Purnell: report

         Hezekiah Johnson & Joshua Duer to view estate of Rebecca
F. 18   Kellam (of John), in care of Hannah Kellam, guardian: report;
         due 1/4 of real estate of John Kellam, 440 acres, & right of
dower; sworn before Philip Quinton

F. 19   Apprentice; Ezekiel Smashy (of James), 14
         Bound to; William Cropper
         Trade; Shoemaker
         Sureties; Hillary Pitts, Thomas N. Williams

F. 20   Apprentice; Kendal Tubbs (of Joseph), 14 on 8 Dec. next, with
         permission of his mother, Sally Hudson [couldn't write]
         Bound to; Ashur Burrows [also Burroughs], cordwinder & tanner
F. 21   Trade; shoemaker
         In presence of John P. Mitchell, John Postly

         Apprentice; Jesse Crapper (of Jesse), 15 last July, by
F. 22   permission of his mother, Abia(?) Crapper
         Bound to; Isaac I.(?) Evans, cordwainer
         Trade; cordwainer
F. 23   Surety; William Coventon

         Apprentice; James W. Taylor [couldn't write](of Charles), 17
         on 11 May last, by permission of his mother, Hannah Taylor
         Bound to; William Lister, blacksmith
         Trade; blacksmith

F. 24   Apprentice; Handy Smith (of Levi), 16 on 29 Apr. last, by
        permission of his mother
F. 25   Bound to; Elijah Reed [also Read], carpenter & joiner
        Trade; house carpenter & joiner
        Surety; Sterling Jones
        In presence of John Postly, Anderson Patterson

F. 26   Letters of collection granted to John Buckhannon on estate of
        John McGivan

Martha Howard, guardian to Samuel, John & Charlotte Howard, excused
from rendering accounts until they come of age

Isaac Ayres & John Hudson to view estate of Moses Quillen, in hands of
Benjamin Quillen, his next of kin

Rachel Coulborn, guardian to James, Rachel, Charlotte & John Coulborn,
excused from passing accounts

Hezekiah Johnson & Sarah Price, exes. of Arthur Price, to sell
personal estate, except negroes, a still, the new pewter & books

F. 27   John Whittington & William Schoolfield to view estate of
        Isaac Layfield, in care of Joseph Houston, guardian

Jacob Dale & Sterling Jones to view estate of Wingate Smith, in care
of William Smith, guardian

Joshua Hammond, adm. of Solomon Knox, allowed $40 for negro Henry
included in inventory

Littleton Robins & Edward Henry to view estate of John Turpin, in care
of Sewell Turpin, guardian

Littleton Robins & Edward Henry to view estate of Anne Turpin, in care
of Southey Whittington, guardian

Esther Layfield, exe. of Isaac Layfield, to sell personal estate,
except negroes

George Bell & Laban Johnson to distribute negroes from estate of Rouse
Fassitt, in hands of Thomas Fassitt & Sarah, his wife, adms.

Capt. Charles Bennett & Benjamin Dennis, Esq., to distribute [estate?]
of Joshua White among representatives of Barclay White

F. 28   Thomas N. Williams, adm. of Layfield Collier, to sell enough
        personal estate to cover debts

Sarah Townsend, adm. of William Townsend, to place ad in some Delaware
paper for creditors to meet at house of William Hudson, St. Martins,
to receive their share of estate

George W. Purnell & Henrietta Purnell, exes. of Dr. John Purnell, to sell estate

Samuel Dickerson, adm. of Jesse Dickerson, to sell personal estate

F. 29   Receipt of Cornelius Ennis, guardian to Jesse Ennis, for $53.33 (L.20), for land condemned for road

Receipt of John Webb [couldn't write] to James Blades for profits of estate in hands of Solomon Pepper; mentions heirs of W. Melvin Test.; Joshua Duer, Selby Blades

F. 30   John Postly, William Corbin & Maj. John Holland appointed Justices

Guardian bonds;

F. 31   Orphan; Isaac Puzey
        Guardian; John Riggen
        Sureties; James Riggen, Levi Townsend

F. 32   Orphan; John Price
        Guardian; Eliakim Johnson
        Sureties; Thomas Turner [couldn't write], Michael Tarr

F. 33   Orphan; Isaac Benson
        Guardian; William F. Adams
        Sureties; Joseph Schoolfield, Joseph Houston

F. 34   Orphan; William Benson
        Guardian; Robert Sneed
        Sureties; Capt. Joshua Prideaux, Anderson Patterson

Orphan; Arthur Price
Guardian; Michael Tarr
Sureties; Eliakim Johnson, Joshua Tarr

F. 35   Orphan; Benjamin Davis
        Guardian; Annanias Powell
        Sureties; John Tingle, James Selby (of Ezkl.)

F. 36   Orphan Margaret Fassitt
        Guardian; Dr. Thomas S. Fassitt
        Sureties; Laban Johnson, Charles Hammond

F. 37   Orphan; William Price
        Guardian; Sarah Price [couldn't write]
        Sureties; Samuel Bradford [couldn't write], Coulbourn Long

F. 38   Orphan; Molly Rankin
        Guardian; James Selby
        Sureties; John Davis, John J.(?) Williams

F. 39
Orphan; James Rankin
Guardian; James Selby
Sureties; John Davis, John J.(?) Williams

F. 40
Orphan; George Rankin
Guardian; James Selby
Sureties; John Davis, John J. Williams

F. 41
Orphan; Sarah A. Rankin
Guardian; James Selby
Sureties; John Davis, John J. Williams

F. 42
Apprentice; Major Bird
Bound to; Thomas Dryden
Trade; blacksmith
Sureties; Thomas Mitchell, James Riggen

F. 43
Apprentice; Joshua Truitt (of Tabitha), 9
Bound to; Matthew Jones
Trade; farmer
Sureties; John Davis, John Williams

F. 44 Account of sale of negroes from estate of Benjamin E. Bishop, by Frederick Conner, guardian to Levin & Charlotte Bishop; negroes Bridget & Phillis in one lot; Rhoda & child in other lot

Robert M. Richardson, clk.

F. 45
Apprentice; William Long, by permission of his father Levin Long (taylor)
Bound to; James Milliches(?)
Term; 4 years

F. 46
Trade; saddle maker or saddler
In presence of Jesse Bennett, Benjamin Dennis

F. 47
Apprentice; Peter Claywell (of Moses), poor orphan boy, by permission of his mother
Bound to; George Houston [also Holston]
Term; 8 years from 20 Sept. next
Surety; John Houston
Trade; farming

F. 48
In presence of Benjamin Dennis, Jesse Bennett

Sally Patrick, adm. of John Patrick, allowed $41.77 for error in inventory, as proved by oath of Col.(?) Joshua Prideaux

Esther Layfield, exe. of Isaac Layfield, to sell personal estate, except negroes

F. 49 Betsy Holland, adm. of Thomas Holland, to sell personal estate, except negroes

Peter S. Corbin & James B. Selby to view estate of Sarah Purnell, in care of Zipporah Purnell, guardian

Anna Townsend, exe. of Levin Townsend, to sell personal estate

William Corbin & Jonathan Hudson to view estate of Isaac Puzey, in care of John Riggen, guardian

John Taylor & Thomas Slocomb to view estate of John Price, in care of Eliakim Johnson, guardian

Levin Merrill & William Schoolfield to view estate of William Benson, in care of Robert Sneed, guardian

George Bell & Laban Johnson, Esqs., to distribute estate of Rouse Fassitt, in hands of Thomas S. Fassitt & Sarah, his wife, adms.

F. 50   Thomas Slocomb & John Taylor to view estate of Arthur Price, in care of Michael Tarr, guardian

Levin Mitchell & Edward Henry to view estate of Benjamin Davis, in care of Annanias Powell, guardian

George Bell & Laban Johnson to view estate of Margaret Fassitt, in care of Thomas S. Fassitt, guardian

Thomas Slocomb & John Taylor to view estate of William Price, in care of Sarah Price, guardian

John Buchannan, collector of John McGivan, to sell estate

James [surname not given], adm. of Anne Selby, allowed 10% commission on estate

Capt. Levin Mitchell & John Franklin to view estate of Molly, James, George & Sarah Rankin, in care of James Selby, guardian

Time limited for Sarah Townsend, adm. of William Townsend, by order at last term to notify creditors to meet, is extended to 1st of April

F. 51   Charles Hammond, guardian to Isaac Selby, to expend 8% per annum of principle of orphan's estate for education

Charles Hammond, guardian to Nancy Selby, [same as above]

Rev. Samuel McMasters & John Whittington to distribute negroes & legacies from estate of Isaac Layfield, in hands of Esther Layfield, exe.

Esther Layfield, exe. of Isaac Layfield, & Isaac Layfield, devisee of the deceased's apportion the rent due from the tenant of [blank] exex., taking the part of the rent that accrued before the death of the deceased the devisee after [blank, very confusing entry]

Adm. dbn granted to Sarah Rackliff on estate of John Rackliff, Sen.

F. 52   John Holland & Jesse Bennett to view estate of Nehemiah S. &
        Daniel G. Robins, in care of Thomas R. Handy, guardian

Isaac Layfield, devisee of Isaac Layfield, vs. Esther Layfield, exe.
of Isaac Layfield; plaintiff entitled to all corn & other annual crops
that was growing in the actual or fancy(?) of the devisor himself at
the time of his death

F. 53   Special Court, Jan. 9, 1801, at request of Isaac Ayres;
        William Corbin, John Holland present

Isaac Ayres vs. Mary Purnell, relict of Elisha; letters of adm. to be
taken on estate

Isaac Ayres vs. Mary Purnell, exe. of Elisha; Col. Samuel Handy,
McKimmy Porter & Col. John Gunby to arbitrate

Joseph Houston & Zadok Wheeler to view estate of Isaac Benston, in
care of William F. Adams, guardian

Mary Gunn, exe. of Henry Gunn, to sell personal estate

F. 54   Joseph Houston & Zadok Wheeler to view estate of Thomas
        Benson, in care of Michael Cluff, guardian

Elizabeth Townsend, adm. of Capt. Levin Townsend, to sell negro girl
Rachel & other personal estate, with cattle & horses, to pay debts

Letters of adm. granted to Isaac Brittingham on estate of Solomon
Brittingham

F. 55   Special Court, Jan. 23, 1801, at request of Esther & Peter
        Waters; William Corbin, John Holland present

Adm. of estate of Patrick Waters granted to Esther & Peter Waters

Esther & Peter Waters, adms. of Patrick Waters, to sell personal
estate, except negroes, to pay debts

Adm. of estate of Nehemiah Dorman granted to Matthias Dorman

F. 56   Tues., Feb. 10, 1801   All Justices present

Levin Pollitt, Esq., Sheriff

Orphan; William Price
Guardian; Samuel Bradford [couldn't write]
Sureties; Selby Parker, Curtis Henderson

F. 57   Orphan; Joseph Nicholson
        Guardian; John Dickerson
        Sureties; William Dickerson [couldn't write], Thomas Dryden

F. 58
Orphan; Levi Richardson
Guardian; Joseph Richardson
Sureties; John Bishop, Thomas Mitchell

F. 59
Orphan; James Brevard
Guardian; Adam Brevard
Sureties; Hillary Pitts, John Fassitt

F. 60
Orphan; Nancy Nicholson
Guardian; Betty & William Dickerson [neither could write]
Sureties; Thomas Dryden, George Houston

F. 61
Orphan; Peter White
Guardian; George Hayward
Sureties; John Townsend, Valentine Dennis

Orphan; Joshua Davis
Guardian; Coulborn Long [signed Colvern]
Sureties; Hampton Long, Phillip Morris [couldn't write]

F. 62
Orphan; Edward Davis
Guardian; Colvern Long
Sureties; Hampton Long, Phillip Morris

F. 63
Apprentice; James Jones, mulatto
Bound to; William Corbin
Trade; common labourer
Sureties; Jonathan Hudson, Jun., John Riggen

F. 64
Apprentice; Jemima Jones, mulatto
Bound to; William Corbin
Trade; kitchen servant
Sureties; Jonathan Hudson, Jun., John Riggen

F. 65
F. 66
Apprentice; Leonard Jones, mulatto
Bound to; William Corbin
Trade; common labourer
Sureties; Jonathan Hudson, Jun., John Riggen

F. 67
F. 68
Apprentice; John Jones, mulatto
Bound to; William Corbin
Trade; common labourer
Sureties; Jonathan Hudson, John Riggen

F. 69
Apprentice; Levin Jones, mulatto
Bound to; William Corbin
Trade; common labourer
Sureties; Jonathan Hudson, Jun., John Riggen

F. 70
F. 71
Apprentice; Henry Riggen, 10
Bound to; Levin Blake
Trade; shoemaker
Sureties; Maj. Edward Henry, Zadok Purnell, Esq.

F. 72	Jacob Teague & Jesse Bennett to view estate of Levi Richardson (of Levi), in care of Joseph Richardson, guardian;
F. 73	sworn before Peter S. Corbin: report
F. 74	John N. Whittington & William Schoolfield to view estate of Isaac Layfield, in care of Joseph Houston, guardian; sworn
F. 75	before Anderson Patterson: report on estate of Isaac Layfield (of George)
F. 76	Joseph Houston & Zadok Wheeler to view estate of Isaac Benson, in care of William F. Adams, guardian; sworn before
F. 77	Levi Henderson: report on estate of Thomas & Isaac Benson (of
F. 78	Elias), in care of Michael Cluff & William F. Adams,
F. 79	guardians; mentions 1/3 of land belongs to William Benson, in care of Robert Sneed, guardian
F. 80	Levin Mitchell & John Franklin to view estate of Molly, James, George & Sarah A. Rankin, in care of James Selby,
F. 81	guardian; sworn before Thomas N. Williams: report; 120 acres
F. 82	Levin Mitchell & Edward Henry to view estate of Benjamin Davis, in care of Annanias Powell, guardian: report; 100
F. 83	acres; Powell's wife has right of dower
F. 84	Apprentice; James Lambden, 15 on 25 Oct. 1800, by permission of his mother, Mary Roach Bound to; John Hall Trade; shoemaker Surety; Esme Burton [also Ismey Buntg][Bunting?] In presence of Levi Henderson, Anderson Patterson
F. 85	Apprentice; Robert Hall, by permission of his father Jesse, of Somerset Co. Bound to; John Hall Trade; shoe & boot maker
F. 86	Surety; Zadok Wheeler In presence of Levi Henderson, Anderson Patterson
F. 87	Apprentice; Charles Tunnell, of Accomack Co., VA, 16 on 10 Mar. next, by permission of his father Charles Bound to; William Tingle Trade; hatter
F. 88	In presence of Wm. Whittington, John C. Handy
F. 89	Apprentice; William Richardson, by permission of his father Whittington Richardson [couldn't write] Bound to; Joseph Bishop Trade; house joiner Witness; John Bishop N. B.- apprentice born Sept. 12, 1781

F. 90	Apprentice; John Bartlet Cameron, by permission of his father William Bound to; John White (of Southy) Term; till 21, on 6 Mar., 1811 Trade; carpenter
F. 91	In presence of John Gunby, Jesse Bennett
F. 92	Apprentice; Levi Henderson, by permission of his mother Susanna Bound to; Levi Houston Trade; cooper Surety; James Henderson In presence of Levi Henderson, Anderson Patterson
F. 93	Apprentice; Robert Mears Baker (of Hancock), 16 on 21 Apr. next, by permission of his mother Martha Johnson, wife of James Bound to; Able Hickman, cart wheel wright Trade; cart wheel wright Term; till 1806
F. 94	Surety; William Dale, Joshua Prideaux Before Thomas N. Williams, Henry Bell
F. 95	Apprentice; Moses Tubbs (of John), 5 on 7 Apr. next; his mother also dead Bound to; James Tubbs, house carpenter Trade; house carpenter before John Postly, Thomas N. Williams Surety; Asher Burroughs
F. 96	Capt. Charles Bennett & Benjamin Dennis, Esq., to distribute estate of Joshua White among representatives of Barclay White; sworn before Peter S. Corbin, Jan. 16, 1801
F. 97	1) To William White; negro woman Hetty, 4/5 of woman Hannah 2) To Henry White; negro boy Elijah, woman Jany(?), 1/5 of Hannah, 1/5 of man Elijah 3) To Peter White; negro woman Sally, 4/5 of man Elijah
F. 98	At request of Dr. Thomas Fassitt, who intermarried with adm. of Rouse Fassitt, George Bell & Laban Johnson appointed to divide negroes from estate; sworn before John Postly, 9 Dec., 1800 1) To Dr. Thomas S. Fassitt & wife; negro man Tony, 47; slim Jacob, 19; Paul, 28; Peter, 1; Rhoda, 42; Rose, 70
F. 99	2) To Mrs. Zipporah Fassitt; James, 47; Jacob, 23; James, 70; Daniel, 8; Lanty, 6; Susa, 1; Rhoda, 30 3) To Mrs. Peggy Fassitt; Isaac, 47; little Jacob, 16; Pleasant, 24; Cool(?), 72; Priss, 6; Sall, 18

Mary Purnell, exe. of Elisha Purnell, to pay to Isaac Ayres L.7/17/8 as cost of suit in which said Ayres was sued for land sold him by Elisha Purnell

F. 100	17 Feb., 1801	Saml. Handy McKimmey Porter John Gunby

Petition of Peter S. Corbin, adm. dbn of Daniel Robins; a dispute exists between Eleanor Fallarton, adm. of William Fallarton, of PA, plaintiff, & your petitioner, in the general court of this
F. 101   state; asks persons to be chosen to settle dispute; granted

John Fassitt, adm. of William Fassitt, allowed L.43/13 for property inserted in inventory, but claimed by James Fassitt under the will of his father, John Fassitt; list

William Selby & William Quinton, exes. of Samuel Nicholson, to sell negro & tools

F. 102   By agreement between Leonard Jones, master, & Leah Jones, mother of Effe, James, Jemima, John & Leonard Jones; master released from recogenzance entered into to said apprentices

William Melvin, guardian to Thomas Robertson, to sell negro girl Esther, & he may apply L.20/17/6 to his own use for advances made by him for education & maintainance of ward in 1799 & 1800

William Q. Dixon, guardian to Thomas W. Dixon, discharged from passing accounts

Thomas Hall, adm. of Joshua Bowen, to sell perishable estate

Elisha Purnell & Littleton R. Purnell appointed to arbitrate between Eli Hudson & wife, exes. of Joseph Ennis, & Samuel Ennis, on
F. 103   accounts 1 & 2

Register to enquire of Anna Messick, adm., if estate of George Messick has increased or decreased, & adjust accounts

Admx. of Stephen Roach, Sen., allowed for negroes Titus & Sylvia out of inventory, & Register to strike distribution

William Tingle vs. Daniel Tingle, adm. of Elijah Tingle; adm. to shew cause why personal estate should not be sold prior to Aug. next

Dr. Thomas S. Fassitt & Zadok Sturgis to distribute negroes of James Parker, deceased, in hands of Milby Purnell, adm.

Colborn Long & wife discharged from guardianship to William Price

John Taylor & Thomas Slocomb to view estate of William Price, in care of Samuel Bradford, guardian

Capt. John Rock & George Hayward to view estate of Joseph Nicholson, in care of John Dickinson, guardian

F. 104   Capt. Jacob Teague & Jesse Bennett, Esq., to view estate of Levi Richardson, in care of Joseph Richardson, guardian

George Rice, adm. of John S. Bratten, to advertise in Cowan's paper in Easten for creditors to exhibit claims

Register to strike distributions of estates of John & Lambert Collier, & also of Sarah Collier, deceased [also Collyer]

Thomas N. Williams, adm. of Layfield Collyer, allowed for crop on hand on devised lands as improperly appraised

Annanias German, adm. of Purnell Henderson, to sell estate

Citation at instance of David Wilson, exe. of William Morris, for Nancy Morris to shew cause why part of estate was concealed

Mary Gunn, guardian to Henry & George Gunn, to get into staves or otherwise sell timber within certain parcel of out ground

F. 105   At instance of Thomas Dixon & others, securities of Henry Gunn, deceased, Mary Gunn, adm., to sell estate to satisfy debts due to Edmond or Levin Dickerson for purchase money of two tracts of land called 'Partners Choice' & 'Bucks Point'

Joshua Prideaux, guardian to Elizabeth Marshall, discharged from passing accounts

Benjamin Wails, John Stevens & wife, exes. of John Marshall, ordered to pay L.25 to Esme Waller, William Kellam & wife

George Bell & James King to view estate of James Bravard, in care of Adam Bravard, guardian; guardian to fell timber & get it into shingles or otherwise sell the same

F. 106   Isaac Layfield, devisee, by Joseph Houston, guardian, vs. Esther Layfield, adm. of Isaac Layfield; Rev. Samuel McMasters & John Whittington to distribute crop on land devised to Isaac by Isaac, deceased

Peter S. Corbin, adm. dbn of Daniel Robins, allowed L.5, the appraised value of negro Sophia, included in inventory & since dead

Daniel Tingle, exe. of Elijah Tingle, to sell estate

Capt. Thomas Hall & Eli Hudson to view estate of Joshua & Edward Davis, in care of Colbourn Long, guardian

Colborn Long & wife, exes. of Edward Davis, allowed for horse & cow included in inventory & since dead

When John Williams & wife find new security for administration of estate of John Turpin, James A. Collins & John Bratten, original securities, discharged: new securities; Isaac Ayres, Thomas N. Williams

F. 107   Thomas N. Williams, Esq., adm. of Layfield Collyer, to give notice in Cowan's paper at Easton for creditors to exhibit claims

Register's report of distribution of estate of William Townsend among creditors confirmed

At instance of George Rosse, adm. dbn of Eleanor Stevens, Isaac Cowper, one next of kin, to shew cause why account of Levin Townsend, late adm., should not be passed; Isaac Cowper, by James P. Wilson, his counsel, appears & consents to account being passed

Will of Thomas Powell, Sen., transmitted by Register of Anne Arundel Co. under special act of Assembly, to be admitted to probate, which is proved by oath of John Postly, Esq., he having first renounced appointment of exe. & the bequests therein made him

New seal now in this office with impression of an eagle hovering her young - Motto Orphans Court Wor. County - "Momento Mori" be received

John Riggin, guardian to Isaac Puzey, to sell estate

F. 108   John Puzey, late guardian to Isaac Puzey, allowed $17.29

John Bishop & Lanta Wright, adms. of John Wright, to give notice in Cowan's paper at Easten for creditors to exhibit claims

John P. Mitchell, adm. dbn of Joshua Mitchell, discharged

Received Oct. 23, 1797, of Benjamin Aydelott, L.6/3/11 for balance of two years accounts with James Aydelott

John Massey   William Aydelott

Received Oct. 23, 1797, of Benjamin Aydelott, L.6/3/11 for balance of two years accounts with James Aydelott

    her   John Massey
Test.; Ann X Smith
    mark

Received Jan. 7, 1797, of Benjamin Aydelott, guardian to James Aydelott, deceased, payment of 1/3 part of James' estate

    her   William Aydelott
Anne X Smith
    mark

          Received Jan. 7, 1797, of Benjamin Aydelott, guardian to
F. 109   James Aydelott, deceased, payment of 1/3 part of James'
          estate
    her   John Massey
Anne X Smith
    mark

F. 110   Tues., Apr. 14, 1801   John Postly, William Corbin present

Orphan; John Evans
Guardian; George Dikes
Sureties; James Bacon, John White

F. 111   Orphan; Nancy Evans
         Guardian; George Dikes
         Sureties; James Bacon, John White

F. 112   Orphan; Sally Evans
         Guardian; George Dikes
         Sureties; James Bacon, John White

         Apprentice; Severen Britt
         Bound to; Joshua Evans
F. 113   Trade; cordwainer
         Sureties; Robert Nairn, Peter White

F. 114   Apprentice; John Blake, 9 on 21 Dec. last
         Bound to; John Bounds
         Trade; farmer
F. 115   Sureties; Major Dorman, James Smith

F. 116   Apprentice; Hannah Blake, 1 last Aug.
         Bound to; Major Dorman
         Trade; spin & weave
         Sureties; John Bounds, James Smith

F. 117   Apprentice; Isaac Tindall, 11 last Aug.
         Bound to; Obed Brittingham
         Trade; farmer
F. 118   Surety; John Allen

F. 119   In pursuance of order dated Feb. 10, 1801, directing me to
         sell negro girl Esther, property of Thomas Robertson, minor,
to satisfy claim for education & maintainance, my being the highest
bidder, she was struck off to me at $104.; Apr. 14, 1801, William
Melvin makes oath regarding above sale

William Corbin & Thomas Dixon, Esq., to view estate of John Flemming,
         deceased, as far as Joshua & James Flemming are concerned, in
F. 120   behalf of William Warwick & Elinor, his wife, guardians;
         Sworn before Jesse Bennett: report, exclusive of widow's
F. 121   thirds

F. 122   William Corbin & Jonathan Hudson to view estate of Isaac
         Pewsey, in care of John Riggen, guardian: report; mentions
widow's thirds; mentions late guardian

F. 123   Apprentice; Peter Dickerson, born 8 May, 1784, by permission
         of his father, William, planter in Indian Town
         Bound to; George Nelson, house joiner & carpenter
         Trade; house carpenter & joiner
F. 124   in presence of Patrick Waters

'15'

F. 125   Edmond Crapper, exe. of Edmond Crapper, allowed $65 in commissions & $40 for maintaining an old negro woman

F. 126   Tues., June 9, 1801   All Justices present

F. 127   Apprentice; John S.(?) Allen, 17
Bound to; William Duncan
Trade; farmer
Sureties; Joshua Hammond, John Ward

F. 128
F. 129
F. 130   George Bell & Laban Johnson to view estate of Margaret Fassitt (of Rouse), in care of Dr. Thomas S. Fassitt, guardian: report; includes plantation where Jackson Turner lives, plantation where James Steel lives, plantation adjoining Reuben Crapper, plantation where Elijah Fassitt lives; no slaves or working beasts on plantations

F. 131   George Bell & James King to view estate of James Brevard, in care of Adam Bravard, guardian: report; no improvements, land low & not possible to reclaim without ditching; one negro boy Daniel, 7

F. 132
F. 133   Thomas Slocomb & John Taylor to view estate of William Price, in care of Sarah Price, guardian; sworn before John Cottingham: report

F. 134
F. 135   Thomas Slocomb & John Taylor to view estate of Arthur Price, in care of Michael Tarr, guardian; sworn before John Cottingham: report; 50 acres

F. 136   John Taylor & Thomas Slocomb to view estate of John Price, in care of Eliakim Johnson, guardian; sworn before John Cottingham: report

F. 137
F. 138
F. 139
F. 140   Peter S. Corbin & James B. Selby to view estate of Sarah Purnell, in care of Zipporah Purnell, guardian; sworn before John Holland: report; mentions land next to Gunby's Mill; mentions widow's dower; tenement occupied by widow Brittingham; father is John Scott Purnell, deceased

F. 141   Apprentice; Burton Bradford (of Levin), 18 on 2 Oct. last, by permission of his mother, Nanny
Bound to; Peter Lister, blacksmith
Trade; blacksmith
Surety; John Massey
In presence of John Postly, Thos. N. Williams

F. 142   Apprentice; William Powell Rean, 12 on 20 Jan. last, at request of Isaac Lewes, who intermarried with John Rean's widow; John Rean, former master; William illegitimate son of Comfort Rean, deceased
Bound to; Isaac Lewes [couldn't write]
Trade; farming

(cont.)

F. 143
Test.; Henry Bell, John Postly
Surety; Zadok Lewes

F. 144
Apprentice; Shadrack Melly Turner, 12 on 21 Feb. last, by permission of his father Samuel, of Sussex Co., DE [couldn't write]
Bound to; Samuel Gray
Trade; farming & miller's business
Surety; James Johnson

F. 145
Apprentice; Peter George, 11
Bound to; Noble Dryden, Jun., farmer & chair maker
Trade; farmer, chair maker
Sureties; Noble Dreadon, John Taylor
Before Jno. Holland, Peter Spencer Corbin

F. 146
Apprentice; Jesse, mulato
Bound to; James Cottingham
Trade; farming
Sureties; Elijah Willyss, Wm. Bacon
Before Thos. Dixon, William Corbin

F. 147
Apprentice; James Ruark, 2 on 26 May last, by permission of his mother, Priscilla Ruark
Bound to; William Butler
Trade; common labour such as farmer's business
Sureties; Jonathan Noble, Rackliff Morris
Before John Cathell, Isaac Hearn

F. 148
Capt. Charles Bennett & Benjamin Dennis, Esq., to distribute estate of Joshua White, Jun., among sons of Barclay White; Before Jesse Bennett;

F. 149
1) To William White; 1/3 of 2/3 of negro man Limas(?)
2) To Henry White; 1/3 of 2/3 of negro man Limas
3) To Peter White; 1/3 of 2/3 of negro man Limas

Sarah Newton, exe. of Levin Newton, to sell personal estate, except legacies

Esther & Peter Waters, adms. of Patrick Waters, to advertise in Cowan's paper at Easton for creditors to exhibit claims

F. 150
Elijah Brittingham, exe. of John Penewell, to sell personal estate

Peter Chaille, Esq., exe. of William Allen, allowed 10% commission in passing final account & L.11/9 on account of Esme Bayley's claim, miscalculated by former Register

Timothy Irons & John Dorman, guardians to Thomas, William & Littleton Dorman, to sell negroes

'17'

Michael Tarr, guardian to Arthur Price, to clear land to make 10 acres, which shall be laid off by John Taylor & Thomas Slocomb, the receivers(?)

John Holland, exe. of Jonathan Hutcheson, to advertise in Cowan's paper at Easton for creditors to exhibit claims

Esther Layfield, guardian to Thomas Layfield, to cut as much dead cypress as necessary for repairing mill, education of orphan & completing dwelling house

F. 151   George Purnell, exe. of Betsy Gunn, to sell estate

George Purnell, adm. dbn of Samuel Gunn, to advertise in Cowan's paper at Easton & Wayne's Philadelphia paper for creditors to exhibit claims

F. 152   Tues., Aug. 11, 1801   All Justices present

Orphan; John Bowen
Guardian; Elizabeth Bowen [couldn't write]
Sureties; Thomas P. Rackliff, Robert Hudson

F. 153   Orphan; Kitty Bowen
          Guardian; Elizabeth Bowen
          Sureties; Thomas P. Rackliff, Robert Hudson

F. 154   Orphan; Joshua Bowen
          Guardian; Elizabeth Bowen
          Sureties; Thomas P. Rackliff, Robert Hudson

          Orphan; Sally Bowen
          Guardian; Elizabeth Bowen
F. 155   Sureties; Thomas P. Rackliff, Robert Hudson

          Orphan; Hetty Bowen
          Guardian; Elizabeth Bowen
F. 156   Sureties; Thomas P. Rackliff, Robert Hudson

          Orphan; Sally Newton
          Guardian; Sarah Newton [couldn't write]
F. 157   Sureties; Shadrach Sturgis, Laban Hudson [couldn't write]

          Orphan; Nancy Newton
          Guardian; Sally Newton [signed Sarah]
F. 158   Sureties; Shadrach Sturgis [couldn't write], Laban Hudson

Orphan; Charlotte Newton
Guardian; Sally Newton [signed Sarah]
Sureties; Laban Hudson, Shadrach Sturgis

F. 159   Orphan; Polly Turner
          Guardian; Alexander McAllen [signed McKallen]
          Sureties; Levi Houston, William Esham

F. 160   Orphan; Sally Turner
         Guardian; Alexander McKallen
         Sureties; Levi Houston, William Esham

         Orphan; Mary Warren
F. 161   Guardian; Thomas Dale
         Sureties; Joshua Prideaux, Thomas N. Williams

         Orphan; Isaac Warren
         Guardian; Thomas Dale
F. 162   Sureties; Joshua Prideaux, Thomas N. Williams

         Apprentice; Isaac Henderson (of Purnell)
         Bound to; George Truitt (of Patey)
         Trade; farmer
F. 163   Sureties; James A. Collins, John Davis

         Apprentice; John Turnwell[?](of Thomas), 13
         Bound to; John Hudson
F. 164   Trade; shoemaker
         Surety; Angello Atkinson

F. 165   Jackson Brown, apprentice, discharged from apprenticeship to
         Andrew Brown, master

         Apprentice; Jackson Brown (of William), 11
         Bound to; John Hudson
         Trade; shoemaker
F. 166   Surety; Angello Atkinson

F. 167   Apprentice; Ned Taylor, son of Lina, mulatto, 13
         Bound to; William Corbin
         Trade; farmer
         Sureties; Zadok Townsend, Samuel Dorman

F. 168   Capt. George Hayward & John Rock to view estate of Joseph
         Nicholson, in care of John Dickerson, guardian; sworn before
F. 169   Zadok Purnell: report; no slaves, 130 acres

F. 170   Maj. John Holland & Jesse Bennett to view estate of Nehemiah
         S. & Daniel G. Robins, in care of Thomas R. Handy, guardian;
F. 171   sworn before Peter S. Corbin; report

F. 172   Littleton Robins, Sen., & John Bishop to view estate of
         William & John H. Bishop, in care of George Truitt, guardian;
F. 173   sworn before Elisha Purnell: report; 40 acres

F. 174   William Corbin & Thomas Atkinson to view estate of Jonathan
         Watson, in care of Major Hudson, guardian; sworn before Thos.
F. 175   Dixon: report

F. 176   Apprentice; George Noble, son of Mary, 5 on 28 Apr. last
         Bound to; William Littleton [couldn't write]
         Trade; common labour
F. 177   Surety; Thomas Lewis
         Before Boaz Walston, John Cathell

         Apprentice; William Gullet, son of Elizabeth, 10 on 28 Mar. last
F. 178   Bound to; Whittington Cox [couldn't write]
         Trade; common labour
         Sureties; William Bigland, William Bruington, Jun. [couldn't write]
F. 179   Before Boaz Walston, John Cathell

         Apprentice; Charles Dickenson (of Jesse), 17 on 20 May last, his mother also dead
         Bound to; Henry Burrows [also Burroughs], cordwainer
         Trade; cordwainer
F. 180   Test.; John Postly, Thos. N. Williams
         Surety; George Truitt

         Apprentice; Nathaniel Brittingham, by consent of his mother
F. 181   Bound to; Elijah Nelson, blacksmith
         Trade; blacksmith
         Term; 7 years
         Surety; John Allen
         Before Jno. Holland, Peter S. Corbin

F. 182   Apprentice; George Peters, free mulatto, with consent of his mother
         Bound to; Littleton Taylor
         Trade; labour
         Term; 15 1/2 years
         Sureties; John Tull, Hope Taylor
         In presence of Thos. Dixon, Jno. Holland

F. 183   Apprentice; Sally Riggen, 10 on 31 July last
         Bound to; Levin Derickson
         Trade; spinster
         Sureties; Robert Nairne, Isaac Collins
         In presence of Trustees for the Poor; Saml. Handy, Wm. Selby, George Hayward

F. 184   Apprentice; Ephriam Peters, 19, by consent of his mother
         Bound to; Ebenezer Hall
         Trade; common labour
F. 185   Surety; Isaac Hearn (of John)
         In presence of Boaz Walston, Isaac Hearn

         Apprentice; Isaac Dreadon [listed once as Brittingham], 10 on 11 July last, by application of Thomas Dreadon, guardian
         Bound to; James Merrill
         Trade; cooper
                                (cont.)

F. 186   Surety; Levin Merrill
           Before Anderson Patterson, Levi Henderson

           Apprentice; James Taylor, 12 on 11 Aug., 1801, by permission
           of his father, Joseph
F. 187   Bound to; Elijah Bennett [Barnett?. couldn't write]
           Trade; farming
           Surety; Ephraim Furness
F. 188   Before Levi Henderson, Anderson Patterson

Dr. Thomas S. Fassitt & Zadok Sturgis, Esq., to distribute estate of
James Parker, in hands of Milby Purnell & wife, adms.; sworn before
           Esme Purnell;
F. 189   1) To Milby Purnell; negroes Guy the elder, Stephen, Dinah
           the younger
2) To Sarah Parker (orphan); Sambo, Dinah the elder, Jack, Minto(?),
Guy the younger, Caesar

John Williams & Henrietta, his wife, vs. George Rice, adm. of John S.
Bratten; two notes of hand on Dr. Edward Rownd, amounting to L.5/10/2
1/2 were put in hands of John S. Bratten for the use of Henrietta by
Littleton R. Purnell for articles purchased by him at sale of John
Turpin's estate, of whom Henrietta is adm., which notes were not
delivered to her by said Bratten in his lifetime; George Rice to
deliver notes

List of Legacies in William Allen's estate paid by Peter Chaille,
           acting exe.; memorandum of negroes freed by will;
F. 190   1) To Warner Mifflin; negroes Bob, Amus(?), James, Philliss
           2) To Elizabeth Teacle; woman Nan
3) To L. Dennis; boy Peregrine
4) To J. Dennis; boy James
5) To Esme Bailey; Daniel, Dick
6) To Jane Cotman; L.25, 1st wife's wearing apparel
7) To P. Chaille; Tom
8) To Sally Hall; Lucy
9) To Susannah Gunby; Liddy
10) To William Handy; silver watch

           Petition of Cornelius Ennis, Sen., guardian to Rachel Ennis
F. 191   (of Cornelius, Sen.); negro woman Sabro had one child, now
           has four; Esther, 6; Sinah, 4; Sall, 2; David, 2 months:
cannot bare expense; court orders sale of Sabro, Sall & David

Capt. Thomas Taylor & Rowland E. Bevans to view estate of Nancy
Newton, in care of Sarah Newton, guardian

Levi Sturgis, guardian to John Williams, discharged from passing
accounts

Isaac Cottingham, guardian to Luke Townsend, discharged from passing
accounts, as no profit is arising from estate

'21'

Copy of will of William Franklin, from Registry of Philadelphia, filed by Sarah Franklin, one exe.; Levin Derickson, one exe., refuses to act

F. 192 Peter Delastatius, guardian to Elizabeth Walton, to apply up to 10% of principle for ward's education

View of estate of Peggy Fassitt to be recinded & Thomas S. Fassitt, guardian, to rent real estate

John Dorman, guardian to Littleton & Thomas Dorman, discharged from passing accounts until estate is L.50

George Truitt, guardian to William & John Bishop, to give each 3 months schooling

David Stevenson, adm. of James Stevenson, allowed 10% commission on collection of monies due, as he had extraordinary trouble collecting

David Stevenson, adm. of James Stevenson, discharged from prosecuting any further suits against Zadok Purnell, Sen.

Peter Chaille, exe. of William Allen, allowed 10% on monies
F. 193 paid creditors & 7 1/2% on residue of estate

Hillary Pitts vs. George Rice, adm. of John S. Bratten; amicable suit to be filed to determine title of property of negro Levin

William Corbin, adm. of William Brown, allowed 10% on balance of estate

By consent of James McFadden, his guardianship to Sally & Polly Turner recinded

Benjamin Gunby & Benjamin Aydelott to view estate of Polly & Sally Turner, in care of Allexander McAllen, guardian

James Franklin, adm. of Ebenezer Franklin, to sell personal estate as soon as inventory is made

Arthur McAllen, adm. of Morgan Bradshaw, to sell estate

F. 194 Part of view of estate of Robert & Milby Kerby, relating to valuation, rescinded; guardian to rent estate

John Postly, Esq., trustee of Milby Powell, allowed 5% on inventory

Laban Johnson, exe. of Mary Lawrence, allowed 10% on balance of money in his hands as compensation for collecting

Benjamin Dennis & Charles Bennett to view estate of Henry & Peter White, in care of George Hayward, guardian; guardian to sell estate, except negroes

Account of stock lost from Jesse Ennis' estate, by Cornelius Ennis, guardian

F. 195   Register to deduct 4 sheep & 2 cattle mentioned above

Register to settle what sum should be deducted from estate of Rachel Ennis, orphan, recovered of Cornelius Ennis, guardian, by representatives of Nelly Ennis, for property paid to guardian by mistake

Distribution of estate of Samuel Dorman, by William Selby (S. H.) & McKimmey Porter, rescinded & they to strike distribution; Charles Townsend, exe.

Peter Chaille, exe. of William Allen, to retain $200 to prosecute a suit vs. James Duer in Court of Chancery

F. 196   Tues., Oct. 13, 1801   All Justices present

Orphan; Anne Gillett
Guardian; Samuel McMasters
Sureties; John C. Handy, Ezekiel Wise

F. 197   Orphan; Nehemiah Redden
          Guardian; John Payne
          Sureties; James B. Selby, Thomas Milbourn

          Orphan; John Selby (of Daniel)
F. 198   Guardian; James Selby (of Jno.)
          Sureties; Selby Parker, Robert M. Richardson

William Davis & Mary, his wife, discharged from guardianship to Peter Parker

          Orphan; Peter Parker (of Jno.)
          Guardian; Selby Parker
F. 199   Sureties; Alexander McAllen, James Selby (of Capt. John)

Orphan; John Rackliffe
Guardian; William Winder, Sen.
Sureties; Zadok Sturgis, Edward H. Rownd

F. 200   Orphan; Rider Henry Rackliffe
          Guardian; William Winder, Sen., of Somerset Co.
          Sureties; Zadok Sturgis, Edward H. Rownd

          Orphan; Charlotte Rackliffe
F. 201   Guardian; William Winder, Sen., of Somerset Co.
          Sureties; Zadok Sturgis, Edward H. Rownd

          Orphan; Kitty Henry(?) Rackliffe
          Guardian; William Winder, Sen., of Somerset Co.
F. 202   Sureties; Zadok Sturgis, Edward H. Rownd

F. 203   Orphan; Elizabeth Truitt
         Guardian; Anne Truitt, of Talbot Co.
         Sureties; Samuel Stevenson, Peter Truitt

F. 204   Apprentice; Mitchell Hudson (of John), 14
         Bound to; Timothy Irons
         Trade; tanner & currier
         Sureties; William Corbin, Angello Atkinson

F. 205   Apprentice; Levin Taylor [also Tyler], 17 Aug. last
         Bound to; John Ward
         Trade; cordwainer
         Sureties; Joshua Evans, Peter Evans

F. 206   Apprentice; Samuel Whittingham (of Heber), 14 on 2 Apr. last
         Bound to; James Marshall
         Trade; cabinet maker
         Sureties; William Stevenson, Samuel Stevenson

F. 207   Capt. Thomas Taylor & Rowland E. Bevans to view estate of
         Nancy Newton, in care of Sarah Newton, guardian; sworn before
F. 208   Jno. Holland: report; 71 acres as of her half; no slaves

F. 209   Thomas Selby & Kendall Patty to view estate of Kendal
         Collyer, in behalf of Sarah Collyer, guardian to Lambert
F. 210   Collyer; sworn before Thomas N. Williams: report

John P. Mitchell & Richard Sampson to view estate of John Baker, in
care of Edward Hammond, guardian; report

F. 211   Benjamin Aydelott & Benjamin Gunby to view estate of Polly &
         Sally Turner, in care of Alexander McKallen, guardian; sworn
F. 212   before Peter S. Corbin: report

List of sales of property of Levi Puzey, in care of John Riggen,
guardian; articles sold to Leah Lankford, John Riggen, Thomas Lokey,
         John Dreadon, Mary(?) Pewsey, John Powell, Pierce Rygen,
F. 213   Lowden Rygen, Purnell Pewsey, Addams Denston, James
         Brodwaters: letter of Pierce Riggen to William Corbin; I will
swear to above sale when I can

         Account of sale of property (negroes excepted) of Henry &
F. 214   Peter White, by Capt. George Hayward, guardian; list of
F. 215   articles sold; Capt. George Hayward swears to above sale
         before William Corbin

         Apprentice; John Scott, 15 on 13 Sept., 1801, son of Rebecka
         Lewes
F. 216   Bound to; James Lewis
         Trade; common labour
         Surety; William Littleton [couldn't write]
F. 217   Before Boaz Walston, Isaac Hearn

'24'

F. 218
Apprentice; William Massey (of John), 10 last Apr., by permission of his mother, Sarah
Bound to; William Covington [also Coventon]
Trade; to make pine furniture, farming
Sureties; Zadok Sturgis, Samuel Holland
Before John Postly, Henry Bell

F. 219
Apprentice; Henry Gunby Bell, 10 last July, by permission of his mother, Ruth Bell
Bound to; Ava(?) Melvin
Trade; farming
Sureties; John Melvin
In presence of Levi Henderson, Anderson Patterson

F. 220   John Williams, adm. of John Hudson, to sell personal estate

Samuel McMasters, guardian to Anna Gillett, to account for profits on estate, and a new view & estimate to be returned

Joshua Duer & Nehemiah Holland to view estate of Nehemiah Redden, in care of John Payne, guardian

Peter S. Corbin & William Holland, Jun., to view estate of John Selby (of Danl.), in care of James Selby, guardian

F. 221
James Selby, adm. of Daniel Selby, to sell personal estate (negroes excepted)

William Davis & Mary, his wife, guardians to Salley & John Parker, to apply up to $10 [10%?] of principle yearly to educate them

Esther Layfield, exe. of Isaac Layfield, to sell as many negroes as needed to pay debts

Account of sale of negro woman Esther, from estate of John Turpin, by Sewell Turpin, guardian; account received, guardian allowed 3% commission

F. 222   Adm. dbn granted to James Franklin on estate of Esther Ironshire

Isaac Collins & Tabitha, his wife, adms. of William Stevenson, allowed lowest priced mare in inventory; mare of no value, since lost

Elzey Maddux, guardian to Lazarus Maddux, allowed L.84, if it doesn't exceed profits of estate, for maintainance of William Maddux

Stephen Roach vs. A. Messex, exe. of George [Messex?], late guardian; George Pollitt & Stephen Disharoon to revalue estate of said Stephen

Mecken & Cochran vs. George Purnell, adm. dbn of Samuel Gunn; petition to have protested bill of exchange & amount tendered at last term passed, if no objections; George Purnell appears, by William
(cont.)

F. 223   H. Winder, his counsel, & objects, as plaintiff neglected making claim in due time

George Purnell, adm. dbn of Samuel Gunn, & exe. of Betty Gunn, late adm., allowed for articles in original inventory

Hannah Tull, exe. of John Tull, deceased, by John Tull, one representative; Register to receive receipts of all representatives now of age & of the guardians of those underage, in case John Tull becomes guardian

Distribution already struck on estate of John Wise rescinded & negro girl Sarah & two children, included in inventory, to be allowed Tabitha Wise, exe., & debt due from Levin Martin, returned sperate, to be deducted; new distribution to be struck

F. 224   Ezekiel Wise, for representatives of John Wise, vs. Tabitha Wise, exe.; above order, allowing debt due from Levin Martin, objected to; rescinded

Lanta Purnell, adm. of John S. Purnell, late adm. of Rosanna Martin, to retain 6% commission on sale of Rosanna's estate & to account with Thomas Martin, adm. dbn of Rosanna, for balance

William Winder, Sen., granted adm. dbn on estate of John Rackliff, Jun.

George Bell & Levin Mitchell to view estate of John, Rider H., Charlotte & Kitty H. Rackliff, in care of William Winder, Sen., guardian; guardian to lease real property

William Winder, Sen., exe. of Sarah Rackliff, to sell personal estate (except negroes)

F. 225   John A. Townsend, exe. of Leah Townsend, to sell personal estate, negroes & legacies excepted

Elizabeth Truitt, guardian to Ann Truitt, to demand & receive all property of minor & in particular negro girl Minty, in hands of Levinia Truitt, exe. of Rownds Truitt, late guardian

F. 226   Tues., Dec. 8, 1801   All Justices present

F. 227   Orphan; John Selby (of Danl.)
Guardian; Maj. William Holland
Sureties; Peter S. Corbin, William Holland, Jun.

Orphan; Revel Horsey, of Worcester Co.
Guardian; Stephen Horsey, of Somerset Co., father
Sureties; Benjamin Gunby, Henry Smith

F. 228   Orphan; Hetty Horsey, of Worcester Co.
Guardian; Stephen Horsey, of Somerset Co., father
Sureties; Benjamin Gunby, Henry Smith

F. 229   Orphan; Sally Horsey, of Worcester Co.
         Guardian; Stephen Horsey, of Somerset Co., father
         Sureties; Benjamin Gunby, Henry Smith

F. 230   Orphan; Edward Horsey, of Worcester Co.
         Guardian; Stephen Horsey, of Somerset Co., father
         Sureties; Benjamin Gunby, Henry Smith

F. 231   Orphan; Lambert Horsey, of Worcester Co.
         Guardian; Stephen Horsey, of Somerset Co., father
         Sureties; Benjamin Gunby, Henry Smith

         Apprentice; Heber Whittingham (of Heber), 18
         Bound to; James Marshall
         Trade; cabinet maker
F. 232   Sureties; John Selby, William Marshall

F. 233   Apprentice; Robert Henderson, 17, son of Nancy
         Bound to; George Bratten
         Trade; house carpenter
F. 234   Sureties; John C. Handy, Eli Hudson

F. 235   Peter S. Corbin & William Holland, Jun., to view estate of
         John Selby (of Danl.), in care of James B. Selby, guardian:
F. 236   report; mentions two tenements where William & Henry Selby
F. 237   live; also land adjoining Thomas Taylor

         Apprentice; Jehu Powell (of Mordicai), both parents dead
         Bound to; Handy Powell, cordwainer
F. 238   Trade; cordwainer (shoe & boot maker)
         Term; till 21 in Dec., 1806
         In presence of John Postly, Thos. N. Williams
         Sureties; Jesse Powell, John Tingle

F. 239   Apprentice; Joseph Gullett, 4 on 15 Mar. last, by consent of
         his mother Polly
         Bound to; Isaiah Smith
         Trade; common labour
F. 240   Surety; Joshua Trader
         Before Boaz Walston, John Cathell

         Apprentice; John Pruitt, 16 on 10 Feb. next, by permission of
         his father, Elijah Pruitt [couldn't write]
         Bound to; William M. Bevans, house carpenter & joiner
F. 241   Trade; house carpenter & joiner
         In presence of Jesse Bennett, John Gunby

F. 242   Apprentice; Thomas Johnson, 4, orphan of the poor house
         Bound to; John Bishop (of William)
         Trade; farming
         Sureties; Josiah Bratten, Levi Bishop
         By the Trustees for the Poor; Saml. Handy, McKimmy Porter,
         Wm. Selby

F. 243 Anna Truitt, guardian to Elizabeth Truitt (of Edward), vs. Lavinia Truitt, exe. of Rownds Truitt; defendant to pay plaintiff $21.97, profits from estate due from Rounds Truitt, late guardian

Peter S. Corbin, adm. dbn of Daniel Selby, to sell indian corn

Jesse Powell, exe. of Thomas Powell, allowed 6% commission on estate

Stephen Horsey, guardian to Revel, Hetty, Sally, Edward & Lambert Horsey, discharged from passing accounts

F. 244 Arthur McAllen, adm. of Morgan Bradshaw, to sell negro Jacob, it appearing that property already sold is insufficient to pay debts

William Corbin, adm. of William Brown, allowed 10% commission on inventory & $4.50 for cost of suit commenced against William Cammock, for negro Flora, in Somerset Co.

Peter S. Corbin, adm. dbn of Daniel Selby, to buy negroes winter clothes

Register to receive list of accounts settled by John P. Marshall, exe. of Isaac Marshall

Register to receive list of accounts settled by John P. Marshall, exe. of John Marshall

F. 245 Isaac Puzey, Sen., deceased, by John Riggen, guardian to Isaac Pewsey, one representative; Register to strike distribution of estate among widow, & Levi, Sena(?) & Isaac, the children

Levi Pewsey, deceased, [as above]

Sena Pewsey, deceased, [as above]

James B. Robins to receive profits of estate of John & Ann Moore (of William) & apply a sum up to $12 each for their education, maintainance & clothing

F. 246 Received Dec. 7, 1801, of Betsy [also Betty] Schockly, guardian to Benjamin Shockley (of Benjamin), L.20/7/6

Test.; Boaz Walston   Benjamin Schockley

F. 247 John Postly, John Holland, Zadok Sturgis appointed Justices

John F. Meuer(?)   Alexander C. Hanson, Chanc.

F. 248 Tues., Feb. 9, 1802   All Justices present

Littleton Robins & other creditors vs. Edward Henry, exe. of William Purnell; plaintiffs appeared by Josiah Bayley & Ephraim K. Wilson, their solicitors; state estate was by his will to be used to pay debts; estate is underappraised; ask that exe. account for
F. 249 sales; Edward Henry appears, with William Polk & James P. Wilson, Esqs., his attorneys; denies charges; case continued
F. 250 for a year; defendant, Maj. Henry, appoints William Winder as
F. 251 his counsel; Court finds for plaintiffs, property to be sold, after advertising in ten places in Buckingham, Quopence & Boguetanorton Hundreds; 13 Feb., 1802, Edward Henry appeals
F. 252 to next General Court for the Eastern Shore on the 2nd Tues of Apr. next; record of case to be sent to Appellant Court, with certificate stating that Edward Henry was granted
F. 253 letters adm. cwa; William Purnell died 30 Jan., 1798; exe. paid out L.1243/14 1/2

Jacob Dale discharged from guardianship to John P. Dale

F. 254
Orphan; John Postly Dale
Guardian; George Truitt (of P.)
Sureties; Annanias Powell, Jacob Dale

F. 255
Orphan; Aary(?) Henderson
Guardian; Elijah Stevenson
Sureties; Levi Houston, James Henderson

F. 256
Orphan; Parker Bowen
Guardian; William Caudery [also Caudry]
Sureties; John Caudery, John Caudery

F. 257
Orphan; Stephen Ennis
Guardian; Samuel Ennis
Sureties; Ephraim K. Wilson, James Selby (of Ezkl.)

F. 258
Orphan; Joseph Ennis
Guardian; Samuel Ennis
Sureties; James Selby (of Ezkl.), Littleton R. Purnell

F. 259
Orphan; Mary Ennis
Guardian; Samuel Ennis
Sureties; James Selby, Littleton R. Purnell

F. 260
Orphan; Samuel Ennis (of Joseph)
Guardian; Samuel Ennis
Sureties; James Selby (of Ezkl.), Littleton R. Purnell

F. 261
Orphan; Elizabeth Bishop
Guardian; John White
Sureties; Peter Waters, John Allen

F. 262
Orphan; Charlotte Maddux
Guardian; Mills Bevans
Sureties; Rowland Bevans, Sen., James Bevans

F. 263
Orphan; Daniel Maddux (of Worcester Co.)
Guardian; William Maddux (of Somerset Co.)
Sureties; James Bacon, Joseph Scott

F. 264
Orphan; Marcey Maddux (of Marcey)
Guardian; Jacob Richards
Sureties; Rowland Bevans, Sen., James Bacon

On suggestion of Samuel Ennis & Thomas P. Rackliffe, in behalf of Jesse Ennis, minor, of improper conduct in Cornelius Ennis, guardian, in not rendering fair accounts of his ward's property, guardianship revoked; Benjamin Purnell appointed guardian

F. 265
Orphan; Jesse Ennis (of Cornelius)
Guardian; Benjamin Purnell
Sureties; Samuel Ennis, Sewell Turpin

F. 266
Apprentice; Milby Young, 16
Bound to; Bailey Young
Trade; cypress cooper
Sureties; John Tunnell, Isaac Henderson

F. 267
Apprentice; Jenny Harmen, 9, daughter of Sophia Harmen
Bound to; John Townsend
Trade; spin & weave
Sureties; William Flemming, Jacob Teague

F. 268
Apprentice; Joshua Harman, 7 next June, son of Sophia Harman
Bound to; John Townsend
F. 269
Trade; farmer
Sureties; William Flemming, Jacob Teague

F. 270
Apprentice; Nancy Henderson (of Purnell), 11
Bound to; George W. Purnell
Trade; knit, sew, spin & weave
F. 271
Sureties; Elisha Purnell, Samuel Ennis

F. 272
Apprentice; Richard Ball (of Richard), 17
Bound to; John Davis
Trade; blacksmith
Sureties; Richard Ward, John Dunkin

F. 273
Apprentice; John Linch (of Elisha), 16
Bound to; Eli Hozier
Trade; house carpenter
F. 274
Sureties; Benjamin Timmons, John Davis (B. S.)

F. 275
Apprentice; James Jarman, 15
Bound to; Samuel Long
Trade; farmer
Sureties; Edward Henry, Sewell Turpin

F. 276   Jacob Dale & Sterling Jones to view estate of Wingate Smith,
F. 277   in care of William Smith, guardian: report; mentions land
         adjoining John Smith

F. 278   Joshua Duer & Nehemiah Holland to view estate of Nehemiah
F. 279   Redden, in care of John Payne, guardian; before Jesse
         Bennett: report

         George Bell & Levin Mitchell to view estate of John, Rider
F. 280   Henry, Charlotte & Kitty Henry Rackliff, in care of William
F. 281   Winder, Sen., guardian; before John P. Marshall: report;
         mentions land in Synepuxent Neck; house where Elijah Bethard
         lives; house where Arthur Tracy lives; no slaves; land at
F. 282   Newport neck where Nathaniel Brittingham lives

[paper glued in to cover end of F. 282 & beginning of F. 283]

F. 283   Benjamin Dennis & Charles Bennett to view personal property
         of Peter & Henry White, in care of George Hayward, guardian:
F. 284   report; list of articles

F. 285   Apprentice; William Long, 19 on 19 Oct. next, by permission
         of his father, Levin Long
         Bound to; Silas C. Bush
         Trade; sadler
F. 286   In presence of Anthony Bacon, Elisha Purnell

         Apprentice; Peter Dicks, free mulatto, son of Nancy Dick
F. 287   Bound to; John Allen, Jun.
         Trade; making coarse or common shoes
         Sureties; John White (of Southey), Frederick Conner
         By Trustees for the Poor; Saml. Handy, McKimmy Porter, Geo.
         Hayward, Wm. Selby

F. 288   Apprentice; Samuel Davis (of Benjamin), 11 last Christmas
         Bound to; Holland Smock, farmer
         Trade; farming
F. 289   Sureties; John Williams, Annanias Jarman
         Before Thos. N. Williams, Nixon Davis

         Apprentice; William Bradford, 17 on 12 Jan. last, by
         permission of his father Avery Bradford
F. 290   Bound to; Henry White, blacksmith
         Trade; blacksmith
F. 291   In presence of John Postly, Thos. N. Williams

         Apprentice; Milby Royal [also Royals], 5, abject son of Hessy
         Bound to; Severen Pruitt, planter
         Trade; farming
F. 292   Sureties; Selby Pruitt, John Taylor
         By Trustees for the Poor; Wm. Selby, Saml. Handy, McKemmy
         Porter

F. 293   Apprentice; Nancy Handy, 7, daughter of John Handy
         Bound to; Selby Prewitt [also Pruitt], waterman
         Trade; spin & weave
         Sureties; Severen Prewitt, John Taylor
         By [as above]

F. 294   Belitha Baynum, exe. of William Baynum, to sell up to $200 of
         estate to settle debts

Timothy Irons, guardian to William & Betsy Dorman, allowed $24 for taking up negroes belonging to orphans

John Dunbar, adm. of James Dunbar, discharged from passing account or exhibiting inventory, upon proof that there is no estate

Rev. Samuel McMasters & Joseph Houston to view estate of Ary Henderson, in care of Elijah Stevenson, guardian

Sarah Maddux & Jacob Richard, adms. of Marcey Maddux, to sell personal estate, negroes & plate excepted

F. 295   Elizabeth Brittingham, adm. of Elijah Brittingham, allowed
         L.24 for education & maintainance of his children

Capt. Benjamin Gunby to settle dispute between John McHenry, & Elizabeth Brittingham, adm. of Elijah Brittingham

John Riggin, guardian to Isaac Pewsey, to account for amount of sale & not the inventory of negroes

Nixon Davis & Charles Hammond to distribute personal estate of Ezekiel Knox, in hands of Barnaby Henderson & wife, adms.

Thomas Fassitt (of John), vs. James Fassitt, exe. of Elijah; exe. to settle account of plaintiff against deceased amounting to $70 for a balance due in guardian account

Sterling Jones vs. William Winder, Esq., adm. dbn of John Rackliff; petition to adjust accounts

F. 296   Dr. Stephen White vs. William Winder, adm. dbn of John
         Rackliff; Co. John Postly & Maj. Edward Henry to settle
         dispute

William Winder, adm. dbn of John Rackliff, vs. Edward Harmonson(?); petition to adjust accounts against defendant; ordered that plaintiff be discharged from further prosecuting the claims for more than L.59/10/11

William Winder, adm. dbn of John Rackliff, to advertise in the Herald, Cowan's paper at Easton, for creditors to exhibit claims

Mary Ann Rice, adm. of George Rice, to advertise in the United States Gazette at Philadelphia, Cowan's paper at Easton & in Yanas(?) & Brown's paper at Baltimore for creditors to exhibit claims

Jesse Powell, exe. of Belitha Powell, allowed 6% commission on estate

Capt. Levin Mitchell, Joshua Prideaux & William Polk, Esq., to arbitrate counter claims between William Winder, Esq., adm. dbn of John Rackliffe, & Thomas S.(?) Fassitt & Sarah, his wife, admx. of Rouse Fassitt

F. 297   William Winder, Esq., adm. dbn of John Rackliffe, discharged from prosecuting a claim against John Fassitt for $150, dated 29 May, 1798, Thomas Fassitt, Esq., having made oath that he saw debt paid

Benjamin Bishop, orphan of Samuel, by Frederick Conner, adm. of Samuel; orphan in lingering dropsical condition; part of estate to be applied to his support & relief

John Bishop & Littleton R. Purnell to view estate of Stephen Ennis, in care of Samuel Ennis, guardian

John Bishop & Littleton R. Purnell to view estate of Joseph, Mary & Samuel Ennis (of Joseph), in care of Samuel Ennis, guardian

Matthew Dorman, adm. of Nehemiah Dorman, to advertise in Cowan's paper at Easton for creditors to exhibit claims

F. 298   William Handy & John Cottingham to view estate of Charlotte Maddux, in care of Mills Bevans, guardian

William Handy & John Cottingham to view estate of Daniel Maddux, in care of William Maddux, guardian

William Handy & John Cottingham to view estate of Marcy Maddux (of Marcey), in care of Jacob Richards, guardian

Representatives of Cornelius, Sen., have recovered L.8/9 from Cornelius Ennis, guardian to Rachel Ennis, which had been received as ward's property

Eleanor Stevens, deceased, by Elizabeth Townsend, adm. of Capt. Levin Townsend; George Rosse, Esq., adm. dbn, to pass all accounts paid by Levin Townsend, adm., in his lifetime

Representatives of Ebenezer & Amutual Franklin to be allowed their shares of negro Caleb, appraised as property of Ebenezer Franklin, deceased, by James Franklin, exe.

F. 299   Jesse Bennett, adm. of John Scarbrough, to sell up to L.50 of personal estate

Rebecca Taylor, adm. of Thomas Taylor, to sell personal estate

John Cottingham & William Handy to distribute estate of Marcy Maddux

State vs. Cornelius Ennis, guardian to Rachel Ennis; guardian has violated order of Court for sale of negroes by suppressing notice of sale, in order to defraud orphan; order rescinded, guardian has no further power to act under same

F. 300   Cornelius Ennis, guardian to Jesse Ennis, to deliver to Benjamin Purnell, present guardian, whole estate; Littleton R. Purnell & Thomas P. Rackliff to view estate

Received July 8, 1801, of Purnell Johnson, adm. of Sarah Trader, $78.24, in full of my mother's estate

Wit.; Purnell Trader   Joshua Trader

Received July 8, 1801, of Purnell Johnson, adm. of Sarah Trader, $78.24, in full of Sarah's estate

Wit.; Amelia Johnson   Henry White

F. 301   Special Court, Mar. 16, 1802, by request of James Broadwater & Major White; John Holland, Zadok Sturgis present

James Broadwater & Major White vs. Levi Holland, exe. of Levi Holland; petition for counter security; agreement with Mary & Polly Holland for faithful performance by Levi Holland, Jun., as exe. of his father, Levi

F. 302   Mary Gunn, adm. of Henry Gunn, allowed $10 for loss of stock

Peter S. Corbin, adm. dbn of Daniel Selby, to advertise at Snow Hill, Col. Chaille's store, Causton's mill, Sandy Hill & Peter Corbin's store for creditors to exhibit claims

F. 303   Tues., Apr. 13, 1802   All Justices present

Orphan; Betsy Holloway
Guardian; Jedida Holloway [signed Giddia, she couldn't write]
Sureties; Joseph Holloway, Joshua Prideaux

F. 304   Orphan; Hannah Holloway
          Guardian; Jedida Holloway [signed Giddia]
          Sureties; Joseph Holloway, Joshua Prideaux

F. 305   Orphan; Thomas Holloway
          Guardian; Jedida Holloway [signed Giddia]
          Sureties; Joseph Holloway, Joshua Prideaux

F. 306   Orphan; Micajah Selby (of James)
          Guardian; Joseph Delastatius
          Sureties; William Selby (S. H.), John Selby (of Parker)

'34'

F. 307
Orphan; Patsey Taylor
Guardian; Rebecca Taylor [couldn't write]
Sureties; Hezekiah Johnson, Rowland E. Bevans

F. 308
Orphan; Betsy Taylor
Guardian; Rebecca Taylor
Sureties; Hezekiah Johnson, Rowland E. Bevans

F. 309
Orphan; Sally Taylor
Guardian; Rebecca Taylor
Sureties; Hezekiah Johnson, Rowland E. Bevans

F. 310
Apprentice; Henry P. Sturgis (son of Priscilla Sturgis), 10 on 9 Aug. next
Bound to; James Bratten
Trade; farmer
Sureties; Joseph Stevenson, Joshua Sturgis

F. 311
Apprentice; James Knox (of James), 17 on 16 Nov. last
Bound to; Parker Selby
Trade; taylor
Sureties; William Selby (of Zadok), George Tarr

F. 312
Apprentice; Mitchell Henderson (of Isaac), 16
Bound to; John Taylor, Jun.
Trade; shoe & boot maker
F. 313
Sureties; Zadok Sturgis, Esq., Frederick Conner

F. 314   John Cottingham & William Handy to distribute estate of
F. 315   Marcey Maddux; before James Brodwatters
    1) to Danl., orphan of Marcey, Wm. Maddux, guardian; negroes Adam, Martha, Priester, Attalanta
    2) to Charlotte, orphan of Marcey, Mills Bevans, guardian; negroes Littleton, Jane, Lovey, Harriet
F. 316   3) to Sally, daughter of Marcey, of age; negroes Joe, Isaac, Nancy
    4) to Marcey Maddux, orphan of Marcey, Jacob Richards, guardian; negroes Levin, Tabitha

William Handy & John Cottingham, Esq., to view estate of Daniel Maddux (of Marcey), in care of William Maddux, guardian; before John
F. 317   Cottingham: report; mentions manner plantation where Marcey
F. 318   Maddux lived; small plantation near Capt. Brodwaters; total
F. 319   600 acres

William Maddux, of Somerset Co., guardian to Daniel Maddux (of Marcey), to receive estate from Sally Maddux & Jacob Richard:
F. 320   account; received negro man Adam, Martha, boy Priester, girl Attalanta

William Handy & John Cottingham, Esq., to view estate of Marcey Maddux (of Marcey), in care of Jacob Richards, guardian; before John
F. 321   Cottingham: report; mentions manner plantation where Marcey
(cont.)

F. 322	Maddux lived; small plantation near Capt. Broadwaters; total
F. 323	600 acres
F. 324	William Handy & John Cottingham to view estate of Charlotte Maddux, in care of Mills Bevans, guardian; before John
F. 325	Cottingham: report; [same as above]
F. 326	Littleton R. Purnell & Thomas P. Rackliff to view estate of
F. 327	Jesse Ennis, in care of Benjamin Purnell, guardian; before
F. 328	Benjamin Dennis: report; mentions house in possession of Elias Pointer; negro men David & Sam, boy Will, girl Leah; offers evidence that house dwelt in by Elias Pointer is his
F. 329	property & he has since removed it
F. 330	Account of property of Jesse Ennis (of Cornelius), received by Benjamin Purnell, guardian, from Cornelius Ennis, Sen., late guardian; negroes David, Sam, Will, Leah; Nelly's part
F. 331	John Bishop & Littleton R. Purnell to view estate of Stephen Ennis, in care of Samuel Ennis, guardian; before Benjamin Dennis: report
F. 332	John Bishop & Littleton R. Purnell to view estate of Joseph
F. 333	Ennis, in care of Samuel Ennis, guardian; before Benjamin Dennis: report
F. 334	John Bishop & Littleton R. Purnell to view estate of Mary
F. 335	Ennis, in care of Samuel Ennis, guardian; before Benjamin Dennis: report
F. 336	John Bishop & Littleton R. Purnell to view estate of Samuel
F. 337	Ennis (of Joseph), in care of Samuel Ennis, guardian; sworn before Benjamin Dennis: report
F. 338	Apprentice; Peggy Ballard, 8, by consent of her mother, Betty Ballard, free negro [couldn't write] Bound to; Capt. Josiah Hubbell Trade; common & usual labour for free female negroes
F. 339	In presence of Anthony Bacon Betty Ballard, being a name she obtained, being one of those distinguished as the children of none or no one
F. 340	Apprentice; James Smith, 11 on 27 Aug., 1802, by consent of his mother, Sarah Smith Bound to; Samuel Blades Trade; farming
F. 341	In presents of Anderson Patterson, Levi Henderson Sureties; James Blades, Handy Blades
F. 342	Apprentice; Sally Shepherd [listed once as Henderson], 9 Bound to; Jacob Henderson [couldn't write] Trade; spinster Sureties; Thomas Milbourn, Jun., Levin Matthews

(cont.)

'36'

By Trustees for the Poor; Wm. Selby, Saml. Handy, McKimmy Porter

F. 343

Apprentice; Jesse Ennis (son of Cornelius, Sen.), with consent of Benjamin Purnell, guardian
Bound to; Thomas Milbourn, carpenter
Trade; house carpenter
Term; until 21 on 13 Feb., 1807

F. 344 In presence of Wm. Holland, Anthony Bacon

F. 345

Apprentice; John Young (of Milby), 19 on 6 May next
Bound to; Bailey [also Bayley] Young, cooper [couldn't write]
Trade; cypress cooper
Surety; Joseph Young
In presents of Edward Stevenson, Edward Lambden

F. 346

Apprentice; John Justice, by consent of Polly Justice
Bound to; William Dunnaway, farmer
Trade; farmer
Term; 14 years
Signed by Mary Justice [couldn't write]
In presence of John P. Mitchell, Joshua Prideaux

F. 347

F. 348

F. 349

Upon application of Elizabeth Townsend, widow of Capt. Levin Townsend, in behalf of Eliza, Eleanor, Maria, Jenny, Sally & Matilda Townsend, orphans of Levin, James Bacon, Esq., appointed trustee for sale of estate, 86 acres of land: sureties; John Cottingham, Levin Pollitt: Act of Assembly passed 31 Dec., 1801, for relief of Elizabeth Townsend & heirs of Levin Townsend, to sell 86 acres cut off from original tract by ditch & road; in presence of Zadok Sturgis, Matthew Hopkins

James Bacon, adm. of John Handy, to advertise in Cowan's paper at Easton & the Baltimore Telegraph for creditors to exhibit claims

Will of Thomas Timmons appointed Stephen & Bassitt Timmons exes; Stephen is out of state, Bassitt granted letters testamentary

F. 350 Jedidah Holloway, adm. of Ebenezer Holloway, to sell such perishable estate as will benefit representatives

Samuel Ennis & Purnell Porter to view estate of John, Hetty, Kitty & Sally Bowen, in care of Elizabeth Bowen, guardian

Robert Hudson, adm. of James H. Hudson, to sell personal estate

Esther Layfield, adm. of Isaac Layfield, allowed 31/10 1/2 for error in sale of corn

Elijah Records, guardian to Sally, Outten & Mary Gornwell (of Major), to apply 10% of principle & all of interest to their education & maintainance

F. 351   Register to strike distribution of estate of John Pennewell among creditors, & Elizabeth Brittingham, adm., allowed for claims of Joshua Prideaux, Joseph Miller, Alexander Franklin & John Franklin, amounting to L.23/8 out of inventory, for benefit of widow & orphans

Esther Layfield, adm. of Isaac Layfield, to retain L.50 for cost of suit in County Court

Benjamin Bishop (of Samuel), by Frederick Conner, adm. of Samuel; adm. allowed to retain orphan's distributive share of father's estate till Feb. 1803

Edmund Crapper, in behalf of Mrs. Nancy Morris, vs. Edward Davis, adm. of Ezekiel, who was adm. of James Davis; adm. to pay said Nancy $11.53

F. 352   Samuel Ennis, guardian to heirs of Joseph Ennis, vs. Eli Hudson & wife, exex. of Joseph Ennis; John Bishop & Littleton R. Purnell to distribute personal estate

Jan. 9, 1802, received of Edmund Crapper in full of my share of estate of Edmund Crapper, Sen.
                                                his
Test.; Jacob Hopkins   John X Crapper
                                                mark

Jan. 9, 1802, received of Edmund Crapper my share of estate of Edmund Crapper, Sen.
                                        Jacob Hopkins
Wit.; Josiah Crapper

Jan. 9, 1802, received of Edmund Crapper my share of estate of Edmund Crapper, Sen.
                                        Josiah Crapper

Apr. 23, 1802, received of Edmund Crapper my share of estate of Edmund Crapper, Sen.
                                        William Crapper

Apr. 23, 1802, received of Edmund Crapper my share of estate of Edmund Crapper, Sen.
                                        Saml. Porter

William Selby, one security, vs. John Tunnell & wife, exex. of James Selby; petition for counter security

F. 353   Tues., June 8, 1802   All Justices present

Orphan; Sally Hutcheson (of Worcester Co.)
Guardian; George Truitt (of Delaware)
Sureties; James Martin, Thomas Martin

F. 354   Orphan; Purnell F. Smith
            Guardian; George W. Purnell
            Sureties; Zadok Sturgis, Alexander Franklin

F. 355   Orphan; Daniel Dykes
            Guardian; Sarah Dykes [couldn't write]
            Sureties; William Dryden, Isaac Houston (of Jno.)

            Samuel Ennis & Purnell Porter to view estate of John, Hetty,
F. 356   Kitty & Sally Bowen, in care of Elizabeth Bowen, guardian;
F. 357   before Jesse Bennett, Elisha Purnell: report

            Rev. Samuel McMasters & Joseph Houston to view estate of Ary
F. 358   Henderson (of Outen), in care of Elijah Stevenson, guardian;
F. 359   before Levi Henderson: report; 148 acres

            Nixon Davis, Esq., & Charles Hammond to distribute estate of
F. 360   Ezekiel Knox between widow & representatives;
            1) to John M. Nox; negro woman Esther
F. 361   2) to Martha Nox; man Levin, girl 18 months old

            Apprentice; Lemuel Henderson (of Bishop), 16 next Mar., by
            permission of former master, Joseph Bishop
F. 362   Bound to; Andrew Tull, carpenter & wheel right
            Trade; carpenter, cart wheel right
            Sureties; John Rich, Edward McGee
            Before John Postly, Henry Bell

F. 363   Apprentice; Stephen Laws, 11 on 1 July, 1801, by permission
            of his mother, Nancy Laws
            Bound to; Isaac Ironshire Evans, shoe & boot maker
            Trade; shoe & boot maker
F. 364   In presence of Thomas N. Williams, William Dale
            Sureties; William McGregor, John Jones William [mistake?]

Catherine Rodgers, guardian to Mitchell Rodgers, to spend 10% of
estate for education & maintainance

John Taylor, Jun., guardian to John & Susanna Aydelott, discharged
from passing accounts

            Peter S. Corbin & Nancy Davis, adms. of Charles Davis,
F. 365   allowed 10% commission on estate

Selby Parker, guardian to Henry Bethards, discharged from passing
accounts

George Truitt, guardian to William & John Bishop, to spend 10% of
principle for education & maintainance

Capt. Littleton Robins & James Bacon to settle dispute between John
Bishop & Mary Anne Rice, exe. of George Rice

John Bowhannan [Buchannan], adm. of John McGiveran, allowed 10% commission on balance of property & on payments

Zadok Sturgis & John Holland, Esqs., to settle dispute between Lanta Purnell, adm. of John S.(?) Purnell, & Capt. Robert M. Richardson

F. 366　Since Joshua Dryden is incapable of working at blacksmith's trade, he is discharged from apprenticeship to Joshua Sturgis

Dr. Thomas S. Fassitt & Sarah, his wife, admx. of Rouse Fassitt, allowed L.1550 on a written contract between deceased & Col. William Morris, so soon as title shall be made by representatives of Rouse Fassitt, in land purchased by him from Howard Aydelotte, to James Fassitt

Barnaby Henderson, adm. dbn of Ezekiel Knox, allowed L.10 out of distribution already struck for two oxen lost

Received Feb., 19, 1801, of John Stevens, $310.49, in full for Sally Marshall's personal estate fell to her by her father's death

Test.; Sally Pollitt　　　　　William Allen Marshall

Received Apr. 24, 1801, of John Stevens, $274.65, being in full for balance of my estate, which fell to me by my father's death

Test.; Saml. Sloan　　　　　Polly Marshall

F. 367　John Tunnell & wife, exex. of James Selby, having failed to give counter security to William Selby, one security, ordered that attachment issue be granted in favour of plaintiff to take the property out of the hands of the defendants

'40'

BOOK 8, JBR 9, 1802 - 1804

MICROFILM: CR 46,719-1

MSA No.: CM 1123-8

Worcester County Orphans Court Proceedings, JBR 9, 1802 - 1804

F. 1   Tues., Aug. 10, 1802   John Postly, John Holland, Zadok Sturgis Justices

Levin Pollitt, Esq., Sheriff   James B. Robins, Reg.

Orphan; William Henderson
Guardian; Levi Houston
Sureties; Edward Lambdon, Ephraim Furniss

F. 2
Orphan; Zipporah Schoolfield
Guardian; Sarah Redden [couldn't write]
Sureties; Joshua Sturgis, Isaac B. Schoolfield

F. 3
Orphan; John Prideaux
Guardian; James Collins
Sureties; Nathaniel Bowen, Josiah Collins

Orphan; Joshua Prideaux
Guardian; James Collins
Sureties; Nathaniel Bowen, Josiah Collins

F. 4
Orphan; Samuel Gunn (of Saml.)
Guardian; Samuel Hopkins
Sureties; William Stevenson, James Handy (Major)

F. 5
Orphan; Martha Knox
Guardian; John M. Knox & Mary, his wife
Sureties; Curtis Henderson, William Hogshiare(?)

Barzilla Parker discharged from guardianship to Sacker Parker, Jun.

F. 6
Orphan; Sacker Parker
Guardian; Lemuel Parker
Sureties; Hezekiah Davis [couldn't write], Daniel Jones

Orphan; Thomas Newbold (of Thomas)
Guardian; Nancy Kerby
Sureties; Jacob White, Thomas N. Williams

F. 7
Apprentice; Rowland Brittingham (of William), 13 on 1 July last
Bound to; James Dennis
Trade; make good common shoes
Sureties; Valentine Dennis, Nathaniel Bowen

F. 8
Apprentice; Sampson, orphan negro boy, 6
Bound to; Levin Pollitt, Esq.
Trade; farmer
F. 9   Sureties; James Bacon, William Townsend

'42'

F. 10	Apprentice; John Prideaux (of John), 15 Bound to; Josiah Collins Trade; shoe maker Sureties; Eli Hudson, William Bowen
F. 11 F. 12	Littleton Robins & James Bacon to settle dispute between John Bishop, claimant, & Mary Ann Rice, exe. of George Rice; Mary to pay to John Bishop L.325/5/11 & to furnish a copy of such articles as Mrs. Attalanta Wright got from said George as are charged against him, the said claimant
F. 13	Zadok Sturgis & John Holland, Esq., to settle dispute between Lanta Purnell, adm. of John S. Purnell, & Robert M. Richardson; Robert to pay Lanta L.17/9/5 1/4 & 200 bushels of indian corn on board said Richardson's vessell to Richmond to be accounted for & paid to heirs of John S. Purnell; also L.12/1 for negro hire
F. 14	Order passed at Feb. term referring dispute between Dr. Stephen White & William Winder, adm. dbn of John Rackliffe, to Col. John Postly & Edward Henry rescinded; matter referred to Maj. Edward Henry Zadok Purnell, Esq.; William Winder to pay Stephen White L.26/3/8; receipt for payment
F. 15 F. 16	Josiah Mitchell, Joshua Townsend, William Stevenson & William Purnell (C. N.) to settle dispute between John Postly, Esq., exe. of Jesse Duncan & adm. dbn of John Duncan, & representatives of Jesse & John Duncan; representatives to pay to John Postly L.12/18/9 3/4 for overpayment to creditors; list of payments due from Thomas Duncan, Charles Duncan, James Duncan, Levin Duncan, Lucy Duncan, Truitt Davis, Wm. Smith, Elisha Wheeler
F. 17	Edward Davis & Thomas Rigsby bound to Thomas P. Rackliffe on adm. of estate of Ezekiel Davis; in presents of Elezebeth Davis
F. 18	Apprentice; Zipporah Simpson, 7 Bound to; Arthur Tracy Sureties; Thomas M. Purnell, John Davis By Trustees for the Poor; McKimmey Porter, George Hayward, Saml. Handy
F. 19	Apprentice; Isaac Noble (son of Mary), 4 on 3 Oct. next Bound to; John Adkins Trade; common labour Surety; Ayres Parker In presence of Boaz Walston, John Cathell
F. 20 F. 21	Apprentice; James Guthrey (of William), by consent of his mother Hannah Tarr [couldn't write] Bound to; James Trahearn [also Trayhearn] Trade; mariner in coasting business & trade of the bay Term; untill 21, on 24 Feb., 1808 In presence of Anthony Bacon, Jesse Bennett

Thomas Dale, guardian to Mary Warren to receive her estate

F. 22 Thomas Dale, guardian to Isaac Warren (of Isaac), 8, to receive his estate

David Cathell, deceased, by John Cathell, Esq., exe.; petition to sell & prayer to retain certain articles inventoried out of sale

Elizabeth Bowen, guardian to John, Catherine, Esther & Joshua Bowen, to apply 10% of principle for education & maintainance

Thomas Parramore, adm. dbn. of John Parramore, to sell certain articles

F. 23 Edward Stevenson & Littleton Long to view estate of William Henderson, in care of Levi Houston, guardian

Elizabeth Townsend, adm. of Levin Townsend, to advertise in Cowan's paper at Easton for creditors to exhibit claims

Charles Hammond & Barnaby Henderson to view estate of John & Joshua Prideaux, in care of James Collins, guardian

Peter S. Corbin & Joseph Delastatius to view estate of Sarah & Nancy Sturgis (of Joshua), in care of Joanna Sturgis, guardian

Sarah Patrick, adm. of John Patrick, allowed 10% of L.42/19/10, that sum being paid in Philadelphia out of money left there by deceased

John Cathell, Esq., exe. of David Cathell, allowed for negro Sandy, since dead

F. 24 Elizabeth Fassitt, adm. of James M. Fassitt, allowed $66.66 for two horse since dead

James Bacon & Matthew Hopkins to make distribution of partnership between Dr. John Neill & exes. of Dr. John Purnell

Peter Parker, adm. of Comfort Laws, states most of estate is repleved out of his hands since inventory; adm. to have till a decision of said writ of replevin for all goods so repleved

Negro Anus(?), by his will, gave his estate to Leonard Jones, exe., for purchase of his wife, Dinah, a slave; exe. allowed L.25, the price paid for said Dinah

Thomas N. Williams, adm. of Layfield Collier, to advertise in Cowan's paper at Easton for creditors to exhibit claims

F. 25 John Postly, Edward Henry & Levin Mitchell to settle dispute between William Winder, adm. dbn of John Rackliffe & John Rackliff, Jun., & Alexander Franklin, adm. of Levin Riley

William Dale, Sen., guardian to Mary & Isaac Warren, discharged from passing accounts

Isaac Brittingham, adm. of Solomon Brittingham (who died in Baltimore), allowed L.10 for funeral expenses & $16 for travelling to Baltimore to collect property

Register to collect $4 from Jesse Powell, exe. of Belitha Powell, for 600 shingles omitted in inventory

Register to strike distribution of estate of Mary Truitt, in hands of Annanias Powell, adm. dbn.; also, adm. allowed 5% on estate, he being exe. of Thomas Webb, late exe. of deceased

F. 26   William Selby vs. John Tunnell & wife; defendants to give security for guardianship

Daniel Cottingham, guardian to James Tilghman, discharged from passing accounts, as orphan will be of age Oct. next

Peter S. Corbin to sell negroes Comfort & her child, & old Dover

Adm. dbn on estate of Rouse Fassitt granted to Dr. Thomas S. Fassitt

If no guardian is appointed for Margaret Fassitt by 3rd Friday of Sept., Thomas S. Fassitt, present guardian, to rent real property for a time not exceeding three years

Charles Hammond & Esme Purnell to view estate of Martha Knox, in care of John M. Knox & Mary, his wife, guardians

Register to strike distribution of estate of William Maddux between Lazarus, Elzey & Thomas Maddux, John Puzey & Mary, his wife, George Puzey & Sophia, his wife (mother of deceased)

F. 27   Account on estate of Joseph Ennis, by Eli Hudson & wife, admx., has error in payment to Samuel Handy as $21.37; should be $8.11

Register to state account on estate of Jane Bevans, allowing $5 paid to William Handy; exe. allowed 2% on estate

Samuel Hopkins, guardian to Samuel Gunn, to receive from Ephraim K. Wilson, Esq., balance of rent of real property of orphans of Samuel Gunn, deducting what was paid to Maj. George Purnell

Bassitt Timmons, exe. of Thomas Timmons, allowed 10% commission on payment of debts & 5% on estate

John Hudson, by his will, gave to his wife, Mary, furniture which was sold by order of Court; Register, in making distribution of estate, to rate said articles at price sold; adm. allowed 10% on estate

Nancy Kerby, adm. cwa of Capt. Thomas Newbold, to sell personal estate (except negroes)

F. 28   John J. Williams & Henrietta, his wife, vs. Mary Anne Rice, adm. dbn of John S. Bratten; attachment issued to compel compliance with order

John Townsend & Benjamin Dennis, Sen., to view estate of Sacker Parker, in care of Lemuel Parker, guardian

Ephraim K. Wilson, Esq., exe. of Levin Handy, to account for interest on list of sperate debts & sales

Stephen Davis, adm. of Nehemiah Hayman, allowed 10% on payment of debts & on balance of estate

F. 29   [blank]

F. 30   Tues., Oct. 12, 1802   All Justices present

Orphan; James Rigsby
Guardian; Milby Purnell
Sureties; William Marshall, Samuel R. Smith

F. 31   Orphan; Betsy Rigsby
           Guardian; Milby Purnell
           Sureties; William Marshall, Samuel R. Smith

           Orphan; John Bradshaw
F. 32   Guardian; Margaret Bradshaw [couldn't write]
           Sureties; Alexander McAllen [also McKallen], Samuel Taylor

           Orphan; Polly Bradshaw
           Guardian; Margaret Bradshaw
F. 33   Sureties; Alexander McAllen, Samuel Taylor

Orphan; Betsy Bradshaw
Guardian; Margaret Bradshaw
Sureties; Alexander McAllen, Samuel Taylor

F. 34   Apprentice; Charles Dougal (of James H.), 15
           Bound to; William M. Bevins
           Trade; house carpenter & joiner
           Sureties; Samuel R. Smith, John Johnson (of Leonard)

F. 35   Apprentice; Stephen Jackson, free negro, 17
           Bound to; James A. Collins
           Trade; farmer
F. 36   Sureties; George Bratten, Luke Teeling

F. 37   Apprentice; John Blair (of John), 16
           Bound to; George Bratten
           Trade; house carpenter
           Sureties; James A. Collins, Luke Teeling

F. 38   Apprentice; Asa Bell (of Robert), 15
        Bound to; Peter Truitt
        Trade; farmer
        Sureties; Ephraim K. Wilson, Esq., Peter Waters

F. 39   Apprentice; Levin Bishop (of Benjamin), 13, by consent of
        Frederick Conner, guardian
        Bound to; Samuel Porter
        Trade; farmer
F. 40   Sureties; Edmond Crapper, William Crapper

        Apprentice; Harry Harmon (son of Leah), 11
F. 41   Bound to; Levin Matthews
        Trade; farmer
        Sureties; Thomas Milbourn (of John), Jacob Henderson

F. 42   Apprentice; John Bell (of John), 13
        Bound to; Major Tarr
        Trade; shoemaker
F. 43   Sureties; Thomas Dryden, Elijah Tarr

        Edward Stevenson, Esq., & Littleton Long (of Littleton) to
F. 44   view estate of William Henderson (of John), in care of Levi
        Houston, guardian; before Edwd. Lambden: report; mentions
F. 45   River plantation & Woods plantation

        Apprentice; Catrin Tarr, orphan of the Poor House, 7
F. 46   Bound to William J.(?) Houston
        Trade; spinning, weaving & other work belonging to the duty
        of a woman
        Sureties; Robert J. H. Handy, Zadok Sturgis
        By the Trustees for the Poor; Saml. Handy, William Selby,
        Geo. Hayward

Thomas S. Fassitt, Esq., guardian to Margaret Fassitt, to sell
livestock

F. 47   Milby Purnell, adm. of Thomas Rigsby, to sell personal estate

Ann German, exe. of Purnell Henderson, allowed 10% on striking
distribution of estate

Edmond Crapper & John Walker to view estate of James & Betsy Rigsby,
in care of Milby Purnell, guardian

Hezekiah Johnson & Richard Sturgis, Sen., to view estate of John,
Polly & Betsy Bradshaw, in care of Margaret Bradshaw, guardian

Adm. on estate of Elisha Purnell granted to Sarah Purnell

James Dennis, exe. of Littleton Dennis, to sell personal estate

F. 48   Annanias German, exe. of Purnell Henderson, to apply 1/3 of
        estate of Thomas Henderson, orphan of Purnell, to his
support, as his property will not support him

Peter Parker, one security of Polly Newbold vs. Nancy Kerby, adm. of
Thomas Newbold, who was guardian to John K. Taylor; Col. John Postly &
Isaac Evans to ascertain estate of John K. Taylor which is intermixed
with that of Thomas Newbold

William Selby (of Zadok) vs. John Tunnell & Mary, his wife; order for
plaintiff to take property rescinded, as debts are satisfied;
defendant to retain property as testamentary guardian to orphans of
James Selby

Register to strike distribution on estate of Levin Newton; exe.
allowed 4% for settling estate

F. 49   Littleton Robins vs. Edward Henry, exe. of William Purnell
        (C. N.); caveat against any accounts on estate being allowed;
plaintiff to shew his objections

Received Apr. 20, 1802, of Mrs. Sarah Bravard, exe. of John Bravard,
for Anna Bravard, in full for her share of her father's estate; negro
man Rich, women Sue & Rhoda, boys Isaac & Littleton; list of articles

Test.; Edward Bridle(?)   John Fassitt, Jun., for his wife

Received Oct. 12, 1802, of Mrs. Sarah Bravard, exe. of John Bravard,
my share of my father's & grandfather's estates: list; L.9 left me
from Adam Bravard, deceased

Test.; Adam Bravard   Ebenezer C. Bravard

Received Apr. 9, 1802, of Sarah Bravard, exe. of John Bravard; list;
L.10 left me by my grandfather

Test.; Adam Bravard   John Bravard (son)

F. 50   [blank]

F. 51   Nov. 27, 1802, special Court at request of Dr. Thomas S.
        Fassitt; John Postly, Zadok Sturgis present

Laban Johnson, Levin Mitchell & Maj. Edward Henry to distribute
livestock from estate of Rouse Fassitt between Zipporah & Margaret
Fassitt

Isaac Brittingham, adm. of Solomon Brittingham, allowed 10% on estate

F. 52   Tues., Dec. 14, 1802   All Justices present

        Orphan; James Gray (of Johnson)
        Guardian; Abisha Davis & Martha, his wife
F. 53   Sureties; Adam Bravard, John Bravard

           Orphan; Johnson Gray (of Johnson)
           Guardian; Abisha Davis & Martha, his wife
           Sureties; Adam Bravard, John Bravard

F. 54   Orphan; William Gray (of Johnson)
           Guardian; Abisha Davis & Martha, his wife
           Sureties; Adam Bravard, John Bravard

           Orphan; Thomas Simpson Gray (of Johnson)
F. 55   Guardian; Abisha Davis & Martha, his wife
           Sureties; Adam Bravard, John Bravard

           Orphan; Tubman Gray
F. 56   Guardian; Abisha Davis & Martha, his wife
           Sureties; Adam Bravard, John Bravard

           Orphan; Martha Johnson Gray
F. 57   Guardian; Abisha Davis & Martha, his wife
           Sureties; Adam Bravard, John Bravard

           Orphan; James Selby
           Guardian; Rowland E. Bevans
F. 58   Sureties; Peter S. Corbin, William M. Bevans

Orphan; Tabitha Selby
Guardian; Rowland E. Bevans
Sureties; Peter S. Corbin, William M. Bevans

F. 59   Orphan; Nancy Selby
           Guardian; Rowland E. Bevans
           Sureties; Peter S. Corbin, William M. Bevans

           Apprentice; John Right (son of Leah Blake), 11 last Sept.
           Bound to; James Jones, Jun.
F. 60   Trade; farmer
           Sureties; John Allen, Benjamin Gunby

F. 61   Abisha Davis & Martha, his wife, admx. of Johnson Gray,
           allowed $260 for negroes Euphemia & Milby, appraised in
inventory & since dead

Hillary Pitts, James Fassitt & George Bell to view property of James,
Johnson, William, Tubman, Thomas S. & Martha Johnson Gray, in care of
Abisha Davis & Martha, his wife, guardians

John J. Williams & Henrietta, his wife, admx. of John Turpin, sold
negro Adam; sale to be ratified at sale price instead of inventory
valuation

William Selby, exe. of Zadok Selby, allowed L.9/4/6 from 8 Apr., 1795,
till one year after letters granted for judgement recovered against
him as exe. by Joshua Duer, & L.3/13/4 for a judgement of Morgan
Bradshaw

'49'

F. 62   James Dennis, exe. of Littleton Dennis, allowed 15 months to
        pass final account

George Rosse, Esq., adm. dbn of Eleanor Stevens, to receive estate
unadministered & undistributed in hands of Elizabeth Townsend, adm. of
Levin Townsend, late adm. of said Eleanor

Letter from John Whittington renouncing his right of adm. as exe. of
Levin Selby; letters granted to Selby Parker, one exe.

Selby Parker, exe. of Levin Selby, to sell stock

George Rosse, Esq., adm. dbn of Eleanor Stevens, to advertise in
Federal Ark at Dover & the Star at Easton for creditors to exhibit
claims

F. 63   Maj. William Holland appointed guardian to George & Henry
        Selby (of Daniel)

Letters of collection on estate of Col. Peter Chaille granted to
Anthony Bacon; Joshua Flemming & William Tingle appointed appraisers

Anthony Bacon, collector of Col. Peter Chaille, to sell personal
estate

Benjamin Dennis & William Quinton to distribute estate of Angelo
Atkinson between five youngest children & widow

William Handy & Comfort, his wife, guardian to orphans of Angello
Atkinson, in account at Feb. term, 1792, charged themselves with negro
boy Orris as increase of estate said to be born since death of said
Angello, which proved to be born of wench not belonging to deceased

F. 64   Samuel Nicholson, deceased, late adm. of Isaac Nicholson, had
        estate appraised, but never returned inventory & has since
sold large part of estate; inventory & sales ratified; William Quinton
& William Selby, adms. dbn, to retain enough of Samuel's estate to
make good any deficiency in Isaac's

Rev. Samuel McMaster & Joseph Houston to distribute estate of James
Selby, in care of Rowland Bevans, guardian to Tabitha, James & Nancy
Selby

F. 65   John Postly, Zadok Sturgis & Littleton Robins, Sen.,
        appointed Justices

        John F. Mercer   Al. Hanson, Chanc.

Wit.; Honourable Alexander C. Hanson, Chancellor

F. 66   Tues, Feb. 8, 1803   All Justices present

'50'

```
           Orphan; Thomas Smock (of Levi)
           Guardian; Purnell Porter
           Sureties; James Bowen, William Hammond, Jun.

F. 67      Orphan; James Dickerson
           Guardian; William Dickerson
           Sureties; James Brodwatter, George Houston [also Holston]

           Orphan; Peter Dickerson
F. 68      Guardian; William Dickerson
           Sureties; James Brodwatter, George Houston

           Orphan; Nancy Newton
F. 69      Guardian; Jesse Sturgis
           Sureties; Nehemiah Holland, Michael Tarr
           In presence of Matthew Hopkins

           Orphan; Charlotte Newton
           Guardian; Jesse Sturgis
           Sureties; Nehemiah Holland, Michael Tarr
F. 70      In presence of Matthew Hopkins

           Orphan; Sally Newton
           Guardian; Jesse Sturgis
           Sureties; Nehemiah Holland, Michael Tarr
           In presence of Matthew Hopkins

F. 71      Orphan; Elijah C. W. Perdue
           Guardian; James W. B. Perdue
           Sureties; John K. H. Perdue, Dennis Hudson [couldn't write]

           Apprentice; Ebenezer Powell (of Milby), 15
           Bound to; John Powell
F. 72      Trade; shoe & boot maker
           Sureties; Sterling Jones, Handy Powell

F. 73      John Lewis discharged from apprenticeship to John Brittingham

           Apprentice; John Lewis (of Scarbrough), 16 last Dec.
           Bound to; Lemuel Henderson
           Trade; Farmer
F. 74      Sureties; Bayly Young, Joseph Young

F. 75      Apprentice; Esme Webb (of John), 15
           Bound to; Timothy Irons
           Trade; tanner & currier
           Sureties; Thomas Milbourn, Solomon Townsend

F. 76      Apprentice; Edward Hudson (of James H.), 15
           Bound to; Isaac Cottingham
           Trade; carriage maker
F. 77      Sureties; Frederick Conner, Purnell H. [blank]
```

F. 78 Edmond Crapper & John Walker to view estate of James & Betsy Rigsby (of Thomas), in care of Milby Purnell, guardian;
F. 79 before Esme Purnell: report; mentions old place where Thomas Rigby formerly dwelt; out plantation by Purnel Porter

F. 80 Hezekiah Johnson & Richard Sturgis, Sen., to view estate of John, Polly & Betsy Bradshaw (of Morgan), in care of Margaret Bradshaw, guardian; before Benjamin Dennis & A. Bacon:
F. 81 report; mentions manor plantation; out plantation called 'Thornsberry': test.; James Willis, Elisha Jones

F. 82 Peter S. Corbin & Joseph Delastatius to view estate of Sally & Nancy Sturgis, in care of Joanna Sturgis, guardian, lately intermarried with Robert Cluff; before Wm. Holland: report;
F. 83 guardian is widow; mentions negro girl Tally or Tal, given to Sally by her grandfather Major Guy; mentions manner plantation & three out places; one occupied by Caleb Watson, free negro; one in possession of Joseph Callahan; other in possession of negro Jacob; mentions Jobe, an old negro

F. 84 Samuel Handy & McKimmey Porter to arbitrate between Fisher
F. 85 Richardson & John Selby, adm. of Ann Walton; John Selby to pay Fisher Richardson L.15

F. 86 Apprentice; Benjamin Twigg, 13 (son of William Twigg & wife, both deceased)
Bound to; John Johnson
Trade; common labour
Surety; Joshua Johnson
Before Boaz Walston, John Cathell

F. 87 Apprentice; Esther & Allice Roberts, daughters of Sarah Roberts [couldn't write]
Bound to; Zepheniah Benston
Term; until 16, 6 years
Trade; any honourable vocation
In presents of Andn. Patterson, Edw. Stevenson

F. 88 Apprentice; Samuel Twigg, 18 next Mar. (son of William & his wife, both deceased)
Bound to; Benjamin Johnson, Jun.
Trade; common labour
Surety; Benjamin Johnson, Sen.
F. 89 Before Boaz Walston, Isaac Hearn

F. 90 Apprentice; Thomas Hadder (of John), 17 on 28 Feb. 1803, by consent of his mother Catherine
Bound to; John Sears [couldn't write]
Trade; farmer
Sureties; Annanias Bradford, Benjamin Timmons
Before Thomas N. Williams, John Davis

'52'

F. 91	Apprentice; James Roberts, son of Esther Roberts [couldn't write] Bound to; Zepheniah Benston In presents of Edward Stevenson, Benjamin Aydelott
F. 92	Apprentice; Henry Fedderman (of Josiah), 16, by consent of William Fedderman, guardian Bound to; John Peden (of Somerset Co.), spinning wheel maker Trade; spinning wheel maker In presence of Edwd. Stevenson, Benjamin Aydelott
F. 93	Apprentice; Parker George, son of Elizabeth George [couldn't write] Bound to; Levin Merrill Term; 12 years, 9 months, 10 days Trade; any honourable vocation, make cooper's ware Before Edwd. Stevenson, Benj. Aydelott
F. 94	Apprentice; John Brittingham, 15 on 29 June next, by consent of his mother Mary Bound to; Joshua Johnson Trade; common labour Surety; John Johnson Before Boaz Walston, John Cathell
F. 95 F. 96	Apprentice; Joseph Taylor (of Joseph), 15 on 12 Mar., 1803 Bound to; Archibald Gault Trade; coasting or mariner's business Sureties; Isaac Ayres, George Davis Before Thomas N. Williams, William Dale

Col. Samuel Handy & John Cutler, Esq., to value parcel of ground adjoining store house, belonging to heirs of Samuel Gunn, & guardians to let same to Anthony Bacon for three years

F. 97 F. 98 F. 99 F. 100	Leah, Ann, Noah & Nancy Henderson, by their solicitor William Whittington, Esq., vs. Sinah Slocomb, exe. of William Henderson; state that Sinah is concealing estate & that she be compelled to file complete inventory; John Dennis, Esq., counsel for defendant, exhibits additional inventory; mentions hire of negroes Stephen & Harry

Col. Samuel Handy & McKimmey Porter to settle dispute between Fisher Richardson & John Selby, adm. of Anne Walton

Arthur McAllen, adm. of Morgan Bradshaw, to sell negro Peter

Register to strike distribution of estate of Levi Holland; Levi Holland, exe., allowed 10% commission

Joshua Prideaux, Esq., to settle dispute between Peter Parker & Elizabeth Selby, exe. of Thomas Selby

Andasia Smock & Samuel Porter, adms. of Levi Smock, to sell personal estate

F. 101   Jesse Bennett, Esq., adm. of John Scarbrough, allowed 10% on inventory

John Holland, Peter S. Corbin & Rowland Bevans, Esqs., to settle dispute between Hezekiah Taylor, & Comfort Newton & Jesse Sturgis, adms. of Sarah Newton

James Dennis, exe. of Littleton Dennis, to advertise at Snow Hill, Boguetanerton, Queponco & Indian Town for creditors to exhibit claims

John Logan, exe. of William Gillitt, allowed 10% for his trouble selling estate

Laban Johnson & Lemuell Showell to view property of Robert & Milby Kerby, in care of Thomas Franklin & wife, guardians

William Winder, Esq., exe. of Sarah Rackliff, allowed $50 for negro boy who died

F. 102   Register to audit accounts of Nathaniel Davis, adm. of James Johnson

Comfort Newton & Jesse Sturgis, adms. of Sarah Newton, to sell personal estate

Nancy Kerby, adm. of Thomas Newbold, to advertise in Duane's paper at Philadelphia for creditors to exhibit claims

John P. Marshall, Esq., exe. of Isaac Marshall, allowed 5% on inventory

Boaz Walston & Purnell Johnson, Esqs., to view estate of Elijah C. W. Perdue, in care of James W. B. Perdue, guardian

Hillary Pitts, James Fassitt & George Bell to view estate of James Gray, in care of Abisha Davis & wife, guardians

F. 103   Elizabeth Payne, adm. of Jacob Payne, to sell personal estate

Peter S. Corbin & John Holland, Esqs., to view property of Micajah Selby, in care of Joseph Delastatius, guardian

Henry Parker, exe. of Schoolfield Parker, allowed 5% on money collected & 10% on payment of debts

William Winder, Esq., exe. of Sarah Rackliff, allowed 5% on estate

William Winder, Esq., adm. dbn of John Rackliff, allowed 5% on debts collected

William Winder, Esq., exe. of Sarah Rackliff, to transfer 13 shares in Bank of Columbia to each representative, viz.; John, Ryder, Charlotte & Kitturah Rackliffe

F. 104   Peter S. Corbin & Rowland Bevans to pay of representatives of Levin Newton out of property left by Sarah Newton, former guardian, now in possession of Comfort Newton & Jesse Sturgis, adms. of Sarah

Anthony Bacon, collector of Col. Peter Chaille, states that two beds appraised in inventory were seized by Sheriff to satisfy county levy; ordered deducted from inventory

William Burbage vs. William Winder, adm. dbn of John Rackliffe; L.50, being two notes of hand deposited with deceased on Thomas Smith, to be suspended as credit on land from said Burbage to deceased [confusing]

F. 105   Register to ascertain & liquidate what sum has been paid by exe. of Thomas Purnell (W. N.) to adm. of David Stevenson

Nathaniel Davis, adm. of James Johnson, allowed L.4 for council fees

Thomas Taylor & Rowland Bevans to view estate of Nancy Newton, in care of Jesse Sturgis, guardian to Nancy, Sally & Polly Newton, & to sell personal property

James Cottingham & wife, guardians to George & Susannah Cottingham, to dispose of $12 worth of timber, to be applied to their support

F. 106   Part of lands formerly valued as property of John, Rider, Charlotte & Kitturah Rackliff are entailed; guardian to have George Bell & Levin Mitchell revalue land

Whereas life estate of Sarah Marshall is represented to be determined by which means the lands held by her has become property of John P. Marshall the proper heir; Sewell Turpin, Esq., & Thomas P. Rackliffe to view estate in care of John P. Marshall, Esq., guardian

William Selby, security, vs. John A. Townsend, exe. of Leah Townsend; exe. to shew cause why he has not returned full inventory & list of debts due

Sinah Slocomb, exe. of William Henderson, to retain $60 for prosecuting three suits in Somerset Co. against William Coulbourn, Mary Coulbourn & Michael Benston

F. 107   Exes. of John Sturgis, Sen., allowed 10% commission on inventory

F. 108   Tues., Apr. 12, 1803   All Justices present

'55'

Orphan; Nancy Jones
Guardian; Major Guy
Sureties; Joseph Delastatius, John Neill
In presence of Matthew Hopkins

F. 109   Orphan; James Dryden (of David)
Guardian; Samuel Dryden
Sureties; William Dryden, Samuel Hopkins
In presence of Matthew Hopkins

F. 110   Orphan; George Selby (of Danl.)
Guardian; William Holland, Sen.
Sureties; John Williams, Selby Parker

F. 111   Orphan; Henry Selby (of Daniel)
Guardian; William Holland, Sen.
Sureties; John Williams, Selby Parker

Lemuel Henderson discharged from apprenticeship to Andrew Tull

F. 112   Apprentice; Lemuel Henderson (of Bishop), 17
Bound to; Samuel Stevenson
Trade; farmer
Sureties; John Stevenson, Sen., John A. Townsend

F. 113   Apprentice; James Prideaux (of Thomas), 11 on 10 Mar. last
Bound to; William J. Houston
Trade; farmer
F. 114   Sureties; Joseph Houston, George Houston (of John)

F. 115   Apprentice; Micajah Selby (of James), 15 on 28 Feb. last
Bound to; Major Tarr
Trade; shoe & boot maker
Sureties; Daniel Patrick(?), John J.(?) Purnell
F. 116   Joseph Delastatius, guardian

F. 117   Apprentice; Severin Taylor (of Daniel), 15 on 2 Feb. last
Bound to; Daniel Patrick
Trade; shoe & boot maker
Sureties; John S. Purnell, Major Tarr

F. 118   Rowland Bevans & Thomas Taylor to view estate of Nancy Newton
F. 119   (of Levin), in care of Jesse Sturgis, guardian; before John
Holland: report; 1/2 belongs to orphan

F. 120   Charles Hammond & Esme Purnell to view estate of Martha Knox, in care of John M. Knox & Mary, his wife, guardians; before
Nixon Davis: report; orphan owns 1/2 of estate; mentions
negro man Levin

F. 121   Report of James Bacon, trustee for sale of part of Levin
Townsend's real estate, authorized by Act of Assembly 2 Nov.,
(cont.)

F. 122   1801; Major White highest bidder at $8.51 per acre; 81 3/4
          acres; before James Cottingham; map of tract, laid off by
Joshua Duer

F. 123   Apprentice; Isaac Tull, by consent of his father John
          Bound to; Samuel M. Duer (of Somerset Co.)
          Trade; blacksmith
F. 124   Test.; Benj. Aydelott, Edward Stevenson

          Apprentice; John S. Lamberson, by consent of his father Smith
          [couldn't write]
          Bound to; Samuel M. Duer (of Somerset Co.)
          Trade; blacksmith
F. 125   test.; Edward Stevenson, Benj. Aydelott

          Apprentice; Nancy McGath, mulatto, 9 on 29 Jan. last, by
          consent of her mother
          Bound to; George Mosly [couldn't write]
          Trade; common labour
F. 126   Sureties; Levin Handy, John Umsted(?)
          Before Boaz Walston, John Cathell

F. 127   Apprentice; Rhoda McGath (daughter of Milly), mulatto, 9 on
          29 Jan. last
          Bound to; George Mosley
          Trade; common labour
          Sureties; Levin Handy, John Umsted
F. 128   Before Boaz Walston, John Cathell

          Apprentice; James Alexander, by consent of his mother
          Elizabeth, of Virginia [couldn't write]
          Bound to; Jesse Boston
          Term; 5 years from 25 Jan. last
          Trade; carpenter & joiner
F. 129   Before Edwd. Stevenson, John Williams

          Apprentice; Lemuel Bowen (son of Jepthah), 19 on 9 instant
          Bound to; Peter Lister, blacksmith
          Trade; blacksmith
F. 130   In presence of Thos. N. Williams, Wm. Dale, Isaac Ayres

          Apprentice; Major Taylor (son of William), 10 last Aug.
          Bound to; Matthias Lindsey, blacksmith
F. 131   Trade; blacksmith
          Test.; Saml. A. Harper, W. Holland

          Apprentice; Peter H. Henderson (son of Jenkins)
          Bound to; John Hall
          Term; till 21; 7 years & 11 months
F. 132   Trade; shoe & boot maker
          Test.; Edward Stevenson, Benj. Aydelott

Peter S. Corbin & Rowland E. Bevans to distribute estate of Levin
Newton, left by will & his deceased widow, who was guardian
F. 133   to representatives; Jesse Sturgis present guardian: report;
1) to Comfort Newton (daughter of Levin)
2) to Jesse Sturgis, guardian to Nancy Newton
3) to Polly Newton (daughter of Levin)
4) to Jesse Sturgis, guardian to Sally & Charlotte Newton
5) to his supposed son Josiah Newton

F. 134   Account of property received by Jesse Sturgis, guardian to
         Sally & Charlotte Newton, representatives of Levin Newton:
F. 135   list; also legacy to Nancy Newton

         Account of sales of property of Nancy, Sally & Charlotte
F. 136   Newton, by Jesse Sturgis, guardian: report; Peter S. Corbin
         makes oath on above sales before Jno. Holland

F. 137   Report on partnership of Neill & Purnell; Dr. John S.
         Purnell, deceased, by John Neill & George W. Purnell, exes.;
         James Bacon & Matthew Hopkins to settle accounts; Dr. George
F. 138   W. Purnell, exe., chargeable for L.1085/18/4; Dr. Neill
         chargeable for debts due from Andrew Aitkin, George Bayly,
         Robert Graham, Solomon Hopkins, George Hayward, suit against
F. 139   John Tunnell(?); mentions accounts against Benjamin Purnell
         (merch.): list of accounts assigned to Dr. Neill, as balance
due him; Col. Levin Handy, Joseph Delastatius, John Townsend (mill),
Rowland Bevans, Sen., Joseph Scott, Mrs. Brumbly, Major Guy, Ephraim
Smullen, Mrs. Otwell, Solomon Townsend, James Bennitt, Thomas Victor,
Jun., William Schockley, Mrs. Williams, McKimmey Scarbrough, Handy
Mills, Daniel Selby, Giles Jones, Zadok Selby, Milby Atkinson,
         Littleton Riley, James Mallett, Grace Cottingham, Miss
F. 140   Barshaba Richards, Richard Ward, Capt. Matthias Davis, Levi
         Townsend, John Bonnewell, Wm. Bishop, Sen., Rackliff Pointer,
John Reed (Matty), Zadok Townsend, James Trippe, Mrs. Hayward,
Angello Atkinson, Mrs. Evans (widow of Jno.), Valentine Dennis, James
Atkinson, Jun., Stephen Allen, Matthias Lindsey, Maj. John Holland,
Mrs. Townsend (of Major), Samuel Johnson, John Selby (of Parker),
George Martin, Sen., John Mallitt, Josiah Bratten, Tabitha Selby,
Joshua Flemming, Sen., John Hudson (of Major), Sacker Pepper, Mrs.
Newton (of Selby), Col. James Houston, David Price, Samuel Stevenson,
Capt. Nehemiah Holland, Elgate Ruke,, Samuel Shockley, Joel Nelson,
Capt. Thomas Hall, Benjamin Aydelott, Joshua Sturgis (B. S.), Thomas
Jones (Quepo.), Levin Selby, Mrs. Bishop (of Chas.), James Marshall,
James Trehern, Jonathan Stevenson, Lemuel Bishop, John Taylor (B. S.),
Thomas Blake, Eliakim Johnson, Jun., John Atkinson, Thomas Stevenson,
Henry Smock, William Ishum, John Stevenson, Sen., Nathan Cottingham,
Parker Selby (of Zadok), Edward Stevenson, Miss Betsy Wise, Mrs. Selby
         (of John, Nesx.), Jabez Stevenson, Mrs. Parker (widow of
F. 141   Charles), Daniel Duffy, Henry Scarbrough, Turner Davis, Capt.
         James Cottingham, John Cottingham (of Thos.), Jacob Richards,
Denny Bishop, John Ayres, Mrs. Sturgis (Boguetn.), Micajah Selby,
Jackson Turner, Robert Hudson, Sen., Levin Long, Rev. Samuel
McMasters, Samuel Ennis, Wm. Whittington, Esq., Wm. Taylor (of Jno.,
                                 (cont.)

'58'

B. S.), John Lane, Charles Townsend, John Caudrey, Jun., Joseph
Stevenson, Capt. Thomas Martin, Thomas Shockly, William Turner,
Purnell Bishop, Capt. George Martin, Jun., Ephraim Wilson, Esq.,
Pompey Polk, William Bevans, Sen., Maj. Wm. Holland, Jacob Teague,
Samuel Nicholson, William Polk, Esq., Major Lindsey, Levin Layfield,
James Nairne, Betsy Gunn, John Taylor (I. Town), Mrs. Townsend (of
Levin), Col. James Martin, William Powell, Peter Evans, Wm. A.
Marshall, Robert Handy, Solomon Eshom, George Nelson, Samuel Mills,
Wm. Bennett (seaside), Purnell Hill, Thomas Dryden, James Givans,
Isaac Cottingham, John Johnson (of Leod.), Jonah Nelson, Levin Hill,
Charles Bishop, Sen., George Selby, John Fassitt (Synpt.), Edward
Scarbrough, Andrew Brown, Peter Truitt (of Wm.), Hezekiah Johnson,
   Hannah Bishop, John Wright, Jun., Daniel Cottingham
F. 142 List of accounts allotted to Dr. John Neill as his share of
  debts deemed good; Thomas Martin (of Thos.), John Wallop,
Tabitha Wise, John Caudrey, Sen., Polly Ware, Kellam Lankford, Capt.
George Richardson, William Hozier, Mrs. Stevenson (mill), Dennis
Carey, Wm. Purnell, Esq. (C. N.), James Atkinson, Sen., Moses
Claywell, Wm. S. Hill, Benja. Purnell (I. Town), John Caudrey, Jun.,
Obediah Jones, Nancy Purnell (I. Town), John Riggen, John Hudson
(shoemaker), Benjamin Bishop (seaside), Sally Hopkins, Philip Marsh,
Elijah Ricketts, Wm. Dennis (of Shalmz.), Elisha Gunby, Nathaniel
Bratten, Stephen Sturgis, Henry Turner, Mrs. Long (widow of Wm.),
Daniel Price, Peter Jones, Thomas Purnell (of Wm.), Levi Crapper,
Margaret Truitt, Wm. Porter, Richard Sturgis, Jonathan Hutcheson,
Mary Townsend, Peter Tarr, Stephen Sturgis, Mrs. Johnson (of Geo.),
Denny Truitt, Shadrach Sturgis, Leonard Johnson, Sally Wise, Thomas
Rigsby, James Selby, Joseph Ennis, widow Allen (seaside), George
Puzey, Mrs. Nicholson (widow of Jos.), Jeremiah Hales, John Purnell
   (of Thos.), John Johnson (cooper), Kellam Truitt, Littleton
F. 143 Robins, Jun., Rosanna Martin, Wm. Claywell, Isaac
  Brittingham, John Holston (of R.), Isaac Holston, William
Price, Nancy Ennis, Stephen Purnell, Esq., James B. Robins, Edward
Dymock, Michael Tarr, Mrs. Hammond (of Wilson), Jesse Riggen, John P.
Marshall, Esq., Parker Dukes, Daniel Price, Moses Claywell, George
Truitt, Jun., Asa Bowen, Sewell Dryden, Laban Hudson, John Dorman,
Jacob Purnell (negro), Hinman Cowley, Levin Godfrey, James Bennitt
(Matty.), John Payne, Denwood Townsend, Tom Wilson (negro), Levi
Merrill, William Davis (Wilton's mill), Thomas D. Shockley, Elisha
Jones, Nelly Guttry, Major Reed, Samuel Mallitt, Johnson Hayman, Rev.
David Ball, Dennis Carey, Barnaby Henderson, Capt. Charles Bennitt,
John Done, Esq., James Stevenson, Henry Cottingham, Zadok Sturgis,
Esq., John Savage, Patrick Waters, Sen., Mary Martin, Mrs. Stevenson
(of James), Thomas Milbourn, Col. Thomas Martin, Mrs. Bevans (of Wm.),
Benjamin Purnell (carpt.), Mrs. Parker (of Chas.), Peter S. Corbin,
William Harper, Mrs. Shockley (of Wm.), John Shockly, George Rice,
   Samuel Smith, Mrs. Nancy Handy, John Dennis (St. Martins),
F. 144 Edward Stevenson, Philip Quinton, Sen., Esq., Thomas Outten,
  Wm. A. Selby, Mrs. Polly Smith, Mrs. Lanta Purnell, Levi
Outten, Samuel Banks, Capt. Robt. M. Richardson, Samuel Parker
(carpt.), John Scarbrough, Jun., Ephraim Tilghman, Daniel Davis, John
White (of S.?), Jonathan Eshom, Mrs. Elizabeth Rosse, Thomas Claywell,
Capt. Rowland Bevans, Lemuel Selby, John Jones (of Giles), James
        (cont.)

'59'

Houston, Jun., Isaac Nicholson, Timothy Irons, Edward Robins, Miss
Leah Martin, John Cutler, Esq., William Quinton, Samuel Gunn,
Alexander McAllen, James Selby (of Jno.)
List of accounts allotted to Dr. George W. Purnell, exe. of Dr. John
Purnell; Maj. George Purnell, Maj. Wm. Purnell, Anne Robins, Thomas
Purnell (of Thos.), Zadok Purnell, Esq., Benjamin Purnell (merch.),
Isaac Marshall, Comfort Purnell, Elisha Purnell, Esq., Henry Gornwell,
Jenny Greer, Elijah Laws, John McCauley, Jun., James Reed,
F. 145   Anderson Parker, Dolly Allen (negro), Levi Jones, John
Franklin, Sen., Leah Hales, John Wright, Sen., William
Slocomb, Wm. Davis (B. S.), Wm. Porter, Mrs. Perkins, Jonathan
Hutcheson, Capt. George Hayward, George Murray(?), John S.(?) Purnell,
Whittington Richardson, Benja. Scott (S.? Point), Isabella Robins,
Jesse Jones, Levi Hudson, William Dreadon, Sen., Jesse Steel, Jesse
Mumford, Euphemia Brittingham, Betsy Purnell (of Thos.), Rosanna
Martin, Miss Polly Spence, Elisha Purnell (Quepo.), Ebenezer Franklin,
Sarah Purnell (I. Town), Miss Sally Spence, Mrs. Sarah Marshall,
Littleton R. Purnell, Solomon Bradford, Nancy Henderson, Mary Purnell,
Rev. David Ball, Isaac Riley, Capt. Littleton Robins, Riley Marchment,
Capt. George Spence, James Dennis (seaside), Zadok Sturgis, Esq.,
Joshua Prideaux, John S. Purnell, Esq., Paul Grant(?), William
Houston, Elizabeth Rosse, John Cutler, Esq., Samuel Gunn
F. 146   List of debts on books of Neill & Purnell deemed desperate;
widow Hudson (Town?), Harris P. Corbin's place, Parker Selby
(of Math.), Wm. Tarr, Wm. A. Selby, Wm. Pruitt, Sen., Joshua
Beachboard, Zedekiah Bradford, John Handy (nes.?), Robert Richardson,
Wm. Brittingham, Rives R. Townsend, George Gunn, Samuel Bishop
(taylor), Wm. Purnell, Esq. (C. N.), John Sturgis (S. Hill), Polk or
Pope (near Atkinson's mill), Mrs. Paramore, Ralph Holston, Levin
Townsend (of Laz.), Hessey Mason, Mrs. German, Geo. Wise, Thomas
James, Eliza Carey, Edward Davis, Wm. Townsend (of Laz.), Daniel
Sturgis (B. S.), Thomas Mallany, Geo. Dashiell (joiner), [blank]
Outten (ship carpt.), Mrs. Mumford, Wm. Bennett (of Wm.), Baham(?)
Armstrong, Indian Sarah, Saml. Dreadon (of Jno.), John Reed
F. 147   (Quepo.), negro Hope(?), Elijah Christopher, James America,
Jonathan Hutt, Ephraim Collins, Nancy Henderson (of Levin),
Elijah Bowen, Sophia Davis, John Ball, Henry Cauper(?), Mrs. Hopkins
(of Luke), Peter Evans, Isaac Riggen, John Reed (Davis mill), Mrs.
Hales, Saml. Scarbrough, Polly Dennis, Anna Pollit, Sarah Richardson,
Levin Parsons, negro Jess, Daniel Price, John Henderson, Sally Kellam,
Purnell Smith, Esther Newton, negro Titus' wife, Benjamin Bevans, Mrs.
Townsend (of Barcley), Jabez Willis, Joshua Fisher (negro), Rhoda
(widow of Joshua), Omey(?) Pepper, [blank] Shockley, Betsy Mallott,
Joseph Furrow(?), [blank] Donohoe, Josiah Dickerson, Benjamin Tull,
Martha McGan(?), Mrs. Riggen, Levi Davis, Geo. Richardson (of
Charles), Joseph Tilghman, James Boston, Jeremiah Armstrong, Jesse
Armstrong, Tabitha McFadden, Sally Pointer, John Tarr, Wm. Selby
(Ac.), Azariah Purnell (negro), Ezekiel Butler, William Milbourn,
Mitchell Wise, Lydia Davis, Wm. Morris (const.), John Ricketts,
[blank] Wilson (caulker), Levin (mulatto), Sarah Africa,
F. 148   Nancy Pointer, Lanty Pepper, Mrs. Guttry (of Wm.), Capt. Wm.
Valance, Rachel Hancock, Mrs. Moore (w. of Thos.), Sabastin
Lankford, Wm. Ball, Mrs. Shockley, Nancy Brittingham, David Taylor,
(cont.)

'60'

James Amwood, Leah Harman, Elisha Bowen, Wm. Dykes, Abisha Davis, John Dykes, [blank] Hook, Levin Sturgis, Severn Rock, Southey Miles, [Mrs.?] Willis (widow of Jabez), James McFadden, Robert Taylor, Rachel Nimber, Robert Rowan, Peter Tull, Ezekiel Knox, Pruitt Crother (?) (of Selby), Jones Forest, Lowder Smullen, William Sturgis, Jonathan Watson, Wm. Porter (taylor), Wm. M. Robins, Joseph Evans, James Jones, Elijah Brittingham, John Sturgis (of Levin), Mrs. Truitt (widow Little Wm.), John Allen, Jun., Mrs. Givans, Sarah Johnson, Wm. Downs, Moses Hudson, Jun., Thomas Irons, John Brazier, Samuel Payne, Peter Townsend, James Johnson, Isaac Purnell, David Dreadon, James Chericks, Elijah Tarr (Harelip?), John Green, James Davis, Cornelius Morris, Sally Coston, Moses Greer, [blank] Mitchell, Ayres Taylor
F. 149 (N. S.), Coulbourn Long, Joshua Butler, Charles Godfrey, David Gunby, Levin Riggen, Zadok Claywell, Maj. Wm. Chaille, Mrs. Jones (widow of James), Sally Murphy, Chloe Cashaby, [blank] widow Morris, widow Steel, Rachel Brittingham, Nehemiah Tarr, Samuel Henderson, Eli Pepper, Alexander Richardson, Sampson Davis, Samuel Beazy, Maj. Jas. Townsend, Mrs. Molly Wise, Wm. Beachboard, John McIver, Betty Truitt, Tesa(?) Tarr, John White (caulker), Jonathan Hammond, Jack Fisher (negro), Levin Matthews, Elijah Tarr, Lazarus Townsend, Henry Parker (forest), Levin Townsend (B. S.), Levina Burch, Samuel Hopkins, Littleton Reed, William Trehern, Gilbert Townsend, Mary Black, Tabitha Johnson, John Richardson, Francis Rosse, John McIver (for Hugh Connelly), Elizabeth Marshall, Thomas Bruff, James Lecount, Micajah Hudson, John Timmons, John Steel, William Hammond, Thomas Robinson, Shadk. Coston's wife's mother, Betty Hornes(?), Eli Pepper, Ceazar (negro preacher), John P. Truitt, Jeremiah Taylor George Spence (negro), Charles Richardson, Obed Brittingham,
F. 150 Capt. James Conner, Aaron Hudson, [blank] Pruitt (of Wm.) Hugh Stevenson, Jesse Simpson, Robt. Gibbs, Eli Adams, M. Bennitt, John Holston, Sen., Wm. Selby (Matty), John Hoolbrook, John Chaille, Mrs. Adkins, [blank] Stanford (cooper), Noah Riggen, Joseph Riggen, Mrs. Betsy Martin (widow of Levin), Levin Holston, Lizy Taylor, Nancy Tarr, John Bowen, Mrs. Stevenson (Quepo.), Bowan (at Purnell's mill), Maj. James Handy, Indian Sarah's daughter, John Redden, Caleb Rain, Patrick Waters, Jun., Wm. Caudrey (B. S.), Brittingham (sister to Beaza?), Belitha Hales, [blank] Douglass (seaside), Thomas Bevans, Geo. Burch, Matthias Nicholson, Moses Chaille, Dennis Conner (of D.), [blank] Laws, Peter Duer, Wm. Bevans (near __?__), Samuel Devorix, Wm. Deverix, Charles House (N. S.), Wm. Willis, James Smyth (carpt.), William Hughes, [blank] Coulborn (forest), Kendal Taylor, George Holston, David Ward, Robert Butler, Wm. Caudrey, John S. Bratten, John Jones (forest), John Colborn, Lazarus Harmon, Jesse Hughes, John Davis, James Robinson, Wm. Shockley, Selby Newton, Elisha Johnson, Jesse Marchment, Chapman (Accomack), Wm. Hudson (town), Levi Bishop, Bowdoin Hammond,
F. 151 Betsy Hook, Adam Stevenson, Col. Peter Chaille, George Rosse, Esq., John McDonald, John Redden, Wm. Townsend, [blank] Bower (schoolmaster), Jet (negro), Daniel Young, Levin Sturgis, Starling Hudson, Ephraim (negro) Spence, Peter Redden, Sam Givans, Abel Wright, Levin Townsend (of Laz.), Polly Nicholson, John Milbourn, Wm. Bowden, Marge(?) Jones, John Bowen, John Hudson, Esther Pettitt, John Henderson, Elijah Potter, [blank] Jones (Quepo.), Teackle Taylor,
(cont.)

James Willis, James Dredon, Isaac Hodge, Flora (?, free woman), Thomas Bowen, Jeremiah Harmon, John Floyd, Solomon C. Porter, Betty Ballard, Capt. John Hall, Peter White, Mrs. Handy(N. S.), Jabez Brumbly, [blank] Jones (at H. Parkers), John Sturgis, Mrs. Bevans (near Coston's?), Jno. McIver (for Jas. Goodman), Esau Pilchard, Wm. Selby (Matty.), Sarah Townsend (of Laz.), Chas. Parker, Curtis Henderson, Moses Parker

F. 152 List of debts collected on books of Caleb Powell, by John Postly, Esq., returned in a schedule by Zadok Sturgis, Sheriff; Presgrave Williams, John Smith, Elsey Smith, Joseph Dunbar, Rebecca Belts, Milby Griffin, Thomas Dale, Jesse Timmons, Esther Bethard, James Bethard, Annanias Laws, Sacker Taylor, Solomon Williams, Edmond Ronnells, Sewell Turpin, Samuel Williams, Isaac Long, William Richards, John Richards, James Steele, Milby Bowen, Jackson Turner, Isaac Warren, Isaac Richards, Henry Schoolfield, William Burbige, Isaac Bethard, Benjamin German, Saul Gundy [Gunby?], Armwell Holloway

F. 153 Account of Col. John Postly, who was appointed collector of Caleb Powell, late exe. of Milby Powell; cash retained by Catherine Powell, guardian to Henry & George H. Powell, orphans of Milby

F. 154 Kitturah Milbourn, adm. of Thomas Milbourn, to sell property up to $1500 (except negroes)

Laban Johnson & James Selby to view estate of Betsy, Thomas & Hannah Holloway, in care of Jedida Holloway, guardian

John Williams & Henrietta, his wife, admx. of John Turpin vs. Sewell Turpin, guardian to John Turpin, & Southey Whittington, guardian to Anne Turpin, orphans of John Turpin; guardians to repay
F. 155 overpayment of orphans distributive shares

James Bacon, adm. of John Handy, allowed 10 % on inventory

Cornelius Ennis, guardian to Rachel Ennis, to sell negro girl Esther

John Powell & Charles Walston to view property of James Dryden, in care of Samuel Dryden, guardian

Nancy Kerby, adm. of Thomas Newbold, to sell personal estate

F. 156 William Caudry, guardian to Parker Bowen, to sell negro Lit(?)

David Johnson & Lemuel Showell to view property of Milby & Robert Kirby, in care of Thomas Franklin, guardian

Sewell Turpin, guardian to John Turpin, to apply L.5 of principle yearly for his support & education

Zadok & Mary Sturgis, exes. of John Sturgis, allowed L.11/5/0 for mare that died

Fisher Walton, by his will, gave his wife Anne whole estate; L.50 is due Brown, Litler & Co. of Philadelphia; James Selby, adm. of Anne, to retain L.50 for payment of debt

F. 157   John Postly, Esq., guardian to Molly Morris, allowed 10% on profits of estate

John & Jesse Duncan, deceased, by John Postly, Esq., who was exe. of Jesse & adm. dbn of John; award against representatives ratified

Caleb Powell, one exe. of Milby Powell, allowed 10% in settling his accounts with guardian of orphans

Admx. allowed for negro woman Leah appraised in estate of Charles Rackliff, Jun., now dead

F. 158   Attachment issue ordered against Stephen Redden & Daniel Hancock for disobeying order in favour of Sarah Redden; also to shew cause why they have not delivered estate of Zipporah Schoolfield

Sewell Turpin, guardian to John Turpin, to retain L.26/5/6 3/4 overpaid by adms. of John Turpin above orphans' share of estate

Received of Laban Hill L.166/16/8, a dividend of Lewis Davis' estate

19 Mar., 1803   Selby Hudson
                                  Levin Davis
Test.; James Dale   Comfort Davis
      Jens. Knox??????

N. B. - There is a negro man, Isaac, valued at &70, the overplus paid in cash being L.96/16/8

F. 159   [blank]

F. 160   Tues., June 14, 1803   All Justices present

Orphan; Hugh Mills Stevenson (of Jonathan)
Guardian; Curtis Henderson & Lydia, his wife [she couldn't write]
Sureties; Nathaniel Bowen, Thomas N. Williams

F. 161   Orphan; Leah Davis (of Ezekiel)
         Guardian; Purnell Porter
         Sureties; Thomas N. Williams, Milby Purnell
F. 162   In presence of Matthew Hopkins

Laban Johnson & James Selby (of Zekiel) to view estate of Hannah,
         Thomas & Betsy Holloway, in care of Jedidah Holloway,
F. 163   guardian; before Richard Sampson: report; 160 acres; negro
         man David, 21

F. 164	Peter S. Corbin & John Holland to view estate of Micajah Selby, in care of Joseph Delastatius, guardian; before Wm.
F. 165	Holland: report; 150 acres

	Hillary Pitts, James Fassitt & George Bell to view estate of James, Johnson, William, Tubman, Thomas Simpson & Martha Gray, in
F. 166	care of Abisha Davis & wife, guardians; For James, sworn
F. 167	before Richard Sampson; for Johnson, sworn before Thos. N.
F. 168-9	Williams; for William, sworn before William Dale; for Tubman,
F. 170	sworn before William Dale; for Thomas S., sworn before Thomas
F. 171	N. Williams; for Martha, sworn before Thomas N. Williams:
F. 172	report; 375 acres; mentions clearing where Isaac Warrington lives; clearing where Powell Pennewell lives; small field adjoining to Stephen Anderson's lot; mentions Mrs. Davis' thirds

F. 173	John Postly & Isaac Evans to ascertain what part of estate of John Kirby Taylor (of George) was remaining in the hands of Thomas Newbold, deceased: witness; John Holland, Esq.; sister Mary Taylor married Thomas Newbold; Thomas became guardian upon
R. 174	her death; Thomas & wife obtained judgement at Feb. 1801 term against Leah Taylor, adm. of George, for property in possession of George, which descended to his children by death of Sarah Kerby; John Kirby Taylor's estate in hands of Thomas Newbold - negro Isaac 24, girl Belinda 6; adm. of Thomas Newbold to deliver to Peter Parker above articles for use of John K. Taylor

F. 175	William Handy & Thomas Robins Handy became bond for eight children of Angello Atkinson, deceased, viz; Sarah Williams (wife of Isaac), Joshua, Isaac, Angello, George, Betsy, Benjamin & Anne; William Handy, on 15 Jan., 1793, bought lands of
F. 176	Angello Atkinson; in presence of John C. Bacon, Rhodes Clark [couldn't write]

F. 177	Apprentice; John Cottingham Johnson (of Levi), 8 on 12 Feb. next Bound to; John Reed, waterman, alias coaster Trade; coaster or waterman Sureties; John Taylor (bl.smith), Charles Pruitt By Trustees for the Poor; Saml. Handy, McKimmey Porter, Wm. Selby

F. 178	Apprentice; John Stapleford (son of William), of Somerset Co., 19 next Dec. Bound to; Jonathan Parsons Trade; common labour Surety; Elijah Parsons Before Boaz Walston, John Cathell

F. 179	Apprentice; Charles Ware, by consent of Stephen Sturgis, guardian Bound to; John Taylor, shoe maker Trade; shoe maker
F. 180	In presence of Jesse Bennett, John Williams

F. 181 Apprentice; Thomas Garretson Crapper, poor boy, 15
Bound to; James Wonnell, Jun., farmer
Trade; farming
Sureties; Robert Nairne, Moses Carey
By Trustees for the Poor; McKimmey Porter, Wm. Selby, George Hayward

F. 182 John Selby, adm. of Ann Walton, allowed 10% on sale of estate

Purnell F. Smith, by George W. Purnell, guardian, vs. James A. Collins & Peggy Williams, adms. of Isaac Williams; Maj. Edward Henry & Thomas N. Williams to ascertain what property of Purnell F. Smith was in hands of Isaac Williams, late guardian, at his death; also what property is entitled to the dividend of said Purnell's father's estate; also to a deed of gift from his father

Curtis Henderson & Lydia, his wife, admx. of Jonathan Stevenson, allowed 7 1/2% commission

James A. Collins & Peggy Williams, adms. of Isaac Williams, allowed L.57/19/3 for saving crop

James Atkinson, exe. of Robert Atkinson, allowed 10% on inventory

Stephen Redden & Daniel Handcock, exes. of John Redden, allowed 10% on balance of last account

F. 183 Nathaniel Bowen, exe. of John Bowen, allowed $239.99 in final account for appraised value of negroes Cudge & Jenny, included in inventory, but manumitted by deceased's will 12 months after his death

Nathaniel Davis, guardian to James Brittingham, to apply L.2/10 of estate for support & education

James Selby, adm. of Walton Collins, to sell horse

Hezekiah Johnson & Sarah Price, exes. of Arthur Price, to sell still

George Richardson, adm. of Benjamin Purnell, to sell estate

F. 184 John Bishop & Lanta Wright, adms. of John Wright, allowed 10% on estate, half of which to be returned by John Bishop

Register to charge Richard H. Handy, guardian to Charlotte Round, for sum allowed for board

Edward McGee objects to James A. Collins & Peggy Williams, adms. of Isaac Williams, passing any accounts

F. 185 Tues., Aug. 9, 1803   John Postly, Zadok Sturgis, Littleton Robins present

Orphan; William Whittington Jarman (of Belitha)
Guardian; James Jarman
Sureties; Curtis Henderson, Joshua Phillips

F. 186   Orphan; James Jarman (of Belitha)
          Guardian; James Jarman
          Sureties; Curtis Henderson, Joshua Phillips

F. 187   Orphan; Esther Selby (of Levin)
          Guardian; Elisha Gunby
          Sureties; John N. Whittington, William A. Marshall
          In presence of Matthew Hopkins

Elijah Stevenson discharged from guardianship to Arey Henderson; Levi Henderson new guardian

F. 188   Orphan; Arey Henderson (of Outten)
          Guardian; Levi Henderson
          Sureties; Levi Houston, William F. Adams
          In presence of Matthew Hopkins

Sewell Turpin discharged from guardianship to John Turpin; William Turpin new guardian

F. 189   Orphan; John Turpin (of John)
          Guardian; William Turpin
          Sureties; Sewell Turpin, John Richards
          In presence of Matthew Hopkins

          Orphan; Elizabeth Selby (of James)
F. 190   Guardian; William Selby (of Accomack Co., VA)
          Sureties; Rowland Bevans, Ephraim K. Wilson
          In presence of Matthew Hopkins

Timothy Irons discharged for guardianship to William Dorman; Samuel Dorman new guardian

          Orphan; William Dorman (of Samuel)
F. 191   Guardian; Samuel Dorman
          Sureties; John Dorman, Henry Townsend

Edward Hammond & wife discharged from guardianship to John B. Baker; Seth Whaley new guardian

          Orphan; John B. Baker (of Levin)
F. 192   Guardian; Seth Whaley
          Sureties; John P. Mitchell, Levin Mitchell

          Orphan; James Bruff (of James)
F. 193   Guardian; Zipporah Bruff
          Sureties; Joshua Prideaux, Joseph Bruff

	Orphan; Catherine Selby (of Thomas)

F. 194   Orphan; Catherine Selby (of Thomas)
         Guardian; Elizabeth Selby
         Sureties; Isaac Ayres, Selby Parker

F. 195   Orphan; Peggy Selby (of Thomas)
         Guardian; Elizabeth Selby
         Sureties; Isaac Ayres, Selby Parker

Orphan; Martha Selby (of Thomas)
Guardian; Elizabeth Selby
Sureties; Isaac Ayres, Selby Parker

F. 196   Orphan; Kendal Selby (of Thos.)
         Guardian; Elizabeth Selby
         Sureties; Isaac Ayres, Selby Parker

F. 197   Orphan; Thomas Selby (of Thomas)
         Guardian; Elizabeth Selby
         Sureties; Isaac Ayres, Selby Parker

F. 198   Apprentice; John Gibbs (of John), 17 on 21 May last
         Bound to; Joshua Evans
         Trade; boot & shoe maker
         Sureties; Timothy Irons, John Deckerson

F. 199   David Johnson & Lemuel Showell to view estate of Milby &
F. 200   Robert Kirby, in care of Thomas Franklin & wife, guardians;
         before Abisha Davis: report; 190 acres; half of small greas
         [grist] mill

F. 201   Rowland E. Bevans, guardian to Tabitha & Nancy Selby (of
         James, P. Creek), to receive estate from John Tunnell & Mary,
his wife, exex. of James Selby: list of property; negro men Jack,
         George, Ned; boys Levin & Handy; women Grace, Dinah & Bet;
F. 202   girl Milly; mentions note of William Selby

                               Saml. McMaster
                               Joseph Houston

Rowland E. Bevans, guardian to James Selby (of James, P. Creek), to
         receive estate from John Tunnell & Mary, his wife, exex. of
F. 203   James Selby: list; negro boy Leges(?)

                               Saml. McMaster
                               Joseph Houston

F. 204   Cornelius Ennis, guardian to Rachel Ennis, to sell negro
         Esther; sold to Boaz Ennis for L.61

Petition of Annanias Dale & William Perkins for counter security from
Sally Tubbs, exe. of Joseph Tubbs, lately intermarried with Henry
Hudson

(cont.)

F. 205 In presence of;   James Selby (of Zekele)
        Matthew Hopkins   Josiah Mitchell

F. 206 Apprentice; Benjamin Schoolfield, by consent of his mother,
        Leah Schoolfield, widow of Stephen [she couldn't write]
        Bound to; William Smith, hatter
        Term; till 21, Dec. 13, 1808
        Trade; hatter
F. 207 In presents of Edward Stevenson, Benj. Aydelott

In consideration of $60, to be paid by Lazarus Harman, I do discharge
his son Lloyd from indentures of apprenticeship to me

Test.; John Worrelaw(?)   Outterbridge Horsey

        Apprentice; Lloyd Harmon, 17 on 2 July last, by consent of
        his father, Lazarus [couldn't write]
        Bound to; John Bishop, merchant, coasting trade
        Trade; coasting trade
F. 208 In presence of Matthew Hopkins, John A. Townsend

F. 209 Apprentice; James Morris Bowden (son of Hessey Murphy), 8 on
        13 Sept., 1803
        Bound to; Solomon Smith
        Trade; common labour
        Surety; William Richardson
F. 209b Before Boaz Walston, Isaac Hearn

Petition of William Selby & William Quinton, exes. of Samuel Nicholson
& adms. dbn of Isaac Nicholson; ask court to charge estate of Samuel,
brother & late exe. of Isaac, with errors made while he was exe.;
granted

F. 210 Jacob Boston, guardian to Levin Henderson, discharged from
        passing accounts

William Watts & Sarah, his wife, admx. of John S. Purnell, allowed in
final account for lowest priced yoke of oxen in inventory, the most
valuable horse & one cow, lost by providential accident

Thomas S. Fassitt, Esq., guardian to Margaret Fassitt, to rent real
estate in occupation of Handy Davis

Littleton Long & Anderson Patterson to view estate of Arey Henderson,
in care of Levi Henderson, guardian

John Postly, Edward Henry & Levin Mitchell to settle dispute between
William Winder, adm. dbn of John Rackliff, & Alexander Franklin, adm.
of Levin Riley

        Maj. Edward Henry & John Richards to view property of John
F. 211 Turpin, in care of William Turpin, guardian

Barnaby Henderson & Elizabeth, his wife, guardians to John, Esther & Sarah Bowen, discharged from passing accounts

Joseph Houston & Thomas Merrill to view estate of James, Tabitha & Nancy Selby, in care of Rowland Bevans, guardian

Rowland E. Bevans, adm. of Ephraim Henderson, to sell personal estate

Levin Mitchell, exe. of Joshua Mitchell, to sell perishable property

William & Betsy Pollitt, adms. of Samuel Pollitt, to sell corn brandy & other perishable articles

F. 212   John O. Sturgis & Samuel A. Harper, Esq., to view estate of Hugh M. Stevenson, in care of Curtis Henderson & Lydia, his wife, guardians

John P. Mitchell & Abisha Davis, Esqs., to distribute personal estate of Levin Baker, deceased, between widow & John B. Baker

Register to open accounts on estate of Belitha Powell & allow Jesse Powell, exe., for debts paid

Lilla(?) Ward vs. Esther Ward, exe. of Jesse Ward; plaintiff entitled to loom, warping bars & box in inventory, but given to her by deceased

F. 213   Henry Hudson & Sarah, his wife, exex. of Joseph Tubbs, allowed for mare since dead & beef killed for food; also for debt due Dr. Purnell, for finishing crop & for fees paid Col. Handy, late Register

Jesse Powell, adm. dbn of John Powell, allowed 5% on estate

Samuel Ennis, guardian to Mary, Samuel & Joseph Ennis, passed account for time he boarded orphans; did not include time they were boarded & clothed by Eli Hudson

Jacob Richards & Sally Maddox, admx. of Marcy Maddox, allowed 5% on balance of estate

F. 214   Annanias Powell, adm. of Thomas Webb, allowed sum paid William Reily Evans for balance due him from estate of Mary Truitt, which deceased administered

Thomas Parramore, guardian to Thomas Parramore, to retain amount of costs expended

Exes. of Arthur Price, with consent of guardian of several minors, to sell negroes

Sarah Redden vs. Daniel Handcock & Stephen Redden, exes. of John Redden; negro Stephen, mentioned in marriage contract between plaintiff & deceased, to be considered separate property of Sarah & she to relinquish claim to other negroes in estate

F. 215   Milby Purnell, adm. of Thomas Rigsby, to advertise in Duane's
         paper at Philadelphia & Cowan's paper at Easton for creditors
to exhibit claims

From distribution of John Turpin's estate, it appears that Southey
Whittington, guardian to Anne Turpin, received more than her share;
guardian to sell negro Lucy & her child, Sarah

Register to deduct $67.73 from inventory of estate of Robert Atkinson
before distribution for property purchased by Milby Atkinson as
settlement of award in Worcester Co. Court; also $40, a debt due from
Elijah Sturgis, to be charged to adm.

Levin Mitchell, exe. of Joshua Mitchell, was asked by deceased to
purchase mourning dresses for his sister & two nieces, & for Patty
Hadder, but made no provision in will; expense allowed

F. 216   George Truitt & Sally, his wife, guardian to John & William
         Bishop, to give orphans three months schooling

Joshua Prideaux & William Hudson to distribute estate of Thomas Selby
among next of kin

Charles Bennett & Sarah, his wife, ask court to not allow Isaac Ayres
to pass accounts on estate of Benjamin Purnell, Jun.

James Houston, in consideration of $50, quits all claims to shares of
estate of John Parramore & Mary, his wife, due his wife Mary, daughter
of said John & Mary; in presence of Matthew Hopkins

F. 217   Thomas Parramore, for $50, quits all claims on estates of his
         parents, John & Mary Parramore; in presence of Matthew
Hopkins

List of property from estate of Purnell F. Smith remaining in hands of
Isaac Williams, late guardian; adm. of said Williams allowed for same

F. 218   [blank]

F. 219   Tues., Oct. 11, 1803   John Postly, Zadok Sturgis present

Orphan; Levin Selby (of Levin)
Guardian; Selby Parker
Sureties; Levin Pollitt, Elijah Colbourn

F. 220   Orphan; Elizabeth Selby
         Guardian; Selby Parker
         Sureties; Levin Pollitt, Elijah Coulbourn

         Orphan; Peggy Handy (of James)
F. 221   Guardian; Nancy Handy
         Sureties; Charles Bennett, Ephraim K. Wilson

F. 222
Orphan; George Handy (of James)
Guardian; Nancy Handy
Sureties; Charles Bennett, Ephraim K. Wilson

Orphan; Levin Handy (of James)
Guardian; Nancy Handy
Sureties; Charles Bennett, Ephraim K. Wilson

F. 223
Orphan; Matthias Handy (of James)
Guardian; Nancy Handy
Sureties; Charles Bennett, Ephraim K. Wilson

F. 224
Orphan; Arthur Price (of Arthur)
Guardian; Matthias Lindsey
Sureties; James Givan, Ephraim Tilghman
In presence of Matthew Hopkins

F. 225
Orphan; Samuel Adams Milbourn
Guardian; Kitturah Milbourn
Sureties; Samuel A. Harper, William Harper

F. 226
Orphan; Levin Townsend (of Levin)
Guardian; William Hudson
Sureties; John Ayres, Robert J. H. Handy

Orphan; Euphemia Townsend (of Levin, Indian Town)
Guardian; William Hudson
Sureties; John Ayres, Robert J. H. Handy

F. 227
Apprentice; Purnell Brittingham (of Elijah)
Bound to; Benjamin Gunby, planter & miller
Trade; farmer & miller
F. 228
Sureties; John Selby, Michael Tarr
In presence of John Gunby, John Holland

Apprentice; William Magar, 21 on 15 Nov., 1812, by consent of his mother Milly [couldn't write]
Bound to; Josiah Hubbell
Trade; mariner
In presence of McKimmey Porter, James Givan

F. 229 Peter S. Corbin, adm. dbn of Daniel Selby, allowed 10% on estate

Laban Johnson & Laban Hill to distribute estate of Levin Baker, in hands of Jonathan Baker, adm. dbn

Jonathan Baker, adm. dbn of Levin Baker, to sell orphans' shares of estate

James Bevans & Levin Sturgis to view estate of Arthur Price, in care of Matthias Lindsey, guardian

Nancy Handy, adm. of James Handy, to sell personal estate

'71'

F. 230 Adam Bravard, guardian to James Bravard, discharged from passing accounts untill profits accrue

Lemuel Parker, guardian to Sacker Parker, discharged from passing accounts, as there is no profit from estate

John Cottingham & Thomas R. Handy to view estate of Samuel A. Milbourn, in care of Kitturah Milbourn, guardian

Letters of adm. dbn cwa on estate of Levin Townsend granted to William Hudson & Priscilla, his wife

William Hudson & Priscilla, his wife, adm. dbn cwa of Levin Townsend, to sell stock & perishable property

Betty Kellam, adm. of Joseph Kellam, to sell negro Bob, two horses & perishable property

F. 231 John Benston & wife, exex. of Isaac Layfield, allowed costs of suit against Anderson Patterson

Edward Stevenson & Edward Lambden to distribute estate of Isaac Layfield, in possession of John Benston & wife, exex.

John Benston & wife, guardian to Thomas Layfield, discharged from passing accounts

Edward Henry & Thomas N. Williams to view estate of Mary Mitchell, in care of Levin Mitchell, guardian

John Holland & George Truitt, exes. of Jonathan Hutcheson, allowed 10% on sale of estate

F. 232 Nancy Richardson, adm. of Robert M. Richardson, to sell stock & perishable property

Lydia Warren, adm. of Dr. John Warren, allowed for horse that died with the glanders; before Thos. N. Williams

William White (of Barclay) vs. John Taylor, late guardian; guardian to deliver to him his estate

William Selby & William Quinton, exes. of Samuel Nicholson (late guardian to Nancy Nicholson), to exhibit amount of charges against ward & credits for profits on her estate

F. 233 Isaac Ayres, guardian to Harrison A. & William S.(?) Schoolfield, to charge himself L.11/5/6, the profits of their estate since 1800

F. 234-7 [blank]

F. 238 Tues., Dec. 13, 1803 John Postly, Littleton Robins present

Robert Nairne, Esq., Sheriff

Orphan; Isaac Selby (of William)
Guardian; Charles Hammond
Sureties; Samuel Handy, George Hayward

F. 239 Orphan; Nancy Selby (of William)
        Guardian; Charles Hammond
        Sureties; Samuel Handy, George Hayward

        Orphan; James Dryden (of David)
F. 240 Guardian; Kendal Crapper
        Sureties; Nathaniel Bowen, Barnaby Henderson

        Apprentice; Laban Baker (of Zadok), 15
        Bound to; James Dickerson
        Trade; shoe maker
F. 241 Sureties; John P. Mitchell, Seth Whaley

F. 242 Apprentice; Isaac Waters (of Patrick)
        Bound to; Daniel Patrick
        Trade; cordwainer
        Sureties; Maj. John Purnell, Matthias Dorman

F. 243 Apprentice; James Dryden (of David), 10 next Feb.
        Bound to; Kendal Crapper
        Trade; blacksmith
F. 244 Sureties; Nathaniel Bowen, Barnaby Henderson

F. 245 Littleton Long & Anderson Patterson to view estate of Ara
        [also Arey] Henderson (of Outten, granddaughter of Jacob), in
        care of Levi Henderson, guardian; before Edward Stevenson:
F. 246 report; mentions negro woman Lydda; widow's thirds

F. 247 John Cottingham & Thomas R. Handy to view estate of Samuel A.
        Milbourn, in care of Kitturah Milbourn, guardian; before
F. 248 Benjamin Dennis: report; mentions improvements in Nasswadux
        on Pocomoke River; negro man Abraham, Leah 33, James 16,
F. 249 Henry 9, Levin 9, Linda 11; improvements on forest place;
        improvements on plantation on the seaside; 200 acres on
Carey's Creek(?) & binding on Pocomoke River & land near Mr. Bell's
called 'Wilderness' or 'Desert'; widow's dower

F. 250 James Bevans & Levin Sturgis to view estate of Arthur Price,
        in care of Matthias Lindsey; before W. Holland: report; 50
F. 251 acres

The Orphans Court of Somerset Co. appointed Littleton Dennis & Samuel
        Smith to view estate of Thomas Benston, in care of Michael
F. 252 Cluff, guardian; before Jno. Fleming: report; [says no land
F. 253 & then proceeds to report on improvements on land]

Test.; Geo Handy, Register of Wills for Somerset Co.

F. 254	John O. Sturgis & Samuel A. Harper to view to view estate of Hugh M. Stevenson, in care of Curtis Henderson & wife, guardians; before Jesse Bennett: report; one plantation, 90 acres
F. 255	Maj. Edward Henry & Thomas N. Williams to view estate of Mary Mitchell, in care of Levin Mitchell, testamentary guardian:
F. 256	report; negro Isaac 23, Plem 23, Zeb 19, Charles 17, Nancy 25, Rachel 24, Hector 55, George 60, John 5, Stephen 3, Caleb 2, Hager 70, Dinia 60, Sarah 5, Minter 5, Sue 10 months, Comfort 5 months
F. 257	William Winder, adm. dbn of John Rackliff, Sen. & Jun. vs. Alexander Franklin, adm. dbn of Levin Riley; John Postly, Edward Henry & Levin Mitchell to settle dispute; estate of
F. 258	Levin Riley is indebted to estates of John Rackliff, Sen. & Jun., for L.12/14/5 1/2; [account of how sum was figured];
F. 259	mentions Mr. Reyley's mother, deceased, Adam Bravard
F. 260	Southey Whittington, guardian to Anne Turpin (of John), to sell negro woman Lucy & her child; sold at Maj. Benjamin Conner's store in Somerset Co.; bought by Southey Whittington
F. 261	Apprentice; Robert Johnson (of Robert, his mother also deceased), 18 & 5 months Bound to; William Collier, Jun., house carpenter & joiner Trade; house carpenter & joiner Sureties; William K__?__, Jesse Powell Before Abisha Davis, Richard Sampson
F. 262	Apprentice; Thomas Dennis, 8 on 1 Jan. next, by consent of his father Zedekiah [couldn't write] Bound to; Obediah [also Obed] Latchum Trade; taylor
F. 263	In presence of Abisha Davis
F. 264	Apprentice; Mary Dennis, 7 on 1 Mar. next, by consent of her father Zedekiah Bound to; William Hudson [couldn't write] Trade; taylor Before Abisha Davis
F. 265	Apprentice; Polly Carter (daughter of Jesse), 10 on 22 Dec., 1803 Bound to: William Daily [also Dayly] Trade; spinning & weaving, & other things what is common for women to do Surety; Thomas Layfield Before; Boaz Walston, Isaac Hearn
F. 266	William Truitt (of Belitha), 10 Oct. last, by consent of his mother Bound to; George Wainright [also Winright, couldn't write]

(cont.)

Trade; common labour until 16, then put to some other trade
Surety; John Schockley

F. 267 Before Boaz Walston, John Cathell

Michael Cluff, guardian to Thomas Benston, to expend whole estate for education

Henry & Sarah Adams, admx. of William F. Adams, to sell corn brandy, fodder & tobacco

John P. Mitchell & Robert Mitchell to divide negroes from estate of Levin Baker among widow & orphans

John P. Marshall, Esq., exe. of Elizabeth Marshall, to sell representatives estate (except negroes & wearing apparel)

F. 268 James Selby, adm. of Walter Collins, to sell personal estate

Hezekiah Johnson, adm. of Michael Tarr (of Saml.), to sell personal estate

Exes. of Arthur Price allowed for L.11/10/0 spent for board of Priscilla Price, one orphan, & for her funeral

Edward Hammond, Sen., & Nixon Davis, Esq., to settle dispute between John Williams & wife, & William Hammond, Sen., late guardian

Benjamin Purnell & McKimmey Porter to view property of Isaac & Nancy Selby, in care of Charles Hammond, guardian

F. 269 George Bell, Hillary Pitts & James Fassitt to view estate of heirs of Johnson Gray, in care of Abisha Davis & wife, guardians

Levin Mitchell & Edward Henry to distribute personal estate of William Stevenson

John Selby, adm. of Ann Walton, to advertise in __?__ & Brown's (?) paper at Philadelphia for creditors to exhibit claims

Matthias Lindsey, guardian to Arthur Price, to clear 5 acres of land

Charles Hammond, guardian to Isaac & Nancy Selby, to sell estate allotted to them from estates of Parker & Glippery(?) Selby (except negroes)

F. 270 Abisha Davis & Martha, his wife, guardians to James, Johnson, Tubman, Thomas, William & Martha Gray, to cut dead timber & apply proceeds to education

Robert Hudson, guardian to Nathaniel Richards, allowed for employing Milby Atkinson to keep negro child, & for 6 years maintaining negro girl Leah

Turner Davis & John Powell to ascertain sum due Samuel Dryden, late guardian to James Dryden

F. 271   Littleton Robins, John Bishop & Isaac Franklin appointed Justices

Robt. Bowie   Al. Hanson, Chanc.

Wit.; Honourable Alexander Contee Hanson, Chancellor

F. 272   Tues., Feb. 14, 1804   All Justices present

Orphan; Isaac Benston (of Elias)
Guardian; Levin Henderson
Sureties; James Henderson, Joseph Houston
In presence of Matthew Hopkins

F. 273   Orphan; Matilda Townsend (of Capt. Levin)
         Guardian; Betsy Tarr, wife of Peter
         Sureties; George Miles, Michael Tarr

         Orphan; Maria Townsend (of Capt. Levin)
F. 274   Guardian; Betsy Tarr, wife of Peter
         Sureties; George Miles, Michael Tarr

         Orphan; Jane Townsend
F. 275   Guardian; Betsy Tarr, wife of Peter
         Sureties; George Miles, Michael Tarr

         Orphan; Sally Townsend
         Guardian; Betsy Tarr, wife of Peter
F. 276   Sureties; George Miles, Michael Tarr

Orphan; Selby Johnson (of Geo.?)
Guardian; Levin Hill
Sureties; John Allen, Frederick Conner
In presence of Matthew Hopkins

F. 277   Orphan; George Johnson
         Guardian; Levin Hill
         Sureties; John Allen, Matthias Lindsey

         Orphan; Eleanor Townsend (of Levin)
F. 278   Guardian; John C. Bacon
         Sureties; William Corbin, Anthony Bacon
         In presence of Matthew Hopkins

         Orphan; Charles Morris (of Phillip)
         Guardian; Amelia Morris [couldn't write]
F. 279   Sureties; William Jones, William Hogshare [also Hogshier]
         In presence of Matthew Hopkins

| | Orphan; Peter Morris (of Philip)
| | Guardian; Amelia Morris
| | Sureties; William Jones, William Hogshare
| F. 280 | In presence of Matthew Hopkins

Apprentice; Thomas Powell (of Thomas), 16 on 3 May next
Bound to; Capt. John Fassitt
Trade; coasting business
Sureties; Sewell Turpin, Thomas Rackliffe

| F. 281 | Apprentice; John Goote (of William), 11
| | Bound to; Obediah Carey
| | Trade; cooper
| F. 282 | Sureties; Robertson Lamberson, Elisha Jones

| F. 283 | Apprentice; Thomas Goote (of William), 13 on 24 Jan. last
| | Bound to; Robertson Lamberson
| | Trade; cordwainer
| | Sureties; Obediah Carey, William Aydelott

| F. 284 | Apprentice; James Davis (of William), 14
| | Bound to; Elisha Jones
| | Trade; carpenter
| F. 285 | Sureties; William Aydelott, Benjamin Aydelott

| | Apprentice; James Trader (of Jonathan), 11 on 19 May next, by consent of his mother
| | Bound to; John Long
| F. 286 | Trade; taylor
| | Sureties; Levin Long, Littleton Davis

| F. 287 | Apprentice; Kendall Webb (of Thomas), 14 on 7 Jan. last
| | Bound to; John Powell
| | Trade; shoe & boot maker
| | Sureties; William Jones, Elijah Reed

| F. 288 | Apprentice; John Trader (of Jonathan), 7 on 28 Oct. last
| | Bound to; Robert Blair
| | Trade; coasting business
| F. 289 | Sureties; Zadok Sturgis, James Collins (Queponco)

| F. 290 | Apprentice; John Prideaux (of John)
| | Bound to; Thomas Patrick
| | Trade; shoe & boot maker
| | Sureties; James Collins, Isaac Franklin

| F. 291 | Apprentice; Levi Robertson (of John), 15 on 19 June next, by consent of his mother
| | Bound to; Jesse Riggen
| | Trade; common plantation business, use of tools, shop joiner
| F. 292 | Sureties; Joshua Evans, George Houston (of John)

F. 293   Apprentice; Henny George, 10
         Bound to; William Bennitt (of James)
         Trade; common house business; weaving, spinning & c.
         Sureties; John Hall, John Spencer

F. 294   Apprentice; Benjamin Tull (of Benjamin), 14, by consent of
         his mother
         Bound to; Ezekiel Coston
         Trade; farmer
F. 295   Sureties; Levin Pollitt, Esq., John Allen

         Apprentice; Branson Collins, 15, mulatto, son of Mary Collins
F. 296   Bound to; John Williams
         Trade; common plantation business
         Sureties; Joshua Fleming, Sen., Andrew Brown

F. 297   Apprentice; Stephen Johnson, 13, mulatto, son of Esther
         Bound to; Joshua Fleming, Sen.
         Trade; common plantation business
         Sureties; John Williams (Neswadix), Andrew Brown

F. 298   Apprentice; James Bevans (of William), 18
         Bound to; Isaac Brittingham
         Trade; common plantation business
F. 299   Sureties; Solomon Townsend, Timothy Irons

F. 300   Joseph Houston & Thomas Merrill, Sen., to view estate of
         Tabitha, James & Nancy Selby, in care of Rowland Bevans,
F. 301   guardian; before Edward Stevenson: report

F. 302   Richard Sampson & Abisha Davis to view estate of John B.
F. 303   Baker, in care of Seth Whaley, guardian; before James Law:
F. 304   report; 138 acres

         Turner Davis & John Powell to view estate of James Dryden, in care of
         Kendal Crapper, guardian, & to ascertain anything due Samuel
F. 305   Dryden, late guardian; before John Cathell: report; 50 acres
         in Wicomico Hundred

F. 306   Annanias Powell & William Perkins, sureties for Sally Tubbs
         (now married to Henry Hudson) on her adm. of estate of Joseph
         Tubbs, requested counter security, which has not been given; estate
         appraised by David Johnson & Lemuel Showell; before Joseph
F. 307   Gray: [gives inventory]

         Alexander Massey, security for Martha Baker, on estate of
F. 308   Handcock Baker (she now wife of James Johnson), asks counter
         security of said James: said James' securities; Joseph Gray,
         David Johnson; in presence of James Law, Levin Derickson

F. 309   Edward Stevenson & Edward Lambden to distribute estate of
         Isaac Layfield, in hands of John Benston & Esther, his wife,
         exex.; distribution took place at house of John Benson on 9
                                  (cont.)

F. 310   Nov., 1803; Robert Snead & wife not present;
          1) to Levin Henderson & Nancy, his wife; negro woman Charity & child
          2) to James Barrot & Caty, his wife; boy Elijah
          3) to Joseph Houston, guardian to Nancy & Isaac Layfield (of George); bonds from Levin Henderson & James Barrot
          4) shares belonging to Mary Patterson's children, wife of Anderson, also to Robert Snead & wife, & Thomas Layfield, together with Mrs. Benson's thirds, left in hands of Mrs. John Benson

F. 311   Apprentice; Thomas Carey (of Shadrach), 10 on 2 Feb. next, by consent of his mother Betsy Holloway
          Bound to; Kendal Merrill
          Trade; seemster, otherwise taylor
F. 312   In presence of Thomas N. Williams, John Davis
          Sureties; William Riley, Elijah Brittingham

F. 313   Apprentice; John Henderson (of Purnell), 11 on 23 Feb. next
          Bound to; Peter Lister [also Lyster]
          Trade; blacksmith
F. 314   In presence of Thos. N. Williams, John Davis
          Sureties; William Lister, Levi Mills

F. 315   Apprentice; William Trehearn, by consent of his father William [couldn't write]
          Bound to; John Worrilaw, blacksmith
          Trade; blacksmith
          Term; 9 years
F. 316   Witness; Matthew Hopkins

F. 317   Apprentice; James Butler, 11 on 9 June next, by consent of his father Samuel [couldn't write]
          Bound to; Samuel Lokey, carpenter [couldn't write]
          Trade; carpenter
F. 318   Before James Brodwatter, Wm. Holland

          Apprentice; John Hook, poor orphan, by consent of his mother Mary Hook
          Bound to; John McCalley, Jun. [also McCauley], shoe maker
F. 319   Term; till 6 Apr., 1808
          Surety; Samuel Porter
          Trade; shoe maker
          Before Jesse Bennett, Nixon Davis

F. 320   Apprentice; James Taylor, poor child
          Bound to; Daniel Handcock, farmer
          Trade; farmer
F. 321   In presence of Wm. Holland, Samuel A. Harper

John Fassitt, adm. of William Fassitt, & his partner in trade, allowed for debts paid as agreed to by all representatives except James Fassitt

Sewell Turpin & Thomas Rackliff to view estate of John P. Marshall, in care of John P. Marshall, guardian

Purnell Johnson & Boaz Walston, Esqs., to view estate of Elijah C. W. Perdue, in care of James W. B. Perdue, guardian

F. 322 James Jarman, apprentice to Samuel Long, has been taken by his father to Delaware; Samuel Long discharged

John Fassitt, adm. of William Fassitt, allowed 6% on distribution balance

Littleton Dennis, one valuer of estate of Thomas Benston, lying in Somerset Co., states that farm needs barn; Michael Cluff, guardian, to build

F. 323 Peter Tarr & Betsy, his wife, admx. of Capt. Levin Townsend, allowed 5% on estate, including monies arising from sale of lands under an Act of Assembly; also widow allowed 1/8 part of land sold & 1/3 part of remainder

Peter Tarr & Betsy, his wife, admx. of Capt. Levin Townsend, allowed L.2/18 for Dr. John Sloan's claim, upon producing receipt from Levin Pollitt, his agent; also 50 shillings for expenses in Council's advice & $573.90 for sum due on bond of Levin Townsend to William Townsend

William, John & Anthony Bacon, exes. of James Bacon vs. Peter Tarr & Betsy, his wife, admx. of Levin Townsend; there remains money in hands of exes. of James Bacon, late trustee for sale of real estate of Capt. Levin Townsend; exes. to retain money for payment of Betsy Gunn

F. 324 John Cottingham & William Corbin, Esqs., to distribute estate of Levin Townsend, leaving in hands of admx. enough to pay claims

Peter Tarr & Betsy, his wife, guardian to Maria, Jane, Sally & Matilda Townsend, to sell estate (except negroes, a still & bedding)

John Cottingham & William Corbin, Esqs., to view estate of Eleanor Townsend, in care of John C. Bacon, guardian; guardian to sell personal property

John Cottingham & William Corbin, Esqs., to view estate of Maria, Jane, Sally & Matilda Townsend, in care of Peter Tarr & Betsy, his wife, guardians

F. 325 Benjamin Bishop, one child of Samuel Bishop, died during his minority; his share of his father's estate to be paid by Frederick Conner, adm. dbn, to John White, guardian to Elizabeth Bishop, only surviving child

William Hudson, exe. of Leah Townsend, allowed 5% on estate

Register, in settling accounts of Leah Townsend, late exe. of Levin Townsend, to allow 5% on inventory for her trouble settling same; also, William Hudson & Priscilla, his wife, adm. dbn of Levin Townsend, allowed 5% on inventory

George Truitt, guardian to John P. Dale, discharged from passing accounts

State at instance of James Selby, adm. of Walton Collins vs. Sewell Dryden & Martha, his wife; citation for detaining goods of said Walton; Martha to deliver bedstead to adm.

F. 326   Received Feb. 8, 1804, of Levi Houston, in full of real & personal estate

Test.; James Dickeson   William Henderson

Received Dec. 14, 1803, of William Hammond, Sen., guardian to Mary Hammond, L/44/9/6. in full for her share of her father's estate

Test.; Nixon Davis   John Williams

F. 327   Special Court, Mar. 16, 1804, at request of John Selby; all Justices present

William Caudrey & wife discharged from guardianship to Parker S. Bowen; John Selby new guardian

F. 328   Orphan; Parker Selby Bowen
Guardian; John Selby
Sureties; William Jones, Barnabas Henderson

Order of 14 Apr. last for William Caudrey & wife, guardians to Parker S. Bowen, to sell negro Lit, rescinded

Nathaniel Franklin, adm. dbn of William Franklin, to sell personal estate (except negroes)

F. 329   Special court, Mar. 20, 1804, at request of John Stevens; all Justices present

John Stevens & Elizabeth, his wife, by William Whittington, Esq., their solicitor, vs. David, Esme, Samuel, Molly & Nancy Richardson, children & co-heirs of George Richardson, deceased; John & Elizabeth Stevens state that a paper purporting to be will of George Richardson, who died on or about 4 Mar. instant, has been preferred for
F. 330   probate & is not his will; he was greatly addicted to liquor; he could not read or write; Elizabeth is co-heir of George; ask that will be rejected & adm. of estate be granted to them; if will is accepted, they accept negro man Abner bequeathed to John Stevens

F. 331   Will of George Richardson;
          1) to my son-in-law John Stevens & my daughter Elizabeth
          Stevens all my part of my mills & mill lands, 1100 acres; 2 acres I
          bought from Alexander McAllen; all lands I own except that bought of
          Thomas Martin; they to support my five younger children, David, Esme,
          Samuel, Molly & Nancy; friend Thomas Robins Handy appointed
F. 332   trustee to assist in maintaining other children; George
F. 333   Hayward trustee if said Handy cannot serve; John Custis Handy
          trustee if said Hayward cannot serve
          2) Son-in-law John Stevens to sell land I bought of Thomas Martin near
          Thomas Victor's; money to be applied to discharge of debts
          3) to son-in-law John Stevens negro man Abner
          John Stevens appointed exe.
                                                              his
F. 334   4 Feb., 1804   George X Richardson
                                                             mark

Witnesses; William Handy, John Rock, James Davis

Subpena issued for David, Esme, Samuel, Molly & Nancy Richardson

F. 335   David, Esme, Samuel, Molly & Nancy Richardson appear by
          Thomas Martin, Esq., guardian; no nothing of above matters

F. 336   Deposition of William Handy; was requested by George
          Richardson on 2 Feb. last to write will; did not feel he was
F. 337   of sound mind; could not sign name; talked of killing
          someone; asked Moses Hudson & Dr. Savage to tell Mr.
Richardson or his son-in-law that will would not stand

F. 338   Deposition of John Rock; found Mr. Richardson intoxicated,
          not capable of making will

          Deposition of James Davis; called by Capt. Richardson to
F. 339   witness will; he was intoxicated, not of mind to make will

F. 340   Will rejected by Court

          Apprentice; Daniel Harmon, mulatto, 17 on 4 July last, son
          of Esther Harmon
          Bound to; John Stevens
          Trade; common labour
F. 341   Sureties; John Rock, George Hayward

          Apprentice; Henry Harmon, mulatto, 16 on 25 Nov. last, son of
F. 342   Esther Harman
          Bound to; John Stevens
          Trade; common labour
          Sureties; John Rock, George Hayward

F. 343   John Stevens, adm. of George Richardson, to sell personal
          estate (except negroes)

Received Feb. 20, 1804, of John Fassitt, exe. of William, $129.96, my part of William Fassitt's estate

Wit.; Thos. Fassitt   Sewell Turpin

Received Feb. 20, 1804, of John Fassitt, exe. of William Fassitt, $129.96, my 1/8 part of William's estate

Wit.; Thomas Fassitt   Thos. P. Rackliffe

Received Feb. 21, 1804, of John Fassitt, exe. of Wm. Fassitt, $129.96, my 1/8 part of William's estate

Wit.; Thos. Fassitt   Sally Fassitt

F. 344   Received Feb. 21, 1804, of John Fassitt, exe. of Wm. Fassitt, $129.96, my 1/8 part of Wm's estate

Wit.; Thos. Fassitt   Edward Bridell

Received Feb. 21, 1804, of John Fassitt, exe. of William Fassitt, $129.96, my 1/8 part of William's estate

Wit.; Edward Bridell   Thos. Fassitt

Received Feb. 27, 1804, of John Fassitt, exe. of William Fassitt, $129.96, my 1/8 part of William's estate

Wit.; Adam Bravard   Elizabeth Fassitt

Received of John Fassitt, exe. of William Fassitt, $129.96, balance of final account of estate of William

Wit.; Thos. Fassitt   James Fassitt

F. 345   Tues., Apr. 10, 1804   All Justices present

          Orphan; Charlotte Maddux
          Guardian; William Bacon
F. 346   Sureties; Jacob Richards, James Bevans

Orphan; David Richardson
Guardian; John Stevens
Sureties; John Rock, William Quinton

F. 347   Orphan; Esme Richardson
          Guardian; John Stevens
          Sureties; John Rock, William Quinton

          Orphan; Samuel Richardson
F. 348   Guardian; John Stevens
          Sureties; John Rock, William Quinton

```
              Orphan; Molly Richardson
F. 349        Guardian; John Stevens
              Sureties; John Rock, William Quinton

              Orphan; Nancy Richardson
              Guardian; John Stevens
F. 350        Sureties; John Rock, William Quinton

Orphan; George Gunn (of Samuel)
Guardian; Esther Purnell
Sureties; George Bratten, Littleton Robins
In presence of Matthew Hopkins

F. 351        Apprentice; James Melvin (of Samuel), 14 on 13 Dec. last
              Bound to; James Davis
              Trade; cask cooper
              Sureties; John Melvin, James Melvin

F. 352        Apprentice; Thomas Melvin (of Samuel), 13 on 15 July next
              Bound to; John Melvin
              Trade; cypress cooper
F. 353        Sureties; James Davis, James Melvin

              Apprentice; Levin Gibbs (of Abraham), 14 on 15 instant
              Bound to; William Tingle
F. 354        Trade; hatter
              Sureties; John Rock, Esme Purnell

F. 355        Apprentice; William Handcock (of Eli), 13
              Bound to; Levin Briddell
              Trade; farmer
              Sureties; David Briddle, Benjamin Briddle

F. 356        Apprentice; Nancy Guthrey (of William), 8 on 5 Nov. last
              Bound to; Eleanor Guthrey
F. 357        Trade; common house business - sew, spin & knit
              Sureties; Severn Guthrey, [blank]

F. 358        Purnell Johnson & Boaz Walston, Esq., to view estate of
              Elijah C. W. Perdue (of James), in care of James W. B.
F. 359        Perdue, guardian; before Isaac Hearn: report; mentions negro
              boy Sevron 13, Rachel 19

F. 360        Laban Johnson, Levin Mitchell & Maj. Edward Henry to
              distribute estate of Rouse Fassitt, in hands of Thomas S.
              Fassitt;
F. 361        1) to Thomas S. Fassitt; livestock
              2) to Zipporah Fassitt; livestock
3) to Margaret Fassitt

F. 362        Distribution of negroes from estate of James Selby by Samuel
F. 363        McMaster & Joseph Houston, delivered to Rowland Bevans,
              guardian;
                              (cont.)
```

1) to Elizabeth Selby; negro man George, man Need, woman Grace
2) to Tabitha Selby; woman Diner, boy Levin, girl Milla
3) to Nancy Selby; boy Handy, girl Betty, man Jack

F. 364	Distribution of estate of Levin Baker by Laban Johnson & Laban Hill, in hands of Jonathan Baker, adm. dbn.; 1) to children [list]
F. 365	2) to Jonathan Baker, his part of his father's estate
F. 366	[cont.]
F. 367	Maj. Edward Henry & Thomas N. Williams, Esq., to ascertain property of Purnell F. Smith (of John), in possession of Isaac Williams, late guardian, at the time of said Isaac's
F. 368	death: report; evidence adduced by Dr. George W. Purnell, guardian, & James A. Collins, adm. of Isaac, examined; mentions negro man Jacob; original distribution made 30 Mar.,
F. 369	1798

BOOK 9, 1804 - 1805

MICROFILM: CR 46,719-2

MSA No.: CM 1123-9

Worcester County Orphans Court Proceedings, 1804-5, JBR-9, Book #2

F. 1 Tues., Apr. 10, 1804 (cont.) All Justices present

Account of sales of property of Betsy, Tabitha & Nancy Selby, sold by Rowland Bevans, guardian; list of sales of estate of James Selby, deceased; items sold to Wm. Q. Dixon, William Bevans, Rowland

F. 2 Bevans, Joseph Houston, Walter Bayne, Henry Selby, Joseph Young; mentions Betsy's third part, to be paid to William Selby; Joseph Houston was clerk for sale of property of James Selby, Sen.; before Edwd. Stevenson; Bevans guardian to Tabitha & Nancy

F. 3 Account of sale of part of personal property of Margaret Fassitt (of Rouse), sold by Thomas S. Fassitt, guardian; paid off by E. Henry, Laban Johnson, Levin Mitchell; list of stock sold to Thomas Franklin, Thomas S. Fassitt, Thos. N. Williams, Dr.

F. 4 White, William Richards, Levi Brimer(?), James Jones, John Davis, William Benston; Edward Henry swears to above sale

F. 5 Surety bond from Milby Purnell, John Purnell (Queponco) & Esme Purnell to Peter Parker & Thomas Jones, who were bound to Milby Parker, guardian to Sarah Parker (of James); before Matthew Hopkins

F. 6 Apprentice; Samuel Holland, by consent of his mother, Sarah Hudson [also Hutson, couldn't write]
Bound to; Stephen Pilchard, blacksmith
Trade; blacksmith

F. 7 in presents of Edward Stevenson, Benj. Aydelott

Apprentice; Zacheus Henderson, by consent of his father, Benjamin
Bound to; James & Caleb Tilghman
Trade; cordwinding
Term; till 10 Feb., 1809

F. 8 In presents of Edward Stevenson, William Melvin

John Williams, master, asks to be released from recognizance entered into by him to Branson Collins, as it appears he has been bound in Somerset Co. & is residing there

John Melvin, adm. of Elijah Nelson, to sell personal estate

F. 9 Jonathan Baker, adm. dbn of Levin Baker, allowed 6% on property

Angello Atkinson, adm. of Joseph Tilghman, excused from exhibiting inventory or rendering accounts, the object in administering being to collect some debts

George Hayward & William Selby to view property of David, Esme, Samuel, Molly & Nancy Richardson, in care of John Stevens, guardian

'87'

Zadok Sturgis & Littleton R. Purnell to distribute negroes from estate of Charles Rackliffe, in hands of Sewell Turpin & wife, admx.

Maj. William Holland, guardian to John, George & Henry Selby, to sell negro girls Leah & Hannah, property of heirs of Daniel Selby

F. 10   John Bishop, adm. of Esther Pettitt, allowed 10% on estate

F. 11   Tues., June 12, 1804   All Justices present

F. 12
Orphan; William Sturgis (of John)
Guardian; Ebben Christopher
Sureties; Robert Nairne, Selby Parker
In presence of Matthew Hopkins

Orphan; Levi Merrill
Guardian; Levin Merrill
Sureties; James Melvin, Joshua Duer

F. 13   Orphan; Matthias Truitt (of Thomas)
Guardian; Littleton Truitt
Sureties; Thomas Whaley, Elijah Fooks
In presence of Matthew Hopkins

F. 14
Orphan; John Round
Guardian; Samuel H. Round [also Rownd], father
Sureties; Thomas Martin (of Thomas), Angello Atkinson

F. 15
Orphan; Henry Round
Guardian; Samuel H. Round, father
Sureties; Thomas Martin (of Thomas), Angello Atkinson

F. 16
Orphan; Martha Round
Guardian; Samuel H. Round, father
Sureties; Thomas Martin (of Thomas), Angelo Atkinson

F. 17
Orphan; Anne Round
Guardian; Samuel H. Round, father
Sureties; Thomas Martin (of Thos.), Angelo Atkinson

F. 18   James Bacon, appointed trustee to sell part of real estate of Capt. Levin Townsend, is since dead; John C. Bacon appointed to compleat sale to Major White: sureties; William Bacon, Anthony Bacon; sale for relief of Elizabeth Townsend & heirs of Levin

F. 19   Apprentice; James Rigsby (of Thomas), 10
Bound to; William Crapper
Trade; shoe maker
Sureties; Stephen White, John Taylor, Jun.

F. 20   Apprentice; Gillis P. Vincent (of George), 9
Bound to; Michael Murray
F. 21   Trade; clerk in retail store
Sureties; Levin Pollitt, John S. Purnell

F. 22   Apprentice; Benjamin Lewis Armstrong, mulatto, 13 last fall,
           son of Hannah
           Bound to; Zadok Sturgis
           Trade; farmer
F. 23   Sureties; Jacob Teague, Selby Parker

F. 24   Esme Purnell & Handy Jones to view estate of Charles & Peter
F. 25   Morris (of Phillip), in care of Amelia Morris, guardian;
           before John Purnell (Quepo.): report; 2/5 of property belongs
F. 26   orphans; mentions widow's thirds, other children

           Account of property of Isaac Benston received by Levin Henderson,
               Sen., guardian, from Henry & Sarah Adams, adms. of William F.
F. 27   Adams, late guardian: report; mentions old negro man Hector

           Apprentice; James Batts, 14 on 25 June, by consent of his
           father Henry [neither could write]
           Bound to; James Fookes (of Jesse)
           Trade; common labour
F. 28   Before John Cathell, John Dashiell

           Apprentice; Isaac Johnson, by consent of David Johnson, who
F. 29   was appointed guardian by will of Joseph Johnson
           Bound to; John Taylor, blacksmith
           Trade; blacksmith
           Term; till 19, but voluntarily binds self till 21
F. 30   Before Joseph Gray, Richard Sampson

Betty Truitt, adm. of Thomas Truitt, to sell enough furniture & stock
to pay debts

Edward Stevenson & Edward Lambden, Esqs., to view estate of Levi
Merrill, in care of Levin Merrill, guardian

           Jonathan Fookes & Billy Fookes to view estate of Matthias
F. 31   Truitt, in care of Littleton Truitt, guardian

Kitturah Milbourn, adm. of Thomas Milbourn, to sell personal estate
(except negroes)

William Fassitt & Thomas Franklin to revalue estate of Lambert
Collier, in care of George Davis & Sarah, his wife, guardians, as barn
has burned

James Dennis & Smith Johnson to view estate of Richard Shockley, in
care of John Shockley, guardian

Levin Mitchell & Edward Henry were appointed to divide estate of
William Stevenson, but said Mitchell is since dead; Edward Henry &
Joshua Prideaux to divide estate

           Alexander Franklin, adm. dbn of Levin Riley, allowed 10% on
F. 32   payment of debts

Sewell Turpin & John Bishop, Esqs., to distribute estates of Parker & Glippery Selby

John Stevenson, guardian to William Henderson, discharged from passing accounts

Thomas & Nancy Dryden, adms. of Isaac Dryden, allowed 7 1/2% on estate

John Bishop, one adm. of John Wright, allowed L.20/15/9 for money advanced to pay debts

F. 33   Attalanta Wright, guardian to Robert, Nancy & John Wright, to retain interest on dividends from father John Wright's estate

F. 34   Tues., Aug. 14, 1804   All Justices present

Orphan; Wealthy Gellett
Guardian; William Bevans
Sureties; Brittingham Bevans, John R. Slocomb

F. 35   Orphan; Mary Mitchell (of Joshua)
Guardian; Elizabeth Smack [also Smock]
Sureties; Peter Evans, Isaac Franklin

F. 36   Orphan; Nancy Green (of Joseph)
Guardian; Daniel Tingle
Sureties; Thomas M. Purnell, Peter C. Evans

F. 37   Orphan; Molly Green (of Joseph)
Guardian; Elizabeth Purnell
Sureties; Thomas M. Purnell, Daniel Tingle

F. 38   Orphan; Lydia Bevans (of Mills)
Guardian; Barshaba Bevans
Sureties; William Bacon, Jacob Richards
In presence of Matthew Hopkins

F. 39   Orphan; Milchah Bevans
Guardian; Barshaba Bevans
Sureties; William Bacon, Jacob Richards
In presence of Matthew Hopkins

Orphan; John Ennalls Scott
Guardian; Sarah Scott
Sureties; Joseph Scott, Jun., James Maddux
In presence of Matthew Hopkins

F. 40   Orphan; William Scott (of John)
Guardian; Sarah Scott
Sureties; Joseph Scott, Jun., James Maddux
In presence of Matthew Hopkins

F. 41 Orphan; Polly Scott (of John)
       Guardian; Sarah Scott
       Sureties; Joseph Scott, Jun., James Maddux
       In presence of Matthew Hopkins

F. 42 Orphan; Levin Scott (of John?)
       Guardian; Sarah Scott
       Sureties; Joseph Scott, Jun., James Maddux
       In presence of Matthew Hopkins

F. 43 Orphan; Henry Scott (of John)
       Guardian; Sarah Scott
       Sureties; Joseph Scott, Jun., James Maddux
       In presence of Matthew Hopkins

Orphan; Susan Scott (of John E.)
Guardian; Sarah Scott
Sureties; Joseph Scott, Jun., James Maddux
In presence of Matthew Hopkins

F. 44 Orphan; George Scott (of John)
       Guardian; Sarah Scott
       Sureties; Joseph Scott, Jun., James Maddux
       In presence of Matthew Hopkins

F. 45 Attalanta Wright, by Littleton R. Purnell, asks to be released from guardianship to John, Nancy & Robert Wright (of John), due to indisposition; Zadok Sturgis, Esq., new guardian

Orphan; Robert Wright
Guardian; Zadok Sturgis
Sureties; John Ayres, James Selby (of Ezl.)

F. 46 Orphan; John Wright (of John)
       Guardian; Zadok Sturgis
       Sureties; John Ayres, James Selby (of Ezekiel)

F. 47 Orphan; Joshua P. Sturgis (of Joshua)
       Guardian; Esther Sturgis [couldn't write]
       Sureties; Zadok Sturgis, Samuel Helman

F. 48 Orphan; Rachel Bassett (of John)
       Guardian; Rachel Bassett [couldn't write]
       Sureties; William Adkins, John Brittingham [neither could write]
       In presence of Matthew Hopkins

F. 49 Orphan; James Smith (of John)
       Guardian; Samuel Bishop
       Sureties; Thomas Mitchell, Selby Parker

F. 50 Orphan; John Payne (of Jacob)
       Guardian; Elizabeth Payne [couldn't write]
       Sureties; Frederick Conner, James Payne

Orphan; Jacob Payne (of Jacob)
Guardian; Elizabeth Payne
F. 51   Sureties; Frederick Conner, James Payne

Orphan; Polly Selby (of Daniel)
Guardian; Fisher Richardson
Sureties; Peter S. Corbin, John Selby, Sen.
In Presence of Matthew Hopkins

F. 52   Indemnity bond from John Stevens, Jacob Richards & Robert J. H. Handy to John Rock, who was bound to said Stevens for guardianship to David, Esme, Samuel, Molly & Nancy Richardson (of George); in presence of Matthew Hopkins

F. 53   Apprentice; Thomas Edgar (alias Thomas Scott), 13, son of Milly Scott
Bound to; Handy Powell
Trade; shoe & boot maker
Sureties; James Selby (of Ezekiel), Nixon Davis

F. 54   Apprentice; Nancy Townsend (daughter of Elias), 10 last Christmas
Bound to; Sewell Dryden
Trade; spin, sew, weave & knit
F. 55   Sureties; Samuel Dorman, Matthias Davis

F. 56   Apprentice; Peter Reed, colored, 8 last Jan., child of Rachel
Bound to; John S. Purnell
Trade; house servant
Sureties; Charles Bennett, Jun., William Stevenson

F. 57   Apprentice; James Melvin (of John)
Bound to; George Houston
Trade; cypress cooper
F. 58   Sureties; Levi Houston, Levi Merrill

F. 59   Lemuel Henderson discharged from apprenticeship to Samuel Stevenson

Apprentice; Lemuel Henderson (of Bishop), 18
Bound to; John Bishop
Trade; farming
Sureties; Selby Parker, George Truitt (of Outten)

F. 60   Jonathan Fooks & Billy Fooks to view estate of Matthias
F. 61   Truitt (of Thomas), in care of Littleton Truitt, guardian;
F. 62   before John Cathell: report; Thomas died intestate, leaving a widow & four children; 65 3/8 acres

         Sewell Turpin & Thomas P. Rackliff to view estate of John P.
F. 63   Marshall, Jun., in care of John P. Marshall, Sen., Esq.,
F. 64   guardian; before Sewell Turpin: report; 600 acres plus marsh

F. 65   Joshua Prideaux, Esq., to settle dispute between Peter Parker & Elizabeth Selby, exex. of Thomas Selby; estate of Thomas Selby to pay Peter Parker L.3/16/7

F. 66   Apprentice; Betty Pruitt, 8 on 6 Dec. last
Bound to; John Smith, Sen.(?)
Trade; spinster & all other house work
Sureties; Sterling Jones, Levin Pollitt
By Trustees for the Poor; Saml. Handy, McKimmey Porter, George Hayward

F. 67   Apprentice; Elijah Shepherd, abject orphan, 5 on 5 Mar. last
Bound to; Joshua Sturgis (of Jacob), planter
Trade; planter
Sureties; James Victor, John Townsend
By Trustees for the Poor; Saml. Handy, George Hayward, Wm. Selby

F. 68   Apprentice; John Clark, abject orphan, 7 on 7 Mar. past
Bound to; Charles Harris, Jun., planter
Trade; planter
F. 69   Sureties; Charles Harris, Sen., Thomas Dryden
By Trustees for the Poor; Saml. Handy, Wm. Selby, George Hayward

Caveat against probate of will of Elizabeth Handcock, by John Handcock & others

Laban Johnson & Maj. Edward Henry to view estate of Peggy Fassitt, in care of Thomas S. Fassitt, Esq., guardian; guardian to rent land

F. 70   John Cathell & Thomas Fooks to view estate of Joshua P. Sturgis, in care of Esther Sturgis, guardian

Thomas N. Williams & Maj. Edward Henry, Esqs., to view estate of Mary Mitchell, in care of Elizabeth Smack, guardian; guardian to rent land

Thomas N. Williams & Edward Henry to distribute estate of Joseph Green, in hands of Josiah Davis, adm. dbn

Register, in settling accounts of Samuel Nicholson, late adm. of Isaac Nicholson, to allow L.52/19/6 for debt paid to John Carter(?), as appears by transcript from Accomack Court

F. 71   Letters of collection on estate of Maj. Levin Handy granted to Tubman Lowes

Daniel Handcock & Curtis Henderson to distribute estate of John Bassitt

William Adams & Kitturah, his wife, admx. of Thomas Milbourn, to sell negroes Hetty & Leah & her young child, born since appraisal

Samuel Bishop, guardian to James Smith, released from rendering accounts

William Winder, exe. of Sarah Rackliff, allowed for 52 shares in Bank of Columbia, as bank refuses to give him control over them unless he takes letters of adm. in District of Columbia

F. 72 Hezekiah Johnson & Joshua Duer to view estate of John & Sarah Payne, in care of Elizabeth Payne, guardian

Thomas & Nancy Dryden, admx. of Isaac Dryden, allowed for three cows which died

Register to charge Southey Whittington, guardian to Anne Turpin, $241 for sale of negro & allow him $80.50 for sum refunded to adm. of her father John Turpin

Laban Johnson & Thomas N. Williams, Esqs., to view estate of John, Rider, Charlotte & Kitty Rackliff, in care of William Winder, Esq., guardian

William Winder, guardian to John, Rider, Charlotte & Kitty Rackliff, to rent real estate

F. 73 John Stevens, adm. of George Richardson, to sell negroes, as estate is insufficient to pay debts; two women named Esther & their children, viz. Jack, Dinah, Sabro (?), Isaac, Comfort & William; also woman Comfort & her child Henny; man Albe(?)

F. 74 Sally Davis, adm. of Kendal Collier, lists stock dead since appraisal; before Thomas N. Williams; Nancy Miller, who lived with Sally, swears to above list; George Davis & Sally, his wife, allowed for loss

Nancy Richardson, adm. of Robert M. Richardson, to complete house started during Robert's lifetime and in danger of being lost

F. 75 William Winder, Esq., adm. dbn of John Rackliffe vs. Thomas Purnell (W. N.); a receipt from P. Townsend to Elijah Fassitt in John Rackliffe's hand to be considered payment, not bond

Charles Bennett & Sarah, his wife, exex. of Benjamin Purnell, Sen., vs. Edward Robins; defendant to shew cause why he should not give receipt for legacies bequeathed in will to his wife & children; states property received as gift before will; claims nothing under will

F. 76 Charles Bennett & Sarah, his wife, exex. of Benjamin Purnell, Sen., vs. John Stevens, adm. of George Richardson; defendant to shew cause why he should not give receipt for legacies bequeathed by will to intestate's wife & child; states legacies received by said George in his lifetime for his daughter Polly & her child, & that Nancy received her legacies before her marriage to said George

James A. Collins & Peggy Williams, adms. of Isaac Williams, allowed for costs & damage of a suit commenced against deceased in his lifetime by Boaz Ennis

John Bishop, George Hayward & Rowland E. Bevans to distribute estate of Daniel Selby

F. 77 Tues., Oct. 9, 1804 All Justices present

   Orphan; Levin Townsend (of Levin)
   Guardian; Frederick Conner
   Sureties; Levin Conner, Joshua Sturgis
F. 78 In presence of Matthew Hopkins

Order appointing Peter Tarr & Betsy, his wife, guardians to Maria, Jane, Sally & Matilda Townsend, rescinded; George Miles new guardian

   Orphan; Maria Townsend (of Capt. Levin)
   Guardian; George Miles
F. 79 Sureties; Cornelius Dickerson, Timothy Irons

Orphan; Jane Townsend (of Capt. Levin)
Guardian; George Miles
Sureties; Cornelius Dickerson, Timothy Irons

F. 80 Orphan; Sally Townsend (of Capt. Levin)
   Guardian; George Miles
   Sureties; Cornelius Dickerson, Timothy Irons

   Orphan; Matilda Townsend (of Capt. Levin)
F. 81 Guardian; George Miles
   Sureties; Cornelius Dickerson, Timothy Irons

   Apprentice; Harry Handy, free negro, 4 on 20 Mar. last, son of Susanna Handy
   Bound to; John R. Slocomb
F. 82 Trade; farmer
   Sureties; Ephraim K. Wilson, Peter S. Corbin

F. 83 Apprentice; Jenny Handy, free negro, 2 on 1 Mar. last, daughter of Susanna Handy
   Bound to; John R. Slocomb
   Trade; spin, knit & sew
   Sureties; Ephraim K. Wilson, Peter S. Corbin

F. 84 Apprentice; Southey Whittington Gellett (of Ayres), 16 last June, by consent of John Whittington, guardian
   Bound to; George Nelson
F. 85 Trade; house joiner & carpenter
   Sureties; George Bratten, Alexander McAllen

F. 86 Apprentice; Stephen Ennis (of Joseph), 16 last Jan., by consent of his guardian, Samuel Ennis
         (cont.)

	Bound to; George Bratten
	Trade; house carpenter
F. 87	Sureties; George Nelson, James A. Collins

F. 88 Apprentice; Levin Townsend (of Levin), 13 on 13 July last
Bound to; Levin Conner
Trade; house carpenter
Sureties; Frederick Conner, Joshua Sturgis

F. 89 Edward Stevenson & Edward Lambden to view estate of Levi
F. 90 Merrill, in care of Levin Merrill, guardian; before William Melvin: report; mentions ground lying in Newtown, 1/4 acre; negro boy Jack, 16

F. 91 William Selby & George Hayward to view estate of David, Esme, Samuel, Molly & Nancy Richardson, in care of John Stevens,
F. 92 guardian: report; tract called 'Defiance', 666 2/3 acres;
F. 93 blacksmith shop, property of George Martin's representatives, 1/6 part to Mrs. Elizabeth Marshall Stevens; negroes Zadok (blacksmith), Jacob, Abel, old negro Dinah

F. 94 Daniel Handcock & Curtis Henderson to distribute estate of John Bassitt: report; to daughters Sophia Parsons, Rachel Bassitt; widow's dower

F. 95 James Victor, adm. of Richard Ward, to sell personal estate

Isaac Ayres & Thomas Franklin to view estate of Lambert Collier, in care of George Davis & Sarah, his wife, guardians

William Schoolfield, guardian to Sally Merrill(?), to sell $20 worth of timber for education & maintenance

Samuel Dorman, guardian to William Dorman, discharged from rendering accounts

F. 96 William McGregor & William Lister to distribute personal estate of Robert Mitchell

Polly Mitchell, adm. of Levin Mitchell, to sell perishable property

Order entered at June term, 1803, allowing James A. Collins & Peggy Williams, adms. of Isaac Williams, for saving crop rescinded; allowed L.59/18/4, amount fixed by Edward Henry & Thomas N. Williams

Mistakes were made in inventory of estate of Joseph Green, returned by Mary Green, late adm., on 2 June, 1800; Josiah Davis, adm.
F. 97 dbn, has charged himself with these amounts; Register to rescind distribution & strike a new one

Elizabeth Purnell, guardian to Molly Green, to sell personal estate

Daniel Tingle, guardian to Nancy Green, to sell personal estate

William Quinton & Jackson Turner to view estate of Henry & Peter White, in care of George Hayward, guardian

William Corbin & John Cottingham to view property of Maria, Jane, Sally & Matilda Townsend, in care of George Miles, guardian

F. 98   Seth Whaley, guardian to John B. Baker, vs. Edward Hammond, Sen., & wife, admx. of Levin Baker; states Levin Duncan devised articles to said Baker's wife, now Mrs. Hammond, for life; she married Levin Baker, who died; Abisha Davis & John P. Mitchell to appraise estate of Mary Hammond as estate of Levin Baker

Adm. of estate of Capt. Levin Townsend, granted to Betsy Townsend, revoked; granted to George Miles

George Miles, adm. of Capt. Levin Townsend, vs. Peter Tarr & Betsy, his wife, late admx.; estate to be delivered to said George

F. 99   Received Oct. 9, 1804, of Rachel Bassett, exe. of John Bassett, $30.38, my share of estate

                              George Parsons(?)

Received Oct. 9, 1804, of Rachel Bassett, exe. of John Bassett, $27.38, my share of estate

                              William Bassett

F. 100 [blank]

F. 101 Tues., Dec. 11, 1804   All Justices present

Orphan; Nancy Jones
Guardian; William Jones, father
Sureties; William Holland, Sen., Samuel A. Harper

F. 102 Orphan; John Richardson
        Guardian; Nancy Richardson
        Sureties; Col. Thomas Martin, Samuel R. Smith

F. 103 Orphan; Mary Richardson
        Guardian; Nancy Richardson
        Sureties; Thomas Martin, Samuel R. Smith

F. 104 Apprentice; Harry Armstrong, mulatto, 15 Dec. last, son of Betsy
        Bound to; John Taylor
        Trade; shoe maker
        Sureties; John A. Townsend, Stephen Sturgis

F. 105 Daniel Handcock & John Givans to view estate of Rachel
F. 106 Bassitt (of John), in care of Rachel Bassitt, guardian;
F. 107 before James Houston: report; 129 acres; widow's dower

William McGregor & William Lister to distribute estate of Robert
         Mitchell, in hands of Matthias Warren & wife, admx.: report;
F. 108   1) 1/3 to Matthias Warren & wife; negroes James 13, Isaac 10,
         Sampson 2, Chloe 29, Fanny 1; list of articles
F. 109-10 2) 2/3 to representatives; list; negroes man Hope, Abram 28,
F. 111   Ben 23, Elijah 17, George 11, Arnell(?) 4, Milla 24, Rhoda 8,
F. 112   Sarah 5, Huldah 4; Distribution ratified

         Apprentice; William Smith Drummond, born 19 Jan., 1787, by
         consent of his mother, Ann Robinson Drummond, of Accomack
         Co., VA
         Bound to; George Nelson, house carpenter & joiner
         Trade; house joiner & carpenter
F. 113   In presence of Richard Wimbrough, Joel(?) Nilson

F. 114   Apprentice; John Pollitt (son of Samuel)
         Bound to; James Gibbons, of Somerset Co., joiner
         Trade; house carpenter & joiner
         Signed by Betsy Pollitt
         Before John Cathell, Isaac Hearn;
         N. B.; John Pollitt was 17 on 28 Nov., 1804

William Corbin & John Cottingham to distribute estate of Capt. Levin
Townsend, in hands of George Miles, adm.

F. 115   Letters of adm. dbn granted to Elizabeth Smack on estate of
         Joshua Mitchell

William Holland & Fisher Richardson, guardian to John, George, Henry &
Polly Selby, to sell negro man Abram

Matthias Warren & Elizabeth, his wife, guardians to Julianna Mitchell,
to sell personal estate (except negroes, plate & 1 dozen china plates)

William McGregor & Hillary Pitts to view estate of Julianna Mitchell,
in care of Matthias Warren & Elizabeth, his wife, guardians

Tubman Lowes, collector of Maj. Levin Handy, to sell personal estate

F. 116   Eli Hudson & Nancy, his wife, exex. of Joseph Ennis, allowed
         10% on payment of debts & 6% on remainder

John Dennis & John Duncan to view property of James & William Jarman,
in care of James Jarman, guardian

Handy & Mary Jones, exes. of Jesse Jones, allowed for articles burnt
in barn of Charles Hammond

Rowland Bevans, guardian to Tabitha, Elizabeth & Nancy Selby, allowed
10% on sale of property

State of accounts of Cornelius Ennis, guardian to Rachel Ennis, to be
reported by Register

F. 117   Samuel Parker & others vs. William Riley & Elizabeth Wright,
         adms. of Hezekiah Wright; adms. to sell personal estate

F. 118   Tues., Feb. 12, 1805   All Justices present

         Orphan; Joseph Harrison (of John)
         Guardian; Joseph U. Crockett (of Sussex Co., DE)
         Sureties; Levin Derickson, Jesse Powell
F. 119   In presence of Matthew Hopkins

Orphan; George Harrison (of John)
Guardian; Joseph U. Crockett (of Sussex Co., DE)
Sureties; Levin Derickson, Jesse Powell
In presence of Matthew Hopkins

F. 120   Orphan; John Nelson (of Elijah)
         Guardian; Sophia Nelson [couldn't write]
         Sureties; William Melvin, Sen., Avery Melvin [signed Avra]
         In presence of Matthew Hopkins

         Orphan; Susanna Nelson (of Elijah)
F. 121   Guardian; Sophia Nelson
         Sureties; William Melvin, Sen., Avery Melvin
         In presence of Matthew Hopkins

         Orphan; Patsey Melvin (of William)
         Guardian; Nehemiah Blake [couldn't write]
F. 122   Sureties; John Tindall [couldn't write], Avry Melvin
         In presence of Matthew Hopkins

         Orphan; Westly Melvin (of William)
         Guardian; Nehemiah Blake
F. 123   Sureties; John Tindall, Avra Melvin
         In presence of Matthew Hopkins

         Orphan; Nancy Holland (of Thomas)
         Guardian; Fisher Richardson
F. 124   Sureties; Samuel R. Smith, Henry Parker
         In presence of Matthew Hopkins

Orphan; John Turpin (of John)
Guardian; Sewell Turpin
Sureties; Littleton R. Purnell, Thomas P. Rackliff
In presence of Matthew Hopkins

F. 125   Orphan; Sally Smock (of Levi)
         Guardian; Thomas N. Crapper
         Sureties; Ephraim K. Wilson, Samuel Bishop
         In presence of Matthew Hopkins

         Apprentice; Levin Henderson (of Samuel), 10 on 16 Mar. next,
         by consent of his mother
         Bound to; William Bradford
                        (cont.)

F. 126   Trade; farming
          Sureties; Frederick Conner, Curtis Henderson

F. 127   William Corbin & John Cottingham to view estate of Maria,
          Jane, Sally & Matilda Townsend, in care of George Miles,
F. 128   guardian; before Thos. N. Williams: report; mentions widow &
F. 129   heirs that are of age; negroes Ned, Rhoda, Rachel, Silva &
F. 130   Lindy; 500 acres

Laban Johnson & Thomas N. Williams to view estate of John Rackliff,
          in care of William Winder, guardian; before William McGregor:
F. 131   report; mentions lands entailed to said John by one ancestor,
F. 132   now leased to Kirk Gunby in Synepuxent Neck; other lands
          belonging to Rider, Kitturah & Charlotte Rackliff; land
F. 133   called 'Cedars'; land leased to Nathaniel Brittingham
          called 'Newport'

F. 134   Laban Johnson & Thomas N. Williams to view estate of Rider
F. 135   Rackliff, in care of William Winder, guardian; before William
F. 136   McGregor: report; [same as above, minus John's land]

F. 137   Laban Johnson & Thomas N. Williams to view estate of Kitturah
          Rackliff, in care of William Winder, guardian; before William
F. 138-40 McGregor: report; [same as above, minus John's land]

Laban Johnson & Thomas N. Williams to view estate of Charlotte
          Rackliff, in care of William Winder, guardian; before William
F. 141-43 McGregor: report; [same as above, minus John's land]

Maj. Edward Henry & Thomas N. Williams to distribute estate of Joseph
          Green, in hands of Josiah Davis, adm. dbn: report; negroes
F. 144   Bob 40, Sacre 30, George 23, Peter 21, Charles 7; Milby 4 &
          Sacre 18 months, born since appraisal; Esther 43, Jenny 25,
Rody [Rhoda] 14, Betty 9
          1) to Josiah Davis; negroes Peter, Sacre, Esther, Sacre
F. 145   2) to Nancy Green; negroes Bob, Milby, Rhoda, Betty
          3) to Molly Green; negroes George, Charles, Jenny
List of goods remaining in hands of Josiah Davis, adm. dbn;
F. 146-7 [another list of negroes]
          1) to Josiah Davis; [same as above]
          2) to Nancy Green, in hands of Daniel Tingle, guardian
F. 148   3) to Molly Green, in hands of Elizabeth Purnell, guardian

John Cottingham & William Corbin to distribute estate of Capt. Levin
          Townsend, in hands of George Miles, adm.;
F. 149   1) to John Corbin & Eliza, his wife; negro boy James;
          mentions William Corbin, James Brodwatter, John C. Bacon
2) to Eleanor Townsend; negro boy Harry
          3) to Maria, Jane, Sally & Matilda Townsend; remainder of
F. 150   estate; above will give refund if Peter & wife claim widow's
          thirds

F. 151   John White, guardian to Elizabeth Bishop (of Samuel), to receive property of ward from Frederick Conner, adm. dbn of Samuel; her share is $197.93; also received $171.21 from estate of Benjamin Bishop (of Samuel), who died a minor

F. 152   Elizabeth Purnell, guardian to Molly Green (of Joseph), to sell personal estate (except negroes);
F. 153   Daniel Tingle, guardian to Nancy Green (of Joseph), to sell personal estate: report; sold to Joshua Gray, James Bennett,
F. 154   Nath. Brittingham, Samuel Long, Caleb Hancock(?), James Willis, Joseph Miller, Dr. George W. Purnell, James Jones,
F. 155   Josiah Davis, Edmond Crapper, James Franklin, William Duncan, William Richards, Isaac Holston, Henry Davis, Obediah
F. 156   Brittingham, Isaac Long, Handy Powell, Elizabeth Purnell, Dr. Stephen White, John Richards, Thomas N. Williams, James Selby, John Powell, John J.(?) Williams, George Taylor, Edward Walker, William Smashey, Kendall Merrill, James Truitt, Levi Mills,
F. 157   Samuel Findley, Belitha Burbage, Henry Burroughs, Jacob White, Robert McNeill, Levin Stuart, Alexander Massey, Daniel Tingle

F. 158   Apprentice; Levin Selby (son of Micajah), 15
         Bound to; John T. Taylor, shoe maker, of Snow Hill
         Trade; shoe maker
F. 159   In presence of W. Holland, J. Hubbell

         Apprentice; John Tull, by consent of his father John
         Bound to; James Tilghman
         Trade; cordwinding
         Term; till Jan. 1, 1809
F. 160   Before John Williams, Benj. Aydelott

         Apprentice; Isaac Claywell, by consent of his mother, Rhoda
F. 161   Robertson
         Bound to; James Sturgis
         Term; till 21, on 7 Nov., 1817
         Trade; shoe maker or cordwinder
F. 162   In presence of Jesse Bennett, John Bishop

         Apprentice; William Powell, by consent of his father Levin
         Bound to; Samuel M. Duer (of Somerset Co.), blacksmith
         Trade; blacksmith
F. 163   In presents of Benj. Aydelott, Edwd. Stevenson

F. 164   Petition for sale of Col. Zadok Purnell's estate, who died intestate; signed by Littleton Robins, Mary Purnell, Esther Purnell, Lanta Purnell, William P. Marshall, Elizabeth Purnell, Hetty Purnell, Zipporah Purnell, Joshua Prideaux, Thos. Purnell (of Wm.), Edward Henry, John P. Marshall, Saml. Ennis, Zadok Purnell, John Purnell; Littleton Robins, Joshua Prideaux & Zadok Purnell,
F. 165   adms. of Col. Zadok Purnell, to sell personal estate (except negroes, wearing apparel & legacies)

James Laws, Jun., & David Johnson to view estate of Joseph & George Harrison, in care of Joseph U.(?) Crockett, guardian

Benjamin Aydelott & James Davis to view estate of John & Susanna Nelson, in care of Sophia Nelson, guardian

Outten & Purnell Toadvine, exes. of Capt. William Toadvine, to sell personal estate

Handy Mills & Rowland Bevans to view estate of Nancy Holland, in care of Fisher Richardson, guardian

John Davis & James A. Collins to view estate of John Turpin, in care of Sewell Turpin, guardian

F. 166   Rowland Bevans & Handy Mills to distribute estate of Thomas Holland, in hands of Fisher Richardson & Besty [Betsy?], his wife, admx.

As personal estate of Caleb Tingle is insufficient to pay claims, John Tingle, exe., to ascertain amount of claims & assets, & what proportion each legacy will abate

Nancy Spence, exe. of George Spence, allowed $50 for boat accidentally sunk in bay

Rowland Bevans, adm. of Ephraim Henderson, allowed L.28/14/6 for note of deceased given to John Tunnell, who deposited same with Ephraim Furniss for collection & is removed out of state

F. 167   Letter of collection granted to Handy Powell on estate of Thomas Scott

Thomas Hall, exe. of Joshua Bowen, allowed 7 1/2% on estate

Rebecca Taylor, guardian to Betsy, Sally & Patsey Taylor, excused from rendering accounts, as there are insufficient profits to support them

William Riley & Elizabeth Wright, adms. of Hezekiah Wright, allowed full time to settle estate as they fear estate insufficient to discharge debts & claims

Thomas Holland, heretofore adm. of Nimrod Jacobs, sold estate for $178.75; Fisher Richardson & Betsy, his wife, adms. dbn, to retain $156.12 paid on claims

F. 168   Fisher Richardson & Betsy, his wife, admx. of Thomas Holland, allowed 5% on estate

Received Feb. 8, 1805, of Thomas Parramore, Sen., of Northampton Co., VA, as adm. of my father's estate & my guardian, my full share of my father's estate & profits from my estate

(cont.)

Test.; Sally Stran(?)   John Parramore
      Margaret Parramore

Received Dec. 8, 1804, of Thomas Parramore of Northampton Co., who was
guardian to my wife & adm. of John Parramore, my wife's father, her
full share of estate & profits

Test.; Thos. Parramore   Thos. Jacobs, Jun.
      John Parramore

F. 169   William Riley & Elizabeth Wright, adms. of Hezekiah Wright,
         to advertise in Smith's paper at Easton for creditors to
exhibit claims

F. 170   Special Court Mar. 22, 1805, by request of Joshua
         Townsend; Littleton Robins, John Bishop present

Orphan; James Townsend (of Major)
Guardian; John A. Townsend
Sureties; Josiah Bratten, Jacob Teague

F. 171   John Tingle, exe. of Caleb Tingle, allowed 10% on payment of
         debts & 5% on estate

F. 172   Littleton Robins, John Bishop & Edward Henry appointed
         Justices

Robt. Bowie   Al. Hanson, Chanc.

Witness; Honourable Alexander Contee Hanson, Chancellor

F. 173   Tues., Apr. 9, 1805   All Justices present

Orphan; Nancy Newton (of Levin)
Guardian; Samuel Cowley
Sureties; Rowland E. Bevans, John Selby

F. 174   Orphan; Charlotte Newton (of Levin)
         Guardian; Samuel Cowley
         Sureties; Rowland E. Bevans, John Selby

Cornelius Ennis discharged from guardianship to Rachel Ennis;
Rackliffe Pointer new guardian

         Orphan; Rachel Ennis (of Cornelius)
F. 175   Guardian; Rackliffe Pointer [couldn't write]
         Sureties; Benjamin Purnell, Levi Merrill

         Orphan;; John Powell (of John)
F. 176   Guardian; Keziah(?) Powell
         Sureties; Jesse Powell, Hillary Pitts

F. 177
Orphan; Dixon Quinton Henderson (of John)
Guardian; Josiah Long [couldn't write]
Sureties; Jesse Henderson, Levi Merrill
In presence of Matthew Hopkins

F. 178
Orphan; Sally Laws Henderson (of John)
Guardian; Josiah Long
Sureties; Jesse Henderson, Levi Merrill
In presence of Matthew Hopkins

William Holland, Sen, discharged from guardianship to John Selby; Fisher Richardson new guardian

F. 179
Orphan; John Selby (of Daniel)
Guardian; Fisher Richardson
Sureties; Peter S. Corbin, John Selby, Jun.

Peter Claywell discharged from apprenticeship to George Holston

F. 180
Apprentice; Peter Claywell (of Moses), 18 Sept. next
Bound to; William Claywell
Trade; farmer
Sureties; Samuel R. Smith, Joshua Evans

F. 181
Apprentice; Jesse Ward (of Jesse), 15 on 25 Feb. last, by consent of his mother
Bound to; Moses Benston
Trade; shoe & boot maker
Sureties; William Handcock, Daniel Handcock (of Wm.)

F. 182
Apprentice; William Ennis, 9 on 16 Feb. last, son of Polly
Bound to; Josiah Collins
Trade; shoe maker
F. 183
Sureties; William Jones (of Jesse), John Harris

F. 184
Apprentice; James T. Morris (of Phillip), 16 on 24 Jan. last
Bound to; Andrew Tull
Trade; wheel wright
Sureties; Thomas Jones, John Purnell (Queponco)

F. 185
Apprentice; John McDaniel (of William), 17, by consent of his mother
Bound to; Shadrach Lane
Trade; taylor
F. 186
Sureties; Major White, Parker Selby

F. 187
Apprentice; Peter Hudson, 15 on 11 Jan. last, by consent of his mother Mary
Bound to; George White
Trade; farmer
Sureties; James Givans, Joshua Sturgis

'104'

F. 188 Apprentice; Harry Johnson, free mulatto, 15 on 1 Jan. last
        Bound to; John Ward
        Trade; coasting business
F. 189 Sureties; William Savage, Thomas Milbourne

F. 190 [written along edge of page;] Error, this recognizance taken
        at June term, 1805

Apprentice; Milly Noble, 9 on 16 July last, daughter of Sarah Noble
(alias Parker)
Bound to; Daniel Patrick
Trade; common house business; spin
Sureties; Col. Samuel Handy, McKimmey Porter

F. 191 William McGregor & Hillary Pitts to view estate of Julianna
        Mitchell (representative of Robert), in care of Matthias
F. 192 Warren & Elizabeth, his wife, guardians; William sworn before
        Abisha Davis; Hillary sworn before William McGregor: report;
F. 193 514 acres; negro men Abram & Elijah, woman Milla, girls Rhoda
        & Serah; men Hope & George (blind), expense to estate; boy
F. 194 Arnell(?) 4, girl Huldah 4; Mrs. Warren's thirds

        James Law, Jun., & David Johnson to view estate of Joseph &
F. 195 George Harrison (of John), in care of Joseph U. Crockett,
        guardian; before Abisha Davis: report

F. 196 Benjamin Aydelott & James Davis to view estate of John &
        Susanna Nelson, in care of Sophia Nelson, guardian; before
F. 197 Edwd. Stevenson: report; 24 acres; widow's thirds

        Apprentice; Levin Blake, 5, abject son of Harmon Blake
        Bound to; John Tarr (of Eli), planter [couldn't write]
        Trade; planter
F. 198 Sureties; John Selby, Jun., Jesse Sturgis
        By Trustees for the Poor; Saml. Handy, Sen., McKimmey Porter,
        George Hayward

        Apprentice; Milby Townsend, 14 on 1 Apr. instant, by consent
        of his father Elias [couldn't write]
        Bound to; Joseph Allen, boot & shoe maker
F. 199 Trade; boot & shoe maker
F. 200 In presence of Thomas N. Williams, Chas. Dingle(?)

        Apprentice; William Silverthorn (of Wm.), 16, by consent of
        Ralph Genkins, guardian, both of Accomack Co., VA
        Bound to; Samuel H. Maddux, house carpenter & joiner
        Trade; house carpenter & joiner
F. 201 In presents of Edwd. Stevenson, Benj. Aydelott

        Apprentice; Rebecca Pruitt, 7, abject daughter of Walter
F. 202 Pruitt
        Bound to; Benjamin Johnson, Jun., planter
        Trade; domestic business; spinning, weaving, & c. & c.
                         (cont.)

'105'

       Sureties; Charles Hammond, John Bevans
       By Trustees for the Poor; McKimmey Porter, Charles Bennett,
       George Hayward

       Apprentice; Nancy Justice, 8 on 9 Feb. last, daughter of Mary
F. 203 Justice
       Bound to; Johnson Hayman
       Trade; domestic business; spinning, weaving, sewing & c. & c.
       Sureties; John Tilghman, Solomon Shockley
       By Trustees for the Poor; McKimmey Porter, Saml. Handy, Sen.,
       George Hayward

F. 204 Apprentice; Parker Selby Bowen
       Bound to; John F. Taylor, shoe & boot maker
       Trade; shoe & boot maker
F. 205 In presence of Jesse Bennett, Matthias Davis
       Sarah Caudrey, mother of Parker, states that he will be 14 on
       17 June next

       Apprentice; David Dixon Henderson (son of Benjamin D.)
F. 206 Bound to; James Tull, carpenter in Newtown
       Trade; house carpenter & joiner
       Term; 4 years, 6 months
F. 207 In presence of Benj. Aydelott, Edwd. Stevenson

Elizabeth Smack, adm. of Joshua Mitchell, to sell personal estate
(except negroes & wearing apparel)

John Stevens, adm. of George Richardson, to advertise in Smith's paper
at Easton for creditors to exhibit claims

F. 208 John Stevens, adm. dbn of Benjamin Purnell, to adv. in
       Smith's paper at Easton for creditors to exhibit claims

William Handy, adm. of James Handy, to advertise in Baltimore
Telegraph for creditors to make distribution

Mary Martin, exe. of George Martin, allowed 6% on passage of her
second account, filed 16 Nov., 1799

Anna Bowen, guardian to Comfort Bowen, discharged from passing
accounts, orphan being of age in Aug. next

William Handy, Zadok Sturgis & Joshua Flemming to distribute three
negroes recovered of John Taylor, adm. of Barcley & Joshua White,
between heirs Henry, Peter & William White

F. 209 Polly Smith, exe. of Walter Smith, allowed 8% on estate

Joseph Nicholson, by his will, left part of personal estate to be sold
by Isaac Nicholson, exe.; list of sales filed 14 Oct., 1800, shows
gain beyond appraisal; Register to strike new distribution

Stephen White, Zadok Sturgis & Laban Johnson to settle dispute between Zadok Purnell, Jun. & Littleton Robins, Joshua Prideaux & Zadok Purnell, Esqs., adms. of Col. Zadok Purnell; petition to have his account against deceased allowed; objected to by adms.

Col. John Postly & Lemuel Showell to view estate of John Powell, in care of Keziah Powell, guardian

John Postly & Lemuel Showell to distribute estate of John Powell, deceased

F. 210   John Postly, Lemuel Showell & William McGregor to distribute estate of Belitha Powell, in hands of Jesse Powell, exe.

George Davis & his wife, admx. of Kendal Collier, allowed 8% on estate after deductions for loss of stock

William Winder, Sen., guardian to Charlotte & Kitty Rackliffe, states profits from estate not sufficient for support & education; ordered to continue them in school one year & make up deficiencies out of principle

William & Betty Dickerson, guardians to Nancy Nicholson, to sell negro Moses

F. 211   William Hudson & Comfort, his wife, guardians to Nancy Knox, to sell negro Rachel & her two children, Levin & Isaac

Rowland Bevans & William Holland, Jun., to view estate of John Selby, in care of Fisher Richardson, guardian

Fisher Richardson, guardian to John Selby, to keep orphan constantly at school

Register, on settling accounts of Levin Mitchell on estate of Joshua Mitchell, allowed 6% on inventory

Received Jan. 9, 1796, of Abijah & Isaac Bethard, exes. of Daniel Coe Bethard, items willed to me in my father's will; list

F. 212   Wit.; John Postly   her
                                     Elizabeth X Bethard
                                             mark

Received Jan. 9, 1796, of Abijah & Isaac Bethard, exes. of Daniel Coe Bethard, items willed to me in my father's will; list

Wit.; John Postly   her
                                        Mary X Betherd
                                             mark

Received Jan. 9, 1796, of Abijah & Isaac Betherd, exes. of Daniel Coe Bethard, items willed to me by my father; list
                              (cont.)

Wit.; John Postly   Benjamin Batherd

Received Jan. 9, 1796, of Abijah & Isaac Betherd, exes. of Daniel Coe Betherd, items willed me by my father; list

Wit.; John Postly   his
                                       James X Betherd
                                             mark

F. 213   Received Jan. 9, 1796, of Abijah & Isaac Bethard, exes. of Daniel Coe Betherd, items willed me by my father; list

Wit.; John Postly   Richard Bathard

Received Jan. 15, 1796, of Abijah & Isaac Betherd, exes. of Daniel Coe Betherd, items willed to Esther Betherd by her father, she being a minor; list

Wit.; John Postly   Richard Bathard

Received 5 Feb., 1799, of Abijah & Isaac Betherd, exes. of Daniel C. Betherd, my share of my father's estate

Test.; John Postly   Benjamin Bathard

Received 5 Feb., 1799, of Abijah & Isaac Betherd, exes. of Daniel C. Betherd, my share of my father's estate

Test.; William McGregor   Richard Bathard

Received 5 Feb., 1799, of Abijah & Isaac Betherd, exes. of Daniel C. Betherd, my share of my father's estate
                                             her
Test.; John Postly   Mary X Betherd
                                             mark

F. 214   Received 5 Feb., 1799, of Abijah & Isaac Betherd, exes. of Daniel C. Betherd, my share of my father's estate

Test.; John Postly   her
                                      Esther X Betherd
                                             mark

Received 5 Feb., 1799, of Abijah & Isaac Betherd, exes. of Daniel C. Betherd, my share of my father's estate
                                             his
Test.; Elsea(?) Smith   James X Bathard
                                             mark

Received 5 Feb., 1797, of Abijah & Isaac Betherd, exes. of Daniel C. Betherd, my wife Elizabeth's share of her father's estate

Test.; William Truitt   Caleb Powell

Received 22 Sept., 1803, of Elizabeth Selby, exe. of Thomas Selby, $315, my share of my father's estate

Test.; John Postly   James Selby

F. 215   Received 13 Nov., 1807, of Elizabeth Selby, exe. of Thomas Selby, $315, my share of my father's estate

Test.; Wm. Fassitt   John Selby

F. 216   Tues., June 11, 1805   All Justices present

F. 217   Orphan; William F. Riley (of Levin)
         Guardian; Alexander Franklin
         Sureties; Joseph Miller, Isaac Franklin

Orphan; Littleton Richards (of John, of Isaac)
Guardian; Polly Richards
Sureties; William Truitt (of Nehemiah, couldn't write), John Smith (of Thos.)

F. 218   Orphan; John Richards (of John, of Isaac)
         Guardian; Polly Richards
         Sureties; William Truitt (of Nehemiah), John Smith (of Thos.)

F. 219   Apprentice; Milly Noble, 9 on 16 July last, daughter of Sarah Noble (alias Parker)
         Bound to; Daniel Patrick
         Trade; house business; spin
         Sureties; Col. Samuel Handy, McKimmey Porter

F. 220   Isaac Ayres & Thomas Franklin to view estate of Lambert &
F. 221   Molly Collyer (of Kendal), in hands of George Davis & Sarah, his wife, guardian; before William Dale: report; lands where John Fisher now lives in Synepuxon Neck called 'Carmaal'(?)

F. 222   Apprentice; Jesse Justice, child of the Poor House, 7
         Bound to; William Hudson (of John) [couldn't write]
         Trade; farmer
F. 223   Sureties; Samuel Porter, John Killam Truitt
         By Trustees for the Poor; George Hayward, Samuel Handy, Charles Bennett

         Apprentice; Noah Cox, 11 in Apr., 1805, son of Elizabeth
         Bound to; James Parker
         Trade; farmer
F. 224   Sureties; George Parker, Levin Smith [couldn't write]
         Before John Cathell, John Dashiell

Zadok Sturgis, guardian to Robert Wright, to expend $30 for education

F. 225   William Gordy, exe. of William Gordy, to sell personal estate (except legacies), giving notice at Salisbury

Col. Samuel Handy & Peter S. Corbin to view estate of William F. Riley, in care of Alexander Franklin, guardian

Nixon Davis & Thomas Duncan to view estate of Littleton & John Richards, in care of Polly Richards, guardian

Thomas S. Fassitt, guardian to Margaret Fassitt, to keep orphan at a boarding school for one year

John Stevens, adm. dbn of Benjamin Purnell, allowed $46 for note to Thomas Fassitt assigned to Sewell Turpin in July, 1802

F. 226 Selby Parker, exe. of Levin Selby, sold real estate, but now doubts that he was empowered to do so; exe. allowed to convey land & strike distribution on balance after payment of debts

F. 227-30 {blank}

F. 231 Tues., Aug. 13, 1805 All Justices present

F. 232 Orphan; Noah Gordy (of William)
Guardian; Betsy Gordy [couldn't write]
Sureties; Stephen Mitchell [couldn't write], Samuel Helman
In presence of Matthew Hopkins

F. 233 Orphan; Leonard Gordy (of William)
Guardian; Betsy Gordy
Sureties; Stephen Mitchell, Samuel Hilman
In presence of Matthew Hopkins

F. 234 Orphan; Betsy Gordy (of William)
Guardian; Betsy Gordy
Sureties; Stephen Mitchell, Samuel Hilman
In presence of Matthew Hopkins

John Selby (Queponco) discharged from guardianship to Parker S. Bowen; William Jones new guardian

F. 235 Orphan; Parker S. Bowen (of Capt. John)
Guardian; William Jones (of Jesse)
Sureties; James Selby, Barnaby Henderson

F. 236 Orphan; William H. Tilghman (of Caleb)
Guardian; Sally Tilghman
Sureties; John Hall, Daniel Cottingham

Maj. William Holland discharged from guardianship to Henry & George Selby; Fisher Richardson new guardian

F. 237 Orphan; Henry Selby (of Daniel)
Guardian; Fisher Richardson
Sureties; Handy Mills, Robert Smith
In presence of Matthew Hopkins

F. 238
Orphan; George Selby (of Daniel)
Guardian; Fisher Richardson
Sureties; Robert Smith, Handy Mills
In presence of Matthew Hopkins

F. 239
Orphan; Molly Purnell (of John, W. N.)
Guardian; Elizabeth Purnell
Sureties; Daniel Tingle, Thomas N. Williams

Orphan; Thomas Purnell (of John, W. N.)
Guardian; Elizabeth Purnell
Sureties; Daniel Tingle, Thomas N. Williams

F. 240
Orphan; Sally Purnell (of John. W. N.)
Guardian; Elizabeth Purnell
Sureties; Daniel Tingle, Thomas N. Williams

F. 241
Orphan; Zadok(?) Purnell (of John, W. N.)
Guardian; Elizabeth Purnell
Sureties; Daniel Tingle, Thomas N. Williams

F. 242
Orphan; Sarah Parker (of James)
Guardian; Milly Purnell [couldn't write]
Sureties; William A. Marshall, William Purnell

F. 243
Orphan; Betsy Rigsby (of Thomas)
Guardian; Milly Purnell
Sureties; William A. Marshall, William Purnell (of Levi)

F. 244
Jacob Teague & Josiah Bratten bound to John A. Townsend, exe. of Leah Townsend: sureties; John Purnell (of Thos.), Thomas Mitchell

F. 245
Apprentice; Henry Davis, mulatto, 10 on 21 Mar. last, son of Nancy Collick
Bound to; John Cutler
Trade; common labour
Sureties; Levi Merrill, Thomas Mitchell

F. 246
Apprentice; Jesse Dick, 11, son of negro Nanny, late slave of Valentine Dennis
Bound to; Valentine Dennis
Trade; farmer
F. 247
Sureties; John C. Handy, Esq., William Davis (Indian Town)

F. 248
Apprentice; Henry Selby (of Daniel), 13, by consent of his guardian
Bound to; Samuel R. Smith
Trade; seafaring business; art of navigation by plain sailing
Sureties; Jacob Richards, Fisher Richardson

F. 249
Apprentice; William Johnson, mulatto, 11 on 22 Dec. last, son of Tabitha

(cont.)

             Bound to; Josiah Hubbell
             Trade; coasting business
F. 250   Sureties; Joshua Prideaux, John Rock

             John Davis & James A. Collins to view estate of John Turpin
F. 251   (of John), in care of Sewell Turpin, guardian; before Nixon
             Davis: report; mentions orphans of John Turpin, viz. Anny,
F. 252   John & William; widow; old house where Jacob Hopkins lives

Zadok Purnell, Jun., vs. Littleton Robins, Joshua Prideaux & Zadok
             Purnell, adms. of Col. Zadok Purnell; Stephen White, Zadok
F. 253   Sturgis & Laban Johnson to settle dispute: witness;
        Littleton Robins, Sen., Esq.; subscribers meeting at Berlin
award L.94 to Zadok Purnell, Jun., from adms. of Col. Zadok, which he
had received from Col. Thomas Purnell's estate as guardian to said
Zadok, Jun.

F. 254   Isaac Evans & Joshua Prideaux ordered at Dec. term, 1791, to
             divide personal estate of Stephen Hill, deceased; before
John Wise, Register; account of estate paid to orphans by former
guardian, Hillary Pitts, to present guardians, William Parker & Isaac
Hill, 14 Jan., 1792;
1) to Micah Hill; negro Milby 6
2) to Rebecca Hill; Thomas 57, Leah 23, Levin 19, Cartshala(?) 12,
Lanty 4, Comfort 2
3) Hillary Pitts relinquishes all right to negroes Bowden & Minta, to
Rebecca, which negroes are run away

F. 255   Apprentice; William O. Bennett (of William), by consent of
             his mother
             Bound to; Littleton Furniss
             Trade; seaman
             Surety; Edwd. Lamden
             In presents of Edwd. Stevenson, William Schoolfield

F. 256   Rackliffe Pointer, guardian to Rachel Ennis, to sell negro
             Sall; money to be applied to claim of Cornelius Ennis, late
guardian

Matters in dispute between Maj. William Holland, late guardian to
John, Henry & George Selby, & Fisher Richardson, present guardian,
referred to John C. Handy & John Cutler, Esqs..

Outten & Purnell Toadvine, exes. of William Toadvine, to advertise in
Smith's paper at Easton & the Telegraph at Baltimore for creditors to
exhibit claims

Nancy Handy, adm. of Maj. James Handy, to advertise in Thomas P.
Smith's paper at Easton for creditors to exhibit claims

F. 257   William McGregor & Jacob White to view estate of Molly,
             Thomas, Zadok & Sally Purnell, in care of Elizabeth Purnell,
guardian

'112'

Nixon Davis & Esme Purnell to view estate of Sarah Parker, in care of Milly Purnell, guardian

Thomas D. Purnell, exe. of Milby Purnell, to sell personal estate (except negroes)

James Selby & Mary, his wife, exes. of Rev. John Rankin, to sell personal estate; allowed $14.25 for devise to deceased's widow for sale of 233 3/4 acres of land

F. 258 Esther Sturgis, exe. of Joshua Sturgis, allowed 10% on payment of debts

Levin Mitchell, late exe. of Joshua Mitchell, allowed 10% on payment of debts

F. 259 Tues., Oct. 8, 1805 All Justices present

F. 260 Orphan; William Drummond Davis (of Thomas, of Major)
Guardian; Henry Davis
Sureties; Thomas Collins, Daniel Hardnett [also Hartnitt]

Levin Merrill discharged from guardianship to Levi Merrill; William R. Merrill new guardian

F. 261 Orphan; Levi Merrill (of Levi, Pitts Creek)
Guardian; William R. Merrill
Sureties; Levi Merrill, Daniel Hartnett

Orphan; Thomas Gordy (of William, Sen.)
Guardian; William Gordy
Sureties; Samuel Gordy, George Smith (B. S.)

F. 262 William Smith discharged from guardianship to Wingate Smith; Belitha Griffin new guardian

Orphan; Wingate Smith (of Levi)
Guardian; Belitha Griffin [couldn't write]
Sureties; Thomas N. Williams, Sterling Jones

F. 263 Apprentice; William Blake, 10, by consent of his father Harmon
Bound to; James Davis
Trade; waterman
Sureties; John Johnson (of Leonard), Zadok Townsend

F. 264
F. 265 Frederick Conner, guardian to Levin Townsend (of Levin), to receive his estate from Priscilla Hudson, adm. of William Hudson, late guardian: report; negro boy Harry; his share of estate of his mother Leah

F. 266 Rackliffe Pointer [couldn't write], guardian to Rachel Ennis (of Cornelius), to sell negro Sall; bought by said Rackliffe: Test.; Matthew Hopkins

'113'

F. 267-9
F. 270
Matthias Warren & Elizabeth, his wife, guardians to Julianna Mitchell (of Robt.), to sell personal estate (except negroes & plate); inventory given; William McGreger, clerk of sale

F. 271
Apprentice; David Long, by consent of his father David
Bound to; Isaac Taylor
Trade; house carpenter & joiner
In presents of Jesse Henderson, John Stevenson, Edward Stevenson

F. 272
Apprentice; Peter Dorman, by consent of his mother Tabitha Dormand [couldn't write]
Bound to; John Willis, shoe maker [couldn't write]
Trade; shoe maker
Term; 6 years, 1 month
Before James Brodwatter, John Williams

F. 273-8 [blank]

F. 279 Thomas D. Purnell, exe. of Milby Purnell, to advertise in Rels's(?) Philadelphia Gazette & the Star at Easton for creditors to exhibit claims

Charles Hope & Benjamin Aydelott to view estate of William D. Davis, in care of Henry Davis, guardian

Edward Stevenson & Edward Lambden to view estate of Levi Merrill, in care of William R. Merrill, guardian

Wilson Maddux, exe. of Hezekiah Maddux, allowed for crops which are devised & mistakenly appraised in inventory

Wilson Maddux, exe. of Hezekiah Maddux, to sell personal estate

Littleton Davis & Annanias Bradford to view estate of Wingate Smith, in care of Belitha Griffin, guardian

F. 280   Elizabeth Johnson, exe. of Laban Johnson, to sell part of estate

Col. Samuel Handy & George Hayward to view estate of John & Molly Richardson, in care of Nancy Richardson, guardian

Maj. Edward Henry & Thomas N. Williams to divide personal estate of John Purnell (W. N.), in hands of Elizabeth Purnell, adm.

Elizabeth Purnell, guardian to Zadok & Sally Purnell (of John, W. N.), to sell orphans' personal estates (except negroes)

Thomas Collins, adm. of John Collins, to sell personal estate (except corn due for rent)

F. 281   Stephen Anderson, adm. dbn of William Campbell, to sell personal estate

Nixon Davis & Thomas Duncan to appraise estate of Molly(?) Purnell, deceased

In consideration of L.130/11, paid to me by George W. Purnell, my late guardian, I quit claim to any other estate belonging to me

In presence of John S. Spence   Purnell F. Smith

F. 282   [blank]

F. 283   Tues., Dec. 10, 1805   Littleton Robins, Edward Henry present

Thomas Franklin & Charlotte, his wife, discharged from guardianship to Robert Kerby; Jacob White new guardian

F. 284
Orphan; Robert Kerby (of John)
Guardian; Jacob White
Sureties; Robert Nairne, Thomas D. Purnell

F. 285
Samuel McMasters & Anderson Patterson to view estate of Wealthy Gillett (of William), in care of William M. Bevans, guardian; before Benj. Aydelott: report; 63 acres; widow's thirds

F. 286
F. 287
John Dennis & John Duncan to view estate of James & William Jarman, in care of James Jarman, guardian; before Benjamin Johnson, Jun., & Matthias Davis: report

F. 288
F. 289
Littleton Davis & Annanias Bradford to view estate of Wingate Smith, in care of Belitha Griffin, guardian; before Thos. N. Williams: report; 50 acres

F. 290
Edward Henry & Thomas N. Williams to distribute estate of John Purnell (W. N.), in hands of Elizabeth Purnell, adm., between widow & representatives;
1) to Mary D.(?) Purnell; negro Stephen 19
2) to Thomas Purnell; Levin 28
3) to Zadok Purnell; Titus 32
F. 291   4) to Sarah Purnell; Jane 16; list
5) to widow Elizabeth; Charles 33, Bridgett 50, Grace 13

F. 292
Collins,
F. 293
Elizabeth Purnell, guardian to Sally & Zadok Purnell (of John), to sell their personal estates (except negroes): report; Sarah's estate sold to Stephen Crapper, James A. Isabiah Crapper, Warrington Davis, Peter C. Evans, James Franklin, Zadok Purnell, Jun., Bowdon(?) Robins, James Selby, George Taylor; Zadok Purnell's estate sold to Annanias Lewis; Before William Dale

F. 293b
F. 294
Benjamin Purnell & McKimmey Porter to view estate of Isaac & Nancy Selby, in care of Charles Hammond, guardian: report; negroes Bob 24, Levin 9, Hetty 6, Gatty 3

John Taylor, Hugh Ware & Attalanta [also Lanty], his wife, & James Taylor & Betty Taylor agree to a division of estates of Elias & Betty Taylor, their father & mother, having each received their share from Betty Taylor; in presence of P. Quinton

F. 295 Apprentice; James Bennett (of William), by consent of his mother Rebecca
Bound to; John Hall, shoe & boot maker
Trade; shoe & boot maker
F. 296 Surety; Eph. Furniss
In presence of Edwd. Stevenson, William Schoolfield

John Holland & John Taylor to view estate of William Price, in care of Samuel Bradford, guardian

John Stewart, adm. of Levin H. Smith, to sell personal estate

Henrietta Devorix vs. Elizabeth Devorix, adm. of John Devorix; states she is entitled to property claimed by her under a gift from her father

Thomas D. Purnell, exe. of Milby Purnell, to sell negroes

F. 297 Esme Purnell & Thomas D. Purnell to view estate of Betsy Rigsby, in care of Molly Purnell, guardian

Elizabeth Devorix, adm. of John Devorix, to sell personal estate (except negro boy, corn & pork)

John Stevenson vs. Isaac Collins & Tabitha, his wife, admx. of William Stevenson; citation issued against goods of defendant

Thomas N. Williams & William McGregor to view estate of Robert Kerby, in care of Jacob White, guardian

Sarah Hindman, adm. of James Hindman, to sell personal estate

F. 298 Received Dec. 8, 1805, of Rachel Parsons, L.6/8, my share of estate
          Jonathan Parsons

Received Jan. 6, 1806, of my unkle George Truitt, as my guardian; list; mother's wearing apparel; obligations on Mrs. Nancy Richardson & Henry Richardson; obligation on McKemmy Porter; my aunt Maryan Rice; Thomas Martin, Esq., attorney, for his advice

Wit.; Mary Hodgson   Sally Hodgson

F. 299-300 [blank]

F. 301 Following proceedings omitted in their proper place at Aug. term, 1805;

John Stevenson vs. Dr. Isaac Collins & Tabitha, his wife, admx. of
William Stevenson; John Stevenson appears, by Ephraim K. Wilson, Esq.,
his solicitor, & exhibits bill of complaint; your petitioner's father,
William Stevenson, died leaving considerable estate; Tabitha
Stevenson, adm., intermarried with Isaac Collins; estate more than
        enough to pay debts without touching negroes; adms. sold
F. 302   estate & negroes for sums far above value & applied same to
        their own use & didn't account for it; asks for just & fair
accounts from adms.; gives inventory of estate appraised 3 Aug., 1797;
        negroes Bobb(?) 37, George 17, Levin 17, Jesse 14, Charles
F. 303-6 12, Hess 17, Minty 15; [inventory continues]

Creditors; Wm. Covington, John Rankin
Near kin; Isabbella Miller, Nancy Mills
Appraisers; John Postly, Josiah Mitchell

Tabitha Stevenson makes oath to above inventory before Levin Handy,
Register

F. 307   1st account of Isaac Collins & Tabitha, his wife, admx. of
        William Stevenson, 2 Sept., 1797; mentions monies paid to
James Fassitt, William Lister, Isaac Franklin, John Massey, Isaac
Ayres, Dr. James Wilson, Levin Handy (Register)

F. 308   2nd account, 7 Sept., 1798; monies paid to James Marshall,
        Sally Franklin (one representative of Edward Vandome, his
bill obligatory to said Vandome by Col. Z. Purnell), Joshua Mitchell,
William Lister, Levin Pollitt, Dr. Thos. S. Fassitt, Isaac Marshall
        (his bill obligatory due to L. Collyer), Levi Mills (award
F. 309   due out of P. Warren's estate), Isaac Collins, Peter Collier,
Josiah Mitchell, John Postly

        3rd account; monies paid to James Selby & wife, exex. of John
F. 310   Rankin; Joseph Miller; Trustees of Washington Academy;
        William Covington, Samuel Handy, Miss Polly Spence, Mckimmey
Porter

        Isaac Collins & Tabitha, his wife, in consideration of L.105
F. 311   paid by Joshua Mitchell, sell negro Charles 12; in presence
        of John Postly

        Isaac & Tabitha swear to above sale before John Postly

F, 312   John C. Handy, clk.

Subpena issued for Isaac & Tabitha

F. 313   11 Dec., 1804, came William Whittington, Esq., Council for
        defendants; case continued to Apr. term, 1805

        Answer of Isaac & Tabitha; claim only small surplus after
F. 314   debts paid; did sell negroes above appraised value but
        believe all they did was their right; John's part was
                        (cont.)

F. 315 delivered to Levin Dereckson, his guardian; came to final settlement before petition & struck distribution

In pursuance of order in behalf of Levin Derickson & William Franklin, Laban Johnson & Hillary Pitts to appraise estate

F. 316 Inventory of estate of William Stevenson; mentions negroes George 19, Hess 19, Milly 1

Nearest of kin; Nancy Mills, Isabella Miller

Distribution;
1) to widow; thirds
2) to children John, Polly, Sally & Edward

F. 317 Deposition of James Bowen; bought negro Bob from Isaac Collins; thought he belonged to Isaac

Deposition of Levin Derickson; Bob was part of William Stevenson's estate; negro Levin sold by Tabitha before she remarried;
F. 318 negro Charles was part of William's estate, had lived with Joshua Mitchell prior to Mitchell's death

Deposition of Kendall Smack; bought negro Minta & her child of Isaac Collins

Negro Jesse sold for L.80

F. 319 Court orders defendants to pay plaintiff $75.41 1/2

F. 320 Account of how above award was figured; mentions John Stevenson

F. 321 L.2 payed each to William Hill & James Bowen for attendance as witnesses; L.1 to Kendall Smack

BOOK 10, 1805

MICROFILM: CR 46,719-3

MSA No.: CM 1123-10

'119'

Worcester County Orphans Court Proceedings, 1805, Book 5

Book of loose papers related to estate of Col. Zadok Purnell

F. 1   Tues., Oct. 8, 1805

James B. Robins & others, representatives in the 4th degree of Col. Zadok Purnell, vs. Littleton Robins, Sen., Joshua Prideaux & Zadok Purnell, adms. cwa of said deceased; petition of James B. Robins, Littleton Robins, Jun., Joseph Gillis & Mary, his wife, Adam Spence, George Bratten & Elizabeth, his wife, Thomas R. P. Spence, Levin Fountain & Andesiah, his wife, Euphemia Purnell, Robert J. H. Purnell, Gertrude Purnell, Anne Purnell, Molly R. Purnell, Littleton Dennis, James Polk, Walton Purnell, Thomas Purnell, Elizabeth Purnell, William Purnell, William Gibb, Elizabeth P. P. Marshall, John P. Marshall, Jun., Thomas P. Marshall, Sarah White, Zipporah Fassitt, Peggy Fassitt, Thomas Fassitt, John Rackliffe, Charlotte Rackliffe, Rider Rackliffe, Kitty Rackliffe;

F. 2   At the time of his death, Zadok Purnell had one sister living & representatives of other brothers & sisters, some of whom are the children, & your petitioners the grandchildren, whose intermediate ancestors are dead; ask that they receive shares

F. 3   that would have gone to their parents; [list of petitioners repeated]

On 2nd Tues of Oct., 1805, came adms., by William Whittington, their counsel; deny petitioners have rights to parents' shares

F. 4   [blank]

F. 5   Exhibit A; Will of Zadok Purnell;
1) to Zadok Purnell, son of Thomas Purnell (Wallops Neck), all lands I bought of Edward Vandome in Newport Neck
2) to aforesaid Zadok; list

6 Jan., 1805   his
                                    Zadok X Purnell
Wit.; Zadok Purnell   mark
       Geo. W. Purnell
       Catherine(?) Franklin

1 Feb., 1805, came Littleton Robins, Sen., Joshua Prideaux & Zadok Purnell & made oath to above will

F. 6   1 Feb., 1805, came Zadok Purnell & George W. Purnell, witnesses, & made oath to above will; state Zadok was of sound mind

James B. Robins, Register, swears that above is true copy of will

'120'

F. 7   Inventory of estate of Co. Zadok Purnell; mentions negroes
          Peter 55, Ben 45, Nimrod 28, Job 28, Caleb 27, Hope 27,
Reuben 25, James 25, George 23, Stephen 23, Jesse 20, Milby 14, Jacob
9, Levin 5, Samuel 3, Dinah 90, Amy 55, Pleasant 55, Bridget 38,
Rachel 18, Leah 14, Margaret 11, Priscilla 9, Betty 8, Nancy 6

F. 8-20   [inventory continues, original folio numbers 1 - 15]

Appraisers; Thos. N. Williams, Zadok Sturgis
Nearest of kin; John P. Marshall, Esther Purnell

F. 19   [out of order] Legacies given to Zadok Purnell (Wallops
          Neck); negroes Pool 45, Manuel 29, Mingo 22; list

F. 21   Adms. swear to inventory

F. 22   James B. Robins, Register, swears that above is true copy of
          inventory

[After F. 22, Exhibit 2, sale of estate, numbered F. 1-21 with pages
out of order]

F. 14   List of negroes repeated, with Daniel added & Nanny for Nancy

James B. Robins, Edward Robins & Thos. N. Williams, clerks, swear to
above sale

Littleton Robins, Joshua Prideaux & Zadok Purnell, adms. of Col. Zadok
Purnell, to sell personal estate; long report

BOOK 11, MH 7, 1806 - 1809

MICROFILM: WK 740-741-1

MSA No.: CM 1123-11

Worcester County Orphans Court Proceedings, MH-7, 1806 - 1809

F. 1   Matthew Hopkins appointed Register of Wills, 27 Jan., 1806

Robt. Bowie   Wit.; The Honorable William Kilty, Chancellor

In presence of Saml. A. Harper, P. Quinton

Sureties; Robert Nairne, James B. Robins

F. 2   Littleton Robins, Sen., John Bishop, Edward Henry appointed Justices

Robt. Bowie   Al. Hanson, Chanc.

Wit.; The Honourable Alexander Contee Hanson, Chancellor

Tues., Feb. 11, 1806   All Justices present

Robert Nairne, Sheriff

F. 3   Orphan; Mary Bell (of James)
        Guardian; Ann Bell
        Sureties; William Bell, Littleton Davis

Orphan; West Watson (of John)
Guardian; Rebecca Watson [couldn't write]
Sureties; John Handcock, Jonathan Melvin

F. 4   Orphan; Sophia Watson (of John)
        Guardian; Rebecca Watson
        Sureties; John Handcock, Jonathan Melvin

Southey Whittington discharged from guardianship to Anne Turpin; Curtis Jenckins new guardian

Orphan; Anne Turpin (of John)
Guardian; Curtis Jenkins
Sureties; Sewell Turpin, Charles Hope

Sewell Turpin discharged from guardianship to John Turpin; Curtis Jenkins new guardian

F. 5   Orphan; John Turpin (of John)
        Guardian; Curtis Jenkins
        Sureties; Sewell Turpin, Charles Hope

Nehemiah Blake discharged from guardianship to Westly Melvin; James Davis new guardian

F. 6   Orphan; Westly Melvin (of William)
        Guardian; James Davis
        Sureties; John Davis, Avery [signed Avra] Melvin

'123'

Nehemiah Blake discharged from guardianship to Patsey Melvin; James
Davis new guardian

Orphan; Patsey Melvin (of William)
Guardian; James Davis
Sureties; John Davis, Avery Melvin

F. 7
Orphan; Moses Payne (of Jeptha)
Guardian; Stephen Chaille
Sureties; John Payne, John Smith

Orphan; Jesse Waters (of Jesse)
Guardian; William Bennett & Anne, his wife
Sureties; Henry Smock, Shadrach Sturgis

F. 8
Apprentice; Thomas Purnell (of Isaac), 15 on 28 June last
Bound to; McKimmey Porter
Trade; boot & shoe make
Sureties; Sewell Turpin, Nathaniel Brittingham
Memorandum; Thomas Jones, father-in-law [step father?] to
orphan was present

F. 9
Apprentice; Jesse Justice (of Solomon), 7 1/2
Bound to; Isaac Knox
Trade; farmer
Sureties; Edmond Crapper, John M. Knox

F. 10
Nixon Davis & Thomas Duncan to view estate of Littleton &
John Richards (of John), in care of Polly Richards, guardian;
before John Davis: report; 40 acres

F. 11
Thomas N. Williams & Edward Henry to view estate of Mary Mitchell (of
Joshua), in care of Elizabeth Smock, guardian; before William
McGregor; Edward sworn before Thomas: report; land where
Joshua Mitchell lately lived; land where Elizabeth Smack now
lives; Mrs. Smock's thirds; part of tract called 'Striban', 160 acres

F. 12
Edward Stevenson Esq., & Dr. John Stevenson to view estate
of William H. Tilghman, in care of Sally Tilghman, guardian;
before William Schoolfield: report; lott in New Town; 2/3 of
estate to orphan

F. 13
Nixon Davis & Esme Purnell to view estate of Sarah Parker (of
James), in care of Milby Purnell, guardian; before John
Davis: report; 180 acres called 'Discovery'; negro lad Sambo,
girl Minto, boys Jack & Greg

F. 14
William Quinton & Jackson Turner to view estate of Henry
White, in care of George Hayward, guardian; before Jesse
Bennett: report; 1/3 of 140 acres; negroes Jane (old), 1/5 of
Hanna (old) & three finger Lige 36, 1/3 of 2/6 of Limon 60, Lige 15,
Milly & 3 children

F. 15   William Quinton & Jackson Turner to view estate of Peter
        White, in care of George Hayward, guardian; before W.
Holland: report; 1/3 of 140 acres; negroes Lige 21, Sally & child; 4/5
of three finger Lige; 1/3 of 2/3 of Limos(?)

F. 16   Charles Hope & Benjamin Aydelott to view estate of William D.
        Davis, in care of Henry Davis, guardian; before W. Holland:
report; 50 acres

        John Holland & John Taylor to view estate of William Price,
F. 17   in care of Samuel Bradford, guardian; before Saml. A. Harper:
report; 100 acres; widow's dower

        Zadok Sturgis, Esq., & Handy Mills to distribute estate of
F. 18   Jesse Waters, deceased, in hands of William Bennett & Anne,
        his wife, exex.; before Jesse Bennett;
1) to William Bennett, in right of his wife Anne (widow of said
Jesse); negroes Bob & Comfort
        2) to Polly Waters (of said Jesse); negroes Bob 51, Major 3
F. 19   3) to Jesse Waters (of said Jesse), Wm. Bennett & wife,
        guardians; negroes Sarah 23, Harry 1

William & Betty Dickerson, guardians to Nancy Nicholson (of Isaac), to
sell negro Moses; bought by Robert J. H. Handy

        Apprentice; Stephen Mills Matthews, by consent of his father
F. 20   William
        Bound to; Jeremiah Flowers
        Before James Brodwatter, John Williams

        Apprentice; Thomas Daniel, 10 & 2 months, son of Rachel
        [couldn't write]
        Bound to; Covington Townsend [also Coventon, farmer(?)
        Trade; farmer(?)
F. 21   In presents of Wm. Holland, Benj. Aydelott

Apprentice; Ebben Maddux [also Maddox], 17 on 1 Mar. next, son of
Anny, of Somerset Co. [couldn't write]
Bound to; Jonathan Parsons
Trade; farmer
In presence of Isaac Hearn, John Dashiell

F. 22   Apprentice; James Brodwatter, 16 years, 5 months & 24 days,
        son of James, Esq.
        Bound to; John Williams
        Trade; business of the water as a salor or any other business
        except farming
        In presents of John Cottingham, Jackson Turner

        Apprentice; Leah Noble, daughter of Sally Parker (alias
        Noble) [couldn't write]
        Bound to; Robt. M. Merrill
F. 23   Term; till 16, on 14 Dec., 1809
                            (cont.)

Trade; spin on spinning wheel
Sureties; Wm. Harper, Thomas Milbourne
In presents of J. Hubbell, John Ward

Anne Bell & William Bell, adms. of James Bell, to sell personal estate

Thomas N. Williams & William McGregor, Esqs., to view estate of Mary Bell, in care of Anne Bell, guardian

Ezekiel Coston & William Aydelott to view estate of West Watson, in care of Rebecca Watson, guardian

F. 24　Martha Duncan, adm. of John Duncan, allowed full time to settle estate, as it is insufficient to pay debts

Thomas N. Williams & William McGregor, Esqs., to distribute personal estate of John Kerby, in hands of Thomas Franklin & wife, exex.

Curtis Jenckins & John J. Williams, guardians to Anne, John & William Turpin (of John), to sell two small negroes George & Keziah, allotted to orphans from estate of William Turpin

Zipporah Bishop, adm. of Charles Bishop, to sell personal estate

Elisha Jones & Hezekiah Johnson to view estate of Moses Payne, in care of Stephen Chaille, guardian

Bayly Young, adm. of Stephen Roach, to advertise in Thomas P. Smith's paper at Easton for creditors to exhibit claims

Thomas D. Purnell, adm. dbn of Thomas Rigsby, to advertise in Thomas P. Smith's paper at Easton for creditors to exhibit claims

F. 25　Thomas D. Purnell, exe. of Milby Purnell, allowed $5 for boards appraised in inventory, but sold during Milby's lifetime; also $6 for corn growing on land devised to his son

Adm. on estate of John Purnell granted to James Trippe

Adm. on estate of Stephen Toadvine granted to Isaiah(?) Toadvine & Thomas Carey

By consent of representatives, exe. of Capt. Thomas Martin to sell enough personal estate to pay debts, provided Thomas Martin (of Thos.), Sarah Wise & John S.(?) Martin, exes. of Leah Martin, shall consent

Outten Toadvine & Purnell Toadvine, exes. of William Toadvine, to sell land called 'Summerfield', as directed by will

Zadok Sturgis & Handy Mills to distribute personal estate of Jesse Waters, in hands of William Bennett & wife, exex.

Thomas N.(?) Crapper, guardian to Sally Smock, to apply $4 of principle for three months schooling

F. 26 James Selby & Mary, his wife, exex. of Rev. John Rankin, allowed $83.40 for loss of property, 10% for trouble settling estate & for raising three young negroes untill their sale

Col. Thomas Martin, exe. of Thomas Martin, Sen., allowed 7 1/2% on sale of real estate

James Trippe, adm. of John Purnell, to sell personal estate, except negroes Sarah, Amos(?), Jasper, Maria, Daniel (the younger) & Moses

Capt. Charles Bennett & Sarah(?), his wife, exe. of Benjamin Purnell, allowed 10% on payment of debts

Isaiah Toadvine & Thomas Carey, adms. of Stephen Toadvine, to sell personal estate

Isaiah Toadvine & Thomas Carey, adms. of Stephen Toadvine, to advertise in Thomas P. Smith's paper at Easton for creditors to exhibit claims

Rachel Gault, adm. of Archibald Gault, to sell personal estate

F. 27 Received 29, Oct., 1802, of my father Edward Hammon, L.20, for a legacy left me by my aunt Leah Hammond

Test.; Lee Farrington

Rachel
her X mark
Hammon

Received at Snow Hill, 12 Feb., 1806, of William R. Warwick & Elenor Warwick, negro man Harry, 47, my share of my father John Flemming's estate

Josa. Flemming, Jun.(?)

Littleton Robins swears to above transaction by Joshua Fleming

Received at Snow Hill, 12 Feb., 1806, of William R. Warwick & Elenor Warwick, L.5, my share of my father John Fleming's estate

James Fleming

Littleton Robins swears to above transaction

F. 28 Tues., Apr. 8, 1806 All Justices present

Alexander McAllen discharged from guardianship to Sally Turner; Cornelius Dickerson new guardian

Orphan; Sally [also Sarah] Turner (of George)
Guardian; Cornelius Dickerson, Jun.
Sureties; Alexander McAllen, Parker Dickerson

F. 29
Orphan; William Johnson (of Laban)
Guardian; Elisabeth Johnson [couldn't write]
Sureties; Edward Robins, Arthur Tracy

Orphan; Moses Johnson (of Laban)
Guardian; Elisabeth Johnson
Sureties; Edward Robins, Arthur Tracy

F. 30
Orphan; Betsy Aydelott (of Benjamin)
Guardian; Leah Aydelott
Sureties; John Holland, Benjamin Gunby

F. 31
Orphan; James Lambden (of Thomas)
Guardian; Edward Lambden
Sureties; Anderson Patterson, John Hall

Orphan; Robert Lambden (of Thomas)
Guardian; Edward Lambden
Sureties; Anderson Patterson, John Hall

F. 32
Orphan; Kendal Scarbrough (of Kendal)
Guardian; Sarah Hinman [also Henman, couldn't write]
Sureties; John Ayres, Josiah Bratten

Orphan; Nancy Hinman (of James)
Guardian; Sarah Hinman
Sureties; John Ayres, Josiah Bratten

F. 33
Orphan; Zacheus Henderson
Guardian; Benjamin Henderson, father
Sureties; Michael Murray, Littleton Furniss

Orphan; David D. Henderson
Guardian; Benjamin Henderson, father
Sureties; Michael Murray, Littleton Furniss

F. 34
Orphan; William Horsey Henderson
Guardian; Benjamin Henderson, father
Sureties; Michael Murray, Littleton Furniss

Orphan; Sally Quinton Henderson
Guardian; Benjamin Henderson, father
Sureties; Michael Murray, Littleton Furniss

F. 35
Orphan; James Milligan Henderson
Guardian; Benjamin Henderson, father
Sureties; Michael Murray, Littleton Furniss

Orphan; Harriet Henderson
Guardian; Benjamin Henderson, father
Sureties; Michael Murray, Littleton Furniss

'128'

F. 36
    Orphan; Stephen Toadvine (of Stephen)
    Guardian; Isaiah Toadvine
    Sureties; Thomas Carey [couldn't write], Joseph Fookes

Orphan; Hetty Toadvine (of Stephen)
Guardian; Thomas Carey
Sureties; Isaiah Toadvine, Joseph Fookes

F. 37
    Orphan; Gatty Fookes
    Guardian; Joseph Fookes, father
    Sureties; Isaiah Toadvine, Thomas Carey

Orphan; Sally Handy (of Col. Levin)
Guardian; Nancy Handy
Sureties; Thomas N. Williams, Ephraim K. Wilson

F. 38
    Orphan; Esther Handy (of Col. Levin)
    Guardian; Nancy Handy
    Sureties; Thomas N. Williams, Ephraim K. Wilson

Orphan; Milly Selby (of James, of Jno.)
Guardian; Mary Selby
Sureties; John Selby, Sen., Benjamin Aydelott

F. 39
    Orphan; Elisabeth Selby (of James, of Jno.)
    Guardian; Mary Selby
    Sureties; John Selby, Sen., Benjamin Aydelott

Orphan; William Stockley Corbin (of Peter S.)
Guardian; Bowdoin Robins
Sureties; Thomas R. Handy, George Hayward

F. 40
    Orphan; Molly Corbin (of Peter S.)
    Guardian; Bowdoin Robins
    Sureties; Thomas R. Handy, George Hayward

Micajah Hill, one legatee of Schoolfield Parker vs. Henry Parker, adm.; Micajah Hill, by William Whittington, Esq., his solicitor, states will of said Schoolfield bequeathed to said Henry the labour of his negro Frederick until Micajah came of age, on provision that exe. should keep negro old Peg & on her decease Frederick to be
F. 41   delivered up; Micajah is of age; Henry is about to remove to Baltimore; asks that he be directed to deliver legacy

Subpena issued for Henry Parker

F. 42
    Henry Parker, by Ephraim K. Wilson, Esq., his counsel, files answer; old Peg is not dead, so no grounds to deliver boy Frederick

F. 43
    Apprentice; John Pettitt (of Absalom), 15
    Bound to; John Taylor
    Trade; boot & shoe maker
    Sureties; Zadok Sturgis, Littleton R. Purnell, Esqs.

F. 44
Apprentice; Bridget Isaacs, free mulatto, 8 last Christmas, daughter of Esther
Bound to; William Floyd
Trade; spin & weave
Sureties; Joseph Houston, Littleton Riley

F. 45
Apprentice; Laban Hudson (of Sterling), 15 on 30 Aug. last, by consent of his mother
Bound to; John Taylor
Trade; boot & shoe maker
Sureties; Robert J. H. Handy, Joshua Fleming, Jun.

Apprentice; Isaiah Cooper (of Bennett), 13 Sept. next
Bound to; James Riggen
Trade; farmer
Sureties; James Brodwatter, Esq., John Riggen

F. 46
F. 47
Elisha Jones & Hezekiah Johnson to view estate of Moses C. Payne (of Jeptha), in care of Stephen Chaille, guardian; before Saml. A. Harper: report; 1/4 acre; right of dower of Wealthy Beachboard, wife of Joshua, late widow of Jeptha

F, 48
F. 49
John Postly & Lemuel Showell to view estate of John Powell (of John), in care of Keziah Powell, guardian; before Wm. McGregor: report; 150 acres where his uncle Belitha Powell lived, who willed it to him & his two sisters, viz. Esther, who is over 16, & Polly, lately married to Jesse Davis (of Jesse), but guardian is willed 1/4 of profits during her widowhood; report continues

F. 50
Thomas N. Williams & William McGrigor to view estate of Mary Bell (of James), in care of Anne Bell, guardian; sworn before each other: report; lands called 'Polke Neglect', 'Forest Flower' & 'Security Enlarged', 552 3/4 acres; Ann Bell's dower; 40 acres of cypress swamp called 'Tillbury'

F. 51
F. 52
William McGrigor & Jacob White to view estate of Molly Purnell (of John), in care of Elisabeth Purnell, guardian; before Thos. N. Williams: report; 700 acres; mentions thirds that was in possession of & occupied by Mrs. Mitchell, widow of Robert, mother of said John; widow's dower; negro man Stephen; Elizabeth Purnell, guardian to Mary Purnell

F. 53
F. 54
William McGrigor & Jacob White to view estate of Sally Purnell (of John), in care of Elisabeth Purnell, guardian; [same as above]; negro woman Jane; Elizabeth Purnell, guardian to Sarah Purnell

F. 55
F. 56
William McGrigor & Jacob White to view estate of Zadok Purnell (of John), in care of Elizabeth Purnell, guardian; [same as above]; negro man Titus

F. 57
William McGrigor & Jacob White to view estate of Thomas Purnell (of John), in care of Elizabeth Purnell, guardian; [same as above]; negro man Levin

F. 58   George Bell, Hillary Pitts & James Fassitt, Sen. to view
         personal estate of heirs of Johnson Gray, in hands of Abisha
Davis & Martha, his wife, guardians; before Wm. McGrigor: report;
negroes Bob 49, Ned 16, Capril 13, Luke 10, Rose 43, Esther 63;
guardians allowed for maintaining negroes Allen (crippled) 8, Daniel
7, woman Bett(?, lunatic), __?__ 6, Usina 4, Cloe 4, Nancy 2, Sarah 3;
         negro man Jep has the clap(?) & under doctor's care; negro
F. 59   Bett is dead

1805, a bill of lumber got of land belonging to heirs of Johnson Gray;
Abisha Davis swears to bill

John Postly, Lemuel Showell & William McGregor to distribute estate of
         John Powell, deceased, in hands of Jesse Powell, adm. dbn;
F. 60   1) to widow; list; negro woman Sall
         2) to Esther Powell, daughter; list; girl Lanty
3) to Molly Powell, daughter, who married Jesse Davis (of Jesse);
list; man Bob
4) to John Powell, son, share paid to Keziah Powell, guardian

F. 61   John Postly, Lemuel Showell & William McGregor to distribute
         estate of Belitha Powell, in hands of Jesse Powell, exe.;
         1) to Esther Powell; list
F. 62   2) to Molly Powell, who married Jesse Davis (of Jesse); list
         3) to John Powell (of John), share paid to Keziah Powell,
guardian; list

F. 63   Apprentice; Polly Porter, child of the Poor House
         Bound to; Joseph E. Bishop
         Trade; house work; spinning, sewing, weaving
         Sureties; Littleton Riley, William Parker
         By Trustees for the Poor; Samuel Handy, Sen., McKimmey
         Porter, George Hayward

         Apprentice; William Vance, 14, by consent of his father
         William
         Bound to; David Cathell
         Trade; carriage maker
F. 64   In presents of Isaac Hearn, Benjamin Johnson

Sally Gray, exe. of Joseph Gray, to advertise in the Mirror at
Wilmington, DE, & the Star at Easton for creditors to exhibit claims

Elizabeth Selby, exe. of Thomas Selby, to sell wind mill on lands of
Peter Parker

Estate of Zadok Selby, in account(?) with William Selby, exe.(?);
negroes Comfort, Joshua, Able, Charlotte; expenses for apprehending
negro Daniel; Wm. Selby, adm. of Zadok, & Parker Selby swear that
above negroes have died

F. 65   Elizabeth Selby, exe. of Thomas Selby, allowed 6% on estate

James Melvin, adm. of Elijah Nelson, allowed 10% on estate

'131'

Frederick Conner, guardian to Levin & Lotty Bishop, states that life estate of Elizabeth Bishop in land called 'Scarbroughs Castle' is determined; Zadok Sturgis & Ralph Milbourn to view same

Zadok Purnell & Joshua Prideaux, Esqs., to view estate of William Johnson, in care of Elizabeth Johnson, guardian

Zadok Purnell & Joshua Prideaux, Esqs., to view estate of Moses Johnson, in care of Elizabeth Johnson, guardian

James Trippe, adm. of John Purnell, to advertise in Thomas P. Smith's paper at Easton for creditors to exhibit claims

James Trippe, adm. of John Purnell, allowed full time to settle estate, as estate is insufficient to discharge debts

Caleb Williams, exe. of Edward McGee, to sell personal estate (except legacies)

F. 66   Henry Parker, exe. of Schoolfield Parker, allowed 5% on estate

Sarah Franklin, exe. of William Franklin, allowed 7 1/2% on estate

William Corbin & Bowdoin Robins, exes. of Peter S. Corbin, to sell personal estate (except negroes & legacies)

Betty Kellam, adm. of Joseph Kellam, to sell negroes Flora & Abel

Zadok Sturgis & Frederick Conner to view property of Nancy Hinman, in care of Sarah Hinman, guardian

John Cathell & Thomas Fookes to view property of Stephen Toadvine, in care of Isaiah Toadvine, guardian

John Cathell & Thomas Fookes to view property of Hetty Toadvine, in care of Thomas Carey, guardian

Zadok Sturgis & Frederick Conner to distribute estate of James Hinman, in hands of Sarah Hinman, adm.

Edward Lambden, guardian to James Lambden, to receive estate

F. 67   Edward Lambden, guardian to Robert Lambden, to receive estate

List of articles made use of for Samuel & George Gunn, of the property of Betsy Gunn, deceased; list; Tabitha Wise, late adm. dbn, made oath to above list of articles used for orphans of Samuel Gunn

Benjamin Henderson, guardian to Zaccheus, David, William, Sally, James & Harriet Henderson, to receive estate

Joseph Fookes, guardian to Gatty Fookes, to receive estate

F. 68   Adm. dbn on estate of William Henderson granted to John R. Slocomb

Register to strike distribution on estate of Jesse Duncan

Register to charge George Miles, guardian to Maria, Jane, Sally & Matilda Townsend, with profits of estates, & to allow him accounts rendered by Peter Tarr for keeping orphans

John Holland & Robert Cluff to view property of Milly & Elizabeth Selby, in care of Mary Selby, guardian

John Holland & Robert Cluff to distribute estates of James Selby (of Jno.) & his son Parker, in hands of Mary Selby, adm.

John Holland & William Holland, Jun., to view estate of William Corbin, in care of Bowdoin Robins, guardian

Samuel Handy & Samuel R. Smith to view estate of Molly Corbin, in care of Bowdoin Robins, guardian

F. 69   [blank]

F. 70   Tues., June 10, 1806   All Justices present

Orphan; Levin R. Marchment (of Riley)
Guardian; Levi Merrill
Sureties; Benjamin Bishop, Isaac Cottingham

William Dickerson & wife discharged from guardianship to Nancy Nicholson; William Dickerson new guardian

F. 71   Orphan; Nancy Nicholson (of Isaac)
         Guardian; William Dickerson
         Sureties; Selby Parker, Joseph Nicholson

         Esme Purnell & Thomas D. Purnell to view estate of Betsy Rigsby, in care of Milby Purnell, guardian; before Nixon Davis: report;
F. 72   land called 'Sandy Point', 65 acres; lot of 15 acres adjacent to Purnell Porter's land

         Zadok Sturgis & Ralph Milbourn to view estate of Levin &
F. 73   Lotty Bishop, in care of Frederick Conner, guardian: report; land called 'Scarbrous Castle', 153 acres

         Ezekiel Coston & William Aydelott to view estate of West
F. 74   Watson, in care of Rebecca Watson, guardian; before Benj. Aydelott: report; 30-35 acres

         Apprentice; John Clark (of Rhodes), 15 on 27 Feb. last
         Bound to; Joshua Evans
         Trade; boot & shoe maker
         Sureties; Littleton Riley, Patrick Waters
F. 75   Sarah Clark, mother, present

'133'

John Bishop & Sewell Turpin, Esqs., to distribute estates of Parker Selby, Sen., & Glippery Selby, his deceased widow, in hands of Charles Hammond;
1) to Milby Selby Purnell, legacies bequeathed to him by his grandfather Parker Selby; list
    2) to Anne Purnell; 1/2 of negroes; Lish 23, Levin 7 months,
F. 76   Jacob 9, Milby 4, Abel 9; list
    3) to Isaac & Nancy Selby, children of William Selby, deceased, & grandchildren of Parker & Glippery; 1/2 of
F. 77   negroes; Bob 23, Levin 10, Hetty 7, Gatty 3; list
    4) to Isaac Selby, a still left in hands of Chas. Hammond, guardian, a legacy from his grandfather Parker Selby, Sen.
5) articles left in hands of Charles Hammond, adm.; list; includes 190 lb. of pork at David Bowen's

F. 78   Apprentice; Moses Fisher, 15 & 8 months, son of Patience [couldn't write]
    Bound to; William Aydelott, farmer
    Trade; farmer
    In presence of Wm. Holland, Benj. Aydelott

Levi Merrill, guardian to Levin R. Marchment, allowed $10 out of principle for three months schooling

F. 79   John McDaniel was bound at Apr. term, 1805, to Shadrach Lane, now deceased, to learn taylor's trade; Nancy Lane, widow, asks that residue of time be assigned to Parker Selby; granted

Charles Hammond, adm. of Glippery Selby, allowed 5% on inventory & list of sperate debts

Charles Hammond, adm. of Glippery Selby, allowed $972.76 3/4, amount of specifics delivered to Anne Purnell; also legacies paid Milby Purnell & Isaac Selby agreeable to their grandfather's will; balance retained by him as guardian to Isaac & Nancy Selby

F. 80   [blank]

F. 81   Tues., Aug. 12, 1806   All Justices present

Orphan; William Benston (of Elias)
Guardian; John Taylor, Sen.
Sureties; Michael Tarr, Eliakim Johnson

Jeremiah Flowers' petition for guardianship of Ritta Flowers; states that Ritta, his brother's daughter, under 16, has right to sundry negroes, which some years past were stolen from Dorchester Co., & are now in possession of Mr. Prentiss, in VA, who took them from Eleazer Johnson, who stole them; Ritta is in Kentucky & doesn't know where negroes are

F. 82   Orphan; Ritta Flowers (of Julius Augustus)
    Guardian; Jeremiah Flowers
    Sureties; Ephraim Tilghman, John Selby, Jun.

Apprentice; William Christie (of William), 13 in Oct. next
Bound to; Lemuel Bowen
Trade; blacksmith

F. 83 Sureties; Thomas Jones, Valentine Dennis

Frederick Conner & Zadok Sturgis to view estate of Nancy
F. 84 Hinman, in care of Sarah Hinman, guardian: report; land
called 'Scarbore Castle', 30 acres, belonging to Nancy &
Sarah Hinman, heirs of James Hinman, in care of Sarah Hinman, guardian

John Cathell & Thomas Fookes to view estate of Stephen
F. 85 Toadvine (of Stephen), in care of Isaiah Toadvine, guardian;
before Nathan Gordy: report; real estate to be divided into 7
equal parts; 207 acres; other farm 159 acres

F. 86 John Cathell & Thomas Fookes to view estate of Nelly [also
Hetty] Toadvine (of Stephen), in care of Thomas Carey,
F. 87 guardian; [same as above]

Zadok Sturgis & Frederick Conner to distribute estate of Kendal
Scarbrough, in hands of Sarah Hinman, adm., between Kendal Scarbrough,
orphan, & his mother, said Sarah, adm. of James Hinman
F. 88 1) to Kendal, son; negro man Levin & woman Rummey(?)
2) to Sarah, late widow of Kendall, who married James Hinman,
deceased; girl Gatty

Thomas N. Williams & William McGrigor, Esqs., to distribute estate of
John Kerby, in hands of Thomas Franklin & Charlotte, his
F. 89 wife: inventory; negroes Ceasar 58, Caleb 45, David 45,
Shedrich 17, Jenny 37, Jenny 18, Rachel 13(?), Esther 14;
F. 90 list; balance of estate $1277.40; will gave property to wife
Charlotte until children come of age;
1) to widow; dower
2) to children Robert, Milby, Molly & William, 1/4 of
F. 91 remainder; Molly died in 1796 leaving no issue; William died
in 1797; Milby died in 1805, part of his estate to Frances &
Lemuel Franklin, his half brothers
Further distribution;
1) to Charlotte; negro man Cesar, woman Sarah; list
F. 92 2) to Robert Kerby; 2/3 of negro man Caleb; man Shederich,
girls Esther & Rachel; list
3) to Frances Franklin; woman Jenny; list
F. 93 4) to Lemuel Franklin; man David; list

Zadok Sturgis & Matthias [Nixon crossed out] Davis, Esqs., to settle
dispute between Purnell Porter & Thomas D. Purnell, exe. of Milby
Purnell; L.3/8/5 due from Thomas D. Purnell to Purnell Porter

F. 94 James Jarman & John Brittingham [couldn't write] vs.
Nathaniel Wilkins & Leah, his wife (formerly Leah Jarman),
F. 95 admx. of John Jarman; claimant asks counter security;
security not given; adm. of estate granted to claimants;
estate to be appraised by Jacob Rownd & Isaac Givan: securities; James
Reed, William Handcock (of Danl.)

F. 96 Apprentice; Zachariah Smith, 16 on 3 Mar. last, by consent of
       his father James, Sen.
       Bound to; William Smith, also son of James, house carpenter &
       joiner
       Trade; house carpenter & joiner
F. 97 In presence of Geo. Kendall, Matthew Hopkins

Apprentice; James Holland, 17 on 1 Mar., 1806, by consent of his
mother Betsy
Bound to; James Tilghman, shoe & boot maker
Trade; shoe & boot maker
Surety; John Hall
In presents of Edwd. Stevenson, William Schoolfield

Thomas Hooper, exe. of Esther Sturgis, to sell personal estate (except legacies)

Adam Bravard, adm. of Ebenezer C. Brevard, to sell personal estate

F. 98 John Cathell, exe. of David Cathell, allowed for negro James,
       in inventory, but since dead

Jesse Bowden, adm. of Jacob Bowden, to sell personal estate

George Hayward & William Quinton to distribute personal estate of
William Smullen(?), in hands of Peter Smullen(?), adm.

Register to strike distribution of personal estate of Thomas Taylor,
between widow & three children; Sally, Betsy & Patsey

Thomas Collins, adm. of John Collins, allowed for saving crop & for
two hogs proved not to belong to estate

John C. Handy, exe. of Thomas Gore(?), allowed for negro Sarah, in
inventory, but since dead

F. 99 John Stevens, adm. of George Richardson, allowed 8% on
       property sold & debts collected

John Stewart, adm. of Levin H. Smith, to advertise in Thomas P.
Smith's paper at Easton for creditors to exhibit claims

Adm. of estate of George Richardson allowed for negro Ledge, included
in inventory under name Elijah, who has since gained his freedom in
Worcester Co. Court

Major Guy, Jun., late exe. of Major Guy, Sen., to be charged with
inventory & debts collected, & allowed for debts paid & for property
which came into hands of adms. dbn

On settling accounts of Major Guy, Jun., as exe. of Major Guy, Sen.,
the exe. of the former to pay adms. of the latter sum due

'136'

Robert Cluff & William Aydelott, adms. dbn of Major Guy, Sen., allowed 4 1/2% on estate & charged with such sums as they shall get from estate of Major Guy, Jun.; distribution to be struck

F. 100　　Register to slate an final account for Milby Purnell, late adm. of Thomas Rigsby

Nancy Jones, by William Jones, guardian, vs. Robert Cluff & William Aydelott, adms. dbn of Major Guy, Sen.; application to have her part of said Major's personal estate delivered up; submitted to Zadok Sturgis, George Hayward & Matthew Hopkins to arbitrate

Bowdoin Robins, guardian to Molly Corbin, to finish house as cheaply as possible on lot divised to her

Thomas D. Purnell, exe. of Milby Purnell, allowed 10% on estate

F. 101　[blank]

F. 102　Tues., Oct. 14, 1806　Littleton Robins, Edward Henry present

Joshua Duer, Esq., Sheriff

Orphan; Noah Henderson (of John T.)
Guardian; Sarah Henderson [couldn't write]
Sureties; Curtis Henderson, George S. Houston

F. 103　　Orphan; Nancy Henderson (of John T.)
　　Guardian; Sarah Henderson
　　Sureties; Curtis Henderson, George S. Houston (of Levi)

Orphan; Joshua Sturgis (of Joshua)
Guardian; Thomas Hooper
Sureties; George Parsons, Jun., Samuel Hilman

F. 104　Orphan; Henry Jarman (of John)
　　Guardian; Nathaniel Wilkins
　　Sureties; Isaac Givan, Round Givans

F. 105　　Orphan; Samuel Gibbons (of Jonathan)
　　Guardian; Isaac Marshall & George H. Gray
　　Sureties; James Law, Jun., Isaac Ayres

George Miles discharged from guardianship to Maria, Jane, Sally & Matilda Townsend; John Corbin new guardian

Orphan; Maria Townsend (of Capt. Levin)
Guardian; John Corbin
Sureties; William Corbin, George Miles

F. 106　　Orphan; Jane Townsend (of Capt. Levin)
　　Guardian; John Corbin
　　Sureties; William Corbin, George Miles

Orphan; Sally Townsend (of Capt. Levin)
Guardian; John Corbin
Sureties; William Corbin, George Miles

F. 107   Orphan; Matilda Townsend (of Capt. Levin)
Guardian; John Corbin
Sureties; William Corbin, George Miles

Apprentice; Esme Bowen (of Elijah), 16 on 7 May last
Bound to; Daniel Patrick
Trade; boot & shoe maker
Sureties; John Bishop, Esq., William Quinton
F. 108   Memorandum; Eleanor Bowen, mother, to supply clothes

Apprentice; John Wright (of John)
Bound to; Daniel Patrick
Trade; boot & shoe maker
Sureties; Thomas N. Williams, Thomas D. Purnell
F. 109   Memorandum; Zadok Sturgis, guardian to John

Apprentice; William Niember (of Hugh), 11 in Mar. last
Bound to; Levin Stewart
Trade; boot & shoe maker
Sureties; Edward Henry, John P. Marshall, Esqs.

F. 110   Whereas James Rigsby was bound to William Crapper at June term, 1804, to learn shoe making & said William is now dead, his widow Leah Crapper asks that court appoint new master

Apprentice; James Rigsby (of Thomas), 14 last Apr.
Bound to; Levin Stewart
Trade; boot & shoe maker
F. 111   Sureties; John Richards, Annanias Bradford

Apprentice; Joseph Taylor (of Joseph), 18 on 12 Mar. last
Bound to; Robert Smith
Trade; mariner to be employed either in the coasting trade or on the high seas
F. 112   Sureties; Samuel R. Smith, John Stevens

Thomas N. Williams & William McGregor to view estate of
F. 113   Robert Kerby (of John), in care of Jacob White, guardian; report; 100 acres; widow Charlotte is now wife of Thomas
F. 114   Franklin; negro men Shedrack & Caleb, girls Esther & Rachel

Col. Samuel Handy & Samuel R. Smith to view estate of Molly Corbin, in care of Bowdoin Robins, guardian; before Josiah Hubbell: report; lott & house in Snow Hill Town

F. 115   Edward Stevenson & Edward Lambden to view estate of Levi
F. 116   Merrill, in care of William R. Merrill, guardian; before Wm. Schoolfield: report; 1/4 acre lot in New Town; negro boy, 18, subject to fits

Nancy Jones, by William Jones, guardian, vs. Robert Cluff & Wm.
Aydelott, adms. dbn of Major Guy, Sen.; Zadok Sturgis, George Hayward
       & Matthew Hopkins to decide what is due said Nancy from
F. 117   estate & how it is to be paid, all legacies already delivered
          except a bed, allotted to Nancy by Major Guy, Jun.; also to
receive $310.60 for her fourth part of estate

Samuel Hopkins, guardian to Samuel Gunn, & Esther Purnell, guardian to
George Gunn, orphans of Samuel, vs. George Ross, Esq.; said Rosse
relinquishes all rights to shed room adjoining said Gunn's storehouse
in Snow Hill & to land it is on, conveyed to him by father of orphans

F. 118   George Hayward & Joshua Fleming to settle dispute between
          John C. Handy, exe. of Mary Handy, & Levin Pollitt

William Handy, Zadok Sturgis & Joshua Fleming to distribute negroes
from estate of Barcley White & Joshua White, Sen., in hands of John
          Taylor, adm.;
F. 119   1) to William White; girl Comfort
          2) to Henry White; boy Levin
3) to Peter White; boy Littleton

Benjamin Henderson, guardian to Zaccheus, David Dixon, William
          Horsey, Sally Quinton, James Milligan & Harriet Henderson, to
F. 120   receive their estate: report; received from William Q. Dixon,
          late guardian to Thomas Q. Dixon, deceased, L.51/3/9. with
Edward Stevenson & Josiah(?) Long, his sureties

          Apprentice; Peter Dubberly, by consent of his father John
          [couldn't write]
          Bound to; Robert M. Merrill
          Trade; hatting
          Term; 4 years, 2 months, 14 days
F. 121   In presents of Josiah Hubbell, John Ward

Apprentice; Daniel Handcock, by consent of his mother Leah, of
Somerset Co. [couldn't write]
Bound to; James Noble [couldn't write]
Term; 6 years, 4 months
Trade; farming
In presents of Benjamin Johnson, Nathan Gordy

F. 122   Apprentice; Walter Turner, 17 on 1 Jan. next, by consent of
          his father Henry, blacksmith
          Bound to; Joseph Kenney [signed Keney], of Somerset Co.
          Trade; shoe maker or chord winder
F. 123   Before John Cathell, Benjamin Johnson

Apprentice; Harriott Nutts, by consent of her father Henry [couldn't
write]
Bound to; Levin Henderson
Term; until 20
Trade; spinning, weaving, sowing & all nessery house business
In presents of Edwd. Stevenson, Wm. Schoolfield

'139'

John Postly, exe. of Betsy Smith, to sell personal estate (except [list])

F. 124   Sarah Hinman, adm. of James Hinman, to sell negro Gatty

Caty Tingle, adm. of James Tingle, allowed 10% on payment of debts

John Brittingham & James Jarman, sureties, to sell estate of John Jarman, taken out of hands of Nathaniel Wilkins & Leah, his wife, admx., by order of court

Caleb Williams, exe. of Edward McGee, to advertise in William Duane's paper at Philadelphia for creditors to exhibit claims

F. 125   Thomas N. Williams & George Hayward to divide estate of Daniel Robins (Bowdoin Robins, adm. dbn), from estate of Peter S. Corbin (William Corbin & Bowdoin Robins, exes.)

Register to slate a final account for Sinah Slocomb, late exe. of William Henderson, Sen., allowing $35.50 for hire of negro Stephen

Exes. of Samuel Nicholson allowed 7 1/2% on estate, after deducting $566.05 due from Samuel to estate of Isaac Nicholson

Adms. dbn of Isaac Nicholson allowed 7 1/2% on estate, including balance due from estate of Samuel Nicholson, late adm.

Thomas D. Purnell, exe. of Milby Purnell, to retain $500 to meet claims in dispute, to wit, Edward Hammond, Sen., Edward Hammond, Jun., John Purnell (Quo.) & Littleton Robins, Sen., & for cost of suits against him in Worcester Co. Court; Register to strike distribution among creditors

[no folios 126 - 152]

F. 153   Col. Samuel Handy & Samuel R. Smith to view estate of William F. Riley, in care of Alexander Franklin, guardian

Adm. of estate of William Holland (of Levi) granted to Thomas Dixon

Ezekiel Smashey was bound to William Crapper, now deceased, at Oct. term, 1800, to learn trade of shoe maker; Leah Crapper, widow, asks that remaining time be assigned to Levin Stewart

Zadok Wheeler, Jun., adm. of Levi Merrill, allowed 10% on estate

Sarah Hinman, adm. of James Hinman, allowed 7% on estate

F. 154   Joshua Prideaux & Thos. N. Williams, Esqs., to distribute negroes & plate from estate of Sarah Rackliffe, in hands of William Winder, exe.

Eben Christopher & Thomas Fookes to view estate of Joshua Sturgis, in care of Thomas Hooper, guardian

Thomas Hooper, guardian to Joshua Sturgis, to sell mare & colt, left to ward by his mother

John Stevens & George Hayward, exes. of Joseph Scott, to sell personal estate (except negroes)

John Givan, Jun., & William Handcock to view estate of Henry Jarman, in care of Nathaniel Wilkins, guardian

William McGregor & Hillary Pitts to view estate of Samuel Gibbons, in care of Isaac Marshall & George H. Gray, guardians

Joshua Prideaux & Zadok Purnell, Esqs., to distribute specifics from estate of Laban Johnson, in hands of Elizabeth Johnson, exe.

Elizabeth Johnson, exe. of Laban Johnson, allowed 6% on estate

F. 155 Isaac Marshall & George H. Gray, guardians to Samuel Gibbons, to build house, & allowed $30 for same on obtaining certificate from Hillary Pitts that work is completed

Mary Perkins, adm. of John Perkins, allowed 6% on estate

Levin Pollitt, adm. of Joseph Bousee, to sell personal estate

John Corbin, guardian to Maria, Jane, Sally & Matilda Townsend, to receive estate

Benjamin Dennis & John Cottingham to reappraise property of Maria, Jane, Sally & Matilda Townsend, in hands of George Miles, late guardian, to be delivered to John Corbin, present guardian

Sarah Henderson, guardian to Noah & Nancy Henderson, to receive their estate

F. 156 William Winder, guardian to John, Charlotte, Kitturah & Rider Rackliffe, allowed to prosecute trespasses on wards' land by Jesse Davis, Henry Davis & [blank] Bratten

William Gibbons & Mary, his wife, file caveat against Levin Pollitt receiving adm. cwa on estate of Joseph Bousee, father of Mary, his only child; caveat dismissed

F. 157 William Winder, guardian to Charlotte Rackliffe, states that she is 16 & wishes to go to a boarding school in Baltimore, but profits from her estate will not cover expense; granted permission to pay extra cost out of principle

Balance due John Selby (of Daniel) from Maj. William Holland, late guardian, is $27.46, the profits of his estate & portion of money from sale of negro Abraham

Received 11 Nov., 1806, from Maj. William Holland, $24.56, the balance
due John Selby
Fisher Richardson, guardian

F. 158   Received 11 Nov., 1806, of Maj. William Holland, $75, balance
due Polly Selby (of Daniel), including 1/4 of 2 years hire of
negro Abraham
Fisher Richardson, guardian

Received 13 Oct. 1806, of Obediah Carey, exe. of Levy Carey, [list],
legacies given to me in my father's will

Test.; Handy Carey   Elisha Carey

Received 13 Oct., 1806, of Obediah Carey, exe. of Levy Carey, [list],
legacies given to me in my father's will

Test.; Wm. Aydelott   Handy Carey

Received 13 Oct., 1806, of Obediah Carey, exe. of Levy Carey, [list],
legacies given to me in my father's will

Levy Carey

Received 13 Oct., 1806, of Obediah Carey, exe. of Levy Carey, [list],
legacies given to me in my father's will
                                           her
F. 159   Test.; Handy Carey   Sarah (Saray) X Carey
                                           mark

Received 13 Oct., 1806, of Obediah Carey, exe. of Levy Carey, [list],
legacies given to me in my father's will

Test.; Wm. Aydelott   Levin Carey

F. 160   Tues., Dec. 9, 1806   Littleton Robins, Edward Henry present

Col. Samuel Handy & George Hayward to view estate of John Richardson
(of Robert Martin Richardson), in care of Nancy Richardson, guardian;
         before J. Hubbell: report; 1/5 of 780 acres on the seaside;
F. 161   part of land occupied by George White, part by Joseph Bishop;
         a mill seat occupied by Nathan Cottingham; a lot in Snow
Hill; widow's dower; five orphans

F. 162   Col. Samuel Handy & George Hayward to view estate of Molly
         Richardson (of Robert Martin Richardson), in care of Nancy
F. 163   Richardson, guardian; [same as above]

         John Givan, Jun., & William Handcock to view estate of Henry
F. 164   Jarman (of John), in care of Nathaniel Wilkins, guardian;
         before Matthias Davis: report; 8 acres

F. 165 Col. Samuel Handy & Samuel R. Smith to view estate of William F. Riley, in care of Alexander Franklin, guardian; before Jesse Bennett: report; lott & house in Snow Hill Town occupied by Littleton Riley; also on lott a hatter's shop,
F. 166 property of Robert Merrill, subject to be removed by him at pleasure; negro lad Jacob

Joshua Dorman & Martha, his wife, admx. of John Duncan, allowed 10% on estate

Robert Smith & Jacob Teague to arbitrate between Edward Hammond & Thomas D. Purnell, exe. of Milby Purnell

Levin Pollitt, adm. cwa of Joseph Bousee, to advertise in Samuel R. Smith's paper at Washington City & in the Federal Gazette at Baltimore for creditors to exhibit claims

Letters of collection on estate of Thomas Clark granted to Joshua Fleming

Nancy Richardson, guardian to John & Molly Richardson, allowed to repair grist mill, provided representatives of Robert M. Richardson, who are of age, agree

F. 167 Nathaniel Bowen, exe. of John Bowen, allowed 5% on $1459.53 & any further desperate debts

Received Oct. 14, 1806, of Sampson [also Samson] Wright & Betsy, his wife, admx. of Henry Smith, $53.97, my part of my father's estate

Test.; Isaac Hearne   her
                              Rosa X Smith
                                    mark

Received Oct. 14, 1806, of Sampson Wright & Betsy, his wife, admx. of Henry Smith, $53.97, my share of my father's estate

Test.; Isaac Hearn   her
                              Betsy X Smith
                                    mark

F. 168 Littleton Robins, Jun., John Bishop & Edward Henry appointed Justices

Robert Wright   W. Kilty, Chanc.

Wit.; The Honourable William Kilty, Esq., Chancellor

       George Miles, adm. of Levin Townsend & late guardian to Maria, Jane,
              Sally & Matilda Townsend, to deliver to John Corbin, new
F. 169   guardian, their estate, to be reappraised by Benjamin Dennis
              & John Cottingham, Esqs.; before Josiah Hubbell; inventory;
negro man Tom & woman Esther (superannuated), man Ned, women Rachel,
                              (cont.)

'143'

Silviah & Linda; still, except privilege of stilling all liquor made of lands of Luke Townsend, agreeable to William B. Townsend's
F. 170 will; [list]; inventoried items to be sold (except negroes)

Orphan; Isaac Davis (of Abijah)
F. 171 Guardian; Benjamin Davis
Sureties; Elijah Reed, Elsea Smith

Daniel Tingle & Littleton Davis to view estate of Isaac Davis, in care of Benjamin Davis, guardian

Benjamin Davis, guardian to Isaac Davis, to receive his estate

Mary Reed & Jesse Sturgis, adms. of John Reed, to sell personal estate

F. 172 Special Court, Jan. 27, 1807, at instance of John Bishop (of William); Littleton Robins, John Bishop present

By consent of legatees of William Bishop, Sen., exe. to sell personal estate (except wearing apparel)

Col. Thomas Martin, adm. dbn of Rosanna Martin, allowed 4% on estate

Lemuel P. Spence appointed Deputy Register of Wills

In presence of Mathias Davis

F. 173 Tues., Feb. 10, 1807   All Justices present

Edward Stevenson vs. Isaac Collins & Tabitha, his wife, admx.
F. 174 of William Stevenson; [repeat of petition & exhibits from 25
F. 175 Oct., 1805 term; case continued until this court session];
F. 176-7 answer of Isaac & Tabitha repeated

F. 178 Fri., Feb. 13, 1807, court orders defendants to pay Edward Stevenson $82.20, the fourth part of increase of his father's estate, one fourth of hire of negro George 9, one fourth of
F. 179 time lost by negro George when sick

Philip Short & Polly (Stevenson), his wife, vs. Isaac Collins
F. 180-5 & Tabitha, his wife, admx. of William Stevenson; [same as above]: wit; Levin Derickson

James Mumford & Sally (Stevenson), his wife, vs. Isaac
F. 186-8 Collins & Tabitha, his wife, admx. of William Stevenson; [same as above up to case continued]

F. 189-91 [blank]

F. 192   Eli Christopher & Shepherd Johnson & Sally, his wife, vs.
          Elijah Christopher, Jun., & Belitha Christopher, devisees of
Elijah Christopher, Sen.; claimants, by William Whittington, Esq.,
solicitor, file caveat against will of Elijah Christopher, Sen., as
will is not signed
Will of Elijah Christopher, 3 Nov., 1802;
1) to wife; plantation; if she should die, to sister-in-law Leah Noble
          2) to son Belitha; list
F. 193   3) to sons Elijah & Belitha; lands after wife's death
          4) Elijah & Belitha appointed exes.

Wit.; Eleazer Johnson, Johnson Hayman, Solomon Kebbel Price

Elijah & Belitha Christopher, by Ephraim K. Wilson, Esq., solicitor,
ask court to accept will

Deposition of Johnson Hayman, 48; Christopher & Eleazer Johnson came
          to field where I & Solomon Kebbel Price were working;
F. 194   declared paper to be his will & asked us to be witnesses; was
          of sound mind; did not sign will, stating his hand trembled;
will written in hand of Eleazer Johnson

Deposition of Solomon Kebble Price, 34; [similar to above]

Deposition of Jonathan Noble, 44; states that Eleazer Johnson lives 17
or 18 miles beyond Milford, DE

F. 195   Will admitted to probate

Sampson Wright's wife, late Betty Smith, was appointed at Apr. term,
1799, guardian to Hetty & William Smith, orphans of Henry; as we are
about to remove to state of Georgia, we wish to relinquish
guardianship; recommend William Dailey as guardian to Hetty & Adam
Moore as guardian to William

F. 196   Orphan; Hetty Smith (of Henry)
          Guardian; William Daily
          Sureties; Adam Moore, John Parker (of Henry)

          Orphan; William Smith (of Henry)
          Guardian; Adam Moore
F. 197   Sureties; William Dailey, John Parker (of Henry)

Frederick Conner discharged from guardianship to Lottee Bishop; Lemuel
Parker new guardian

Orphan; Lottee Bishop (of Benjamin E.)
Guardian; Lemuel Parker
Sureties; John Ayres, Purnell Hill

          Orphan; Hulda Davis (of Benjamin)
F. 198   Guardian; Leah Davis [couldn't write]
          Sureties; Levi Davis, John Wheeler [couldn't write]

Orphan; Peggy Davis (of Benjamin)
Guardian; Leah Davis
Sureties; Levi Davis, John Wheeler

F. 199   Orphan; John Purnell (of Robert)
          Guardian; Kellam Lankford
          Sureties; John Holland, Rowland E. Bevans

          Apprentice; William Clark (of Rhodes)
          Bound to; George Hayward
          Trade; farmer
F. 200   Sureties; John Stevens, Arthur McAllen

          Apprentice; Henry Sturgis, 15 on 2 Aug. next, son of
          Priscilla
          Bound to; James Holland
          Trade; blacksmith
F. 201   Sureties; Levi Merrill, Matthias Davis, Esq.

          Apprentice; Samuel Ennis (of Joseph)
          Bound to; William Round
          Trade; taylor
F. 202   Sureties; John K. Truitt, James Knox

Apprentice; Parker Henderson, 15, by consent of his brother
Bound to; Levin Henderson, cypress cupper
Trade; cypress cupper
Wit.; Edwd. Stevenson, James Tilghman

F. 203   Apprentice; Hannah Showell, by consent of her mother Rachel
          [couldn't write]
          Bound to; Hezekiah Shockley [couldn't write]
          Trade; common work of a woman
          Term; 13 years, 6 months
          Before John Cathell, Nathan Gordy

          Margaret & George Bratten, adms. of James Bratten, to deliver
F. 204   to Margaret Nelson, cow & bed in inventory, but property of
          Margaret

Levin Taylor & wife, guardians to John & Susanna Nelson, excused from
rendering accounts until they each reach 14

William Riley & Elizabeth Wright, adms. of Hezekiah Wright, allowed
10% on estate

Mary Reed & Jesse Sturgis, adms. of John Reed, allowed full time to
settle estate, as it is insufficient to cover debts

Elijah & Belitha Christopher, exes. of Elijah Christopher, Sen., to
sell personal estate

Adm. on estate of James Bratten granted to Margaret & George Bratten

'146'

Leah Aydelott, adm. of Benjamin Aydelott, allowed 10% on estate

F. 205　　John Selby, Jun., adm. of George Selby, to sell personal estate (except negroes & wearing apparel)

Sarah, James & Joseph Moore, exes. of John Moore, allowed 8% on estate

Thomas Mitchell, exe. of Robert Purnell, to sell personal estate, & so much of corn & pork as will discharge execution now levied on property

Zadok Sturgis, Esq., & Ralph Milbourne to view property of Lottee Bishop, in care of Lemuel Parker, guardian

William Holland, Jun., & Nehemiah Holland to view estate of John Purnell, in care of Kellam Lankford, guardian

Margaret & George Bratten, adms. of James Bratten, to sell personal estate (except wearing apparel)

F. 206　　William Gordy, exe. of William Gordy, Sen., allowed $12 for loss of sheep killed by dogs

William Gordy, exe. of William Gordy, Sen., allowed 10% on estate, after deduction of sheep killed by dogs

Adm. cwa on estate of John Ward granted to James Ward & John Dashiell

Nancy Spence, exe. of George Spence, to retain money received of Samuel A. Harper, Esq., for purchase of real estate in & about Caulker's Creek, which was devised by deceased and afterward sold, untill claim of devisee is determined

Nancy Spence, exe. of George Spence, allowed 8% on estate, exclusive of monies from Samuel A. Harper & property lost

F. 207　　Tues., Apr. 14, 1807　　All Justices present

Orphan; Lydia Roach (of Stephen)
Guardian; Mary Roach
Sureties; Littleton Furniss, Edward Lambden

F. 208　　Orphan; Rachel Roach (of Stephen)
Guardian; Mary Roach
Sureties; Littleton Furniss, Edward Lambden

Orphan; Edward Stevenson (of William)
Guardian; Isaac Collins
Sureties; Elijah Reed [also Read], Benjamin Davis

F. 209　　Orphan; Hezekiah Dorman (of Nehemiah)
Guardian; Mary Dorman
Sureties; Rowland E. Bevans, John Selby, Jun.

'147'

F. 210	Orphan; Anne Sheldon Dorman (of Nehemiah) Guardian; Mary Dorman Sureties; Rowland E. Bevans, John Selby, Jun.

Apprentice; Littleton Townsend Warren, 13 on 16 Dec. last, son of
Sally
Bound to; John Hudson
Trade; boot & shoe maker
Sureties; John Taylor (B. S.), Angello Atkinson

F. 211   Apprentice; Abraham Gibbs (of John), 14 on 15 Mar. last
          Bound to; William Tingle
          Trade; hatter
          Sureties; Angelo Atkinson, Jesse Sturgis

F. 212   Apprentice; Peter Riggen, mulatto, 12 on 15 Mar. last, son of
          Jacob
          Bound to; John S. Martin
          Trade; house servant & waiter
          Sureties; Samuel R. Smith, Lemuel P. Spence

F. 213   Apprentice; John Taylor (of James)
          Bound to; James Knox
          Trade; taylor
          Sureties; William Quinton, William Rownd, Jun.

F. 214   Apprentice; Purnell Jones, 9 on 30 Aug. next, son of Milly
          [Milby?]
          Bound to; Edmond Crapper
          Trade; common labour
          Sureties; McKimmey Porter, Jacob Teague

F. 215   William McGregor & Hillary Pitts to view estate of Samuel
          Gibbons (representative of Jonathan), in care of Isaac
F. 216   Marshall & George H. Gray, guardians; before Abisha Davis;
          report; 112 acres, parts of 'Priveledge', 'Second Priveledge'
& 'Conclusion'; 20 acres of river swamp, part of 'Cumberland'

          Zadok Sturgis & Ralph Milbourne to view estate of Lottee [also Lotty]
          Bishop (of Benjamin), in care of Lemuel Parker, guardian;
F. 217   before Jesse Bennett: report; land called 'Scarbrough
          Cassel', 153 acres, belonging to Lottee & Levin Bishop

          Ebben Christopher & Thomas Fookes to view estate of Joshua
F. 218   Sturgis, in care of Thomas Hooper, guardian; before John
          Cathell: report; 208 1/2 acres; negro man Harry, woman Edey

F. 219   Maj. John Holland & William Holland, Jun., to view estate of
          William S. Corbin , in care of Bowdoin Robins, guardian;
F. 220   before J. Hubbell: report; mentions manner plantation,
          Frank's(?) lot, store house lot; 340 or 50 acres called
'Pharsillia'(?); widow's dower; 100 acres of woods bought of Robt.
Purnell

Bowdoin Robins, adm. dbn of Daniel Robins, vs. William Corbin, acting
exe. of Peter S. Corbin; order filed at Oct. term last rescinded;
Thomas N. Williams & George Hayward to ascertain amount of estate of
Daniel Robins, which came to Peter S. Corbin by his marriage with
Comfort Robins, late exe. of Daniel, more than was applied to payment
of debts; 2/3 of estate to be paid to Bowdoin Robins, adm. dbn

F. 221   Littleton Robins vs. Thomas D. Purnell, exe. of Milby
Purnell; Leonard Johnson, Frederick Conner & William Davis
(of Nixon) to settle dispute regarding the deceased not complying with
his covenant in a lease for rent of land of the plaintiff

Court to settle dispute between Zipporah Bishop, adm. of Charles
Bishop, & William A.(?) Marshall

Sewell Turpin, Robert Smith & Matthias Davis to settle dispute between
Samuel Ennis & Thomas D. Purnell, exe. of Milby Purnell

William Hudson & Comfort, his wife, guardian to Nancy Knox (of
    Nehemiah), to sell negro Rachel & her two children, Levin &
F. 222   Isaac, 2/3 of which belongs to orphan; in presents of the
    subscribers; Isaac Hill, Severn Jarvis, Kendell Pattey,
Belitha Collins; bought by William Hudson [also Hutson]

John Corbin, guardian to Maria, Jane, Sally & Matilda Townsend (of
    Capt. Levin), to sell property (except negroes) received from
F. 223   George Miles, late guardian; [list of items sold]

F. 224   John Waters, clerk for sale, swears to above sale; before
    John Williams

Apprentice; Thomas Henderson, 6, child of the Poor House
Bound to; William Bevans
Trade; coasting business
Sureties; William Bacon, Samuel Pettitt
By Trustees for the Poor; Saml. Handy, Chas. Bennett, George Hayward

F. 225   Apprentice; Jenny Sturgis, 10, child of the Poor House
    Bound to; George Hall
    Trade; house work; sewing, spinning & weaving
    Sureties; John Ayres, Thomas Mitchell
    By Trustees for the Poor; Samuel Handy, McKimmey Porter,
    George Hayward

    Apprentice; Leah Marshall, free black, 11 on 15 Feb., 1807
    Bound to; Thomas Brittingham (of Purnell)
F. 226   Trade; sew, spin & wash
    In presence of Edwd. Stevenson, James Tilghman

New warrant for McKimmey Porter & Anthony Bacon to appraise property
of Peter S. Corbin not in 1st inventory

Joshua Fleming, collector of Thomas Clark, to sell property in
inventory

Register to charge Levin(?) Stewart & Mary, his wife, admx. of Azariah
Purnell, $20.93 against sale of part of estate, & allow them for
claims of John Davis, Edward Hammond & Alexander Steel, against
Elizabeth Purnell

James Ward & John Dashiell, adms. of John Ward, to sell personal
estate (except negroes, legacies & wearing apparel)

F. 227   Thomas D. Purnell, adm. dbn of Thomas Rigsby, to strike
distribution among creditors

Nancy Johnson, adm. of William John[son?], to sell personal estate

Thomas Mitchell, exe. of Robert Purnell, allowed full time to settle
estate, as it is insufficient to cover debts

Edward Lambden, guardian to Robert Lambden, admits receiving L.8/16/3,
the orphan's share of his father's estate

James Ward & John Dashiell, Jun., adms. cwa of John Ward, to advertise
in the Federal Gazette at Baltimore & in the Aurora at Philadelphia
for creditors to exhibit claims

John P. Marshall, adm. of Elizabeth Marshall, allowed 8% on estate

F. 228   Nixon Davis & Littleton Davis to view estate of Isaac Davis,
in care of Benjamin Davis, guardian, Daniel Tingle, person
first appointed, being absent

William Hudson & Comfort, his wife, guardian to Nancy Knox, to apply
balance for education

Thomas D. Purnell, exe. of Milby Purnell, to retain, as adm. dbn of
Thomas Rigsby, the proportion due from Milby's estate on his adm. of
Thomas Rigsby

Received 16 Apr., 1807, of Rebeckah Parker, Sen., exe. of my father
William Anderson Parker, negro James, 14 or 15, my share of the estate

Test.; Josa. Fleming, Jun.   William A. Parker

Received Mar. 18, 1807, of Thomas P. Rackliffe, L.60/10/3, all claim
my wife Elizabeth has against him as her former guardian

In presence of Nancy Fassitt   James Fassitt

Received Mar. 10, 1807, of my mother Sarah Bennett (wife of Charles),
my part of my father Benjamin's estate

Test.; Esme Purnell   Elisha Purnell

Received Apr. 21, 1807, of Charles Bennett & wife, the full amount of
my wife Peggy's estate, left her by her father Benjamin Purnell

                              Charles Bennett, Jun.

F. 229   [blank]

F. 230   Tues., June 9, 1807   All Justices present

Apprentice; William Burton [Benton?] (of Michael), 17 on 16 June
instant
Bound to; William Dickerson, Jun.
Trade; cypress cooper
Sureties; Robert Givans, Sen., Robert Givans, Jun.

F. 231   Apprentice; Isaac Puzey (of Isaac), 15 on 9 Feb. last
           Bound to; George Nelson
           Trade; house carpenter & joiner
           Sureties; William Harper, Robert Givan, Sen.

F. 232   Apprentice; Levin Armstrong, mulatto, son of Esther
           Bound to; Robert Givans, Jun.
           Trade; farmer
           Sureties; John Givans, Sen., William Dickerson, Jun.

F. 233   Joseph Scott, Francis Lane & James Bennett bound to Angello
           Atkinson & John Atkinson on said Joseph & Sarah, his wife's,
adm on estate of John E. Scott

           Curtis Jenckins, guardian to Anne & John Turpin, & John J.
F. 234   Williams, guardian to William Turpin (orphans of John), to
           sell two small negroes, George & Keziah (allotted to orphans
from estate of William Turpin); George bought by Joseph Lankford,
Keziah by Jesse Johnson; before Thos. N. Williams

List of articles in estate of Maj. John Purnell, which came to
           knowledge of James Trippe, adm., after return of inventory;
F. 235   [list]; James Trippe swears to above list

           Nixon Davis & Littleton Davis to view estate of Isaac Davis,
F. 236   in care of Benjamin Davis, guardian; before John Davis:
           report; widow's thirds; 5 acres

           Apprentice; Peter Aydelott, born 25 Dec., 1790, by consent of
           his father Benjamin
           Bound to; George Nelson [also Nilson], house carpenter &
           joiner
           Trade; house carpenter & joiner
F. 237   Test.; William Nilson

Thomas S. Fassitt, guardian to Margaret Fassitt, to rent real estate

Nancy Kerby, adm. of Thomas Newbold, to retain $34 to meet claims of
Thomas & William Livermore(?)

'151'

Thomas D. Purnell, exe. of Milby Purnell, to retain $114.33 to meet claims of Thomas Stewart, Edward Hammond, Samuel Ennis & John Hains(?)

James Trippe, adm. of John Purnell (Quepo.), allowed 10% on estate

Mary Reed & Jesse Sturgis, adms. of John Reed, to advertise in Thomas P. Smith's paper at Easton for creditors to exhibit claims

Adam Bravard, adm. of Ebenezer Brevard, to advertise in the Aurora at Philadelphia for creditors to exhibit claims

F. 238 Anthony Bacon & George S. Gunby, exes. of Col. John Gunby, to sell personal estate

Account of property made use of in estate of James Bratten or lost between appraisal & sale; [list]; George Bratten, one adm., swears to above list; Margaret & George Bratten, adms., allowed $10.65 for same

F. 239 List of disbursements in estate of Maj. John Purnell (Quepo.) as returned by James Trippe, adm.; [list]; mentions Mary Purnell; James allowed $68.26 for same

Isaac Collins, guardian to Edward Stevenson, to give his consent to sale of negroes held jointly with the other representatives of his father William Stevenson

Thomas Jones & Levin Holland to pay off Nancy, Hulda & Peggy Davis, three youngest representatives of Benjamin Davis, Sen., out of portion remaining in hands of Leah Davis, adm.

F. 240 Tues., Aug. 11, 1807   All Justices present

Orphan; Patience W. A. Johnson (of William)
Guardian; Nancy Johnson
Sureties; Levin Derickson, Asher Burroughs

Stephen Allen & Leah, his wife, discharged from guardianship to Betsy Aydelott; Samuel Tarr new guardian

F. 241 Orphan; Betsy Aydelott (of Benjamin)
Guardian; Samuel Tarr
Sureties; Michael Tarr, Stephen Allen [couldn't write]

Orphan; John Collins (of John)
Guardian; Thomas Collins
Sureties; Henry Davis, Henry Rowley

F. 242 Orphan; Elisabeth Collins (of John)
Guardian; Thomas Collins
Sureties; Henry Davis, Henry Rowley

Orphan; Mary Collins (of John)
Guardian; Thomas Collins
Sureties; Henry Davis, Henry Rowley

F. 243   Orphan; Susanna Collins (of John)
            Guardian; Thomas Collins
            Sureties; Henry Davis, Henry Rowley

            Orphan; Matilda Selby (of George)
            Guardian; Mary Selby
F. 244   Sureties; John Selby, Sen., John Selby, Jun.

Orphan; George Selby (of George)
Guardian; Mary Selby
Sureties; John Selby, Sen., John Selby, Jun.

            Apprentice; Jacob Johnson Armstrong, mulatto, 16 on 6 Jan.
            next, son of Esther
            Bound to; Joshua Evans
            Trade; shoe maker
F. 245   Sureties; Anthony Bacon, Curtis Henderson

            Apprentice; Rhoda Johnson Armstrong, mulatto, daughter of
            Esther
            Bound to; Joshua Evans
            Trade; house & kitchen servant
F. 246   Sureties; Anthony Bacon, Curtis Henderson

Apprenticeship of Peter Reed, colored child of Rachel, to John J.
Purnell, rescinded; James Fleming new master

            Apprentice; Peter Reed, colored, 11 in Jan. last, child of
            Rachel
            Bound to; James Fleming
F. 247   Trade; house servant & waiter
            Sureties; Littleton Quinton, Joshua Fleming, Jun.

            Apprentice; Samuel Ballard, mulatto, 11, son of Betty
            Bound to; Isaac Cottingham
F. 248   Trade; common labour
            Sureties; Samuel Ennis, John Bishop (of William)

            Apprentice; Experience Ballard, mulatto, 11, daughter of
            Betty
            Bound to; Isaac Cottingham
F. 249   Trade; house servant; spin
            Sureties; Samuel Ennis, John Bishop (of William)

            Sewell Turpin & Robert Smith to settle dispute between Samuel
F. 250   Ennis & Thomas D. Purnell, exe. of Milby Purnell; said
            Purnell to pay said Ennis L.7/13/10

Apprentice; James Ballard, mulatto, by consent of his father John
Bound to; Nehemiah Holland, farmer
Trade; farmer
Term; 11 years
Surety(?); Jno. Holland [couldn't write]
Before Wm. Holland, Benj. Aydelott

F. 251
Apprentice; James Sturgis, 7, child of the Poor House
Bound to; John W. Patterson
Trade; taylor
Sureties; James Patterson, John M. Bowhannon [also Bohannon]
By Trustees for the Poor; Samuel. Handy, McKimmey Porter, George Hayward

F. 252
Apprentice; Peggy Johnson, 13, child of the Poor House
Bound to; James Lecompt
Trade; spin, sew & c.
Sureties; Robert J. H. Handy, Smith Horsey
Before Trustees for the Poor; Samuel Handy, Ephraim K. Wilson, George Hayward

Edward Hammond vs. Thomas D. Purnell, exe. of Milby Purnell; Zadok Sturgis, Thomas N. Williams & Joshua Fleming, Esqs., to settle dispute regarding a note of hand of the plaintiff against the deceased, dated 21 Apr., 1796

Thomas N. Williams, William McGregor & Jacob Dale to settle dispute between Elizabeth Davis & John Davis, adms. of Benjamin Davis, & Sterling Jones

F. 253
Peter Waters' account against estate of Patrick Waters; mentions expense of going to Baltimore to secure & sell negro Stephen, & for his prison charges; cash paid Henry Parker; Peter Waters, surviving adm. of Patrick, charged with same

Estate of Charles Bishop to Zipporah Bishop, adm. [also has exe.]; list

James Fookes, exe. of Jesse Fooks, to sell personal estate

F. 254
Abishai Davis & David John to view estate of Patience W. A. Johnson, in care on Nancy Johnson, guardian

Outten & Purnell Toadvine, exes. of William Toadvine, allowed 10% on estate

Adam Bravard, adm. of Ebenezer C. Brevard, allowed three months to render final account

William Winder, Esq., guardian to John, Rider & Kitturah Rackliffe, to rent real estate

Thomas Mitchell, exe. of Robert Purnell, to advertise in Thomas P. Smith's paper at Easton for creditors to exhibit claims

Peter Waters, surviving adm. of Patrick Waters, allowed 10% on estate

John Bishop, exe. of William Bishop, Sen., to dispose of salt received of Samuel Marrett

John NcCalley & Amelia, his wife, guardian to Charles Morris(?), to rent real estate

F. 255 Elizabeth Davis & John Davis, adms. of Benjamin Davis, to sell deceased's [personal estate?, something left out]

James Trippe, adm. of John Purnell (Quepo.), to retain $500 to meet claim of Zadok Selby against deceased as security of John J. Purnell

F. 256 Tues., Oct. 13, 1807   All Justices present

Orphan; James Sturgis (of John)
Guardian; John Allen (of Jno.)
Sureties; Michael Tarr, Elijah Pruitt [couldn't write]

F. 257 Orphan; John F. Purnell (of Isaac)
Guardian; Thomas Jones
Sureties; James Trippe, Benjamin Bishop

Orphan; Thomas Purnell (of Isaac)
Guardian; Thomas Jones
Sureties; James Trippe, Benjamin Bishop

F. 258 Orphan; Isaac Davis (of Abijah)
Guardian; Thomas N. Williams
Sureties; John Davis, Littleton Davis

Orphan; Sarah D. Adams (of Wm. F.)
Guardian; Henry Adams
Sureties; Joseph Henderson, Thomas Merrill

F. 259 Orphan; Susan Adams (of Wm. F.)
Guardian; Henry Adams
Sureties; Joseph Henderson, Thomas Merrill

Orphan; John Adams (of Wm. F.)
Guardian; Henry Adams
F. 260 Sureties; Joseph Henderson, Thomas Merrill

Apprentice; James Armstrong, mulatto, 16, son of Sarah
Bound to; Dolly Purnell
Trade; farmer
Sureties; Thomas N. Williams, William J.(?) Houston

F. 261 Apprentice; Jacob Armstrong, 14 next Christmas, son of Sarah
Bound to; Dolly Purnell
Trade; farmer
Sureties; Thomas N. Williams, William J.(?) Houston

F. 262 Apprentice; Mary Harmon, mulatto, 8, daughter of Betsy
Bound to; Anna Harmon
Trade; spin, weave & knit
Sureties; Daniel Ruark, John Caudrey, Jun.

F. 263   Apprentice; William Purnell, 14 next Feb., son of Nancy
         Bound to; Edward Dymock, Jun.
         Trade; taylor
         Sureties; Samuel R. Smith, Robert Smith

F. 264   Apprentice; John Cottingham Johnson Price, 12 on 12 Feb.
         next, son of Grace
         Bound to; John K. Truitt
         Trade; farmer
         Sureties; Samuel Porter, Samuel Truitt

F. 265   Apprentice; Peter Dorman (of James), 16 next Mar.
         Bound to; Luke Townsend
         Trade; blacksmith
         Sureties; Thomas R. Handy, Thomas Dryden

F. 266   Abisha Davis & David Johnson to view estate of Patience W. A.
         Johnson, in care of Nancy Johnson, guardian; sworn before
F. 267   William McGregor: report; 105 acres, part of tract called
         'Three Brothers'

Thomas Jones & Levin Holland to distribute estate of Benjamin Davis,
Sen., in hands of Leah Davis, adm. dbn, between Nancy, Hulda & Peggy,
the three youngest children; before Nixon Davis: inventory of
proportional part of estates of Nancy, Margaret & Hulda P. Davis (of
         Benjamin), as paid by Leah Davis, adm. dbn, & guardian to
F. 268   orphans; Levi Davis & John Wheeler, securities;
         1) to Nancy; list
2) to Margaret; list
3) to Huldah Purnell Davis; list

         Thomas N. Williams & William McGregor to ascertain repairs
F. 269   done on estate of Mary Mitchell (of Joshua), by Elizabeth
         Smack, guardian

         James A. Collins & Joseph Miller to value wearing apparel of
F. 270   Edward McGee, deceased; list; Caleb Williams, exe. of Edward,
         to give clothes to William Watson, as directed by will

Leonard Johnson, Frederick Conner & William Davis to settle dispute
between Littleton Robins, Sen., Esq., & Thomas D. Purnell, exe. of
Milby Purnell, regarding a covenant on a lease for rent of land;
Thomas to pay Littleton $60

F. 271   Orphans Court to settle dispute between Zipporah Bishop, adm.
         of Charles Bishop, & William A. Marshall; William to pay
Zipporah $32.85

John Bishop (of Wm.) vs. Zipporah Bishop, adm. of Charles; petition to
pass account against deceased, which is objected to by adm.; Zipporah
to pay John $5.70

F. 272   Apprentice; Wilson Banks, 16 on 13 Feb. next, by consent of
            his father Samuel
            Bound to; John Williams
            Trade; seamans art; following the sea & bay as a salor
            In presence of John Cottingham, James Brodwatter

F. 273   Apprentice; Hes(?) Harmon, 12 on 12 Mar. last, by consent of
            her parents
            Bound to; Nancy Watson
            Trade; spin, knit, sew & the common occupation of house work
            Before Edward Stevenson, James Tilghman

Apprentice; William Sharpley, 10 on 28 Apr. last, by consent of his
mother
Bound to; Moses Benston, shoe maker
Trade; shoe maker
Before Edwd. Stevenson, James Tilghman

F. 273   Apprentice; Isaac Johnson [also Jonson], free negro, 12 on 30
            May next, by consent of his father Isaac [couldn't write]
            Bound to; James Ward
            Trade; labourer & farmer
            In presence of Josa. Fleming, Jun.

F. 275   Apprentice; Sovereign Johnson, free negro, 9 on 10 Aug. next,
            by consent of his father Isaac
            Bound to; James Ward
            Trade; labourer & farmer
F. 276   In presence of Josa. Fleming, Jun.

George Hayward, Littleton R. Purnell & James Trippe to settle dispute
between Charles Bennett & Sarah, his wife, & Dolly Purnell, exe. of
Esme Purnell

Thomas R. Handy & George Hayward to settle dispute between Levin
Black, claimant, use of Henry Bennett, & Zipporah Bishop, adm. of
Charles Bishop; submission of this dispute at Apr. term last rescinded

Thomas R. Handy & George Hayward to settle dispute between Joseph
Bishop & Zipporah Bishop, adm. of Charles Bishop

F. 277   Estate of Joseph Scott, deceased, to John Stevens & George
            Hayward, exes., for items consumed & lost; list

Nehemiah Holland & William Holland, Jun., to view property of James
Sturgis, in care of John Allen, guardian

James A. Collins & Joseph Miller to view wearing apparel of Edward
McGee

William Jones & Barnaby Henderson to view property of Charles Morris,
in care of John McCally & Amelia, his wife, guardians

James Trippe, adm. of John Purnell (Quepo.), to retain $150 to meet claim of Stephen White on suit pending in Worcester Co. Court, for a stack of corn; $16 to meet claim of John M. Rankin; $15 to meet claim of William Purnell

F. 278   James Trippe, adm. of John Purnell (Queponco), to advertise in the Easton Star & notices to be posted at Poplar Town & Snow Hill for creditors to meet at Mrs. Smith's tavern on 20 Nov. next to receive their portion of assets

Allowance made to Joseph Richards & Sally, his wife, & John Hall, exes. of Caleb Tilghman, on 6 Oct. last, for 10% of $1654.28, confirmed

Thos. N. Williams & William McGregor to view repairs done by Elizabeth Smack, guardian, to real estate of Mary Mitchell

William Holland, Jun., & William Aydelott to distribute personal estate of Joshua Sturgis, deceased, in hands of Robert Cluff & Joanna, his wife, admx.

Isaac Lewis, adm. cwa of James Lewis, to sell personal estate

Henry Adams, surviving adm. of William F. Adams, to sell personal estate

F. 279   Esau Boston & Levi Henderson to view property of John, Susan & Sarah D. Adams, in care of Henry Adams, guardian

Rowland E. Bevans, guardian to James Selby, to purchase timber for 1500 fence rails

William Winder, Sen., Esq., adm. of Sarah Rackliffe, allowed for negro man Draper, since dead

Betsy Gordy, guardian to Noah & Leonard Gordy, excused from rendering accounts until they reach 14

William Richards, adm. of Isaac Richards, allowed for corn & pork used in family

William Richards, adm. of Isaac Richards, allowed 10% on estate

Joshua Dorman & Martha, his wife, admx. of John Duncan, to retain $7 to meet claim of John P. Mitchell, Sen.

F. 280   Nathan Rowley, adm. cwa of Richard Rowley, to sell personal estate (except legacies & wearing apparel)

Thomas M. Purnell & George W. Purnell, adms. of Zadok Purnell, Jun., to sell personal estate (except negroes, wearing apparel & corn)

Joshua Prideaux & Thomas S. Fassitt, Esqs., to distribute negroes from estate of Zadok Purnell, Jun., in hands of Thomas M. Purnell & George W. Purnell, adms.

George Hayward & John Stevens, exes. of Joseph Scott, to sell negroes

James Trippe, adm. of John Purnell (Queponco), to have amicable adjustment with James B. Robins, Esq., relative to notes & bonds assigned by said Robins to said Purnell

Thomas Gray, exe. of Eleanor Gray, allowed 6% on inventory

Jacob Dale & Nixon Davis to distribute estate of Isaac Richards (of Isaac), in hands of William Richards, adm.

F. 281   [blank]

F. 282   Tues., Dec. 8, 1807   Littleton Robins, John Bishop present

George Davis & Sarah, his wife, discharged from guardianship to Lambert & Molly Collier; George Davis new guardian

Orphan; Lambert Collier (of Layfield)
Guardian; George Davis
Sureties; Jesse Davis, Absolom Wait [couldn't write]

F. 283   Orphan; Molly Collier (of Layfield)
Guardian; George Davis
Sureties; Jesse Davis, Absolom Wait

F. 284   Orphan; Thomas Purnell (of Jno., Quepo.)
Guardian; Martha Purnell
Sureties; James Trippe, Thomas Jones

Orphan; John Purnell (of John, Quepo.)
Guardian; Martha Purnell
Sureties; James Trippe, Thomas Jones

F. 285   Orphan; Margaret Purnell (of John, Quepo.)
Guardian; Martha Purnell
Sureties; James Trippe, Thomas Jones

Orphan; Mary Purnell (of John, Quepo.)
Guardian; Martha Purnell
Sureties; James Trippe, Thomas Jones

F. 286   Apprentice; Isaac Isaacs, mulatto, 11 next Feb., son of Middlesex Isaacs
Bound to; Francis Lane
Trade; farmer
Sureties; Col. Samuel Handy, Littleton Riley

F. 287
Apprentice; Esau Isaacs, mulatto, 7 next Feb., son of
Middlesex Isaacs
Bound to; Francis Lane
Trade; farmer
Sureties; Samuel Handy, Littleton Riley

F. 288
Apprentice; Littleton Waters (of Patrick), 16 last May
Bound to; Levin Conner
Trade; house carpenter
Sureties; James Trippe, Joshua Sturgis

F. 289
Apprentice; John Bevans (of Benjamin), 15 next Christmas
Bound to; Robert J. H. Handy
Trade; mariner
Sureties; George Hayward, Josiah Hubbell

F. 290
Apprentice; Thomas Owens (of John), 11 on 1 Jan., 1808
Bound to; Charles Fookes
Trade; farmer
Sureties; James Fookes, Seth Fookes

F. 291
Apprentice; Charles Harmon (of Nimrod), 15 last Aug.
Bound to; Thomas N. Crapper
Trade; farmer
Sureties; John Sturgis (Bognetanorten), George Hayward

F. 292
William Jones & Barnaby Henderson to view estate of Charles Morris (of Philip), in care of John McCally & Amelia, his wife, guardians; before J. Hubbell: report

F. 293
F. 294
John Holland & Robert Cluff to view estate of Milly & Elizabeth Selby (of Capt. Jas.), in care of Mary Selby, guardian; before Benj. Aydelott: report; negro Benjamin belonging to Milly, woman Alice(?) belonging to Elizabeth; still belonging to Elizabeth; 385 acres

F. 295
William Holland, Jun., & Nehemiah Holland to view estate of John Purnell, in care of Kellam Lankford, guardian; before Wm. Holland: report; parts of tracts called 'Purnells Lott' & 'Brothers Love', 550 acres; Maj. Wm. Holland's wife's right of dower

F. 296
Maj. Nehemiah Holland & William Holland, Jun., to view estate of James Sturgis, in care of John Allen, Sen., guardian; before Saml. A. Harper: report; tract called 'Middlemore', 18 acres

F. 297
F. 298
John Holland & Robert Cluff to distribute estates of James Selby (of Jno.), deceased, & his son Parker, deceased, in hands of Mary Selby; before Saml. A. Harper:
1) to widow; negroes Cezar, Nice & John; list
2) to John Selby; man Monday; list
3) to Nancy Selby; Patience & Nathan; list
4) to Milley Selby; Benjamin; list
(cont.)

'160'

F. 299   5) to Betsy Selby; woman Nice; list
Nancy's share is $40 more than her due; same to be divided between other children

F. 300   Distribution of negroes & plate of Sarah Rackliffe [blank space where normal intro would be]: report; negro men Draper, Bill, Jesse, Saul & Stephen; lads Draper (dead), Abraham, Richard, Bob, Will, Elijah; women Betty, Rachel, Nancy, Esther, Henny; boys Levin, Hooper (dead), James, Milby, Jacob, Frank; girls Kate, Hannah, Ebby, Sarah, Rachael, Comfort, Lindy, Esther, Mary;

F. 301   born since appraisal, Rachael, Stephen, Levin;
    1) to John Rackliff; negroes Draper 61, Abraham 23, Levin 13, Milby 10, Will 21, Esther 56, Nancy 58, Sarah 18, Esther 9
2) to Charlotte Rackliff; Elijah 20, Bill 49, Richard 23, Levin 9 months, Rachel 62, Hannah 18, Lindy 13, Kate 20
3) to Rider Rackliff; Saul 30, James 11, Jacob 8, Stephen 1, Betty 71, Comfort 14, Henny 29, Mary 7, Rachel 2
4) to Keturah Rackliff; Jesse 44, Bob 21, Stephen 36, Frank 7, Rachel 17, Ebby 18

                                          Joshua Prideaux
                                          Thos. N. Williams

William Winder, guardian to John, Charlotte, Rider & Kiturah Rackliff, representatives of John & Sarah Rackliffe, states that in Nov., 1806, he stated that negroes had not been divided, & as Charlotte

F. 302   was coming of age, a division was needed; court appointed Joshua Prideaux & Thomas N. Williams to make division; only property left is some cattle leased with Newport farm, part of which is since transferred to Sinepuxent farm; hand mill left at latter for use of negro Draper & family there with him; part of Synnepuxent farm entailed to John by will of Charles Rackliff, his great grandfather;
    $40 due from Capril(?) Willey for hire of negro Bill,

F. 303   property of John, Charlotte, Rider & Kiturrah; arrears of
F. 304   negro hire; [list of negroes repeated]; list of bonds from Jackson Turner, John P. Marshall, William Fassitt, Betty Davis, Charles Nutter, Joshua Prideaux, Ephraim K. Wilson, Eli Vinson, Kirk Gunby, Thomas M. Purnell, William Polk; list of arrears

F. 305   of interest due [same list]; list of arrears due from negro hire; Zed. Smock (Jesse), John McDaniel (Hannah), John Larrimore (Saul), Joshua Gray (Richard), John Pruitt

F. 306 - (Elijah), John Rowley (Rachel), James Barclay (Bill)
310   [account of estate continues]

F. 311   Martha Hayman withdraws her caveat against inventory of estate of Rachel Hayman, filed by Isaac Hayman, exe.

Isaac Hayman, exe. of Rachel Hayman, to sell personal estate (except negroes & legacies)

On application of Anthony Bacon & George S. Gunby, exes. of Col. John Gunby, Col. Samuel Handy & George Hayward to ascertain value of negroes

Edward Henry & Thomas N. Williams to view property of Mary Mitchell, in care of Elizabeth Smock, guardian

Nancy Richardson, adm. of Robert M. Richardson, to sell negro woman Comfort & four of her children, Gatty, Zadok, Bob & Amanda, & man Major

William Winder, exe. of Sarah Rackliffe, to retain, as adm. dbn of John Rackliffe, $9938.60, the sum due from her to estate of said John, on which she was late adm.

F. 312   James Bennett, Jun., exe. of James Bennett, Sen., to sell personal estate (except legacies)

Thomas Fookes, adm. of John Owens, to sell personal estate

Martha Purnell, guardian to Thomas, John, Margaret & Mary Purnell, to cut timber in cypress swamp for shingles & apply same to support & education

Thomas Jones & Esther, his wife, admx. of Isaac Purnell, allowed for taxes due George Purnell, late Sheriff

Thomas N. Williams, adm. of Isaac Hill (of Robert), to sell personal estate

James Fookes, exe. of Jesse Fookes, to charge himself $130.50 for lumber shipped to Baltimore by deceased, which was cast away on Tilghman Island

F. 313   Comfort Savage, adm. of John Savage, to sell personal estate

A paper purporting to be the will of Samuel Quillen, exhibited by Priscilla Massey & Laban Taylor, exes. therein named, which is objected to by representatives, not to be admitted until further proceedings; adm. on estate granted to Priscilla & Laban, as Obed Quillen, James Quillen, John Farewell & Peter Quillen have refused to administer estate

Edward Hammond, Jun., adm. of Charles Hammond, to sell personal estate (except negroes, corn, plate & wearing apparel)

Adam Bravard, adm. of Ebenezer C. Brevard, to strike distribution

F. 314
Apprentice; George Isaacs, black, 11, illegitimate, by consent of his mother
Bound to; John Webb, planter
Trade; planter, cypress cooper
Before Edwd. Stevenson, James Tilghman

Apprentice; Samuel Moore [couldn't write], 19 on 3 Feb.(?) last, by consent of his mother
Bound to; Eben [also Ebenezer] Leonard, tanner
(cont.)

Trade; tanner
Test.; Isaac Hearn, Nathan Gordy

F. 315   Apprentice; Robert Peters, illegitimate black, 9 1/2, by
         consent of his mother
         Bound to; Edward Lambden, cypress cooper
         Trade; cypress cooper
         Before Edwd. Stevenson, James Tilghman

F. 316   Special Court, Jan. 26, 1808, at instance of Sarah, James &
         Joseph Moore, exes. of John Moore; Littleton Robins, John
Bishop present

Sarah, James & Joseph Moore, exes. of John Moore, allowed $15.16 for
sundry claims against deceased due in Philadelphia

Whittington Jones, adm. of James Jones, to sell personal estate

F. 317   Littleton Robins, Sen., John Bishop & Zadok Sturgis appointed
         Justices

Robert Wright   Wm. Kilty, Chanc.

Wit.; The Honorable William Kilty, Esq., Chancellor

Tues., Feb. 9, 1808   All Justices present

Nathaniel Wilkins discharged from guardianship to Henry Jarman; Isaac
Givan new guardian

F. 318   Orphan; Henry Jarman (of John)
         Guardian; Isaac Givan
         Sureties; Rownd Givan, John Truitt [couldn't write]

         Apprentice; Seth Porter (of Solomon), 16 on 30 May last
         Bound to; John Dukes
         Trade; farmer
F. 319   Sureties; Arthur Rowley, Ralph Milbourn

         Apprentice; Edward Knox (of Elijah), 17
         Bound to; Daniel Patrick
         Trade; boot & shoe maker
         Sureties; Joshua Fleming, Esq., Littleton Riley
F. 320   George Thomas, guardian to Edward

Apprentice; John Bishop (of Charles, of William), 14 on 30
July next
Bound to; Robert Truitt
Trade; mariner
Sureties; John Sturgis, John Laws

F. 321   Thomas N. Williams, William McGregor & Jacob Dale to settle
         dispute between Elizabeth Davis & John Davis, adms. of
Benjamin Davis, & Sterling Jones; Sterling to pay L.13/18/5 1/2

F. 322   Apprentice; David Watson, 14 on 7 May last
         Bound to; Robert Smith & Ralph B. Draper
         Trade; harness making & trimming
         Before Josiah Hubbell, Josa. Fleming(?)

Apprentice; Betsey Massey, illegitimate, 9 on 2 Jan. next
Bound to; Isaac Walter
Trade; spin & other household work
Before Wm. McGregor, Richard Sampson

F. 323   Apprentice; Littleton D. Tubbs, 17 on 11 Aug. last
         Bound to; George Crippen, shoe maker
         Trade; shoe maker
         Before William McGregor, James Laws

         Apprentice; Elisha Brittingham
         Bound to; William P. Bennett
         Term; 7 years, from 13 May next
F. 324   Trade; mariner or seamanship
         Before Edwd. Stevenson, James Tilghman

Apprentice; Peter Tignal, illegitimate, 10 on 18 instant, by consent
of his mother
Bound to; Levin Mills, hatter
Trade; making hats
Before Edwd. Stevenson, James Tilghman

         Elizabeth Smack, adm. dbn of Joshua Mitchell, to deliver to
F. 325   Polly Mitchell, adm. of Levin Mitchell, a silver watch as
         part of said Joshua's wearing apparel

Major Jones, exe. of Daniel Jones, to sell personal estate (except
legacies)

Laban Taylor & Priscilla Massey, adms. of Samuel Quillen, to sell
personal estate

Thomas S. Fassitt & John Davis, Esqs., to distribute negroes from
estate of Isaac Purnell, in hands of Thomas Jones & Esther, his wife,
admx.

John Steward, adm. of Levin H. Smith, allowed 10% on estate

Adam Moore, guardian to William Smith (of Harry), has received $53.97,
orphan's share of his father's estate

F. 326   William Dailey, guardian to Hetty Smith (of Harry), has
         received $53.97, orphan's share of her father's estate

Stephen W. Thorns(?) granted adm. on estate of David Porter, if no
other applications within 14 days

New warrant to William McGregor & Daniel Tingle to appraise personal estate of Abijah Davis, in hands of Littleton Davis, adm. dbn

Register to slate final account of Matthias Davis, late exe. of Abijah Davis, charging him with balance on his account passed 13 Jan., 1794

New warrant for William McGregor & Daniel Tingle to appraise estate of Matthias Davis, in hands of Littleton Davis, exe.

F. 327 Littleton Davis, exe. of Mathias Davis, to retain, as adm.
        dbn of Abijah Davis, balance due from estate of Matthias to estate of Abijah

Jacob White, adm. of Dr. James Wilson, allowed $220, the value of negro Ebben, since runaway

Jacob White, adm. of Dr. James Wilson, allowed 6 1/2% on estate, exclusive of value of negro Ebben

Elizabeth Smack, adm. dbn of Joshua Mitchell, allowed 5% on estate

Samuel Smyly granted adm. on estate of Stouton Ruark, if no one else applies within 14 days

Thomas D. Purnell, exe. of Milby Purnell, exhibits claims on estate heretofore unknown to him, one of Edward Hammond, assigned to Charles Hammond, & one of William Crapper

F. 328 William Adams & Kiturah, his wife, adms. of Thomas Milbourn, allowed $27.46, the cost of defending four suits against them, by James Duer, J. & E. Levering(?), R. & L. McKerin(?) & James Wonnell

F. 329 Tues., Apr. 12, 1808   All Justices present

Orphan; Nancy D. Gunby (of Col. John)
Guardian; George S. Gunby
Sureties; Benjamin Gunby, Anthony Bacon

F. 330 Orphan; Sally W. Gunby (of Col. John)
        Guardian; George S. Gunby
        Sureties; Benjamin Gunby, Anthony Bacon

Orphan; John Gunby (of Col. John)
Guardian; George S. Gunby
Sureties; Benjamin Gunby, Anthony Bacon

F. 331 Orphan; James T. Cathell (of David)
        Guardian; Joshua Cathell
        Sureties; Robert Nairne, Peter Parker

Orphan; James Rigsby (of Thomas)
Guardian; Purnell Porter
Sureties; Robert J. H. Handy, Dennis Hudson [couldn't write]

F. 332   Apprentice; Cyrus Crapper (of Noble), 11
         Bound to; Parker Collins
         Trade; hatter
         Sureties; John Sturgis (Boguetanorton), William Hammond, Jun.

         Apprentice; James Duffy, mulatto, 9 on 8 June next, son of
         Zippy
         Bound to; James Givan
F. 333   Trade; common labour
         Sureties; Joshua Fleming, Esq., James Ward

         Apprentice; Samuel Gunn (of Samuel), 15 on 11 Oct. last
         Bound to; Ralph B. Draper
         Trade; chaise maker
F. 334   Sureties; Joshua Fleming, Esq., Littleton Riley
         Samuel Hopkins, guardian

         Rowland E. Bevans & William Holland, Jun., to view estate of
F. 335   John Selby, in care of Fisher Richardson, guardian; before
         Wm. Holland: report; 1/4 of negroes Leah 11, Hannah 8

         Zadok Purnell & Joshua Prideaux, Esqs., to view estate of
F. 336   William Johnson, in care of Elizabeth Johnson, guardian;
F. 337   before William Dale: report; 105 acres of woods at Crappers;
         negro man Able

         Zadok Purnell & Joshua Prideaux, Esqs., to view estate of
F. 338   Moses Johnson, in care of Elizabeth Johnson, guardian;
         before William Dale: report; plantation where Laban Johnson,
deceased, formerly lived, 400 acres; land on road near St. Martins
         Church; premises at Herrin(?) Creek, 150 acres; negro boy
F. 339   Francis, woman Hannah

William Holland, Jun., & William Aydelott to distribute estate of
         Joshua Sturgis, in hands of Robert Cluff & Joanna, his wife,
F. 340   adms.; before Benj. Aydelott: inventory; negroes Jacob, Job,
F. 341   Moses, John, Rose, Priss, Bett, Pegg; increase includes
         Leah 5, Rachel 4, Custis 1; daughter Leah Sturgis is dead;
F. 342   1) to Robert Cluff & wife; negroes Jacob, Bett, Leah; list
         2) to Jno. Cluff & wife, daughter Sally Sturgis' share;
         Job, John, Priss, Custis; list
F. 343   3) to Nancy Sturgis, daughter; Moses, Peggy, Rachel, Rose;
         list

         Joshua Prideaux & Zadok Purnell, Esqs., to distribute estate
F. 344   of Laban Johnson, in hands of Elizabeth Johnson, exe.; before
         William Dale;
         1) to widow Elizabeth; Ralf 7, Leah 13, Liddy 75; list
F. 345   2) to William Johnson; John 4, Noah 2, Rachel 25, Pleasant 1
F. 346   month; list
         3) to Moses Johnson; Levin 5, Hannah 30, Jiney 7, child
Hester; cash for negroes Susan & Jacob, sold

F. 347   Thomas S. Fassitt & John Davis, Esqs., to divide negroes from
         estate of Isaac Purnell; before Nixon Davis: report; met at
house of Thomas Jones, after giving notice to John P. Marshall, near
friend to Thomas & John Purnell (of Isaac);
1) to widow, now Mrs. Jones; negroes James, Doll & Lynes(?)
2) to Thomas Purnell; Milly & Linda [also Lynda]
         3) to John Purnell; Quash & Levin
F. 348   N. B.- negro Levin born after death of Isaac

Col. Samuel Handy & George Hayward to value negroes from estate of
         Col. John Gunby, in hands of George S. Gunby & Anthony Bacon,
F. 349   exes.; before John Fleming, Jun.: report; Stephen 64, Bob 38,
         Ebben 38, Lott 46, Cosmo 14, Stephen 12, Caleb 12, Esther 39;
negroes that are expenses; Dinah (superannuated), Lydia & her two
children, Comfort 8 & Abner 4

         Isaac Marshall & George H. Gray, guardians to Samuel Gibbons
F. 350   (of Jonathan), to build house; Hillary Pitts to inspect house

Account of sales of negroes from estate of William Stevenson, by Isaac
Collins, exe.;
1) sold to John Stevenson; woman Esther & child Stephen, Amilla 8,
Cloe 4, George 27
2) sold to John Tull; Jesse 6
James Selby clerk for sale

Thomas R. Handy & George Hayward to settle dispute between Joseph
Bishop & Zipporah Bishop, adm. of Charles Bishop; Zipporah to pay to
Joseph L.12/7/6

F. 351   Thomas R. Handy & George Hayward to settle dispute between
         Levin Black, claimant, use of Henry Bennett, & Zipporah
Bishop, adm. of Charles Bishop; Zipporah to pay Levin L.7/11/3; James
Dennis paid for 4 days attendance as witness

F. 352   Robert Smith & Jacob Teague to settle dispute between Edward
         Hammond, Sen., & Thomas D. Purnell, exe. of Milby Purnell;
Thomas to pay Edward $105.39: witnesses; Littleton R. Purnell, Nixon
Davis, Esme Purnell

F. 353   Joshua Prideaux, William McGrigor & John Davis to settle
         dispute between John McVea & Caleb Williams, exe. of Edward
F. 354   McGee; case repeatedly continued; Caleb to pay John
         L.179/14/8; Caleb Williams, by Ephraim K. Wilson, Esq., his
F. 355   attorney, objects; agent for plaintiffs, Arthur Tracy:
         witnesses; Mary Watson, Thomas N. Williams

         Apprentice; John S. Porter, child of the Poor House, 7
         Bound to; James Burnett
         Trade; farmer
         Sureties; Capt. Benjamin Gunby, William Allen
F. 356   By Trustees for the Poor; Samuel Handy, McKimmey Porter,
         George Hayward

Apprentice; James Bootham, [couldn't write], by consent of his mother
Bound to; George Twilley [also Twilly, couldn't write], shew maker
Trade; shew maker
Before Benjamin Johnson, Isaac Hearn

F. 357   Apprentice; Joshua H. Hall, 15 & 1 month, by consent of
         Jonathan Schockley
         Bound to; Purnell Johnson
         Trade; farming
         Before Nathan Gordy, John Dashiell

         Apprentice; Milly Taylor, child of the Poor House, 8
         Bound to; James Merrill
         Trade; spin, sew & c. & c.
F. 358   Sureties; Isaac Cottingham, William Jones
         By Trustees for the Poor; Samuel Handy, Charles Bennett,
         George Hayward

         Apprentice; Parsha Taylor, daughter of Betsy, a child of the
         Poor House
         Bound to; Levin Mills
         Trade; housework
         Term; Till 16, on 1 Dec., 1819
F. 359   Sureties; James Ward, Major Tarr
         By Trustees for the Poor; Samuel Handy, Charles Bennett,
         George Hayward

James Dale & Mary, his wife, admx. of Jonathan Baker, to sell personal
estate (except wearing apparel)

William Holland, Jun., & Purnell Hill to view estate of George &
Matilda Selby, in care of Polly Selby, guardian

Jonathan Watson, exe. of Jonathan W. Watson, allowed 10% on estate

F. 360   Littleton Davis, adm. dbn of Abijah Davis, allowed 7 1/2% on
         estate

George Bratten & Frederick Conner to value repairs put by Alexander
Franklin, guardian to William F. Riley, on the lot in Snow Hill
occupied at present as a tavern by Littleton Riley

Thomas D. Purnell, exe. of Milby Purnell, allowed cost of awards
against him on suits of Edward Hammond, Sen., Samuel Ennis & Littleton
Robins, Sen.; also costs of defending suits of Col. Zadok Purnell,
exe. of Edward Hammond, Jun. & of Edmond Crapper; & for costs of
advertising in Easton & Philadelphia papers for creditors to exhibit
claims

James Ward & John Dashiell, adms. cwa of John Ward, to sell time of
negroes, & legacies

Priscilla Massey & Laban Taylor, adms. of Samuel Quillen, to advertise
in the Evening Post at Baltimore for creditors to exhibit their claims

F. 361 — James Ward & John Dashiell, adms. cwa of John Ward, to sell negroes on Wed., May 18, at Snow Hill

Ebben Christopher & Thomas Fookes to view estate of James T. Cathell, in care of Joshua Cathell, guardian

Joshua Cathell, guardian to James T. Cathell (of David), to receive his estate from John Cathell, exe. of David Cathell

Henry Adams, surviving adm. of William F. Adams, charged $128.15, the gain on sale of estate

John Selby, Jun., adm. of George Selby, having produced a certificate from William Holland & Henry Smock, that a cow & calf was not included in inventory, which he has sold

Thomas Collins, guardian to Elizabeth, Mary & John Collins, states estate of each is only $32.77, & John & Mary are small & unable to work; guardian to retain profits of John's estate for three years for his maintainance, & two years for Mary

F. 362 — Thomas P. Rackliffe & Nathaniel Bowen to view estate of James Rygsby, in care of Purnell Porter, guardian

George Bratten & Margaret Bratten, adms. of James Bratten, allowed 10% on estate

John Bishop, exe. of William Bishop, Sen., allowed 10% on estate

William Riley & Elizabeth Wright, adms. of Hezekiah Wright, allowed cost of suit of Thomas Mitchell & the suit of Ephraim K. Wilson & John C. Handy

William Riley & Elizabeth Wright, adms. of Hezekiah Wright, to distribute balance of estate among creditors

Note on Act of General Assembly concerning wills

F. 363 — Peter Smullen, adm. of William Smullen, allowed 10% on estate

Jesse Sturgis, adm. cwa of Peter Owens, on citation to exhibit inventory, states he has found no property belonging to deceased

Received 11 Feb., 1807, of Sampson Wright & Betty, his wife, late guardians to William Smith, $53.97, his share of his father Henry's estate

Test.; G. Maddux   Adam Moore, present guardian

Received 11 Feb., 1807, of Sampson Wright & Betty, his wife, late guardians to Hetty Smith, $53.97, her share of her father Henry's estate

                                              William Dailey,
Test.; George Maddux   present guardian

F. 364   Isaac Briddle & Nancy, his wife, late Nancy Collier (daughter of Peter), in consideration of L.2000 paid by Catherine Collier, late guardian to Nancy, quit claim to Catherine; in presence of Mr. Fassitt

F. 365   Tues., June 14, 1808   All Justices present

Apprentice; James Hudson (of James H.), 16 on 4 Apr. last
Bound to; Isaac Cottingham
Trade; chaise maker
Sureties; Samuel A. Harper, Esq., John Sturgis (Bogatn.)

F. 366   Apprentice; Levin Selby (of Levin), 15 in Aug. next
Bound to; Stephen Jones
Trade; shoe maker
Sureties; Peter Holland, John Sturgis (Bognetanorton)

F. 367   Apprentice; Jacob America, mulatto, 16, son of Leah
Bound to; James Givan
Trade; common labour
Sureties; Samuel Ennis, Isaac(?) P. Smith

F. 368   Apprentice; William Bishop (of Charles, of William), 16 in July next
Bound to; Isaac Cottingham
Trade; chaise maker
Sureties; Josiah Hubbell, George Hayward

F. 369   Apprentice; Joseph Ennis (of Joseph)
Bound to; Major Tarr
Trade; boot & shoe maker
Sureties; James Ward, William Rownd
Samuel Ennis, guardian

F. 370   Ebben Christopher & Thomas Fookes to view estate of James T. Cathell, in care of Joshua Cathell, guardian; before Nathan
F. 371   Gordy: report; 400 acres in Worcester Co.; lot in Salisbury, Somerset Co, with storehouse & hatters shop

George Bratten & Frederick Conner to ascertain repairs made by Alexander Franklin, guardian to William F. Riley, on a lot in
F. 372   Snow Hill occupied as a tavern by Littleton Riley: report; carpenters William Brown, George Hall, Jesse Hill; brick from Jacob Teague

F. 373   Apprentice; Riley Jones, 14 on 8 Feb. last, by consent of his mother
Bound to; Elijah Reed, house carpenter
Trade; house carpenter
F. 374   Sureties; Adam Bratten, John Davis
In presence of Nixon Davis, Jacob Dale

F. 375
Apprentice; Samuel Tubbs, 17 on 6 Feb. last
Bound to; James Mumford, tanner
Trade; tanner
Surety; Levin Dirickson
Before Wm. McGrigor, James Law

F. 376
Apprentice; Thomas Powell, son of Thomas, child of the Poor House
Bound to; Levin Conner
Trade; farming
Term; till 21, on 27 Apr., 1821
Sureties; Peter Waters, Lemuel P. Spence
By Trustees for the Poor; Saml. Handy, Sen., McKimmey Porter, George Hayward

James Selby, adm. of Walton Collins, allowed 10% on estate

Stephen Allen & Leah, his wife, admx. of Benjamin Aydelott, allowed $5.29, paid to Levin Townsend; paid by Jesse Sturgis

James H. Rowley & Thomas Collins, adms. of William Rowley, to sell personal estate (except negroes & such team(?) & farming utensils needed to finish crop); also to sell moiety of goods held in partnership with Covington Rowley

F. 377
Esther Dale, adm. of Annanias Dale, to sell personal estate (except wearing apparel)

John Bishop, exe. of William Bishop, Sen., not bound to prosecute claim returned desperate against George Rice, dated 1800

Received Mar. 2, 1808, of Adam Bravard, trustee appointed by will of John Bravard to settle estate, $42.31, my share of estate as widow of Ebenezer Bravard, one heir to estate

Wit.; Thos. Fassitt   Rea__?__ Brevard

F. 378   [blank]

F. 379   Tues. Aug. 9, 1808   All Justices present

Orphan; John Rackliffe (of John)
Guardian; James Laird (of Somerset Co.)
Sureties; Ephraim K. Wilson, George Hayward

F. 380
Orphan; Rider Rackliffe (of John)
Guardian; James Laird (of Somerset Co.)
Sureties; Ephraim K. Wilson, George Hayward

F. 381
Orphan; Kitturah Rackliffe (of John)
Guardian; James Laird (of Somerset Co.)
Sureties; Ephraim K. Wilson, George Hayward

Matthias Warren & Elizabeth, his wife, guardians to Julianna Mitchell, her daughter, are both dead; Mitchell Gray new guardian

Orphan; Julianna Mitchell (of Robert)
Guardian; Mitchell Gray
Sureties; Seth Whaley, John Bratten

<blockquote>
Apprentice; Littleton R. Hudson (of John, of Major), 14 on 7 Oct. next, by consent of his mother Mary
Bound to; John Hudson (of Saml.)
</blockquote>

F, 382 Trade; boot & shoe maker
Sureties; John Corbin, John A. Slocomb

<blockquote>
Apprentice; James Armstrong, mulatto, 13, son of Betty
Bound to; Robert J. H. Handy
</blockquote>

F. 383 Trade; mariner
Sureties; George Hayward, Anthony Bacon

F. 384 Apprentice; Anne Kollock, 14, daughter of Sarah
Bound to; Milby Atkinson
Trade; spin, knit, sew & weave
Sureties; Kenda [Kendal?] Smock, Patrick Waters
Esther Kollock, grandmother of Anne, present

F. 385 Nancy Richardson, adm. of Robert M. Richardson; statement of claims against estate; monies collected or due from Benja. Bishop, Saml. R. Smith, Betsy Wise, Azariah Purnell, Robt. Smith, Mary Martin; debts paid to Benjamin Bishop, Samuel R. Smith, Thomas Claywell, Betsey Wise, Samuel A. Harper, Fisher Richardson, Samuel Johnson, Azariah Purnell, Mary Anne Rice (exe. of George Rice), Jno. Bishop, Zadok Sturgis, Patrick Waters, Lanta Purnell, Col.
F. 386 Handy, Isaac Ayres, Levi Merrill, Betty Martin, Zadok Sturgis, Asa Bowen, E. K. Wilson (for defending suit against Robert Handy), W. B. Martin, Peter & J. Hoffman, George Hoffman, John Thompson, Richardson & Rice, John Townsend, Isaac Riggen, John Stevens (adm. of George Richardson), Robt. Nairne (Shrff.), Thompson & Robt. Smith, John C. Handy (clk.), Wm. Whittington, Esq., Thos.
F. 387 Martin, Esq., Levi Outten, Shadrach Lane, John Brazier, Joshua Fleming, Duer & Fleming, Mary Martin, Purnell Bishop, E. K. Wilson, Esq.; cost of suits of John Thompson, Robert Handy, Mary Rice, Polly Smith (exe. of Walter), Mary Anne Rice (exe. of George)

<blockquote>
Apprentice; David Lynch [also Linch], by consent of his mother, Caty Layton [signed Caty Henderson, neither could write]
Bound to; Revel Powders, mill rite
Trade; turner(?)
</blockquote>

F. 388 Term; 5 years, 5 months
In presence of James Law

Betty Hearn & William Parsons, exes. of John Hearn, allowed 10% on estate

Thomas N. Williams & William McGrigor, Esqs., to view property of John Rackliffe, in care of James Laird, guardian

F. 389   Thomas N. Williams & William McGrigor, Esqs., to view property of Rider & Kitturah Rackliffe, in care of James Laird, guardian

James Laird, guardian to John, Rider & Kitturah Rackliffe, to rent real estate

Henry Davis, exe. of Thomas Davis, allowed 8% on estate

Christopher Ball, adm. of Levi Ball, allowed 8% on estate

John Postly, Isaac Ayres & Laban Hill to settle dispute between Henry Hozier & Betty, his wife, Benjamin Westlake & Anne, his wife, Moses Quillen, Elizabeth Quillen & Charlotte Quillen, & Priscilla Massey & Laban Taylor, adms. of Samuel Quillen

John Cottingham & John C. Bacon to distribute negroes belonging to Maria, Jane, Sally & Matilda Townsend, in hands of John Corbin, guardian

F. 390   John Corbin, guardian to Maria, Jane, Sally & Matilda Townsend, allowed 10% on property sold

John Cathell, exe. of David Cathell, allowed for negro Sandy, now dead

John Cathell, exe. of David Cathell, allowed 8% on estate, after deducting for two negroes which are dead

John Dashiell & Thomas Fookes to distribute specifics from estate of David Cathell, in hands of John Cathell, exe.

William McGrigor & Hillary Pitts to view estate of Julianna Mitchell, in care of Mitchell Gray, guardian

Mitchell Gray, guardian to Julianna Mitchell (of Robert), to receive her estate from Matthias Warren, late guardian

Mitchell Gray, guardian to Julianna Mitchell, to rent real estate

F. 391   Caleb Monis & Dolly, his wife, exex. of Esme Purnell, states that estate to be sold for payment of debts is insufficient; to sell stock & furniture

James Knox & Priscilla, his wife, admx. of William Hudson, allowed 8% on estate

Thomas D. Purnell, exe. of Milby Purnell, to retain $169.22 as 1st & 2nd proportions due on claims of Thomas Stewart, Edward Hammond, Sen., & William Crapper against estate

Stephen Purnell, exe. of Thomas Gray, Sen., to sell personal estate (except negroes, & crop of fruit & liquor on main plantation)

John Selby, Jun., adm. of George Selby, allowed 7 1/2% on estate

Levin Pollitt, adm. cwa of Joseph Bousee, allowed 10% on estate

F. 392   Received Sept. 20, 1808, of Elijah Richards, my late guardian, legacies given me by the will of my father Major Gornwell, & $122.02, being notes of John Sturgis & Littleton R. Purnell

Test.; Zadok Sturgis   Sarah (Sally) O. Gornwell

F. 393   Tues., Oct. 11, 1808   All Justices present

Orphan; James McCormack (of Benjamin)
Guardian; James Tubbs
Sureties; Revel Powders, Severn Jarvis [couldn't write]

F. 394   Orphan; John McCormack (of Benjamin)
Guardian; James Tubbs
Sureties; Revel Powders, Severn Jarvis

Orphan; Charlotte Hammond (of Charles)
Guardian; Edward Hammond, Jun.
Sureties; Jethro Morris [couldn't write], Littleton Sturgis

F. 395   Orphan; Edward Hammond (of Charles)
Guardian; Edward Hammond, Jun.
Sureties; Jethro Morris, Littleton Sturgis

Orphan; William Jones (of James)
Guardian; Betsy Jones
F. 396   Sureties; Aaron Hudson, John Webb [couldn't write]

Orphan; Tabitha Quinton Jones (of James)
Guardian; Betsy Jones
Sureties; Aaron Hudson, John Webb

F. 397   Orphan; Stephen Jones (of James)
Guardian; Betsy Jones
Sureties; Aaron Hudson, John Webb

Orphan; Nancy Mitchell Jones (of James)
Guardian; Betsey Jones
Sureties; Aaron Hudson, John Webb

F. 398   Orphan; Sally James Jones (of James)
Guardian; Betsey Jones
Sureties; Aaron Hudson, John Webb

F. 399
       Orphan; William Dryden (of Isaac)
       Guardian; Thomas Dryden
       Sureties; Selby Parker, Thomas Mitchell

Orphan; James Dryden (of Isaac)
Guardian; Thomas Dryden
Sureties; Selby Parker, Thomas Mitchell

F. 400
       Orphan; Nancy Dryden (of Isaac)
       Guardian; Thomas Dryden
       Sureties; Selby Parker, Thomas Mitchell

Orphan; Isaac Dryden (of Isaac)
Guardian; Thomas Dryden
Sureties; Selby Parker, Thomas Mitchell

F. 401   John M. Rankin & Betsy, his wife, late Betsy Purnell, refuse to give counter security to Thomas N. Williams & Daniel Tingle, her securities on guardianship to Molly, Zadok, Thomas & Sally Purnell (of John, Wallops Neck); guardianship revoked

F. 402
       Orphan; Molly O. Purnell (of John, W. N.)
       Guardian; Daniel Tingle
       Sureties; Thomas N. Williams, Ephraim K. Wilson

Orphan; Zadok Purnell (of John, W. N.)
Guardian; Daniel Tingle
Sureties; Thomas N. Williams, Ephraim K. Wilson

F. 403
       Orphan; Thomas Purnell (of John, W. N.)
       Guardian; Thomas N. Williams
       Sureties; Daniel Tingle, Ephraim K. Wilson

Orphan; Sally Purnell (of John, W. N.)
Guardian; Thomas N. Williams
Sureties; Daniel Tingle, Ephraim K. Wilson

F. 404   Apprentice; Eli Collins (of Chambers), 6
        Bound to; Samuel Long
        Trade; farmer
        Sureties; John J. Williams, John Sturgis (Bognetanorton)

F. 405
       Apprentice; William Hopkins (of Luke), 18 in May next
       Bound to; Belitha Hook
       Trade; boot & shoe maker
       Sureties; Patrick Waters, John Sturgis (Bognetanorton)

F. 406   Hillary Pitts & William Mcgrigor to view estate of Julianna Mitchell (of Robert), in care of Mitchell Gray, guardian;
F. 407   before Abisha Davis: report; 514 acres; negro men Abram, Ben, Elijah; women Milley, Rhoda, Sarah; men Hope, George (blind), an expense to estate; Arnel 8, Huldy 8, Handy 4, Elisa 1 1/2

'175'

	Thomas N. Williams & Edward Henry, Esqs., to view estate of
F. 408	Mary Mitchell (of Joshua), in care of Elizabeth Smack, guardian; before John Bishop: report; lands where Josiah
F. 409	Mitchell formerly lived, 466 acres; land where Mrs. Elizabeth Smock lives, includes 150 acres of cypress swamp; negroes
F. 410	Plem 28, Zeb 25, Charles 22, Rachel 29, Nancy 30, Minta 11, John 10, Isaac (runaway), Sarah 55, George 65, Hagar 76

(expense), Stephen 8, Caleb 7, Toney 3, Isaac 1 1/2, Sue 6, Comfort 5, Hetty 1 1/2

	Thomas N. Williams & William McGrigor, Esqs., to view estate
F. 411	of John Rackliffe, in care of Rev. James Laird, guardian; report; land leased to Kirk Gunby, entailed to John, in
F. 412	Synepuxon neck; lands belonging to John, Rider, Kitturah & Charlotte Rackliffe; land called 'Cedars'; land leased to Nathaniel Brittingham in Newport neck; negroes Draper 62,
F. 413	Abraham 24, Levin 14, Milby 11, Will 22, Esther 57, Sarah 19, Esther 10

	Thomas N. Williams & William McGrigor to view estate of Rider
F. 414-5	Rackliffe, in care of Rev. James Laird, guardian; [same as above, minus John's land]; negroes Saul 31 (blacksmith),

James 12, Jacob 9, Stephen 2, Betty 72, Comfort 15, Henney 30, Mary 8, Rachel 3, girl 10 months

	Thomas N. Williams & William McGrigor to view estate of
F. 416	Kitturah Rackliffe, in care of Rev. James Laird, guardian;
F. 417	[same as above, minus John's land]; negroes Jesse 45, Bob 22, Stephen 37, Frank 8, Rachel 18, Ebby 19

F. 418	John Dashiell & Thomas Fookes to distribute personal estate of David Cathell, in hands of John Cathell, exe.; before John

Cathell;
1) to Joshua Cathell, oldest representative of age; negroes Caleb 27, Milcah 11, Milby 40, Stephen 9; list
F. 419   2) to James Thomson Cathell, youngest representative, as delivered to Joshua Cathell, guardian; negro boy Bob, Moses 52, Charles 23, Darkey 21, Sylva 7; $160.31

Littleton Robins, Joshua Prideaux & Zadok Purnell, Sen., on the one part & John P. Marshall, Maj. Edward Henry, Zadok Marshall, Reuben Anderson, Thomas Marshall, Thos. Purnell (of Wm.), Samuel Ennis, William P. Marshall, John Purnell (of Thos..), George W. Purnell (for his mother Mary) & Boaz Ennis, representatives of Col. Zadok Purnell, on the other part, agree to sale of negroes: test.; Zadok
F. 420   Purnell, Jun., Edward Robins; terms of sale;
1) whole representatives, including James B. Robins & Littleton Robins, allowed to bid
2) Thos. Purnell (Wm.), Zadok Purnell, Jun., & George W. Purnell allowed to bid for Pleasant, Leah, Bet & George
3) purchasers bound to same terms as purchasers of other property
4) negroes hired out not to be delivered till term of service expired
5) hire of such negroes to be accounted for by adms.

'176'

F. 421   Apprentice; John [also has George] Wandum, illegitimate, 18
         on 22 Dec. next, by consent of his mother
         Bound to; John Taylor, blacksmith
         Trade; blacksmith
         Surety; Thomas Franklin
         Before Wm. McGrigor, Abishai Davis

F. 422   Apprentice; Jonathan Eshom, 16 on 20 May next, by consent of
         his father Solomon
         Bound to; William Lecompt
         Trade; sadler
         In presence of J. Hubbell

         Levin Derickson & Peter Lister to view property of James &
F. 423   John McCormack, in care of James Tubbs, guardian

James Laird, guardian to John, Rider & Kitturah Rackliffe, to build
new corn house on farm in Synepuxent, to repair another, & to have a
barn on Newport farm scaled with planks on outside, to make it a safe
repository for grain

Leah Crapper & Josiah Bowen, adms. cwa of William Crapper, allowed 6%
on estate

Benjamin Melsin, adm. of Joseph Melsin, to sell personal estate

George Bonnewell & Elizabeth, his wife, guardians to Jacob & John
Payne, to retain profits of estate for their support & education
untill they turn 14

James Davis, guardian to Westly & Patsey Melvin, to give each one
months schooling this year & next

Belitha Burbage & John McCalley & Amelia, his wife, adms. of Philip
Morris, allowed 8% on estate

F. 424   George Hayward & John Stevens, exes. of Joseph Scott, charged
         with amount negroes were sold for a term of years agreeable
to will

James W. B. Perdue, surviving exe. of James Perdue, allowed 8% on
estate

Boaz Walston & Purnell Johnson to distribute personal estate of James
Perdue, agreeable to will, remaining in hands of James W. B. Perdue,
surviving exe.

Littleton Robins, Zadok Purnell & Joshua Prideaux, adms. cwa of Col.
Zadok Purnell, allowed 8% on estate

Joshua Prideaux, Esq., one adm. of Col. Zadok Purnell, to retain
L.5/5/9, balance against deceased

'177'

William Stevenson, adm. of Elijah Stevenson, to advertise in Thomas P. Smith's paper at Easton for creditors to exhibit claims

Order at Dec. term last allowing admx. of Robert M. Richardson to sell negro Comfort & her children Gatty, Zadok, Bob & Amanda, rescinded; adms. to sell man Elijah, woman Rhoda & Gatty & Isaac,
F. 425 children of Comfort, for payment of claims against deceased by the Hoffmans, Levi Merrill & Benjamin Bishop

Belitha Burbage & John McCalley & Amelia, his wife, adms. of Philip Morris, to retain $489.76 to meet claim of Patrick Glasgow

George Hayward & Eleanor Merrill, adms. of Robert M. Merrill, to sell personal estate

Nixon Davis & Thomas Duncan to view property of Charlotte Hammond, in care of Edward Hammond, Jun., guardian

Nixon Davis & Thomas Duncan to view property of Edward Hammond (of Charles), in care of Edward Hammond, Jun., guardian

Samuel McMaster & Joseph Houston to view property of Tabitha, Stephen, Nancy & Sally Jones, in care of Betsy Jones, guardian

Samuel McMaster & Joseph Houston to view estate of William Jones, in care of Betsy Jones, guardian

F. 426 William McGrigor & Edward Bridell to distribute negroes & legacies from estate of Thomas Gray, Jun.(?) (title to negro Leah, in possession of John Lane, in dispute), in hands of Stephen Purnell, exe.

John Davis & Elizabeth Davis, adms. of Benjamin Davis, allowed 8% on estate

As represented by Henry Davis, exe. of Thomas Davis, & confirmed by Charles Hope, one appraiser, an error was made in inventory, showing 50 bushels of corn; should be 27

Thomas Hooper, exe. of Esther Sturgis, allowed 10% on estate

William McGrigor & Edward Henry, Esqs., to view estate of Mary O. Purnell, in care of Daniel Tingle(?), guardian

William McGrigor & Edward Henry, Esqs., to view estate of Zadok Purnell, in care of Daniel Tingle, guardian

Daniel Tingle, guardian to Mary O. Purnell (of John, W. N.), to receive her estate from John N. Rankin & Elizabeth, his wife, late guardians

F. 427 Daniel Tingle, guardian to Zadok Purnell (of John, W. N.), to receive his estate from John M. Rankin & Elizabeth, his wife, late guardians

Thomas N. Williams, guardian to Thomas Purnell (of John, W. N.), to receive his estate from John M. Rankin & Elizabeth, his wife, late guardians

Thomas N. Williams, guardian to Sally Purnell (of John, W. N.), to receive her estate from John M. Rankin & Elizabeth, his wife, late guardians

Edward Henry & William McGrigor, Esqs., to view estate of Thomas Purnell, in care of Thomas N. Williams, guardian

F. 428   Edward Henry & William McGrigor, Esqs., to view estate of Sally Purnell, in care of Thomas N. Williams, guardian

Nov. 16, 1808, I, Richard Shockley, grandson of Richard Shockley, certify that I received of Elijah Shockley (of Benjamin), L.8, the last payment of estate left me by my grandfather

Test.; John Williams   his
   John Dashiell   Richard X Shockley
              mark

F. 429   Special Court, Nov. 25, 1808, at instance of James H. Rowley & Thomas Collins, adms. of William Rowley; all Justices present

James H. Rowley & Thomas Collins, adms. cwa of William Rowley, to sell negroes, team, farming utensils & crop

F. 430   Tues., Dec. 13, 1808   All Justices present

Orphan; Francis Lane
Guardian; John Lane, father
Sureties; Francis Lane, Stephen Anderson

F. 431   Orphan; Henry Rowley (of William)
Guardian; James Henry Rowley
Sureties; John Tarr (of Eli) [couldn't write], Kellam Lankford

F. 432   Orphan; Susanna Rowley (of William)
Guardian; Thomas Collins
Sureties; Killiam Lankford, James Henry Rowley

Killiam Lankford discharged from guardianship to John Purnell; William Holland, Sen., new guardian

Orphan; John Purnell (of Robert)
Guardian; William Holland, Sen.
Sureties; Joshua Duer, George Hayward

F. 433   Orphan; Thomas Nicholson (of Joseph)
Guardian; William Quinton
Sureties; Littleton Quinton, James Fleming

F. 434
Apprentice; Mitchell Rodgers (of Joseph), 14 in Nov. last
Bound to; McKimmey Porter
Trade; boot & shoe maker
Sureties; Edward Hammond, Sen., Edward Hammond, Jun.
Rouse Harrison, father-in-law [stepfather?] to orphan, present

F. 435
Apprentice; William H. Henderson, by consent of his father Benjamin [couldn't write]
Bound to; Isaac Taylor, carpenter
Trade; carpenter
Term; 4 years
Before Edwd. Stevenson, James Tilghman

F. 436
Apprentice; John Warrenton(?), 16 on 6 Apr. last
Bound to; Thomas Brittingham, shoe maker
Trade; boot & shoe maker
Before Edwd. Stevenson, James Tilghman

Apprentice; Henry Parker (of Somerset Co., couldn't write), by consent of his father Samson
Bound to; Joseph Perkins (of Worcester Co.), turner & cart wheel wright
Trade; turner & cart wheel wright
Term; till 28 Nov., 1811
Before Benjamin Johnson

F. 437   John Caudery, Sen., exe. of Polly Bowen, allowed 8% on estate

Sarah Hartnett, adm. of Daniel Hartnett, to sell personal estate (except negro Susan & wearing apparel)

James H. Rowley, guardian to Henry Rowley, to give ward 6 months schooling

Thomas Collins, guardian to Susanna Rowley (of William), states that ward is suffering from swelling of the head & running at one ear, & that profits of estate will not support her; guardian to retain profits for her support

Leonard Johnson & Thomas Hall, adms. of Turbot Wright, to sell personal estate

F. 438
William Holland, Jun., & Nehemiah Holland to view estate of John Purnell, in care of William Holland, Sen., guardian

Amey Furniss, adm. of Littleton Furniss, to sell personal estate (except negroes & wearing apparel)

Thomas N. Williams, exe. of Elizabeth Smack(?), to sell personal estate (except negroes & list)

Sterling Jones, adm. of Caleb Powell, to sell personal estate

George Parsons, Jun., & Elijah Parsons, exes. of George Parsons, Sen., to sell personal estate (except wearing apparel)

Turner Davis, adm. of Henry Davis, to sell personal estate

F. 439   Rowland E. Bevans, adm. of John Cutler(?), to sell personal estate

Rowland E. Bevans, adm. of John Cutler, to advertise in the National Intelligencer at Washington, the Whig at Baltimore & the Star at Easton for creditors to exhibit claims

Received Aug. 8, 1797, of James Duer, one surety for adm. of estate of Jonathan [also John] Cordray, L.28/8/9, my dividend of estate

Test.; John Cutler, Francis Rosse   Nancy Cordray

11 Jan., 1809, Francis Rosse swears to above before Josa. Fleming Jun.

F. 440   Received of James W. B. Perdue, surviving exe. of James Perdue, L. 15, my legacy

By me Louden Perdue   her
                                          Sally X B. Dennis [signed C.]
                                          mark

17 Mar., 1803, received of George Bell & James W. B. Perdue, adms. of James Perdue, items given to Polly K. Perdue, daughter of James; list

Wit.; Louden Perdue(?)   his
                                         Fisher X Taylor
                                          mark

Received Jan. 14, 1809, of James Walker & Bayley Perdue, surviving exes. of James Perdue, L.50, my wife Polly K. Perdue's share of estate of James, her father, in lewe of a young negro

Test.; Benjamin Johnson, Jun.   his
                                             Fisher X Taylor
                                             mark

Received Apr. 11, 1808, of George Bell & James W. B. Perdue, adms. of James Perdue, items given to Elizabeth Perdue, daughter of James; list

Test.; George Vance   his
      Elijah Shaley Perdue   Benjamin X Dennis
                                                mark

Received Sept. 10, 1808, of James W. B. Perdue, exe of James Perdue, L. 50, a legacy to his daughter Elizabeth Ellener Young Perdue

Benjamin Johnson   his
                                           Benjamin X Dennis
                                           mark

'181'

F. 441 Received Jan., 1809, of James W. B. Perdue, surviving exe. of James Perdue, legacy left her by her father

Test.; Louden Perdue

                 her
            Arcady X Perdue
              mark

F. 442 Special Court, Dec. 30, 1808, at instance of Thomas N. Williams, Esq.; John Bishop, Zadok Sturgis present

Orphan; Mary Mitchell (of Joshua)
Guardian; Stuart Williamson
Sureties; Thomas N. Williams, John S. Martin

Edward Henry & William McGrigor, Esqs., to view estate of Mary Mitchell, in care of Stuart Williamson, guardian

F. 442b [writing changes at this point]

Littleton Robins, Sen., John Bishop & Zadok Sturgis appointed Justices

Robert Wright   W. Kilty, Chanc.

Wit.; The Honorable William Kilty, Esq., Chancellor

Tues., Feb. 14, 1809   All Justices present

F. 443 Orphan; Mitchell Rodgers (of Joseph)
Guardian; Rouse Harrison
Sureties; Littleton Davis, Levin Derickson

Orphan; Mordecai Smith (of John, of Thos.)
Guardian; Littleton Davis
Sureties; Seth Whaley, Rouse Harrison

F. 444 Orphan; Daniel Hartnett (of Daniel)
Guardian; Sarah Hartnett [couldn't write]
Sureties; Thomas Collins, James Henry Rowley

Orphan; William Hartnett (of Daniel)
Guardian; Sarah Hartnett
Sureties; Thomas Collins, James H. Rowley

F. 445 Orphan; Nancy Hartnett (of Daniel)
Guardian; Sarah Hartnett
Sureties; Thomas Collins, James Henry Rowley

F. 446 Orphan; Elizabeth Hartnett (of Daniel)
Guardian; Sarah Hartnett
Sureties; Thomas Collins, James H. Rowley

John C. Handy, appointed by will of James Houston, guardian to his son Isaac Houston, refuses appointment; Henry Bennett appointed guardian

Orphan; Isaac Houston (of Col. James)
Guardian; Henry Bennett(?)
Sureties; Jessy Bennett(?), Selby Parker

F. 447
Orphan; Henry Jarman (of John)
Guardian; Benjamin Dennis [couldn't write]
Sureties; John K. H. Perdue [couldn't write], Elijah C. W. Perdue [signed S. W.]

Orphan; George Bishop (of Charles)
Guardian; John Bishop
Sureties; John C. Handy, George Hayward

F. 448
Orphan; Wilson Bishop (of Charles)
Guardian; John Bishop
Sureties; John C. Handy, George Hayward

F. 449
Orphan; Leah Hudson (of William)
Guardian; James Knox
Sureties; Ephraim K. Wilson, George Hayward

Orphan; George Hudson (of William)
Guardian; James Knox
Sureties; Ephraim K. Wilson, George Hayward

F. 450
Orphan; William S. Corbin (of Peter S.)
Guardian; William Corbin
Sureties; Robert J. H. Handy, John F. Atkinson

Orphan; Molly Corbin (of Peter S.)
Guardian; William Corbin
Sureties; Robert J. H. Handy, John F. Atkinson

F. 451
Levi Henderson & Esau Boston to view estate of John, Susan & Sarah D. Adams [also Addams], in care of Henry Adams, guardian; before Edwd. Stevenson: report; 3/4 of 200 acres

F. 452

F. 453
Levin Derickson & Peter Lister to view estate of John & James McCormack (of Benjamin), in care of James Tubbs, guardian; before Abishai Davis: report; John & James entitled to 1/4 of land each; 97 acres on tract called 'Fanels Folly'

Apprentice; Isaac Dick, mulatto, 6 on 1 Mar. next, son of Nancy
Bound to; Littleton Riley
Trade; house servant & waiter
Sureties; Isaac P. Smith, Patrick Waters

F. 454
Apprentice; Moses Claywell (of Moses), 12 in Sept. last
Bound to; George Bratten
Trade; farmer
Sureties; John Blair, Lemuel P. Spence

Thomas S. Fassitt & Joshua Prideaux, Esqs., to distribute
F. 455   negroes from estate of Zadok Purnell, Jun., in hands of
Thomas M. & George W. Purnell, adms.; before Thos. N.
Williams: report;
1) to John Purnell's heirs; Pool (aged), Big Mingo, Milby, Tab, Milby
2) to George W. Purnell; Mannuel (aged), Little Mingo, Elijah,
Pleasant, Sarah
3) to Thomas M. Purnell; Stephen (aged), Littleton, Grace, Comfort,
Dinah, Hetty
Subdivision among John Purnell's heirs;
1) to Mary O. Purnell; Mingo
2) to Thomas Purnell; woman Milby, girl Tab
3) to Zadok Purnell; man Pool
4) to Sally Purnell; boy Mingo

F. 456   John Bishop & Littleton R. Purnell to distribute personal
estate of Joseph Ennis, in hands of Eli Hudson & Nancy, his
wife, exex.; before Joshua Prideaux, 23 Apr., 1802: report;
F. 457   1) to Stephen Ennis, son; negro woman Esther & her child,
Grace
2) to Joseph Ennis, son; man Parker
3) to Samuel Ennis, son; man Ceaser
4) to Milby Ennis, son; man Jack
5) to Eli Hudson & Nancy, his wife, her thirds; man Stephen, girl
Henny

William McGrigor & Edward Briddle to distribute negroes from estate of
Thomas Gray, Sen., as are not legacied, negro Leah excepted
F. 458   (she in possession of John Lane, title in dispute); before
James Law: report;
1) to Elizabeth Gray, the widow; Nocker 56, Isaac 22, George 22,
Rachel 38, Peggy 13
2) to heirs of Sally Lane, wife of John; Sam 52, Brista 21, Hannah 6
3) to Eliza White, daughter of Martha White; Sam 35, Abner 8, Jude 42
Guardian of Eliza White to pay Elizabeth Gray $28.33; heirs of Sally
Lane, her son Thomas excepted, due $3.33

F. 459   Apprentice; Agor [signed Majer, father?] Lewis Jones, by
consent of his parents
Bound to; James Tilghman, shoe maker
Trade; boot & shoe maker
Term; untill 7 Mar., 1813
F. 460   Before Edwd. Stevenson

Apprentice; Peter Tarr, 14 on 5 Oct. next, by consent of his father
Elijah
Bound to; Major Tarr
Trade; cordwainer
In presence of Joshua Evans, Milby Holland

F. 461   Apprentice; William Scott, 18 on 19 Nov. last, by consent of
his mother
Bound to; Thomas Brittingham, shoe maker
(cont.)

Trade; boot & shoe maker
Sureties; William Smith
Before Edwd. Stevenson, James Tilghman

Littleton Davis, exe. of John Smith (of Thos.), to sell personal estate (except legacies)

F. 462　　Eliakim Jones, adm. cwa of John Jones, to sell personal estate (except legacies)

William Parker, adm. cwa of Col. James Houston, to sell personal estate (except negroes)

Samuel Long, exe. of Colevern Long, to sell personal estate

[writing changes at this point]

Littleton Davis, guardian to Mordecai Smith, to sell bed, furniture & chest, legacies from his father

Abisha Davis & Lemuel Showell to view estate of Mordecai Smith, in care of Littleton Davis, guardian

Register to slate an account for Adam Moore, guardian to William Smith, charging him $53.97 for orphan's property

Register to slate an account for Adam Moore, guardian to Hetty Smith, charging him $53.97 for orphan's property

F. 463　　Littleton Dennis, Edward Stevenson & John Stevenson to settle dispute between Bennett H. Clavoe & Amey Furnis, adm. of Littleton Furnis

Benjamin Purnell & John Stevens to view estate of Isaac Houston, in care of Henry Bennett, guardian

Jacob Rownd & William Handcock to view estate of Henry Jarman, in care of Benjamin Dennis, guardian

New warrant for Joshua Prideaux & Thomas S. Fassitt to appraise estate of Zadok Purnell, Jun.

James Knox, adm. dbn of William Hudson, allowed 8% on estate which came to his hands & to the hands of the late admx., with whom he intermarried

James Knox, adm. dbn of William Hudson, to sell time of negro Henny

John Holland & William Holland, Jun., to view estate of William S. Corbin, in care of Bowdoin Robins, guardian

Samuel Handy & Samuel R. Smith to view estate of Molly Corbin, in care of Bowdoin Robins, guardian

Annanias Jones & Joseph Jones, exes. of Joseph Jones, Sen., allowed 7% on estate

F. 464 James Laird, guardian to John, Rider & Kitturah Rackliffe, received $1900 from William H. Winder, adm. dbn of Sarah Rackliffe, for sale of bank stock in the District of Columbia

William Quinton, adm. dbn of Isaac Nicholson, to retain, as guardian to Thomas Nicholson (of Joseph), $36.20, his share of his father's estate, in hands of the deceased as exe. of said Joseph

Mary Sampson, exe. of Richard Sampson, to sell stock & store goods, perishable items & goods in hands of Thomas Williams

[several different handwritings on rest of page]

Special Court, Mar. 10, 1809, at instance of George Hayward & William Handy, exes. of Bowdoin Robins; all Justices present

George Hayward & William Handy, exes. of Bowdoin Robins, to sell personal estate as directed by will

George Hayward & William Handy, exes. of Bowdoin Robins, to advertise in the Republican Star at Easton for creditors to exhibit claims

[writing changes at this point]

F. 465 Tues., Apr. 11, 1809   All Justices present

Selby Parker discharged from guardianship to Levin Selby; Stephen Jones new guardian

Orphan; Levin Selby (of Levin)
Guardian; Stephen Jones
Sureties; Samuel Tarr, John Aydelott

F. 466 Orphan; Leah Jones (of John, Sen.)
Guardian; Sarah Jones
Sureties; Samuel Tarr, Eliakim Jones

Orphan; John Rowley (of William)
Guardian; William Hargis, Sen.
Sureties; James Henry Rowley, Benjamin Bennett

F. 467 Fisher Richardson discharged from guardianship to George Selby; John Selby new guardian

Orphan; George Selby (of Daniel)
Guardian; John Selby (of Daniel)
Sureties; Fisher Richardson, Nehemiah Holland

F. 468 Orphan; Anne Sheldon Dorman (of Nehemiah)
Guardian; John A. Townsend
Sureties; James Townsend, John Townsend

Orphan; Hezekiah Dorman (of Nehemiah)
Guardian; John A. Townsend
Sureties; James Townsend, John Townsend

F. 469
Orphan; Thomas Jones (of Daniel)
Guardian; Comfort Jones [couldn't write]
Sureties; Major Jones, Moses U. Jones

Orphan; Sally Jones (of Daniel)
Guardian; Comfort Jones
Sureties; Major Jones, Moses Upshen Jones

F. 470
Apprentice; Harry Dick, mulatto, 4 in Aug. last, son of Nancy
Bound to; Whittington Richardson
Trade; farmer
Sureties; John Sturgis, John Holston

F. 471
Apprentice; Jacob Harman, mulatto, 11 on 26 June last, son of Leah
Bound to; Frederick Conner, Sen.
Trade; farmer
Sureties; Andrew Brown, James Knox

F. 472
Apprentice; Stephen Harman, mulatto, 9 on 1 Sept. last, son of Leah
Bound to; Abner Conner
Trade; farmer
Sureties; Frederick Conner, Andrew Brown

F. 473
William Holland, Sen., & Nehemiah Holland to view estate of John Purnell, in care of William Holland, Sen., guardian; before W. Holland: report; 2/3 of 550 acres, part of 'Purnells Lot' & 'Brothers Love'

F. 474
F. 475
Benjamin Purnell & John Stevens to view estate of Isaac Houston, in care of Henry Bennett, guardian; before Mathias Davis: report; 950 acres; Henry Bennett's wife Prissy is sister to Isaac

F. 476
Jacob Rownd & William Handcock to view estate of Henry Jarman, in care of Benjamin Dennis, guardian; before John Dashiell: report; 8 acres; widow's dower

F. 477
William Holland, Jun., & Purnell Hill to view estate of George & Matilda Selby, in care of Polly Selby, guardian; before Saml. A. Harper: report; negro lad Tom, women Leah & Jinny; 500 acres called 'Johnsons Discovery'; widow's dower

F. 478
F. 479
Nixon Davis & Thomas Duncan to view estate of Charlotte Hammond, in care of Edward Hammond, Jun., guardian; before Thos. D. Purnell: report of real estate of Charlotte & Edward, her brother; plantation formerly property of William J. Houston, 130 acres, parts of 'Fair Meadow', 'Chance' &
(cont.)

'Discovery'; land formerly property of John Morris, 60 acres, parts of 'Highfield' & 'Bachelors Lott'; land bought of John Challie, 266 acres, parts of 'Purnells Security' & 'Serban'(?); land formerly property of John Rownd, 283 acres, parts of 'Johns Inheritance' & 'Bletinghurst'(?); 1/3 of negro man Lott, girl Nan

F. 480   Nixon Davis & Thomas Duncan to view estate of Edward Hammond, in care of Edward Hammond, Jun., guardian; [same as above];
F. 481   tract called 'Serban' above, listed as 'Shurban'

         John Holland & William Holland, Jun., to view estate of
F. 482   William S. Corbin, in care of William Corbin, Sen., guardian; before W. Holland: report; land where John Hutcheson now
F. 483   lives, 340 or 50 acres; 100 acres of woods bought of Robert Purnell; Mrs. Corbin's dower

William McGrigor & Edward Bridell to settle dispute between Stephen Purnell, exe. of Thomas Gray, Sen., & Samuel Gray, agent for Elizabeth Gray, widow of Thomas, concerning fruit & liquor produced on land laid off as dower for said Elizabeth whilse widow of Joseph Gray, her former husband, which fruit, together with other fruit growing on lands of Thomas Gray, being converted into brandy by said Stephen, Elizabeth's share became uncertain; Elizabeth awarded 80 on 120 gallons produced

         Zadok Sturgis, Thomas N. Williams & Joshua Fleming, Jun., Esqs., to settle dispute between Edward Hammond, Sen., & Thomas D. Purnell, exe. of Milby Purnell, concerning note against deceased, dated 21
F. 484   Apr., 1796; Edward allowed L.7/9/4 on note of L.70/9/4

         Littleton Davis, guardian to Mordecai Smith (of John, of
F. 485   Thos.), to sell bed, furniture & chest, left ward by his father; list; sold for $14.03; Thomas N. Williams, clerk for sale, swears to above sale before Josa. Fleming, Jun.

Apprentice; Samuel Tull, by consent of his parents
Bound to; James Tull (of James), house carpenter & joiner
Trade; house carpenter & joiner
Term; 3 years, 6 months
Signed by John Tull, carpenter [father?, couldn't write]
Before Edwd. Stevenson

F. 486   Apprentice; James Kersy, 8, child of the Poor House
         Bound to; Josiah Bowen
         Trade; farming
         Sureties; James Ward, William Rownd, Jun.
         By Trustees for the Poor; Samuel Handy, McKimmey Porter, George Hayward

         Apprentice; Haste Cathell, 10 on 29 Sept., 1812, by consent of his father Levi
         Bound to; Ebenezer Leonard
         Trade; tanner & currier of leather
F. 487   In presence of Benjamin Johnson, Isaac Hearn

F. 488
Apprentice; Joshua Dale Williams, 7 on 27 Sept. last, son of Eli
Bound to; William Covington, farmer
Trade; farming
Sureties; Isaac Franklin, Peter C. Evans
Before Thos. N. Williams, William Dale

F. 489
Apprentice; Joseph, negro, son of Sarah [couldn't write], formerly property of Henry White (of Stephen)
Bound to; Affradoze Johnson, farmer
Trade; farmer
By Isaac Hearn, Benjamin Johnson
In presence of J. Umsted, Elisha Parker, Jun.

F. 490
Apprentice; Sally Newton, 9 on 10 Oct. next, child of the Poor House
Bound to; James Dennis
Trade; domestic business, spinning, sewing, weaving & c. & c.
Sureties; James Ward, William Davis
By Trustees for the Poor; Samuel Handy, McKimmey Porter, George Hayward

Apprentice; Henry Mills, 14 on 19 Oct. last, by consent of his mother
Bound to; Joseph Stevenson, blacksmith
Trade; blacksmith
Sureties; Levi Henderson
Before Edwd. Stevenson, James Tilghman

F. 491 [writing changes]

Account of expenses of finishing crop of Wm. Rowley, deceased; money paid to Job Ballard, Jorge(?) Marshall, Hory(?) Jones, Jacob Williams, Abraham Jones, Joyce Williams, James Hancock, Thomas Collins, James H. Rowley; James H. Rowley & Thomas Collins, adms.

F. 492
Estate of Richard Rowley, deceased, to Arthur Rowley, adm.; mentions James H. Rowley; before Jesse Bennett; list of property destroyed

Isaac Hayman, exe. of Rachel Hayman, allowed $54.98 for list & for keeping young negroes, Ballard, Caleb & Titus(?)

George W. Purnell & Thomas M. Purnell, adms. of Zadok Purnell, Jun., to sell corn in additional inventory

F. 493 Polly Mitchell, adm. of Levin Mitchell, allowed 7% on estate

Littleton Robins, Joshua Prideaux & Zadok Purnell, adms. cwa of Col. Zadok Purnell, allowed $33 paid negro Peter for maintaining old negro Dinah

John Stevens, adm. of George Richardson, to sell negroes

Benjamin Aydelott & John Aydelott, exes. of William Aydelott, to sell stock of store goods

William Holland, Jun., & William Jones to view estate of George Selby, in care of John Selby (of Daniel), guardian

Arthur Rowley, adm. of Richard Rowley, allowed 8% on estate

Isaac Hayman, exe. of Rachel Hayman, allowed 7% on estate

Major Jones, exe. of Daniel Jones, allowed 8% on estate

James Bevans, adm. of Mills Bevans, allowed $20 for negro child Harry, now dead

James Bevans, adm. of Mills Bevans, allowed 8% on estate

F. 494 Special Court, 21 Apr., 1809, at request of Stephen Townsend & others; all Justices present

[rest of page blank]

F. 495 Tues., June 13, 1809   All Justices present

Apprentice; James Ballard, mulatto, 11 in Apr. last, son of Betty
Bound to; James Handcock
Trade; farmer
Sureties; Dennis Hudson, James H. Rowley

F. 496 Apprentice; James H. Harman, mulatto, 6, son of Polly
Bound to; Daniel Ruark
Trade; farmer
Sureties; James Knox, William Rownd

F. 497 Apprentice; Samuel H. Harman, mulatto, 7 last Christmas, son of Polly
Bound to; Daniel Ruark
Trade; farmer
Sureties; James Knox, William Rownd

F. 498 Joshua Duer, Robert J. H. Handy & Nehemiah Holland to lay off land devised by will of Bowden Robins, dated 10 Feb., 1809 & probated 3 Mar., 1809, to his brother, Daniel Gore Robins, 3/4 of 'Jingoteage' or 'Gingoteague', which was devised by his father Daniel Robins' will to his sons Nehemiah Stockley Robins & Daniel
F. 499 Gore Robins; sworn before Josa. Fleming, Jun.; gives lay of land; mentions land of Solomon Tull; 558 acres

Apprentice; Joshua Nichols, by consent of his parents
Bound to; Peter Evans, shoe & boot maker
Trade; shoe & boot maker
F. 500 Term; 3 years
Signed by Belitha Nicholson
Wit.; Francis Rosse, Kenl. Smack

F. 501
Apprentice; Charlotte Anderson, 11 on 1 Jan. last, child of the Poor House
Bound to; James Gunby
Trade; domestic business; sewing, spinning & weaving
Sureties; Francis Rosse, James Ward
By Trustees for the Poor; Samuel Handy, McKimmey Porter, George Hayward

F. 502
Apprentice; Thomas Carey, 15 on 2 Feb. last, by consent of his mother
Bound to; Solomon Davis, blacksmith
Trade; blacksmith
Sureties; William Lister, George W. Purnell
Before Thos. N. Williams, Wm. McGrigor

F. 503 [blank]

F. 504 Tues., Aug. 8, 1809 All Justices present

Orphan; Polly Melson (of Joseph)
Guardian; Benjamin Melson
Sureties; Elijah Melson, Wilson Maddux

F. 505
Orphan; Benjamin Melson (of Joseph)
Guardian; Benjamin Melson
Sureties; Elijah Melson, Wilson Maddox

Orphan; Samuel Williams Melson (of Joseph)
Guardian; Elijah Melson
Sureties; Benjamin Melson, Wilson Maddox

F. 506
Orphan; Benjamin Aydelott (of William)
Guardian; John Aydelott
Sureties; James Henry Rowley, James Dickeson

F. 507
Orphan; William Aydelott (of William)
Guardian; John Aydelott
Sureties; James Henry Rowley, James Dickeson

Orphan; Betsey Bradshaw (of Morgan)
Guardian; Jonathan Melvin, Sen.
Sureties; James Dickeson, Jonathan Melvin, Jun.

F. 508
Orphan; Theodore Gray (of Jesse)
Guardian; Samuel Gray
Sureties; George Davis [couldn't write], Zeno Powell

Orphan; George Sampson (of Richard)
Guardian; Mary Sampson
Sureties; Arthur Tracy, Elijah Read

F. 509
Orphan; Margaret Dale (of Annanias)
Guardian; Esther Dale [couldn't write]
Sureties; David Gray, Samuel Gray

Orphan; Elizabeth Dale (of Annanias)
Guardian; Esther Dale
Sureties; David Gray, Samuel Gray

F. 510
Orphan; Martha Dale (of Annanias)
Guardian; Esther Dale
Sureties; David Gray, Samuel Gray

Orphan; Molly Dale (of Annanias)
Guardian; Esther Dale
Sureties; David Gray, Samuel Gray

F. 511   Orphan; Elijah Davis (of Henry)
Guardian; Turner Davis
Sureties; Elijah Reed, Major Tarr

Orphan; Levin Jones (of John)
Guardian; Annanias Jones [signed Anias]
F. 512   Sureties; Elijah Read, Joseph Jones

William McGregor & Isaac Franklin, Esqs., to view estate of Mary
Mitchell, in care of Stuart Williamson, guardian; before Thos. N.
Williams: report; land where Josiah Mitchell formerly lived,
F. 513   466 acres; land where Mrs. Elizabeth Smack formerly lived;
150 acres of cypress swamp; land where Zedekiah Bradford
lives in Queponco called 'Golden Valey', 290 acres; negroes
F. 514   Plem 29, Teb(?) 25, Charles 22, Rachel 29, Nancy 30, Minta
11, John 10, Isaac (runaway), George 65, Sarah 55, Hagar 76,
Stephen 8, Caleb 7, Tony 3, Isaac 1 1/2, Sue 6, Comfort 5, Hetty 1
1/2, child of Rachel 4 months

Edward Henry & William McGrigor, Esqs., to view estate of Molly O.
Purnell (of John, W. N.), in care of Daniel Tingle, guardian;
F. 515   before James Law: report; 1/4 of plantation where John
Purnell formerly lived, exclusive of Mrs. Ranken's dower;
land which Mrs. Mitchell, widow of Robert, held after death
F. 516   of her son John, Mrs. Ranken having no dower; grave yard;
negroes Stephen 23, Mingore 24

Edward Henry & William McGrigor, Esqs., to view estate of
F. 517   Zadok Purnell (of John, W. N.), in care of Daniel Tingle,
guardian; [same as above]; widow of Robert Mitchell was
F. 518   mother of John Purnell; negroes Titus 36, Pool 47

Edward Henry & William McGrigor, Esqs., to view estate of Thomas
Purnell (of John, W. N.), in care of Thomas N. Williams,
F. 519   guardian; [same as above]; negroes Leven 32, Millby 98,
Tab 5

F. 520   Abisha Davis & Lemuel Showell to view estate of Mordicai
Smith, in care of Littleton Davis, guardian; before William
McGrigor: report; 1/2 of land belongs to Theodore Gray (of
F. 521   Jesse); two plantations; one at landing where Levin
(cont.)

F. 522   Dirickson lives, one on county road where James Warters lives; houses where Levin Dirickson lives built by Capt. Jesse Gray, deceased, except house where Jesse Mumford lives

F. 523   Lemuel Showell & Abisha Davis, Esqs., to view estate of Theodore Gray, in care of Samuel Gray, guardian; report; [same as above]; has James Waters

F. 524   Edward Henry & William McGrigor, Esqs., to view estate of Sally Purnell (of John, W. N.), in care of Thomas N.
F. 525   Williams, guardian; before James law: report; land where John Purnell formerly lived, exclusive of Mrs. Rankin's right of dower; land which widow of Robert Mitchell held on death of her son John, Mrs. Rankin having no dower; grave yard; negroes Milby 17, Jane 20 & her child

F. 526   Orphan; Edward Hammond (of Charles)
Guardian; Handy Jones
Sureties; John Richards, Edward Hammond, Sen.

Orphan; Charlotte Hammond (of Charles)
Guardian; Handy Jones
F. 527   Sureties; John Richards, Edward Hammond.

Apprentice; Esther Roberts, 12, daughter of Betty
Bound to; Stephen Chaille
Trade; house work; spin & weave
Sureties; Peter Waters, James Jones

F. 528   Apprentice; Elijah Davis (of Henry), 16 on 14 Oct. next
Bound to; Major Tarr
Trade; boot & shoe maker
Sureties; Peter Evans, William Rownd

F. 529   Apprentice; Thomas Davis (of Thomas), 14 on 29 Dec. next
Bound to; Robert Smith & James Givan, trading under the name of Smith & Givan
Trade; chaise maker
Sureties; John Stevens, James Ward

F. 530   Apprentice; George Hutt (of Levin), mulatto, 13 last June
Bound to; Purnell Taylor
Trade; farmer
Sureties; Edward Scarborough, John Ayres

Apprentice; Amey Isaacs, free black, illegitimate, 7 last May
F. 531   Bound to; Esau Pilchard
Trade; common business of house wifry; spinning, weaving & sewing
Before James Tilghman, Edwd. Stevenson

	Apprentice; Henry Dennis, 17 on 15 Nov. next, by consent of his father Valentine
	Bound to; James Ward, Snow Hill
	Trade; boot & shoe maker
F. 532	In presence of Litt. Quinton, Littleton Sturgis

John Postly, Isaac Ayres & Laben Hill to settle dispute between Henry Hosier & Betty, his wife, Benjamin W. Lake & Anne, his wife, Moses Quillen, Elizabeth Quillen & Charlotte Quillen, claimants, & Priscilla Massey & Laban Taylor, adms. of Samuel Quillen, concerning rent on real estate; John Postly, being sick, Wm. Covington to help; Priscilla & Laban to pay claimants $140

F. 533-5 [blank]

F. 536   Tues., Oct. 10, 1809   All Justices present

Orphan; George Noble Fooks
Guardian; Joshua Johnson
Sureties; Eben Christopher, Mathias Davis

	Orphan; Jacob Wheeler (of Zadok)
F. 537	Guardian; Patty Wheeler [couldn't write]
	Sureties; James Dickeson, Shedrach Redden [also Reden]

Orphan; Margaret Beauchamp Wheeler (of Zadok, Sen.)
Guardian; Patty Wheeler
Sureties; James Dickeson, Shadrach Redden

F. 538	Orphan; Henry Wheeler (of Zadok)
	Guardian; Patty Wheeler
	Sureties; James Dickeson, Shadrack Redden

	Orphan; Major Wheeler (of Zadok)
	Guardian; Patty Wheeler
F. 539	Sureties; James Dickeson, Shadrack Redden

Orphan; Job Wheeler (of Zadok)
Guardian; Patty Wheeler
Sureties; James Dickeson, Shadrach Redden

	Orphan; Mary Wheeler (of Zadok)
F. 540	Guardian; Patty Wheeler
	Sureties; James Dickeson, Shadrach Redden

Orphan; James Lewis (of James)
Guardian; James Lewis, Sen. [couldn't write]
Sureties; Isaac Lewis [couldn't write], John Dennis (of Johnson)

F. 541	Orphan; Stephen Townsend
	Guardian; Stephen Townsend, father
	Sureties; James Redden, Fleet Chelton [signed Sleetees Shelton]

'194'

```
         Orphan; James Townsend Melvin
         Guardian; William Melvin, father
F. 542   Sureties; James Burnett, John Melvin
```

Orphan; Hugh M. Stevenson (of Jonathan)
Guardian; Lydia Henderson [couldn't write]
Sureties; John Givan, Robert Givan, Sen.

```
         Orphan; John Henderson (of Curtis)
F. 543   Guardian; John Laws, Jun.(?)
         Sureties; Shipherd Johnson, Milby Adkins
```

Orphan; Elsea Davis (of Henry)
Guardian; Turner Davis
Sureties; Elijah Read, Sampson [also Samson] Davis

```
F. 544   Orphan; Joshua Davis (of Henry)
         Guardian; Turner Davis
         Sureties; Elijah Reed, Sampson Davis
```

```
         Orphan; Martha Davis (of Henry)
         Guardian; Turner Davis
F. 545   Sureties; Elijah Reed, Sampson Davis
```

Orphan; Molly Davis (of Henry)
Guardian; Turner Davis
Sureties; Elijah Reed, Samson Davis

```
         Orphan; Tressey Davis (of Henry)
F. 546   Guardian; Turner Davis
         Sureties; Elijah Reed, Samson Davis
```

Orphan; William J. Stevenson (of John)
Guardian; Peter C. Evans
Sureties; Levin Dirickson, Thomas Selby

```
         Thomas Hargis & Edward Stevenson, Esqs., to view estate of
F. 547   Benjamin Aydelott, in care of John Aydelott, guardian; before
F. 548   James Tilghman: report; negro woman Philess & child; 200
         acres
```

```
         Samuel R. Smith & John Stevens to view estate of Molly
F. 549   Corbin, in care of William Corbin, guardian; before J.
         Hubbell: report; lott in Snow Hill Town, former taylor's shop
```

```
William McGrigor & Asher Burrows [also Burroughs] to view estate of
         Elizabeth, Margaret, Molly & Martha Dale, in care of Esther
F. 550   Dale, guardian; before Abishai Davis: report; land where
         Esther Dale lives, exclusive of Esther's dower; 200 acres
```

```
F. 551   Joshua Prideaux & William McGrigor, Esqs., to view estate of
         Edward Stevenson, in care of Isaac Collins, guardian; before
         Lemuel Showell: report; land where Isaac Collins lives near
                                  (cont.)
```

F. 552   Berlin, lotts #2 & 6; mentions his mother Mrs. Collins' thirds; land in Queponco, 85 acres, lott #3

[writing changes]

F. 553
Apprentice; Levi Jones (of James), 18 on 7 Mar. next
Bound to; Levi Sturgis
Trade; farmer
Sureties; James Sturgis, John Sturgis

F. 554
Apprentice; Giles Jones (of Giles), 13 on 20 Nov. of the present month
Bound to; Thomas Duncan
Trade; farmer
Sureties; Levi Duncan, John Dashiell, Jun.

F. 555
Apprentice; George Harmon, mulatto, 5 on 20 Apr. last, son of Betsy [also Betty]
Bound to; John Townsend (J. T.)
Trade; common labour
Sureties; Robert J. H. Handy, John C. Bacon

F. 556

F. 557
Apprentice; Eli Roberts, mulatto, 13 next Christmas, son of Betty
Bound to; William Veasy
Trade; farmer
Sureties; Wrixham Payne, Daniel Mason

F. 558
Apprentice; Moses Roberts, mulatto, 8 in May last, son of Esther
Bound to; Wrixham Payne
Trade; farmer
Sureties; William Veasy, Daniel Mason

F. 559

F. 560
Apprentice; Thomas Anderson, 10, a child of the Poor House, son of Leah
Bound to; Abel Harmon, Sen. [couldn't write]
Trade; farming
Sureties; John Ayres, Levi Merrill
By Trustees for the Poor; Saml. Handy, George Hayward, Ephm. K. Wilson

F. 561
Apprentice; Stephen Taylor, 15 on 14 Aug., by consent of his father Jeremiah
Bound to; John Bell
Trade; shoe & boot maker
In presence of Francis Rosse

F. 562
Apprentice; David Bowen, 11 on 26 Aug. next, by consent of his father George [couldn't write]
Bound to; William Bowen
Trade; farmer
In presence of Francis Rosse

F. 563   Thomas Hargis & Edward Stevenson, Esqs., to view estate of
         William Aydelott, in care of John Aydelott, guardian; before
F. 564   James Tilghman: report; negro woman Hannah; 200 acres

BOOK 12, MH15, 1809 - 1811

MICROFILM: WK 740-741-2

MSA No.:   CM 1123-12

Worcester County Orphans Court Proceedings, MH-15, 1809 - 1811

F. 1   Tues, Oct. 10, 1809(cont.)   Littleton Robins, Zadok Sturgis,
                                      John Bishop present

        Apprentice; John F. Taylor, 6 on 10 Apr. last, child of the
F. 2   Poor House
        Bound to; Asa Bowen
        Trade; farming
        Sureties; William Bowen, Josiah Bowen
        By Trustees for the Poor; Samuel Handy, Charles Bennett,
        McKimmey Porter

        Apprentice; Thurrowgood [also Thouroughgood] Savage
        Lamberson, 15, by consent of his mother
F. 3   Bound to; William McHenry, farmer
        Trade; farming or husbandry
        Surety; Benjamin Blades
F. 4   Before James Tilghman, Edwd. Stevenson

Thomas Hargis & Edward Stevenson to distribute specifics from estate
of William Aydelott, in hands of Benjamin & John Aydelott, according
        to will; before Benj. Aydelott;
F. 5-7 1) to Mary Aydelott; negro girl Leah, boy Jim(?); list
        2) to John Aydelott; boy Peter, woman Esther, girl Betsy;
        list
F. 8   3) to Benj. Aydelott; women Phylliss & Patience, child
F. 9   Preston, man Robbin; list
F. 10-11 4) to William Aydelott; woman Hannah, boy Henry; list
F. 12   Above distribution ratified

Rouse Harrison & [blank], his wife, guardian to Mitchell Rodgers, to
put new sill under side of dwelling, & sash & glass in windows

William R. Merrill, guardian to Levi Merrell, to settle a well on
property in New Town

F. 13   John Dashiell & Thomas Fookes to view estate of George Noble
        Fookes, in care of Joshua Johnson, guardian

Annanias Powell & Littleton Davis vs. Schoolfield Bradford &
Elizabeth, his wife, & John Davis, adm. of Benjamin Davis; citation
for defendants to shew objections to claims against estate

James H. Rowley, adm. of Coventon Townsend, to sell personal estate

John Laws, exe. of Curtis Henderson, to sell personal estate (except
legacies to his children John & Sally, the wearing apparel, & negroes
Harry & Sarah)

F. 14   Thomas N. Williams & William McGrigor to view property of
        Mary Bell, in care of Edward Briddle & Anne, his wife,
guardians

James Victor, adm. of Richard Ward, allowed 10% on estate

James Victor, adm. of Richard Ward, to retain $53.01 to meet cost of sundry suits, & after deducting claims of preference, Register to strike distribution among creditors of inferior grade

Order passed at Oct. term, 1802, allowing Ephraim K. Wilson, exe. of Col. Levin Handy, interest from debts due & sale of property, rescinded

F. 15   Jonathan(?) & Zeno Powell, exes. of Thomas Powell, allowed value of bed, which was recovered by Eb.(?) Truitt

Joshua Townsend, adm. of Luke Townsend, allowed 10% on estate

New warrant for Nixon Davis & Selby Parker to appraise property of Col. James Houston

John Benson & Esau Boston to view estate of Henry, Major, Job, Jacob, Margaret B. & Mary Wheeler, in care of Patty Wheeler, guardian

John Holland & William Holland to view estate of Dixon Q. & Sally H. Henderson, in care of Josiah Long, guardian

Levin Hill, guardian to Selby Johnson, states that negro James is subject to fits; asks to be allowed for his maintenance

F. 16   Joseph Miller & James Jarman to view property of James Lewis, in care of James Lewis, Sen., guardian

John Tull & Mitchell Gray to distribute negroes from estate of Johnson Gray, in hands of Abisha Davis & [blank], his wife, admx.

Jesse Bennett & Isaac Cottingham to view property of Hugh M. Stevenson, in care of Lydia Henderson, guardian

Thomas D. Purnell & Selby Parker to view property of John Henderson, in care of John Laws, guardian

Peter C. Evans, adm. of John Stevenson, to sell personal estate (except negroes, corn & wearing apparel)

F. 17   New warrant to James Tilghman & John Stevenson to appraise property of James Townsend

Nixon Davis & Jacob Dale to view property of Elsea, Joshua, Martha, Molly & Trissey Davis, in care of Turner Davis, guardian

Nixon Davis & Jacob Dale to view property of Elijah Davis, in care of Turner Davis, guardian

Littleton Davis, exe. of Matthias Davis, allowed 7 1/2% on estate

John Benson & James Tilghman to distribute negroes from estate of Zadok Wheeler, in hands of Patty Wheeler & James Dickeson, exes.

Rowland E. Bevans, guardian to James & Nancy Selby, to make repairs on property; list

F. 18　　John Aydelott, guardian to William Aydelott, to ditch land & clear 15 acres

John Aydelott, guardian to Benjamin Aydelott, to settle a draw well of good cypress hollows & build corn crib

New warrant to Benjamin Aydelott & McKimmey Porter to appraise property of Maj. William Holland

Eben Christopher, adm. dbn of David Porter, to sell negro Caleb

F. 19　　John Laws, exe. of Curtis Henderson, & Lydia Henderson, guardian to Hugh M. Stevenson, to sell negro Harry, 2/3 of whom belongs to ward & 1/3 to estate

F. 20　　Special Court, Nov. 24, 1809, at instance of John Holstone; John Bishop, Zadok Sturgis present

John Holstone, adm. of Nancy Long, to sell personal estate

F. 21　　Special Court, Dec. 6, 1809, at instance of Jacob Teague; all Justices present

Jacob Teague, adm. of John Ayres, to sell personal estate, including equity of redemption of certain negroes mortgaged to Jacob Teague & Josiah Bratten

F. 22　　Tues., Dec. 12, 1809　　All Justices present

　　　　　Orphan; William Isaac Stevenson (of John)
　　　　　Guardian; Peter C. Evans
F. 23　　Sureties; Levin Dirickson, Thomas Selby

Apprentice; William Tarr (of Elijah), 18 on 9 Jan. next
Bound to; John Bell
Trade; boot & shoe maker
Sureties; James Ward, William Round

F. 24　　Apprentice; Jesse Long (of William), 17 on 8 Jan. next
　　　　　Bound to; James Ward
　　　　　Trade; boot & shoe maker
F. 25　　Sureties; William Rounds, John Bell

F. 26　　Apprenticeship of John H. Bishop (of Charles) to Robert Truitt, to learn art of mariner, rescinded

'201'

	Apprentice; John H. Bishop (of Charles), 15 on 30 July last Bound to; Daniel Patrick Trade; boot & shoe maker
F. 27	Sureties; John Bishop (of Wm.), Thomas Jones
F. 28 F. 29	John Dashiell, Esq., & Thomas Fookes, Sen., to view estate of George Noble Fookes, in care of Joshua Johnson, guardian; before Isaac Hearn: report; 336 acres called 'Driskells Industry' & 'Sarahs Choice'
F. 30-1 F. 32	William McGriger & Thomas N. Williams, Esqs., to view estate of Mary Bell, in care of Edward Briddle & Anne, his wife, guardians: report; Mrs. Briddle's dower; 82 acres in woods
F. 33	Joseph Miller & James Jarman to view estate of James Lewis, in care of James Lewis, Sen., guardian; before Mathias Davis: report; 30 acres
F. 34 F. 35-36	Nixon Davis & Jacob Dale to view estate of Elijah, Elsea, Joshua, Martha, Molly & Tressey Davis, in care of Turner Davis, guardian: report; 120 acres; part of 'St. Martins', 'Desert', 'John Lott' & 'Deers(?) Choice'
F. 37 F. 38	Mitchell Gray & John Tull to distribute negroes from estate of Johnson Gray, in hands of Abisha Davis & Martha, his wife, admx.; before William McGrigor: inventory; Jesse 34, Ned 22, Capril 19, Luke 16, Daniel 13, Linty(?) 12, Usina(?) 10, Clary 10, Sarah 9 & 3 months, Nancy 7 & 4 months; men Bob 55 & Allen 14, afflicted; Rose 49 & Esther 69, sickly;
	1) to Abisha Davis & Martha, his wife; Jesse, Luke, Clary, Rose
F. 39	2) to James Gray; Linty(?) 12, Allen 3) to Johnson Gray; Capril 4) to William Gray, deceased; Ned, Esther
	5) to Tubman Gray; Sarah, Nancy 6) to Thomas S. Gray; Us_?_ 10, Bob 7) to Martha Gray; Daniel
F. 40	Apprentice; William Thorns [Thomas?], 3 on 1 Apr., 1809 Bound to; William Gordy Trade; farming Before Isaac Hearn, Nathan Gordy
F. 41 F. 42	Apprentice; Esme Timmons, 16 on 11 Aug. next, son of Thomas [couldn't write] Bound to William K. Hopkins Trade; blacksmith Surety; Elijah Reed In presence of Nixon Davis, Jacob Dale
	Apprentice; Philip Adams, 14 on 20 Jan. next, by consent of his mother Bound to; Levin Mills, hatter

(cont.)

'202'

F. 43   Trade; hatter
        Surety; Thomas Brittingham
        Before Edwd. Stevenson, James Tilghman

F. 44   Apprentice; Tully Sneed [also Snead], 14 on 18 Dec., 1809, by
        consent of his mother
        Bound to; Thomas Brittingham, shoe maker
        Trade; shoe & boot maker
        Surety; Levin Mills
        Before Edwd. Stevenson, James Tilghman

F. 45   Apprentice; Kellam Anderson, child of the Poor House
        Bound to; John Allen, Jun.
        Term; till 21, on 12 Dec., 1823
        Trade; farming
        Sureties; Jesse Sturgis, Purnell Hill
F. 46   By Trustees for the Poor; McKimmey Porter, Charles Bennett,
        Geo. Hayward

        Apprentice; Obed Gault, 15 on 15 Mar. next, by consent of his
        mother
        Bound to; Robert Kerby, shoe & boot maker
        Trade; shoe & boot maker
F. 47   Surety; Levin Derickson
        Before Wm. McGrigor, Abishai Davis

William Parker(?), adm. cwa of Col. James Houston, to sell negroes &
property in additional inventory

F. 48   Thomas Marshall & [blank], collectors of Maj. William
        Holland, to sell whole property, farming utensils & team

Joshua Johnson, exe. of John Fookes, to sell crop

William Melvin & [blank], exes. of James Townsend, to sell crop not
legacied

F. 49   Patty Wheeler & James Dickeson, exes. of Zadok Wheeler, to
        sell crop

William Handy, collector of Daniel Robins, to deliver up specifics to
Daniel G. Robins, adm. dbn.

Francis Rosse, exe. of Elizabeth Rosse, to sell personal estate
(except negroes Bob & Rhoda, & a gold watch

New warrant for George Hayward & Jacob Teague to appraise property of
Col. John Gunby

        Thomas Dukes, adm. of John Dukes, to sell personal estate
F. 50   (except wearing apparel)

Thomas Selby, exe. of Elizabeth Selby, to sell personal estate (except
negroes & wearing apparel)

Hulda Ball, adm. of John Ball, to sell personal estate

William Sturgis, adm. of Stephen W. Thorns [Thomas?], to sell personal estate

F. 51   Jacob White & William McGrigor to view property of William I. Stevenson, in care of Peter C. Evans, guardian

New warrant to William McGrigor & Jacob White to appraise property of John Stevenson

Betsy Rankin, adm. of John Rankin, to sell fodder

John Stevenson, acting exe. of Whittington Jones, to sell property as directed by will

Anthony Bacon & George S. Gunby, exes. of Col. John Gunby, to sell property in additional inventory (except negroes)

F. 52   Anthony Bacon & Matthew Hopkins to settle dispute between Robert J. H. Handy & William Corbin, surviving exe. of Peter S. Corbin

Nehemiah Burbage & Mary Burbage, adms. of Edward Burbage, allowed for oats, corn & fodder fed to stock, & flax & wool used for clothing

F. 53   Special Court, Jan. 26, 1810, at instance of William Jones; all Justices present

Apprentice; Elsea Davis (of Henry), 12 last July
Bound to; Edward Dymock, Jun.
Trade; tailor
Sureties; Barzilla Parker, Littleton Sturgis

F. 54   William Jones, exe. of Eli Bowen, & testamentary guardian to Selby Bowen, to sell personal estate (except negro Stephen)

F. 55   Littleton Robins, Sen., John Bishop & Zadok Sturgis appointed Justices

Edw. Lloyd   W. Kilty, Chanc.

Wit.; The Honorable William Kilty, Esq., Chancellor

Tues., Feb. 13, 1810   All Justices present

Levin Diricken, Esq., Shrff.

F. 56   Orphan; Patty [also Patsey] Taylor (of Thomas)
        Guardian; Samuel Tarr
        Sureties; Stephen Jones, John Aydelott (of Jas.)

F. 57   Orphan; Leah Jones (of John)
             Guardian; William Hancock
             Sureties; Daniel Handcock, William Parker

             Orphan; Charlotte Marchment (of Riley)
             Guardian; George Hayward
F. 58   Sureties; Thomas R. Handy, James Knox

Orphan; Stephen Marchment (of Riley)
Guardian; George Hayward
Sureties; Thomas R. Handy, James Knox

F. 59   Apprentice; Mandey [also Manday] America, mulatto, 13, son of
             Leah
             Bound to; William Selby
             Trade; farmer
             Sureties; John Selby, Parker Selby

F. 60   Apprentice; John Wright (of John), mulatto, 18 on 23 Sept.
             last
             Bound to; John Aydelott (of James)
             Trade; farmer
             Sureties; William Jones, Samuel Tarr

F. 61   Apprentice; Joshua Read (of William), 18
             Bound to; Kendal S. Crapper
             Trade; farmer
F. 62   Sureties; James Givan(?), William P.(?) Crapper

             Apprentice; Josiah Hopkins (of Jacob), 11
             Bound to; Kendal S. Crapper
F. 63   Trade; farmer
             Sureties; Joseph J. Gilliss, William P. Crapper

F. 64   Apprentice; Edmund Hopkins (of Jacob), 13
             Bound to; William P. Crapper
             Trade; house carpenter
             Sureties; Barzilla Parker, Kendal S. Crapper

F. 65   Apprentice; John Richardson (of Robert M.), 15 on 4 Nov. last
             Bound to; Samuel R. Smith
             Trade; bookkeeping by single entry
             Sureties; Stuart Williamson, Thomas Hall

F. 66   John Holland & William Holland to view estate of Dixon Q.
F. 67   Henderson, in care of Josiah Long, guardian; before J.
F. 68   Hubbell & Saml. A. Harper: report (on estates of Dixon Q. &
             Sally Henderson); 1/2 of 240 acres called 'Parramores
Double(?) Purchase'

             John Holland & William Holland to view estate of Sally H.
F. 69   Henderson, in care of Josiah Long, guardian; [same as above]

'205'

F. 70	Thomas D. Purnell, Esq., & Selby Parker to view estate of
F. 71	John Henderson, in care of John Laws, guardian; before
F. 72	Mathias Davis: report; widow's dower; 300 acres

Apprentice; George Blake, 12, son of Leah [couldn't write]
Bound to; Stephen Jones, farmer
F. 73 Trade; farming
F. 74 In presence of Benjamin Bishop, Mathias Davis

Apprentice; Samuel Jones Merrill, 18 on 9 Aug. next, son of George, of Accomac Co., VA
Bound to; William Brown, carpenter
Trade; house carpenter & joiner
F. 75 In presents of Benj. Aydelott

Apprentice; Isaac Bowen, 17 on 23 Mar. next, by consent of his mother
Bound to; Riley [also Ryla] Bowen
F. 76 Trade; different branches of farming
Before Kendal S. Crapper, Thos. D. Purnell

Apprentice; Peter, negro, 11(?) on 1 May next, son of Comfort [couldn't write]
Bound to; Archibald [also Archable] Smith
Trade; farmer
F. 77 In presents of Isaac Hearn, Nathan Gordy

Apprentice; William Christopher, 15 on 20 Oct. next, by consent of his father George, of Somerset Co.
Bound to; Levin Hitch
Trade; boot & shoe maker
F. 78 In presents of Jesse Townsend, John Moore

Apprentice; James Christopher (of James)
Bound to; Levin Smith [couldn't write]
F. 79 Signed by Lowden(?) Christopher [couldn't write]
Before Isaac Hearn, Nathan Gordy

Stephen Purnell, exe. of Thomas Gray, exhibits list of expenses; mentions Nevitt(?) Taylor

F. 80 Mary Newton, adm. of Job Newton, to sell personal estate

Jonathan S. Parsons & Levin Parsons, exes. of Jonathan Parsons, allowed 6% on estate

George Parsons & Elijah Parsons, exes. of George Parsons, Sen., allowed 8% on estate

F. 81 James B. Robins, adm. of Littleton Robins, Jun., to sell personal estate (except negroes & wearing apparel)

Kendal Crapper, guardian to James Dryden, to rent real estate

Stuart Williamson, guardian to Mary Mitchell, to account for rent on land & negroes

Negro Hannah, belonging to representatives of Charles Bishop (of William), has had two children, Levin & Hulda, now in possession of George Truitt & Sarah, his wife, guardians to William & John H. Bishop, orphans of said Charles; 1/3 belongs to guardians, 2/3 to orphans; negroes to be sold

Joseph Stevenson, adm. of Zepheniah Davis, to sell personal estate

F. 82   Handy Jones, adm. dbn of Charles Hammond, to advertise in a paper at Easton for creditors to exhibit claims

Nancy Hammond, adm. of Edward Hammond, Jun., to advertise in a paper at Easton for creditors to exhibit claims

Thomas Hall & Leonard Johnson, adms. dbn of Attalanta Wright, allowed 10% on estate

James B. Robins, adm. of Littleton Robins, Jun., to sell negroes Nance & Esther

Henry Adams, surviving adm. of William F. Adams, allowed 8% on estate

F. 83   Adam Moore, guardian to William Smith, charged with interest on $53.97

William Dailey, guardian to Hetty Smith, charged with interest on $53.97

James H. Rowley, guardian to Henry Rowley, allowed for schooling

Register to state account for Turbot Wright, late exe. of Attalanta Wright, charging him with $154.65 paid John Bishop on deceased's note, dated 8 Aug., 1804

Thomas Fookes, adm. of John Owens, allowed $10.08 for gathering corn

Received 20 Dec., 1809, of Stephen Allen & Leah, his wife, admx. of Benjamin Aydelott (of Wm.), $25.37, my share of my father's estate

John Aydelott   Bety Aydelott

F. 84   Received 20 Dec., 1809, of Stephen Allen & Leah, his wife, admx. of Benjamin Aydelott (of Wm.), $25.37, my wife Polly's share of her father's estate

John Aydelott   Samuel Tarr

F. 85   Special Court, Apr. 2, 1810, at instance of Mary Sampson, exe. of Richard Sampson; all Justices present

Ephraim K. Wilson & William Whittington, Esqs., to adjust accounts between Richard Sampson (Mary Sampson, exe.) & James Givan, surviving partner of Sampson & Givan; account

F. 86   Wm. Whittington & E. K. Wilson award $3528.51 from James Givan to Mary Sampson, exe. of Richard Sampson

Mary Sampson, exe. of Richard Sampson, to sell that part of estate belonging to firm of Sampson & Givan

F. 87   Joshua Johnson, exe. of John Fookes, exhibits list of expenses; list; mentions Betty Willis

F. 88   Henry Bennett, guardian to Isaac Houston, to receive his estate from William Parker, adm. of Col. James Houston

Jesse Bennett, one person appointed to view estate of Hugh M. Stevenson, in care of Lydia Henderson, guardian, is too indisposed to act; Josiah Hubbell & Isaac Cottingham to view property

F. 89   Tues., Apr. 10, 1810   All Justices present

Orphan; Elisa White (of Nathaniel)
Guardian; Seth Whaley
Sureties; Isaac Ayres, John Bratten

F. 90   Orphan; Richard Sampson (of Richard)
        Guardian; James Givan
        Sureties; Zadok Sturgis, William Quinton

F. 91   Orphan; Julianna Ridgeway(?) Sampson (of Richard)
        Guardian; James Givan
        Sureties; Zadok Sturgis, William Quinton

        Orphan; Ara Spence (of George)
        Guardian; Lemuel P. Spence
F. 92   Sureties; Thomas R. P. Spence, John S. Spence

Orphan; James Houston (of James)
Guardian; Gertrude Houston
Sureties; Thomas N. Williams, Robert Nairne

F. 93   Orphan; George Furnis (of Littleton)
        Guardian; Amey Furnis [couldn't write]
        Sureties; James Tilghman, Michael Murray

        Orphan; Delia Furnis (of Littleton)
F. 94   Guardian; Amey Furnis
        Sureties; James Tilghman, Michael Murray

        Orphan; Isaac Furnis (of Littleton)
        Guardian; Amey Furnis
F. 95   Sureties; James Tilghman, Michael Murray

Orphan; Thomas Porter (of David)
Guardian; Levin Hitch
Sureties; Benjamin Johnson, Jun., James Powell

F. 96   Orphan; George Harrison (of John)
        Guardian; Levin Dirickson
        Sureties; William Bell, Littleton Davis

F. 97   Orphan; Joseph Harrison (of John)
        Guardian; Levin Dirickson
        Sureties; William Bell, Littleton Davis

F. 98   Apprentice; Riley Truitt (of William), 16
        Bound to; Seth Whaley
        Trade; farmer
        Sureties; John Bratten, Isaac Ayres

F. 99   Apprentice; Patey Truitt (of William), 18 on 1 Jan. last
        Bound to; Lemuel Timmons
        Trade; farmer
        Sureties; Er(?) Truitt, John Bratten

F. 100 Apprentice; John, negro, son of Lydia (who was manumitted by
        William Lane)
        Bound to; Levi Ellis
        Trade; farmer
F. 101 Sureties; James Davis, John Stevenson

F. 102 Apprentice; William Ward (of Richard), 17 on 30 Mar. last
        Bound to; John Blair
        Trade; house carpenter
        Sureties; John S. Martin, James Givan

F. 103 Apprentice; Levin Heath, mulatto, 13 last Christmas, son of
        Sally Coston
        Bound to; Abel Coston
        Trade; farmer
        Sureties; McKimmey Porter, Handy Jones

F. 104 Apprentice; John Roach, mulatto, 17 next June, son of
        Hager(?) Coston
        Bound to; Shadrach Isaacs
        Trade; common labour
        Sureties; James Bevans, Eliakim Johnson

F. 105 Apprentice; Joshua Ishmael, 10 last Mar., son of Sophia
        Ishmael (late slave of Ezekiel Coston)
        Bound to; John Coston
        Trade; farmer
        Sureties; Benjamin Gunby, Micajah Ayres

F. 106 Apprentice; Samuel Ishmael, 4 last Aug., son of Sophia Ishmael
        (late slave of Ezekiel Coston)
                              (cont.)

'209'

F. 107	Bound to; John Coston Trade; farmer Sureties; Benjamin Gunby, Micajah Ayres
F. 108	Apprentice; Harriot Ishmael, 6 last Mar., daughter of Sophia Ismael (late slave of Ezekiel Coston) Bound to; John Coston Trade; spin & weave, common housework Sureties; Benjamin Gunby, Micajah Ayres
F. 109	Apprentice; James Jones (of Giles), 15 on 27 Apr. last Bound to; Elisha Jones Trade; farmer Sureties; Edward Stevenson, Giles Jones
F. 110	Apprentice; Samuel Mason, 12 on 12 Apr., 1810 Bound to; James Bevans Trade; coasting
F. 111	Sureties; Luke Townsend, Isaac Brittingham

F. 112 Josiah Hubbell & Isaac Cottingham to view estate of Hugh M.
F. 113 Stevenson, in care of Lydia Henderson, guardian; before James Givan: report; 120 acres

F. 114 Samuel McMaster & Joseph Houston to view estate of William
F. 115 Jones, in care of Betsy Jones, guardian; before William Schoolfield: report; one tract 63 acres; another 133 acres; widow's dower

F. 116 Samuel McMaster & Joseph Houston to view estate of Tabitha
F. 117 Q., Nancy M., Sally & Stephen Jones, in care of Betsy Jones, guardian; before William Schoolfield: report; 133 acres held in common by sons Whittington, James, William & Stephen, & daughters Polly, Hannah, Peggy, Tabitha, Nancy & Sally, subject to Betsy's right of dower (widow of James)

F. 118 Thomas P. Rackliffe & Nathaniel Bowen to view estate of James
F. 119 Rigsby, in care of Purnell Porter, guardian; before Thomas D. Purnell: report; tract called 'Sandy Point' adjacent to Capt. Littleton Robin's land, 50 acres; land adjacent to Purnell Porter's land, called 'Pointers(?) Gift to Purnell', 14 acres

F. 120 Dr. John Stevenson & John Hall to view estate of Isaac,
F. 121 Delia & George Furnis, in care of Amey Furnis, guardian; before James Tilghman: report; plantation 75 acres; 3 lots in New Town, one 3/4 acre, one 1/2 acre called shop lot, one 1 3/4 acre; widow's dower

F. 122 Thomas Mitchell, Josiah Bratten & Jacob Teague bound to Robert Nairn & Matthias Davis, on said Mitchell's adm. of estate of Robert Purnell; in presence of Sophia Bratten

'210'

F. 123 Abisha Davis, William McGregor & Thomas N. Williams, Esqs., to settle dispute between Zebulon Gray & Stephen Purnell, exe. of Thomas Gray; L.47/1/10 due from Thomas, Sen., to Zebulon, minus L.3/10/10 paid to Lemuel Showell, attorney for Zebulon

F. 124 Littleton Dennis, Edward Stevenson & Dr. John Stevenson to settle dispute between Bennett H. Clavoe & Amey Furnis, adm. of Littleton Furnis; Amey to pay Bennett L.74/16/5, as balance from firm of Furniss & Clarvoe

Received Nov. 20, 1809, of Henry Cluff, for Amey Furnis, above award

Test.; James Tilghman   Bennett H. Clarvoe

F. 125 Dr. John Stevenson & John Hall to distribute negroes from estate of Littleton Furnis, in hands of Amey Furnis, adm.; before Jas. Tilghman;
1) to Amey Furniss; Sam 22, Alse 15
2) to Isaac Furniss; Vinah 46, Peter 7, David 9
3) to Delia Furniss; Killiam 16, Nasa(?) 6
4) to George Furniss; Chloe 15, Levin 11

F. 126 Apprentice; Levin Clark, illegitimate, 16 on 12 Aug. next, by consent of his mother
Bound to; George Tyer, shoe maker
Trade; shue making
F. 127 Surety; Levi Holloway
Before Abishai Davis, Lemuel Showell

Apprentice; Maria [also Mariah] Tweedle Salisbury Hall, indigent orphan, 11 [couldn't write]
Bound to; James B. Waters
F. 128 In presence of Abishai Davis, Lemuel Showell

Apprentice; Esme Jones, 16 on 26 Apr. last, by consent of his father Obed
Bound to; John T. Taylor
Trade; shoe & boot maker
F. 129 In presence of Jackson Turner, Josa. Fleming, Jr.

Apprentice; John Holloway, 8 on 13 Aug. next, a pauper of the Poor House
F. 130 Bound to; Robert Givan
Trade; farmer
Sureties; Selby Parker, William Townsend (of Bkly.)
By Trustees for the Poor; Samuel Handy, McKimmey Porter, Ephraim K. Wilson

F. 131 William Parker, adm. of Col. James Houston, exhibits list of items used in the family; list; before J. Hubbell

Thomas Hall & Leonard Johnson, adms. of Turbot Wright, exhibit list of expenses; ; list

F. 132   Eliakim Jones, adm. of John Jones (Matty), exhibits account of items used in the family; list; saw taken by Caleb Jones

F. 133   Heirs of Littleton Furniss (Amey Furniss, adm.) exhibit account; mentions Andrew Gilchrist, William Davis, Peter Spiers, Stephen Luds, Joseph Callahan, Jno. W. Patterson, Levin Pilchard, John Young, Somerset (negro), Wm. Whelar, James Bunting, Planner (negro), John R. Slocomb

F. 134   Abisha Davis, William McGregor & Thomas N. Williams, Esqs., to settle dispute between Zebulon Gray & Stephen Purnell, exe. of Thomas Gray, Sen.

Nixon Davis, Jacob Dale & Thomas D. Purnell, Esqs., to settle dispute between Isaac Ayres & Keziah Davis, exe. of Daniel Davis

Purnell Toadvine, exe. of Priscilla Toadvine, to sell personal estate (except legacies)

F. 135   Josiah Collins, adm. of Edmund Reynolds, to sell personal estate

Leah Sturgis, adm. of John O. Sturgis, to sell personal estate

Kenal [Kendal?] S. Cropper, adm. of Henry Gornwell, to sell personal estate

F. 136   John S. Martin & Robert Smith, exes. of Col. James Martin, to sell personal estate (except legacies, wearing apparel & negro Gorge)

James H. Rowley, adm. of Coventon Rowley, to sell personal estate

Jacob Teague, adm. of John Ayres, to advertise in Thomas P. Smith's paper at Easton for creditors to exhibit claims

James H. Rowley, adm. of Covington Townsend, to advertise in the Democratic Press at Philadelphia for creditors to exhibit claims

F. 137   James B. Robins, adm. of Littleton Robins, to advertise in Thomas P. Smith's paper at Easton for creditors to exhibit claims

Esther Buchanan, adm. of John Buchanan, allowed 10% on estate

Eliakim Jones, adm. of John Jones, allowed 8% on estate

James Bennett, Jun., exe. of James Bennett, Sen., allowed 7% on estate

Amey Furnis, adm. of Littleton Furnis, allowed 7 1/2% on estate

New warrant for John Stevenson & James Tilghman to appraise property of Littleton Furnis

Thomas N. Williams & William McGrigor to distribute negroes from estate of Elizabeth Selby, in hands of Thomas Selby, exe.

F. 138   Dr. John Stevenson & John Hall to view property of Isaac, Delia & George Furnis, in care of Amey Furnis, guardian

Dr. John Stevenson & John Hall to distribute negroes from estate of Littleton Furnis, in hands of Amey Furnis, adm.

Register to state account for Whittington Jones, late adm. of James Jones, charging him with property & debts collected

Negroes from estate of Mills Bevans to be sold, as they cannot be equally divided

Amey Furnis, guardian to Delia Furnis, to sell negro Kellam

Order of 17 May last, for sale of negroes from estate of Mills Bevans, rescinded; George Hayward & John Stevenson to divide negroes, now in hands of James Bevans, adm.

F. 139   Abisha Davis & William McGregor, Esqs., to view property of Eliza White, in care of Seth Whaley, guardian

Abishai Davis & Lemuel Showell to view property of Joseph & George Harrison, in care of Levin Dirickson, guardian

F. 140   [blank]

F. 141   Tues., June 12, 1810   All Justices present

Joshua Cathell discharged from guardianship to James T. Cathell, for failing to give counter security to Robert Nairne & Peter Parker, his securities; Eben Christopher new guardian

F. 142   Orphan; James T. Cathell (of David)
Guardian; Eben Christopher
Sureties; Robert Nairn, John Sturgis

F. 143   Orphan; Purnell Johnson Jones (of Matthew)
Guardian; Benjamin Johnson, Sen.
Sureties; George Parsons, Robert Givan, Jun.

Orphan; Nancy Jones (of Matthew)
Guardian; Benjamin Johnson, Sen.
Sureties; George Parsons (of George), Robert Givan, Jun.

F. 144   Orphan; Sally Aydelott (of William)
Guardian; Mary Aydelott [couldn't write]
Sureties; Littleton Riley, John Selby, Sen.

Eben Christopher discharged from guardianship to James T. Cathell; Joshua Cathell new guardian

'213'

F. 145
Orphan; James T. Cathell (of David)
Guardian; Joshua Cathell
Sureties; Levi Cathell, Davis Cathell, Daniel Wails

F. 146
Apprentice; John Jester (of Southy), 16 on 9 instant
Bound to; George W. Hammond
Trade; farmer
Sureties; James Bevans, William Willis

F. 147
Apprentice; John Parker (of John), 16 on 12 Apr. last
Bound to; Robert Givan, Jun.
Trade; house carpenter
Sureties; Peter Parker, Jr., Charles Bennett, Jr.

F. 148
F. 149
John Benson & Esau Boston to view estate of Jacob Wheeler, in care of Patty Wheeler, guardian; before William Schoolfield: report; 60 acres

F. 150
John Benson & Esau Boston to view estate of Job Wheeler, in care of Patty Wheeler, guardian; [same as above]

F. 151
F. 152
John Benson & Esau Boston to view estate of Major Wheeler, in care of Patty Wheeler, guardian; before William Schoolfield: report; 100 acres of cypress swamp; negro Caleb

F. 153
F. 154
John Benson & Esau Boston to view estate of Henry Wheeler, in care of Patty Wheeler, guardian; before William Schoolfield: report; cooper's shop; 180 acres; widow's thirds

F. 155
F. 156
formerly
F. 157
Sewell Turpin & Benjamin Purnell, Esqs., to view estate of Edward Hammond, in care of Handy Jones, guardian; before Saml. A. Harper: report; plantation formerly property of William J. Houston, 132 acres, part of 'Fair Meadow', 'Chance' & 'Discovery'; land bought of John Chaille, 200 acres, part of 'Purnells Security' & 'Sherbourn'; land property of John Morris, 45 acres, part of 'Highfields'; life estate of Sarah Smock (aged woman) in a tract called 'Partnership'; land formerly property of John Round, 240 acres, part of 'Johns Inheritance' & 'Blackinghurst'

F. 158 -
160
Sewell Turpin & Benjamin Purnell, Esqs., to view estate of Charlotte Hammond, in care of Handy Jones, guardian; [same as above]

F. 161
Apprentice; John Fisher, black, illegitimate, 9 on 20 June last, by consent of his mother
Bound to; John Aydelott, farmer
Before Jas. Tilghman, Wm. Schoolfield

Thomas S. Fassitt & Cord Hazzard to settle dispute between Booz Ennis, & Peter Scott & Mary, his wife, exex. of Richard Sampson

Sophia Bradford & Pierce Riggin, adms. of Avery Bradford, to sell personal estate (except legacies & wearing apparel)

John Coston, adm. of Ezekiel Coston, to sell personal estate

F. 162   Hetty Lindsey, adm. of Major Lindsey, to sell personal estate (except negroes & wearing apparel)

John Richards, exe. of Isaac Richards, to sell personal estate

John Richards, adm. of William Wright, to sell personal estate

George Parsons, exe. of Matthew Jones, to sell personal estate (except negroes, crop & wearing apparel)

F. 163   Jesse Sturgis, Sen., adm. of John Reed, allowed 10% on estate

Thomas Mitchell, exe. of Robert Purnell, allowed 10% on estate

Eben Christopher, adm. dbn of David Porter, allowed 10% on estate

It being represented that Booz Ennis, who obtained a judgement against William Riley & Elizabeth Wright, adms. of Hezekiah Wright, has petitioned to be relieved under Act for Relief of Insolvent Debtors, adms. to retain judgement until Trustee complies with said Act

Joshua Cathell, late guardian to James T. Cathel, to deliver property to Eben Christopher, present guardian; John Dashiell & Thomas Fookes to view property

F. 164   James Ward & John Dashiell, adms. of John Ward, allowed costs on suits of the U.S. against them, & costs incurred by Timothy Irons & Valentine Dennis, who were sued as securities

James Ward, one adm. of John Ward, swears that $20.20 returned in list of sperate debts as received from Rowland E. Bevans & $5 received from James Truitt (of Betty), were received for property sold & not for debts

John Dashiell & Eben Christopher to view property of Purnell I. Jones, in care of Benjamin Johnson, guardian

John Dashiell & Eben Christopher to view property of Nancy Jones, in care of Benjamin Johnson, guardian

Henry Bennett, guardian to Isaac Houston, to rent real estate

F. 165-6 [blank]

F. 167   Tues., Aug. 14, 1810   John Bishop, Zadok Sturgis present

F. 168   Orphan; Polly Purnell Mitchell (of John Pope Mitchell) Guardian; Polly Mitchell
Sureties; Robert Mitchell, Stephen Purnell

'215'

Orphan; Rufus Mitchell (of John P.)
Guardian; Robert Mitchell
Sureties; Stephen Purnell, Robert J. H. Purnell [signed Handy]

F. 169 Apprentice; William Furmington (of Charles), 10 on 11 May last
Bound to; William Ball
Trade; farmer
Sureties; John R. Slocomb, Jonathan Cluff

F. 170 Apprentice; John Jones (of Giles), 13 on 25 Mar. last
Bound to; John Spencer, Jun.
Trade; shoe maker
Sureties; Ralph Milbourn, Littleton Quinton

F. 171 Apprentice; Ephraim Armwood, 12 on 15 Mar. last, son of Nancy
Bound to; Obed Taylor
Trade; farming
F. 172 Sureties; John Stevens(?), Robert J. H. Handy

Apprentice; Daniel Armwood, 8 on 20 July last, son of Nancy
Bound to; Obed Taylor
F. 173 Trade; farmer
Sureties; John Stevens, Robert J. H. Handy

Apprentice; Major Armwood, 4 on 10 May last, son of Nancy
Bound to; Obed Taylor
F. 174 Trade; farmer
Sureties; John Stevens, Robert J. H. Handy

F. 175 Jacob White & William McGrigor to view estate of William I. Stevenson (of John), in care of Peter C. Evans, guardian;
F. 176 before Jacob Dale: report; lott #1 near Berlin; lott #5 near Berlin, 55 acres; grandmother's thirds; land in Queponco, lott #4, 100 acres; mother's thirds; estate not being settled, we couldn't value negroes

Certificate from Sussex, Co., Delaware; Samuel Elliot, John
F. 177 Morris & Saml. Hearn to view estate of Samuel U., Benjamin & Polly Melson (of Joseph), in care of Elijah & Benjamin Melson, guardians: report; land on west side of road leading from Indian River to Salisbury
James F. Baylis, clk.

Sewell Turpin & Thomas P. Rackliffe to settle dispute between Edward Davis & Samuel Long, exe. of Colevern Long

F. 178 Account of William Parker, adm. of Col. James Houston; mentions James Duer, Saml. R. Smith; before Mathias Davis

Thomas & William Franklin, exes. of John Franklin, Sen., to sell personal estate (except legacies, negroes & wearing apparel)

F. 179   Sarah Massey & Kendal Massey, adms. of John Massey, to sell personal estate (except negroes, wheat & wearing apparel)

Peter C. Evans, adm. of John Stevenson, to sell corn

Handy Davis, adm. of Thomas [John crossed out] Davis, to sell personal estate (except wearing apparel)

Edward Bredell & Anne, his wife, & William Bell, adms. of James Bell, allowed 8% on estate

F. 180   Stephen Purnell, exe. of Thomas Gray, Sen., allowed 8% on estate

Samuel McMaster, adm. of Edward R. Morris, allowed 6% on estate

William Lister & wife, exex. of David Johnson, to advertise in the American Watchman & Delaware Republican at Wilmington for creditors to exhibit claims

Elijah Melson, guardian to Samuel U. Melson, excused from rendering accounts until he reaches 14

Benjamin Melson, guardian to Polly Melson, excused from rendering accounts until she reaches 14

Kendal S. Crapper, adm. of Henry Gornwell, allowed full time to settle estate, as it is insufficient to cover debts

Thomas N. Williams, Levi Duncan & William McGregor to distribute specifics from estate of John P. Mitchell

F. 181   Order directing Thomas S. Fassitt & William Riley to view estate of George Sampson rescinded; new commission to Thomas S. Fassitt & Cord Hazard

Thomas Franklin & Isaac Ayres to view estate of Lambert Collier, in care of George Davis, guardian

Thomas R. Handy & John C. Bacon to view estate of Lydia & Milcha Bevans, in care of Luke Townsend & wife, guardians

F. 182   Apprentice; John Young, by consent of his father Littleton
Bound to; Ebenezer Leonard
Term; 4 years from 5 Nov. next
Trade; tanner & currier of leather
In presents of Benjamin Johnson

F. 183   [blank]

F. 184   Tues., Oct. 9, 1810   Littleton Robins, Zadok Sturgis present

Orphan; Ezekiel Coston
Guardian; John Coston
Sureties; Benjamin Gunby, John Aydelott (of Wm.)

F. 185 Orphan; Peter Coston (of Ezekiel)
        Guardian; John Coston
        Sureties; Benjamin Gunby, John Aydelott (of Wm.)

        Orphan; John C. Clarvoe
F. 186 Guardian; Bennett H. Clarvoe, father
        Sureties; Edward Lambden, John Marchant

        Apprentice; Thomas Townsend, 12 on 24 May last, son of Eli
        Bound to; William Dryden, Jun.
        Trade; farmer
F. 187 Sureties; Littleton Riley, James Knox

        Apprentice; Coleborn Long (of Coleborn), 16 on 15 Aug. last
        Bound to; William Bishop
F. 188 Trade; hatter
        Sureties; John P. Slemaker, Lemuel P. Spence

F. 189 Apprentice; Joseph McLean (of John), 17 on 13 Apr. last
        Bound to; John P. Slemaker
        Trade; hatter
        Sureties; William Bishop, William Rownd, Jun.

F. 190 William Sturgis, Esq., & George Parsons to view estate of
        James T. Cathell, in care of Joshua Cathell, guardian; before
F. 191 Shipherd Johnson: report; 400 acres in Worcestor Co., part of
F. 192 'Addition to Preston'; lot in Salisbury, Somerset Co.;
        negroes Moses 50, Charles 24, Dareus 21, Bob 13, Silva 6

        Thomas N. Williams, Levi Duncan & William McGrigor to
F. 193 distribute personal estate of John P. Mitchell, in hands of
F. 194 Robert Mitchell, exe.: report; list of articles consumed
        since appraisal;
1) to widow; negro men Cook, Jake, Levin, Elijaham, boy Handy, women
        Peggy, Millia, girls Maria, Rachel; list
F. 195 2) to Robert Mitchell; man Major, boy Lewis, woman Tab, girl
F. 196 Henney; list
        3) to Isaac Mitchell; man Milby, boys Honis(?), Littleton,
        girl Sarah; list
F. 197 4) to John Mitchell; man Harry, boys Ebin, Burton, woman
        Betty; list
        5) to Rufus Mitchell; man Prince, boys Loyd, Abraham, woman
F. 198 Minta; list
        6) to Eloisa Gartrude P. Mitchell; man Limon, woman Lucy,
girl Ebben, boy Ned; list
7) to Mary P. Mitchell; boys David, James, Allen, woman Phillis, girl
        Lovy; list
F. 199 above distribution confirmed

F. 200	Robert Mitchell, guardian to Rufus Mitchell (of John P.), to sell personal estate (except negroes); list; Mitchell Gray, clerk for sale
F. 201	
F. 202	Polly Mitchell, guardian to Polly P. Mitchell (of John P.), to sell personal estate (except negroes); list; Mitchell Gray, clerk for sale
F. 203	Nixon Davis, Jacob Dale & Thomas D. Purnell to settle dispute between Isaac Ayres & Keziah Davis, exe. of Daniel Davis; Keziah to pay Isaac $4
F. 204	Apprentice; Jacob Fisher, by consent of his mother Patience [couldn't write] Bound to; Daniel Handcock (of John) Trade; farming Before Saml. A. Harper, Josa. Fleming, Jr.
F. 205	Apprentice; Robert Armstrong, 11, by consent of his mother Bound to; William A. Marshall Trade; farming Surety; George Truitt Before Thos. D. Purnell, Nixon Davis

Account of John Houston [also Holston], adm. of Mrs. Nancy Long; list; mentions Wm. Devorix, Isaac Hodge, Hannah Armstrong

James Davis & James A. Collins, adms. of John Davis, to sell personal estate

F. 206 Joseph Young, exe. of Zepheniah Benson, to sell personal estate

Polly Mitchell, guardian to Polly P. Mitchell, to sell personal estate (except negroes)

Edward Bredell & Levi Duncan to view estate of Polly P. Mitchell, in care of Polly Mitchell, guardian

Joseph Scott, adm. of James Gunby, to sell negroes

Robert Mitchell, guardian to Rufus Mitchell, to sell personal estate (except negroes)

F. 207 Littleton R. Purnell, exe. of Dennis Hudson, to sell personal estate as directed by will

Sarah Davis, adm. of John Davis, to sell personal estate

[erased] Long & Thomas M. Tull, adms. of Littleton Long, to sell personal estate

Frederick Conner, adm. dbn of John Devorix, to sell personal estate

F. 208 John Bishop & Littleton R. Purnell, adms. of William Davis, to sell personal estate

Mary Newton, adm. of Job Newton, allowed for corn & fodder consumed

Edward Stevenson & John Holland to view estate of Ezekiel & Peter Coston, in care of John Costen, guardian

Joshua Prideaux & William McGriger to distribute negroes from estate of Thomas Selby, Sen., in hands of Thomas Selby, Jun., adm., as directed by will

May 29, 1810, received of Edward Davis, Sen., $134.12, on account of Leah Davis' estate, on order to receive estate out of his hands

F. 209 Test.; William Porter   Purnell Porter

New warrant for John Dashiell & Eben Christopher to appraise property of Matthew Jones

F. 210 Tues., Dec. 11, 1810   All Justices present

Selby Parker discharged from guardianship to Elizabeth Selby; William Parker new guardian

F. 211
Orphan; Elizabeth Selby (of Levin)
Guardian; William Parker
Sureties; William Hammond, Stephen Riley

Orphan; Sally Hudson (of Dennis)
Guardian; William Jones
Sureties; Robert Nairne, Handy Jones

F. 212
Orphan; Gertrude Hudson (of Dennis)
Guardian; William Jones
Sureties; Handy Jones, Robert Nairne

F. 213
Orphan; Polly Hudson (of Dennis)
Guardian; William Jones
Sureties; Robert Nairne, Handy Jones

Orphan; Hetty Hudson (of Dennis)
Guardian; William Jones
Sureties; Robert Nairne, Handy Jones

F. 214 Orphan; Littleton R. P. Hudson (of Dennis)
Guardian; William Jones
Sureties; Robert Nairne, Handy Jones

F. 215
Orphan; Priscilla Hudson (of Dennis)
Guardian; William Jones
Sureties; Robert Nairne, Handy Jones

Orphan; John C. H. Hudson (of Dennis)
Guardian; William Jones
Sureties; Robert Nairne, Handy Jones

F. 216   Orphan; John Devorix (of John)
         Guardian; Frederick Conner, Sen.
         Sureties; Patrick Waters, George Hayward

         Orphan; George Milbourn (of Elijah)
F. 217   Guardian; John Allen, Jun.
         Sureties; John Selby, Jun., Purnell Hill

Evans Hudson & Nancy, his wife, discharged from guardianship to John Richardson; Henry Richardson new guardian

         Orphan; John Richardson (of Robert M.)
         Guardian; Henry Richardson
F. 218   Sureties; Samuel R. Smith, Littleton R. Purnell

Evans Hudson & Nancy, his wife, discharged from guardianship to Mary Richardson; Henry Richardson new guardian

Orphan; Mary Richardson (of Robert M.)
Guardian; Henry Richardson
Sureties; Samuel R. Smith, Littleton R. Purnell

F. 219   Apprentice; John Devorix (of John), 16 in May next
         Bound to; Daniel Patrick
         Trade; boot & shoe making
         Sureties; George Hayward, Patrick Waters

F. 220   Apprentice; Elijah Timmons (of Elijah), 16 on 17 Dec. last
         Bound to; John P. Chaille
         Trade; boot & shoe maker
         Sureties; Levin Dirickson, Jesse Timmons

F. 221   Apprentice; Annanias Timmons (of Elijah), 18 on 30 June last
         Bound to; Benjamin Jarmin
         Trade; farmer
         Sureties; Jesse Timmons, Nehemiah Timmons

F. 222   Apprentice; Levin Henderson (of Samuel), 16 on 16 Mar. last
         Bound to; Joseph Schoolfield
         Trade; farmer
         Sureties; Robert McAllen, James Dickenson

F. 223   Apprentice; Jesse Henderson (of Samuel), 11 on 8 Oct. last
         Bound to; Robert McAllen
         Trade; farmer
         Sureties; Joseph Schoolfield, James Trehearn

F. 224   Apprentice; William, negro, 18 next Apr., son of Rhoda
         (formerly slave of James Trehern)
                              (cont.)

F. 225
Bound to; James Trehern
Trade; coasting business
Sureties; William Rownds, Patrick Waters

F. 226
Apprentice; Levin, negro, 15 last Oct., son of Rhoda
Bound to; James Trehern
Trade; farmer
Sureties; William Rownds, Patrick Waters

F. 227
Apprentice; Littleton, negro, 13 last July, son of Rhoda
Bound to; James Trehern
Trade; farmer
Sureties; William Rownd, Patrick Water

F. 226
Apprentice; William Taylor (of Levin), 13 on 10 Feb. next
Bound to; John T. Taylor
Trade; boot & shoe maker
Sureties; Thomas Dukes, John Laws

F. 229
Apprentice; Benjamin Armstrong, mulatto, son of Betty
Bound to; John Holston
Trade; farmer
Sureties; Peter Waters, William Rownds

F. 230
F. 231
William McGrigor & Abisha Davis, Esqs., to view estate of Eliza White, in care of Seth Whaley, guardian: report; land lying near Herrin Creek; Mrs. Gray's dower, widow of Thomas Gray, Sen.; 410 acres; negroes Luke 36, Sam 36, Henry 33 (infirm), James 11, Abner 8, Jude 43 (infirm)

F. 232
Sewell Turpin & Thomas P. Rackliffe to settle dispute between Edward Davis, Jun., & Samuel Long, exe. of Colvern Long; Samuel to pay Edward L.30/18/5

F. 233
Apprentice; John Slattery [also Slaughtery], 17 on 8 Feb. next, by consent of his mother
Bound to; Jesse Dean [also Deen]
Trade; house carpenter
Sureties; William Davis, Josiah Crapper
Before Kendall S. Crapper, Thomas D. Purnell

F. 234
Apprentice; James Porter, born 13 June, 1804, child of the Poor House, son of Naomi
Bound to; Purnell Johnson
Trade; cooper
Sureties; Barzilla Parker, George Richardson
By Trustees for the Poor; Samuel Handy, Sen., McKimmey Porter, George Hayward

F. 235
William Parker, adm. cwa of Col. James Houston, exhibits list of unadjusted claims; mentions 25 acres sold to Major Clavil in 1800; claim assigned to L. Robins, Esq., against Nathaniel Dixon; suit brought by H. Bennett; John Parmore

James Patterson, exe. of Anderson Patterson, to sell personal estate (except legacies & wearing apparel)

Sarah Bradford, adm. of William Bradford, to sell perishable estate

F. 236   John Benson, adm. of Tabitha Selby, to sell negroes

Edward Stevenson & [blank], adms. of John Hall, to sell personal estate (except negroes & wearing apparel)

James Dickenson & Patty Wheeler, exes. of Zadok Wheeler, to sell negroes

Powell Patey, exe. of John Bradford, Sen., to sell personal estate (except legacies)

F. 237   Pierce Riggin & Loudy(?) Riggin, exes. of John Riggin, to sell personal estate (except wearing apparel)

[this entry crossed out;] Isaac P. Johnson, adm. of Hezekiah Johnson, to sell personal estate (except legacies)

Eleanor Fassitt, exe. of John Fassitt, allowed 10% on payments

George Parsons, exe. of Matthew Jones, to sell personal estate contained in additional inventory

Benjamin Purnell & Thomas P. Rackliffe to view estate of Sally & Littleton Hudson, in care of William Jones, guardian

Joshua Johnson, exe. of John Fookes, allowed 10% on estate

F. 238   Register to state account for Elizabeth Devorix, late adm. of John Devorix, charging her with estate & debts

Jacob Teague & Frederick Conner to view estate of John & Mary Richardson, in care of Henry Richardson, guardian

William Parker, adm. of Col. James Houston, allowed 10% on estate

F. 239   Special Court, Dec. 28, 1810, at instance of Elisha Baynum; John Bishop, Zadok Sturgis present

Elisha Baynum, adm. of William Baynum, to sell personal estate (except corn for rent of plantation where he lives)

F. 240   Special Court, Jan. 25, 1811, at instance of Isaac S. Johnson; all Justices present

Samuel Ennis discharged from guardianship to Joseph Ennis; Stephen Ennis new guardian

'223'

Orphan; Joseph Ennis (of Joseph)
Guardian; Stephen Ennis
Sureties; Frederick Conner, John Harris

F. 241   Samuel Ennis discharged from guardianship to Samuel Ennis;
         Stephen Ennis new guardian

Orphan; Samuel Ennis (of Joseph)
Guardian; Stephen Ennis
Sureties; Frederick Conner, John Harris

F. 242   Apprentice; Nathaniel Beazy, child of the Poor House, son of
         John Beazey
         Bound to; Major Reed [signed Walter Reed, couldn't write]
         Trade; farmer, working in a crop
         Sureties; Purnell Hill, Elijah Pruitt [couldn't write]
         By Trustees for the Poor; Samuel Handy, McKimmy Porter,
         Ephraim K. Wilson

F. 243   Isaac S. Johnson, adm. of Hezekiah Johnson, to sell personal
         estate (except legacies)

Littleton R. Purnell & Thomas P. Rackliffe to view estate of Joseph &
Samuel Ennis, in care of Stephen Ennis, guardian

John Holston, adm. of Nancy Long, allowed 10% on estate

John Holston, adm. of Nancy Long, to retain $114.99 to meet claims of
Sally, Jesse & Katy Long, minors, representatives of William Long,
which was in hands of deceased as admx. of William

F. 244   Littleton Robins, Sen., John Bishop & Zadok Sturgis appointed
         Justices

Edw. Lloyd   W. Kilty, Chanc.

Wit.; The Honourable William Kilby, Esq., Chancellor

Tues., Feb. 12, 1811   All Justices present

         Orphan; Betsey Long (of Littleton, Jun.)
F. 245   Guardian; Anne Long [signed Anna]
         Sureties; Bayly Young, William Henderson [neither could
         write]

         Orphan; Thomas Long (of Littleton, Jun.)
         Guardian; Anne Long
F. 246   Sureties; Bayly Young, William Henderson

Orphan; Henrietta Bradford
Guardian; Sarah Bradford [couldn't write]
Sureties; James Hook, Lemuel P. Spence

F. 247
Orphan; Isaac Toadvine (of Henry)
Guardian; Elijah Ennis
Sureties; Eben Christopher, Turner Davis

F. 248
Orphan; William Spence (of George)
Guardian; Lemuel P. Spence
Sureties; Thomas R. P. Spence, John S. Spence

Orphan; Irving Spence (of George)
Guardian; Lemuel P. Spence
Sureties; Thomas R. P. Spence, John S. Spence

F. 249
Orphan; Littleton Devorix (of John)
Guardian; Frederick Conner, Jun.
Sureties; Frederick Conner, Sen., James Givan

Samuel Bradford discharged from guardianship to William Price; Severn Pruitt new guardian

F. 250
Orphan; William Price (of Arthur)
Guardian; Severn Pruitt [couldn't write]
Sureties; Isaac S. Johnson, John Price

[writing changes]

Orphan; Joshua Davis (of John, Sen.)
Guardian; James A. Collins
Sureties; Matthias Davis, Robert J. H. Handy

F. 251
Orphan; Peggy Davis (of John, Sen.)
Guardian; James A. Collins
Sureties; Matthias Davis, Robert J. H. Handy

Apprentice; Littleton Devorix (of John)
Bound to; Frederick Conner, Jun.
Trade; blacksmith
Sureties; Frederick Conner, Sen., James Givan

F. 252
Apprentice; Tully Sneed (of Robert), 14 on 15 Mar. next
Bound to; William Lecompt
Trade; Saddle & harness maker
Sureties; George Nelson, Francis Ross

F. 253
Apprentice; Isaac Laws (of Major)
Bound to; John T. Taylor
Trade; boot & shoe maker
Sureties; Lemuel P. Spence, Peter Truitt

F. 254
Apprentice; Kellam Riggin, 17 on 19 Jan. last, illegitimate child of Rachel Maddux
Bound to; Thomas Maddux
Trade; shoe maker
Sureties; William Quinton, Robert J. H. Handy

'225'

F. 255   George Hayward & John Stevens to distribute negroes from
         estate of Mills Bevans, in hands of James Bevans, adm.;
F. 256   before J. Hubbell: inventory; negroes Will 26, Hannah 25;
         increase; Ebben 4, Milby 2, Mary 7 months;
1) to Luke Townsend & wife; Hannah, Mary
2) to daughter Lydia A.; Will
3) to daughter Milcha; Eben, Milby

         John Holland, George Hayward & Jesse Bennett to distribute
F. 257   negroes from estate of Morgan Bradshaw, in hands of Arthur
         McAllen, adm.; before Saml. A. Harper;
1) to Robert Johnson; negro Abraham
2) to widow; Priscilla, Maria
3) to Betsey Bradshaw; Comfort (old & infirm), Esther, Peter, Harriott

Sewell Turpin & Thomas P. Rackliffe, Esqs., to settle dispute between
         Joshua Davis & Samuel Long, exe. of Colevern Long (late
F. 258   guardian to Joshua); Samuel to pay Joshua L.30/18/5; Samuel
         objects; Court reexamines case & lowers award to L.27/10/11

Levin Dirickson exhibits bill of complaint against Peter Scott & Mary,
         his wife, exex. of Richard Sampson; Levin obtained judgement
F. 259   in Chancery Court of Delaware against Samuel Dirickson on 27
         July, 1802, by his attorneys Ezekiel Williams & Richard
         Sampson; asks that Peter & Mary pay him anything collected
F. 260   under his judgement; Peter & Mary appear, by William
F. 261   Whittington, their attorney; court grants petition

Sewell Turpin & Thomas P. Rackliffe, Esqs., to settle dispute between
Joshua Davis & Samuel Long, exe. of Colevern Long (late guardian to
Joshua)

         Apprentice; James Baynum (of William), 13 on 8 Apr. next
         Bound to; Jehu [signed Jehew] Powell, shoe maker
         Trade; shoe maker
F. 262   Surety; Elisha Baynum
         Before Wm. McGrigor, Jacob Dale

         Apprentice; Hetty Baynum (of William), 10 next June
F. 263   Bound to; Jehu Powell
         Trade; work necessary for a woman to know
         Surety; Elisha Baynum
         Before Wm. McGrigor, Jacob Dale

F. 264   Apprentice; Mordecai Davis (of John, blacksmith), 16 on 19
         Aug. next, by consent of his mother & stepfather, John &
         Zipporah Jones
         Bound to; Jehu Powell, shoe maker
         Trade; shoe maker
         Surety; Jesse Powell
F. 265   Before Wm. McGrigor, Jacob Dale

Apprentice; Barick, negro, 6 on 13 Nov. last, illegitimate son of
Milly Long
Bound to; Edward Lambden, copper [cooper]
Trade; cypris copper
Before James Tilghman, Wm. Schoolfield

F. 266
Apprentice; Josiah Daugherty, 18 on 19 Oct. next, by consent of his father Nathaniel
Bound to; Joshua Matthews
Trade; ship carpenter
In presence of Francis Rosse, Elizabeth Rosse

F. 267
Apprentice; Henny Hughs, 11 next June, by consent of her father William
Bound to; John Floyd
Trade; spin & weave
Before Geo. Bratten, Saml. A. Harper

F. 268
Apprentice; Betsey Campbell, 9 on 18 Oct. next, child of the Poor House, daughter of Peggy
Bound to; John Johnson (of James) [couldn't write]
Trade; house work
Sureties; John Hall Hill, Parker Dukes
By Trustees for the Poor; Samuel Handy, Ephraim K. Wilson, George Hayward

Janet Read, adm. of Elijah Read, to sell personal estate (except wearing apparel)

F. 269   Esau Boston & Edward Stevenson to view property of Betsey & Thomas Long, in care of Anne Long, guardian

George Hall, adm. of Thomas Hall, to sell personal estate

Isaiah Baker, adm. of Archibald Baker, to sell personal estate (except wearing apparel)

William Pollitt & Joshua Morris to view property of Isaac Toadvine, in care of Elijah Ennis, guardian

William Parsons, adm. of Samuel Parsons, to sell personal estate (except wearing apparel)

Polly Warrington, adm. of Isaac Warrington, to sell personal estate

F. 270   Henry Richardson, guardian to John & Molly Richardson, to repair kitchen, barn & granery belonging to heirs of Robert M. Richardson

James Fleming, adm. of James Devorix, to sell store goods from firm of James Devorix & Co., of which he is the surviving partner

James Fleming, adm. of James Devorix, to sell personal estate (except negroes)

Littleton Robins, Joshua Prideaux & Zadok Purnell, adms. of Col. Zadok Purnell, allowed 8% on estate

Sarah Melvin, exe. of Jonathan Melvin, to sell personal estate (except negroes & legacies)

F. 271 Isaac P. Smith, adm. of Robert Smith, to sell personal estate (except wearing apparel)

James Bevans & Matthias Lindsey to view property of William Price, in care of Severn Pruitt, guardian

Samuel Tarr, guardian to Patsey Taylor, to give ward 6 months schooling & excused from rendering reports

Margaret Hudson & John Bishop, exes. of Robert Hudson, to sell property as directed by will

Jacob Teague & Joseph J. Gillis to distribute specifics from estate of William Bradford, in hands of Sarah Bradford, adm.

F. 272 Thomas N. Williams & William Richards to view property of Joshua Davis, in care of James A. Collins, guardian

Thomas N. Williams & William Richards to view property of Peggy Davis, in care of James A. Collins, guardian

Levin Dirickson, adm. of James B. Waters, to sell personal estate

John Stevenson, exe. of Whittington Jones, to retain, as adm. dbn of James Jones, $1,346.74, amount due from deceased to estate of James

John Stevenson, exe. of Whittington Jones, allowed 5% on estate

John Stevenson, adm. dbn of James Jones, allowed 5% on estate

Selby Parker, late guardian to Levin Selby, to retain $21.48, the sum due him as exe. of Levin's father Levin Selby

F. 273 Received Mar. 9, 1809, of Eliakim Jones, adm. of John Jones, property from will of my father; list

Test.; Jno. Holland   Henry Jones

Jan. 19, 1811, received of Eliakim Jones, adm. of John Jones, property from will of my father; list

   her   Hezekiah Jones
Test.; Sarah X Tarr
   mark

Received Mar. 9, 1809, of Eliakim Jones, adm. of John Jones, property from will of my father; list

(cont.)

Test.; Jno. Holland   Sally Jones

Sept. 17, 1810, received of Eliakim Jones, adm. of John Jones, $329.36 & list, Leah Jones' legacies

Test.; Giles Jones   William Handcock

F. 274   Tues., Apr. 9, 1811   All Justices present

Orphan; William Baynum (of William)
Guardian; James Baynum
Sureties; William Townsend (of Barkley), Belitha Baynum

F. 275   Joshua Cathell discharged from guardianship to James T. Cathell; William S. Handy new guardian

Orphan; James T. Cathell (of David)
Guardian; William S. Handy, Jun.(?)
Sureties; Joshua Cathell (of Somerset Co.), Levi Cathell, Levin Parsons, John W. B. Parsons

F. 276
Orphan; James Devorix (of John)
Guardian; Jesse H. Bennett, Jr. (of Wm.)
Sureties; William Bennett, Sen., Frederick Conner, Sen.

F. 277
Orphan; Major Jones (of Whittington)
Guardian; Jarman Gillett
Sureties; Bayly Young [couldn't write], John R. Slocomb

Orphan; Whittington Jones (of Whittington)
Guardian; Jarman Gillett
Sureties; Bayly Young, John R. Slocomb

F. 278   Orphan; John Clarvoe [also Clavoe]
Guardian; Bennett H. Clarvoe, father
Sureties; Levin Powell, Sen., Fleet Chilton, Ralph Henman

F. 279   Orphan; Benjamin Parsons (of Samuel)
Guardian; William Parsons
Sureties; Jonathan S. Parsons, George Parsons (of Geo.)

F. 280
Orphan; William Richards (of John)
Guardian; William Richards
Sureties; Robert J. H. Handy, George Hayward

Orphan; Mary B. Richards (of John)
Guardian; William Richards
Sureties; George Hayward, Robert J. H. Handy

F. 281   Orphan; Joseph Hutcheson (of Jonathan)
Guardian; John Stevens
Sureties; George Hayward, Joshua Fleming, Jun.

'229'

```
            Orphan; Levi Long (of Littleton)
            Guardian; Samuel Tull
F. 282      Sureties; Edward Lambden, Barzilla Parker

Orphan; Littleton Long (of Littleton)
Guardian; Samuel Tull
Sureties; Edward Lambden, Barzilla Parker

            Orphan; Sally Long (of Littleton)
F. 283      Guardian; Samuel Tull
            Sureties; Edward Lambden, Barzilla Parker

            Orphan; Peggy Long (of Littleton)
            Guardian; Samuel Tull
F. 284      Sureties; Edward Lambden, Barzilla Parker

Orphan; Susan Long [also Susanna] (of Littleton)
Guardian; Samuel Tull
Sureties; Edward Lambden, Barzilla Parker

            Orphan; Polly Rowley (of William)
F. 285      Guardian; Hetty Rowley [couldn't write]
            Sureties; William Jones (of Jno.), Samuel Ball [couldn't
            write]
```

Jonathan Fookes & Elender, his wife, & Ebenezer Hearn & Betty, his wife, vs. Outten Toadvine & Rhoda Toadvine; caveat against will of Nancy R. Toadvine withdrawn; will admitted to probate

```
            Apprentice; Hugh M. Stevenson (of Jonathan), 15 on 12 Mar.
F. 286      last
            Bound to; George Nelson
            Trade; house carpenter & joiner
            Sureties; Frederick Conner, James Holland

            Edward Stevenson & John Holland to view estate of Ezekiel
F. 287      Coston, in care of John Coston, guardian; before James
F. 288      Tilghman: report; mentions Price's place & Moor's place;
            800 acres; orphan entitled to 1/4 of above

            John Holland & Edward Stevenson to view estate of Peter
F. 289-90   Coston, in care of John Coston, guardian; [same as above]
```

Jacob Teague & Frederick Conner to view estate of John Richardson (heir of Robert M.), in care of Henry Richardson, guardian:
F. 291 report; land called 'Middle'; widow's dower; lott Snow Hill; John entitled to 1/5; land where Peter Truitt now lives; land
F. 292 where Levi Sturgis now lives; 508 acres at 'Middle'; mentions land in Mount Ephraim & Durram

```
            Jacob Teague & Frederick Conner to view estate of Mary
F. 293      Richardson (heir of Robert M.), in care of Henry Richardson,
F. 294      guardian; [same as above]
```

F. 295   William Pollett & Joshua Morris to view estate of Isaac
         Toadvine, in care of Elijah Ennis, guardian; before John
F. 296   Cathell: report; one negro, 30; 230 acres

         Edward Briddle & Levi Duncan to view estate of Polly P.
F. 297   Mitchell, in care of Polly Mitchell, guardian; before Robert
         Mitchell: report; 13 acres near head of Curch Branch; negroes
Fillis 60, Davis 14, James 12, Lovy 11, Alen 4

         Thomas N. Williams & William Richards to view estate of
F. 298   Joshua Davis, in care of James A. Collins, guardian; before
F. 299   Wm. McGrigor: report; entitled to 1/9 of 440 acres

         Ebin Christopher & George Parsons (of George) to view estate
F. 300   of James T. Cathell, in care of William Handy, guardian;
F. 301   before Shipherd Johnson: report; 400 acres called 'Addition
F. 302   to Preston'; land in town of Salisbury, Somerset Co.; negroes
         Moses 50, Charles 24, Dareus 21 (infirm), Bob 13, Silvia 6

         Joshua Prideaux & William McGrigor to distribute negroes from
F. 303   estate of Thomas Selby, Sen., in hands of Thomas Selby, Jun.;
         before Peter C. Evans:
1) to Elizabeth Selby, dower; negroes Littleton 17, Eben 9, Elsey 4,
Israel 1, Nell 29, Hess 15, Comfort 11, Amy 8, Lidy 6
2) to John Selby; Jacob 32, Hannah 52
3) to Thomas Selby; Caleb 27
4) to Patty Selby; Elijah 25, Satira(?) 52 (infirm)
5) to Kendal Selby; Jess 23
         6) to Sarah Selby, deceased, or her heirs; Daniel 19
F. 304   7) to James Selby; Sacker 17, Daniel 58 (infirm)
         8) to Peggy Selby; Bob 13, Leah 2, Jenny 52 (infirm)
9) to Kitty Selby; Patt 36 & her infant child; Levin 8

F. 305   Jacob Teague & Joseph J. Gillis to distribute estate of
         William Bradford, in hands of Sarah Bradford, adm.;
F. 306   1) to Sarah Bradford, widow; negro Sarah
F. 307-8 2) to Peter Truitt & wife; list; Rose 7, Isaac 5
F. 309   3) to Henny Bradford, minor; list; Mary 2

F. 310   Dr. John Stevenson & James Tilghman to settle dispute between
         Fleet Chelton, & Edward Stevenson & Rebecca Hall, adm. of
John Hall

Sewell Turpin, William Jones & Thomas P. Rackliffe to settle dispute
between Meshach Melvin & Littleton R. Purnell, exe. of Dennis Hudson

Ambrose White & Joshua Fleming to adjust accounts of late firm of
Handy & Robins, & to ascertain what is due from William Handy & George
Hayward, exes. of Bowdoin Robins, to Thomas R. Handy, surviving
partner in firm

         Apprentice; Ebenezer Hearn, 19 on 8 Mar., 1811, by consent of
F. 311   George Hearn, guardian
                         (cont.)

```
              Bound to; Ebenezer Leonard, tanner
              Trade; tanning & currying leather
              Before William Sturgis, George Maddux

              Apprentice; Thomas Lewis, 9 last Jan., by consent of his
              mother
              Bound to; Thomas Littleton, farmer [couldn't write]
              Trade; farming
F. 312        Surety; Wm. Littleton [couldn't write]
              Before Nixon Davis, Matthias Davis
```

Apprentice; Morris Elzey, 12 on 2 Aug. last, by consent of his mother
Bound to; Isaac Leonard, tailor
Trade; tailor
Before Benjamin Johnson, George Maddux

```
              Apprentice; Samuel Peacock, 13 on 10 Jan. next, child of the
F. 313        Poor House, son of Comfort
              Bound to; John Floyd
              Trade; farming
              Sureties; Robert J. H. Handy, Robert Nairne
F. 314        By Trustees for the Poor; Samuel Handy, Sen., Charles
              Bennett, George Hayward
```

Sarah Harnett, adm. of Daniel Hartnett, exhibits account of items used in feeding cretures & family; list

Sally Davis, widow & adm. of John Davis (of George), exhibits account; list

```
              Thomas Dukes, adm. of John Dukes, exhibits account; list;
F. 315        mentions Ralph Milbourn
```

Sarah Bradford, adm. of William Bradford, exhibits account; list; mentions James Bishop, Thomas Jackson, negro Stephen, George Houston, negro Jacob, Thos. Mitchell

F. 316   List of disbursements in estate of Thomas Davis (of Edward), as returned by Handy Davis, adm.; mentions Elias Burbage

F. 317   William Richards, exe. of John Richards, to sell personal estate (except negroes, bacon, farming utensils & team)

Ebenezer Powell, exe. of Zadok Powell, Sen., to sell personal estate (except legacies)

Susanna Townsend, adm. Pendentelite [during litigation] of Elijah Townsend, to sell personal estate

Nancy Hammond, adm. of Edward Hammond, Jun., to sell negro girl Sarah & boy Zeb

F. 318   Handy Davis, adm. of Thomas Davis, allowed 8% on estate

James Davis, guardian to Wesley & Patsey Melvin, to give each 1 month schooling & to be excused from rendering accounts

Eben Christopher & George Parsons to view property of James T. Cathell, in care of William Handy, guardian

Thomas Dukes, adm. of John Dukes, allowed 10% on estate

Order authorizing Henry Richardson, guardian to John & Molly Richardson, to put new logs under roof of old kitchen rescinded; ordered to build new kitchen

Henry Richardson, guardian to John & Molly Richardson, to repair well

Ordered that $2,935, appraised value of negroes in inventory of estate of Elizabeth Selby, exhibited 9 Jan., 1810, by Thomas Selby, Jun., exe., to be deducted, it appearing that negroes belonged to estate of Thomas Selby, Sen.; Thomas N. Williams & William Hudson to reappraise

F. 319   John Stevenson, adm. of Samuel Gillett, to sell personal estate (except legacies)

Edward Stevenson & James Tilghman to view property of Major & Whittington Jones, in care of Jarman Gillett, guardian

George Hall, adm. of Thomas Hall, to advertise in paper at Easton for creditors to exhibit claims

Register to issue subpena for Levin Parsons & Isaac Hearn & wife to shew cause why will of Sarah Parsons should not be admitted to probate

Thomas N. Williams & James A. Collins to view estate of William Richards, in care of William Richards, guardian

Betsey Jones, guardian to Nancy & Sally Jones, excused from rendering accounts untill they reach 14

Edward Stevenson & Esau Boston to view property of Levi, Littleton, Samuel, Peggy & Susan Long, in care of Samuel Tull, guardian

Thomas N. Williams & Joshua Prideaux to divide negroes from estate of Elizabeth Selby, in hands of Thomas Selby, exe.

F. 320   Thomas Barnes, Jun., & Henry Dickerson, adms. of Thomas Barnes, Sen., to sell personal estate (except negroes, crop & 2 yoke of oxen)

Sarah Bradford, adm. of William Bradford, allowed 8% on estate

Eli Collins, adm. of William Coe, to sell personal estate

New warrant for Thomas N. Williams & Nixon Davis to appraise property of John Davis, Sen.

James Duer, use John Townsend, vs. Purnell Porter, adm. of Leah Davis; motion to pass note of Ezekiel Davis, father of Leah, dated 5 Oct., 1801, against estate as heir of Ezekiel; granted

F. 321   Alexander McAllen & Betsey, his wife, admx. of Joseph Kellam, allowed 8% on estate

James A. Collins & James Davis, exes. of John Davis, Sen., to sell corn in additional inventory

Citation for Schoolfield Bradford & wife, surviving admx. of Benjamin Davis, to give counter security

Jonathan S. Parsons, adm. of Sarah Parsons, to sell personal estate (except legacies)

Peter C. Evans, adm. of John Stevenson, allowed 7 1/2% on estate

F. 322   I, John Freeman, of Baldwin Co., GA, appoint David Parker of said county my attorney to receive of exes. of Rachel Hayman, of Worcester Co., MD, legacies willed by said Rachel to Rebecca Disharoon, my wife

15 Mar., 1818 [10]

Saml. S. Steele, Not. Public

John Freeman
her
Rebeckah X Freeman
mark

I, Thomas H. Kenan, Clerk of Superior Court for said county, certify that Samuel S. Steele is qualified as a Notary Public for the town of Milleageville & county aforesaid; 15 Mar., 1810

July 16, 1810, received of Isaac Hayman, $90, in full for Rebeckah Disharoone's part of Rachel Hayman's estate

Test.; Jno. Dashiell   David Parker

Received Dec. 3, 1807, of Isaac Hayman, exe. of Rachel Hayman, negro girl Esther & list, legacies left me by Rachel

Purnell Johnson   Mary Haman, John Toadvine

Received Dec. 3, 1807, of Isaac Hayman, exe. of Rachel Hayman, negro boy Harry, left to Matty Hayman by will of Rachel Hayman

Test.; William Nutter   David Cathell, Matty Cathell

F. 323   Received Dec. 3, 1807, of Isaac Hayman, exe. of Rachel Hayman, a legase left my two brothers, John & Hezekiah Hayman, & myself, negro woman Ross

Test.; John Cathell

hir
Elezbath X Hayman
mark

Received Dec. 3, 1807, of Isaac Hayman, exe. of Ratchel Hayman, a legusa left him by hir, negro Abel

Test.; James D. Hayman   John Hayman

Received Dec. 3, 1807, of Isaac Hayman, exe. of Ratchel Hayman, a legasy left hir by hir, 1/2 of negro Isaac

Test.; James D. Hayman   Ratchel Hayman

Received Dec. 3, 1807, of Isaac Hayman, exe. of Rachel Hayman, a ligase left him by hir, negro George

Test.; John Cathell   Cornelius Hayman

Received Dec. 3, 1807, of Isaac Haman, my part of Rachell Haman's clothing, left me by will

                                                    hir
Test.; Eben Christopher   Elizabeth X Hayman
                                                    mark

Received Dec. 3, 1807, of Isaac Haman, my part of Rachel Hayman's clothing, left me by will

                                                    her
Test.; Eben Christopher   Rachell X Hayman
                                                    mark

Received Dec. 3, 1807, of Isaac Haman, my part of Rachel Haman's clothing, left me by will

                                                    her
                                                 Mary X Hayman
                                                    mark

Received Dec. 3, 1807, of Isaac Hayman, exe. of Rachel Hayman, $10, left me by will

                                                Talby Hayman

F. 324   [blank]

F. 325   Tues., June 11, 1811   All Justices present

Orphan; Henry Sturgis (of John O., Jun.)
Guardian; Leah Sturgis [couldn't write]
Sureties; Handy Mills, John Hall Hill

        Orphan; John Outten Sturgis (of John O., Jun.)
F. 326   Guardian; Leah Sturgis
        Sureties; Handy Mills, John Hall Hill

        Orphan; Handy Mills Sturgis (of John O., Jun.)
        Guardian; Leah Sturgis
F. 327   Sureties; Handy Mills, John Hall Hill

         Orphan; Sarah Sturgis (of John O., Jun.)
         Guardian; Leah Sturgis
         Sureties; Handy Mills, John H. Hill

F. 328   Orphan; Catherine Sturgis (of John O., Jun.)
         Guardian; Leah Sturgis
         Sureties; Handy Mills, John H. Hill

         Orphan; Levin Jones (of John)
F. 329   Guardian; Annanias Jones
         Sureties; Joseph Jones, William Burbage

         Orphan; Benjamin Barnes (of Thomas, Sen.)
         Guardian; Henry Dickerson
F. 330   Sureties; Cornelius Dickerson, Sen., John Corbin

Orphan; Parker Barnes (of Thomas, Sen.)
Guardian; Thomas Barnes
Sureties; Cornelius Dickerson, Sen., John Corbin

         Orphan; George R. Richardson (of Robert)
F. 331   Guardian; Thomas R. P. Spence
         Sureties; William Quinton, Lemuel P. Spence

         Orphan; Comfort Devorix (of John)
         Guardian; George Hayward
F. 332   Sureties; John Stevenson, Ephraim K. Wilson

Major Dorman vs. Isaac Hayman, exe. of Rachel Hayman; defendant,
having failed to give counter security, attachment issue authorizing
plaintiff to take property of deceased from defendant; William Sturgis
         & Eben Christopher to appraise estate: securities; Joshua
F. 333   Morris, John Givan, Jun.

Annanias Jones & Thomas Timmons [couldn't write], vs. Sterling Jones,
adm. of Caleb Powell; defendant having failed to give counter
         security, he to deliver up estate of deceased to plaintiff;
F. 334   Thomas N. Williams & Jacob Dale to appraise estate:
         securities; Joseph Jones, Nehemiah Timmons

F. 335   James Bevans & Matthias Lindsey to view estate of William
         Price, in care of Severn Pruitt, guardian; before Saml. A.
F. 336   Harper: report

         Apprentice; John Duffy, child of the Poor House
         Bound to; Isaac Porter
         Trade; farming
         Term; till 21, on 1 Jan., 1825
F. 337   Surety; William Whittington, Esq.
         By Trustees for the Poor; Samuel Handy, McKimmy Porter,
         George Hayward

F. 338
Apprentice; Mitchell Dirickson, 9 on 15 Jan. next, by consent of his father Milby [couldn't write]
Bound to; Asa Bell
Trade; common labour
N.B. - Mitchell not to be removed out of county to reside with said master
Test.; Jacob Teage

F. 339
Apprentice; William Read, 16 on 25 Sept., by consent of his mother
Bound to; Jesse Jones, house carpenter
Trade; house carpenter
Surety; William Jones
Before Matthias Davis, Kendal S. Crapper

Apprentice; William Grooms, by consent of his mother Amelia [couldn't write]
Bound to; Levi Townsend, planter
Trade; planter
In presence of John Williams, John Cottingham

F. 340
Dear Sir, I give my son Milby [also Milba] Purnell authority to bind my son William Purnell from 1 Jan., 1811, for term of 4 years

Test. present; Sarah X Purnell
            her
            mark

Zadok Purnell
22 Dec., 1810

F. 341
Apprentice; William Purnell [couldn't write], by consent of his parents
Bound to; Timothy Irons, tanner & currier
Trade; tanner & currier
Term; till 1 Jan., 1815
Sureties; McKimmy Porter, William Townsend
In presence of Josa. Fleming, Jun.

F. 341b
Apprentice; Molly Read, child of the Poor House
Bound to; Peter Sturgis
Trade; weave & other house work

F. 342
Sureties; William Bennett, John White (of Southy)
By Trustees for the Poor; Samuel Handy, Sen., McKimmy Porter, Ephraim K. Wilson

F. 343
Apprentice; Jonathan Layton, 16 on 7 Aug. next, by consent of his father David [couldn't write]
Bound to; Levin Brazier [signed Brasher, couldn't write]
Trade; shoe making
In presence of James Law, David Gray

Richard Handy, adm. dbn of John W. Rownd, allowed 8% on estate, exclusive of negroes runaway or dead

F. 344
Richard Handy, adm. of Peggy W. Rownd, allowed 8% on estate

McKimmy, Lemuel & Thomas Timmons, adms. of Benjamin Timmons, to sell personal estate (except wearing apparel)

Thomas Collins, guardian to Susanna Rowley, allowed $10 for her support, she still being indisposed with same affection as mentioned in order of Dec. term, 1808

James & Samuel McMaster, exes. of Samuel McMaster, to sell personal estate (except legacies, wearing apparel & crop)

James Tilghman, exe. of James Ward, to sell personal estate (except wearing apparel)

F. 345 Henry Richardson vs. Evans Hudson & Nancy, his wife, adms. of Robert M. Richardson; John Ayers, one security, is dead, without sufficiency of property to pay debts & Thomas Martin, other security, has removed to Baltimore Co., & estate is wasted; citation for adms. to shew cause why they should not give counter security

Joshua Holloway, adm. of Joseph Holloway, to sell personal estate (except wearing apparel & crop)

Estate of Edward Hammond, Jun., late adm. of Charles Hammond, became answerable for considerable sums for which he didn't obtain vouchers; he paid $20 to Rachel Jones for keeping illegitimate child of deceased in 1808; $182.80 to James B. Robins, part of judgement of William J. Houston against deceased; allowed $408.69 for claims & payments

F. 346 Edward Hammond, Jun., late adm. of Charles Hammond, allowed for corn & negroes siezed by sheriff to satisfy judgement of William J. Houston

Register to state account for Edward Hammond, Jun., late adm. of Charles Hammond, charging him for inventory, sales & monies collected, & crediting him with claims paid

Edward Hammond, Jun., late adm. of Charles Hammond, sold negro Peg to Daniel Jones, which negro was not in inventory; to be charged for same

Er.(?) Truitt & Sarah, his wife, admx. of Isaac William (of Price), allowed 7 1/2% on estate

James Fleming, adm. of James Devorix, to sell negroes

Evans Hudson & Nancy, his wife, adms. of Robert M. Richardson, to sell negroes

F. 347 John Cottingham & Angelo Atkinson to distribute negroes from estate of Thomas Barnes, Sen., in hands of Thomas Barnes, Jun., & Henry Dickerson, adms.

James Fleming, adm. of James Devorix, allowed for negro Sabro, dead

Mary Ann Rice, adm. dbn of John Bratten, allowed $23.10 for costs recovered against late adm. on suits against Joseph Johnson & adm. of John Waters; also for balance due on Zadok Selby's judgement (use of Peter S. Corbin) against deceased

F. 348 Daniel G. Robins, adm. dbn of Daniel Robins, vs. William Corbin, surviving exe. of Peter S. Corbin; defendant to shew cause why a decree should not be entered up on award obtained against him as exe. of Peter S. Corbin, by Bowdoin Robins, former adm. dbn of Daniel Robins, dated 11 Dec., 1807

Whereas Richard Henry Handy, of Somerset Co., took letters of adm. dbn on estate of my father, John W. Rownd, of Worcester Co., & letters of adm. on estate of Peggy Winder Rownd, his widow, & remaining estate descended to me & my sister, Hetty W. Rownd, only heirs of John & Peggy, & whereas negroes Tom, Jacob, Sall, Rachael & Hannah fled, & Linda died, I release said Henry from responsibility for said negroes

F. 349 Charlotte H. Rownd

In presence of Robt. Lemmon, Esq., Justice of the Peace, Som. Co.

Wm. Done, Clk., Som. Co.

[release as above] Negro Linda listed as Leanden

F. 350 Hetty Winder Rownd
F. 351 [continues]

F. 352 [blank]

F. 353 Tues., Aug. 13, 1811   All Justices present

F. 354 Inventory of property taken out of hands of Isaac Hayman, exe. of Rachel Hayman, by Major Dorman, now of Somerset Co., but now of Worcester Co., to be appraised by William Sturgis & Eben Christopher; before George Maddux: report; negro Stephen 22

F. 355 Polly Warrington, Joshua Holloway & Er.(?) Truitt bound to John Lane, on Polly's adm of estate of Isaac Warrington

F. 356 Apprentice; Ayres Stevens, negro, 1 last Feb., son of Nancy
Bound to; Benjamin Cluff
Trade; common laborer
Sureties; Stephen Pilchard, Selby Blades

F. 357 Apprentice; Levin Duffy, mulatto, 18 last Apr., son of Zipporah
Bound to; William Townsend
Trade; farming
Sureties; John A. Townsend, William Rownd

'239'

	Thomas S. Fassitt & Cord Hazzard to view estate of George
F. 358	Sampson, in care of Peter Scott & Mary, his wife, guardians;
F. 359	before Thos. N. Williams: report; land borders lands of

Elijah Williss & of Arthur Tacey [Tracey?]; lot in Poplar Town, 1 3/4 acres

F. 360 Edward Stevenson & James Tilghman, Esqs., to view property of Major Jones, in care of Jarman Gillett, guardian; before Wm. Schoolfield: report; lot in New Town, 1/4 acre

F. 361
F. 362 Edward Stevenson & James Tilghman, Esqs., to view estate of Whittington Jones, in care of Jarman Gillett, guardian; before Wm. Schoolfield: report; 125 acres; widow's dower

F. 363 Thomas N. Williams & Joshua Prideaux to distribute negroes from estate of Elizabeth Selby, in hands of Thomas Selby, exe.; before Wm. McGrigor;
1) to Kitty Selby, daughter; negroes Sacker 18, Eben 10, Hannah 58, Comfort 12, Amey 9
2) to Patty Selby, daughter; Jacob 33, Littleton 13, Daniel 59 (infirm), Hess 16
3) to Peggy Selby, daughter; David 20, Elsa 5, Israel 2, Nell 30, Lidia 7

F. 364 James Tilghman & Joseph Stevenson (of Jonathan) to settle dispute between Lemuel Henderson & James Patterson, exe. of Anderson Patterson

Nixon Davis & Thomas N. Williams, Esqs., to settle dispute between William Hogshire & Nancy Hammond, adm. of Edward Hammond, Jun.

F. 365 Apprentice; Elsea Jones, 15
Bound to; William Bratten, turner
Trade; turner
Sureties; Henry Bradford, Joseph Mumford [neither could write]
Before Nixon Davis, Jacob Dale

F. 366 Apprentice; George Matthews, 18 on 16 Nov. next, by consent of his father Levi, of Somerset Co.
Bound to; Joshua Matthews
Trade; ship carpenter
In presence of Francis Rosse, Ambrose White

F. 367 Apprentice; Samuel Johnson, by consent of his father James [couldn't write]
Bound to; Isaac Cottingham, carriage maker
Trade; carriage maker
Test.; Saml. A. Harper, Geo. Bratten

Robert Mitchell, exe. of John P. Mitchell, allowed 5% on estate

Sally Stevenson, adm. of Edward Stevenson (of Joseph), allowed 10% on estate

Benjamin Melson, guardian to Polly & Benjamin Melson, to rent real estate

Elijah Melson, guardian to Samuel Melson, to rent real estate

Luke Townsend & wife, guardians to Lydia & Milcha Bevans, to give each 6 months schooling

Hetty Lindsey, adm. of Major Lindsey, allowed 8% on estate

F. 368   Peter Scott & wife, guardians to George Sampson, to rent real estate

John & Jacob Evans, exes. of Jacob Evans, to sell personal estate (except legacies)

John Benson, adm. of Tabitha Selby, allowed 10% on estate

Jarman Gillett, guardian to Major Jones, to rent real estate

William Richards, exe. of John Richards, to sell wheat

F. 369   Statement from Samuell Bradford's 10th account on guardianship of William Price: report; mentions deaths of his brother Peter & sister Drucilla

Aug. 24, 1811, received of Samuel Bradford, $81.87, the property of William Price, & receipt for $50, dated July 25, 1811

Test.; Severn Johnson   Severn Pruitt

F. 370   Account of sale of cattle belonging to heirs of John Rackliffe, sold by James Laird, guardian; sold to Dr. George Purnell, Selby Warren, Maj. Prideaux, Obed Brittingham, Nathaniel Brittingham, Kendel Williams, John Tingle; remainder not sold was appraised by Zadok Powell, William Moore & William Johnson; taken by John Rackliffe & Kirk Gunby; 3 cows taken by James Murray, who married Charlotte Rackliffe

F. 371   James Laird, guardian to Rider & Kiturah Rackliffe, swears to above sale; original appraisal given; cattle on Sinepuxent farm

Report of monies due from Rowland E. Bevans, late guardian to Tabitha Selby; mentions bonds due her from Wm. Selby; from John Tunnell, as part of her father's estate; from John Johnson; from sister Elizabeth, over proportion of negroes received by her; allowance for negro Elijah, who was property of James Selby

F. 372   Received 23 Aug., 1811, of Rowland E. Bevans, late guardian to Tabitha Selby, $140.46, balance due from him to estate of said Tabitha, deceased

                                               Jno. Benson, adm.

'241'

F. 373   Tues., Oct. 8, 1811   All Justices present

Orphan; John Ayres Massey (of John A.)
Guardian; Sarah Massey [signed Sary]
Sureties; Levin Dirickson, Zadok Powell

F. 374
Orphan; Kendal Massey (of John A.)
Guardian; Sarah Massey
Sureties; Levin Dirickson, Zadok Powell (of Zadok)

F. 375
Orphan; Daniel Massey (of John A.)
Guardian; Sarah Massey
Sureties; Levin Dirickson, Zadok Powell

Orphan; Rachel Ironshire Massey (of John A.)
Guardian; Sarah Massey
Sureties; Levin Dirickson, Zadok Powell (of Zadok)

F. 376
Orphan; Louisa Massey (of John A.)
Guardian; Sarah Massey
Sureties; Levin Dirickson, Zadok Powell (of Zadok)

Handy Jones discharged from guardianship to Edward Hammond (of Charles); Edward Hammond, Sen., new guardian

F. 377
Orphan; Edward Hammond (of Charles)
Guardian; Edward Hammond, Sen.
Sureties; Ephraim K. Wilson, Thomas N. Williams

Handy Jones discharged from guardianship to Charlotte Hammond; Edward Hammond, Sen., new guardian

Orphan; Charlotte Hammond (of Charles)
Guardian; Edward Hammond
Sureties; Ephraim K. Wilson, Thomas N. Williams

F. 378   George Truitt & wife, discharged from guardianship to John H. Bishop; Patrick Waters new guardian

Orphan; John Henry Bishop (of Charles)
Guardian; Patrick Waters
Sureties; John Sturgis, Lemuel P. Spence

George Truitt & wife discharged from guardianship to William Bishop; Patrick Waters new guardian

F. 379
Orphan; William Bishop (of Charles)
Guardian; Patrick Waters
Sureties; John Sturgis (Bognetinorten), Lemuel P. Spence

F. 380
Apprentice; James Claywell (of Thomas), 10 on 4 Dec. last
Bound to; Samuel Stevenson
Trade; farming
Sureties; Major Tarr, William Rownd, Jr.

F. 381　Apprentice; Samuel Richardson (of George), 18 on 1 Aug. last
　　　　Bound to; John T. Taylor
　　　　Trade; boot & shoe making
　　　　Sureties; Selby Parker, Levin Derickson

F. 382　Apprentice; Abraham Taylor (of James), 14 on 29 Jan. last
　　　　Bound to; James Knox
　　　　Trade; tailor
　　　　Sureties; John T. Taylor, John P. Slemaker

F. 383　John Dashiell & Eben Christopher to view estate of Purnell
F. 384　Johnson Jones, in care of Benjamin Johnson, Sen., guardian;
　　　　before Benjamin Johnson: report; 140 acres called 'Davises
　　　　Outlet'; widow's dower

F. 385　John Dashiell & Eben Christopher to view estate of Nancy
F. 386　Jones, in care of Benjamin Johnson, Sen., guardian; before
　　　　Benjamin Johnson: report; 80 acres called 'Naboths Vineyard';
　　　　widow's dower

　　　　Thomas N. Williams & James A. Collins to view estate of
F. 387　William Richards (of John), in care of William Richards,
F. 388　Sen., guardian; before Wm. McGrigor: report; 330 acres; 1/3
acres of　of 30 acres bought of Col. John Gunby's heirs; 1/3 on 130
　　　　cypress swamp

　　　　Esau Boston & Edward Stevenson to view estate of Thomas Long,
F. 389　in care of Anne Long, guardian; before James Tilghman:
　　　　report; manner plantation; plantation bought of James
F. 390　Merrill; place bought of Edward Lambden; lands bought of
　　　　Floyd & Ballard Blades; 400 acres; widow's dower

　　　　Esau Boston & Edward Stevenson to view estate of Betsey Long,
F. 391-2 in care of Anne Long, guardian; [same as above]

Thomas N. Williams & William H. Taylor to view estate of John, Daniel,
　　　　Kendal, Rachel & Louisa Massey, in care of Sarah Massey,
F. 393　guardian; before Wm. McGrigor: report; 5/6 of tract where
　　　　John Massey lived, with widow's dower, 164 acres; 5/6 of
F. 394　tract called 'Winchester', 85 acres; 5/6 of lot between
　　　　Berlin & Poplar Town

F. 395　Apprentice; Henry Matthews, 17 on 1 Dec. next
　　　　Bound to; George Nelson
　　　　Trade; house carpenter & joiner
　　　　Sureties; George Bratten, John Dickerson

F. 396　John Cottingham & Angelo Atkinson to distribute negroes from
　　　　estate of Thomas Barnes, Sen., in hands of Thomas Barnes,
　　　　Jr., & Henry Dickerson, adms.;
F. 397　1) to Sophia Barnes, widow; negroes Leonard 24, Leah 33
　　　　2) to Nancy Dickerson; Clem 27
3) to Thomas Barnes; James 23

(cont.)

4) to Priscilla White; Zilf 22
5) to Rosa Barnes; Hetta 12
6) to William Barnes; Love 6
7) to Benjamin Barnes; John 4
8) to Parker Barnes; Stephen 20 months

F. 398 Nixon Davis & Thomas N. Williams to settle dispute between William Hogshire & Nancy Hammond, adm. of Edward Hammond, Jr.; Nancy to pay William $24.95; account of how award was
F. 399 figured; mentions Sally Crapper, Ezekiel Smashey: wit.; John Sturgis

Court to settle dispute between Eli Hudson & Littleton R. Purnell, exe. of Dennis Hudson

Order of Apr. term last for Ambrose White & Joshua Fleming, Jr., to settle dispute between Thomas R. Handy, surviving partner of Handy & Robins, & William Handy & George Hayward, exes. of Bowdoin Robins, rescinded, as Joshua Fleming is since dead; Ambrose White &
F. 400 James Givan to act

Apprentice; Littleton Long, 15 on 15 Feb. next, by consent of his father Levin
Bound to; John T. Taylor
Trade; boot & shoe making
F. 401 In presence of Jesse Bennett, Wm. Rownd

Apprentice; Levin Parsons, negro, 9, by consent of his mother
Bound to; Archibald Smith, farmer
Trade; farming
Before Nathan Gordy, George Maddux

F. 402 Louden & Pierce Riggen, exes. of John Riggen, allowed for expense of clothing negroes hired out; account; before James Tilghman

Turner Davis, adm. of Handy Davis, allowed for family expenses; list

F. 403 Handy Davis, adm. of Thomas Davis, allowed for clothing negroes & family expenses; list; mentions Cornelius Crapper, William Davis, Edward Bolds, Mary Stevenson, Sinah Davis,
Levin D. Burbage

F. 404 Thomas & William Franklin, exes. of John Franklin, Sr., allowed for cost of finishing crop & for items consumed by family; list

F. 405 George Parsons, exe. of Matthew Jones, allowed for saving crop; list; mentions Adam Price; before Josa. Fleming, Jr.

Zipporah Hudson, adm. of Joshua Hudson, allowed for negro George (alias George Miller), who obtained his freedom in Worcester Co. Court & which was affirmed by the Court of Appeals for the Eastern Shore
(cont.)

F. 406   Above judgement sworn to by James Easte(?), clk. for Eastern Shore Court of Appeals

Isaac & Esau Timmons, exes. of Elijah Timmons, to sell personal estate

William B. Bell, adm. of Smith Horsey, to sell personal estate (except negroes & wearing apparel)

Louden & Pierce Riggin, exes. of John Riggin, Sen., allowed 10% on estate

F. 407   Sally Fleming, adm. of Joshua Fleming, to sell personal estate (except plate & wearing apparel); also goods belonging to firm of Joshua & James Fleming to be sold

Turner Davis, adm. of Henry Davis, allowed 10% on estate

Zadok Sturgis, adm. of Littleton Sturgis, to sell personal estate (except negroes, plate & wearing apparel)

William White, exe. of Major White, to sell personal estate (except legacies)

Life estate of Nathaniel White in lands belonging to Eliza White, minor, is determined; William McGrigor & [blank] to view lands, in care of Seth Whaley, guardian

F. 408   Ambrose White, adm. of Joshua Matthews, to sell personal estate

Barney Davis, adm. of Matthias Davis, to sell personal estate

William Richards, guardian to William Richards (of John), to repair barn & corn crib

Elizabeth Rankin, adm. of John Rankin, allowed 10% on estate

Mary Parker, adm. of James Parker, to take property of deceased at appraised value

Josiah Bratten & Joseph J. Gilliss to view property of John H. & William Bishop, in care of Patrick Waters, guardian

F. 409   Stephen Purnell, exe. of Thomas Gray, allowed for negro Leah & sorrel horse sold to John Lane on 8 Nov., 1806, & cost of suit for recovery of same

New warrant for John Cottingham & John Corbin to appraise property of Thomas Barnes, Sen.

Nehemiah Burbage, adm. of Mary Burbage, to sell personal estate

Henry Richardson, guardian to John & Molly Richardson, to rent real estate

Amey Furniss, guardian to Isaac, Delia & George Furniss, to rent real estate

F. 410 Obligations in hands of Stuart Williamson, guardian for rent of lands & hier [hire] of negroes of Mary Mitchell, minor, for 1810; Truitt & Coffin for rent of farm; William Franklin (for hire of negro Isaac), Sam Williams (for Litt), Josiah Hill (Levin), Wm. A. Parker (Minte), James Banum (Plem), Alexander Franklin (Charles), Severn Jarvis (Bob), Josiah Crapper (Lante), George Givan (Rachel) [same as above for 1811;] John Williams (Zeb), James Banum (Plem), James Pitts (Charles), John Lamberson (Minte), William Franklin (Isaac), Bradford & Lister (Litt), Isaac Long (Lott), James Franklin (Lante), Caleb Williams (Sarah), Samuel Tindell (Rachel), Edward Williams (Levin), Jacob White (Bob), Stuart Williamson (Jacob), T. N. Williams (John), [blank] Powell (Amey), Stuart Williamson

F. 411 (Omey), memorandum mislaid (George); rent of farm, Truitt & Coffin; rent of 'Golden Valley' to Kerby Smack; inventory of negroes; Major, Sarah, George, Zeb, Plem, Charles, John, Rachel Sen.,Sue, Toney, Hetty, Mille, Nancy, Minte, Stephen, Caleb, Comfort, Isaac, Mine, Jacob, Bob, Isaac, Littleton, Levin, Milby, Ned, Esther, Amy, Lott & child (dead), Lante, Sarah, Rachel Jun., Omey, Jenny; list of property

F. 412 Oct. 9, 1911, received of Stuart Williamson, late guardian, specifics & negroes above listed

Mary M. Mitchell

John Robins, son of Thomas Robins, deceased, releases Elijah Shockley (of Ben), his guardian, from all claims: wit.; Jesse Townsend

Received Jan. 25, 1811, of George & Elijah Parsons, exes. of George Parsons, $167.79, a legacy from my father

Jehu Parsons

Received Mar. 30, 1811, of George & Elijah Parsons, exes. of George Parsons, $127.79, my part of my wife's father's estate

Test.; James Powell   Zechariah Parsons

F. 413 Received Mar. 30, 1811, of George & Elijah Parsons, exes. of George Parsons, $127.79, my part of my wife's father's estate

Test.; Littleton Weatherly   Joshua Johnson

Received Feb. 2, 1811, of George & Elijah Parsons, exes. of George Parsons, L.10, a legacy left to Obediah Disharoon by said George

Jonathan S. Parsons   Henry Parsons, guardian

Received Jan. 21, 1811, of George & Elijah Parsons, exes. of George Parsons, $617,81, my third part of my husband's estate

Test.; Tempy Disharoon   her
                                                Temporance X Parsons
                                                           mark

Received Jan. 21, 1811, of George & Elijah Parsons, exes. of George Parsons, $127.79, my part of my father's estate, & $40, a legacy

Test.; Tempy Disharoon   Nelly Parsons

Received Feb. 2, 1811, of George & Elijah Parsons, exes. of George Parsons, $127.79, my part of my father's estate

Jonathan S. Parsons   Jordan Parsons

Received Feb. 2, 1811, of George & Elijah Parsons, exes. of George Parsons, $127.79, my part of my father's estate, & $40, a legacy

Jonathan S. Parsons   Henry Parsons

Received June 27, 1810, of George & Elijah Parsons, exes. of George Parsons, L.10, a legacy left me by my grandfather, said George

Zechariah Parsons   Tempy Disharoon

F. 414   Received Oct. 16, 1811, of Robert Mitchell, exe. of John P. Mitchell, $843.23, her part of her father's estate

Test.; Polly Mitchell   Eloisa G.(?) P. Mitchell

Received Oct, 16, 1811, of Robert Mitchell, exe. of John P. Mitchell, $843.23, his part of his father's estate

Test.; Eloisa G.(?) P. Mitchell   John Mitchell

Received Oct. 16, 1811, of Robert Mitchell, exe. of John P. Mitchell, $1129.89, his potion [portion] of his father's estate

Test.; John Mitchell   Rufus K. Mitchell

Received Oct. 16, 1811, of Robert Mitchell, exe. of John P. Mitchell, $843.23, his part of his feather's [father] estate

Test.; Eloisa G. P. Mitchell   Isaac Mitchell

Received Oct. 16, 1811, of Robert Mitchell, exe. of John P. Mitchell, $843.23, of my daughter Polly P. Mitchell's estate

Test.; Eloisa G. P. Mitchell   Polly Mitchell

'247'

Received Oct. 16, 1811, of Robert Mitchell, exe. of John P. Mitchell, $2663.02, for personal estate of John P. Mitchell

Test.; Eloisa G. P. Mitchell   Polly Mitchell

F. 415   [blank]

F. 416   Tues., Dec. 10, 1811   All Justices present

Eli Hudson vs. Littleton R. Purnell, exe. of Dennis Hudson; estate of Dennis Hudson indebted to Eli Hudson for $544.66

F. 417   Stephen Adams vs. Littleton R. Purnell, exe. of Dennis Hudson; Littleton to pay Stephen L.19/17/6

Orphan; James Dukes (of John)
Guardian; John Allen
Sureties; John Selby (of Daniel), Eliakim Jones

Orphan; Henrietta Dukes (of John)
F. 418   Guardian; John Tarr [couldn't write]
Sureties; John Allen, Stephen Sturgis

Frederick Conner, Jun., discharged from guardianship to Littleton Devorix; Edward Dymock new guardian

Orphan; Littleton Devorix (of John)
Guardian; Edward Dymock, Jun.
F. 419   Sureties; Ambrose White, Lemuel P. Spence

Orphan; Betsey U. Finney (of John)
Guardian; Rowland E. Bevans
Sureties; Robert J. H. Handy, Thomas Milbourn

F. 420   Orphan; William Finney (of John)
Guardian; Rowland E. Bevans
Sureties; Robert J. H. Handy, Thomas Milbourn

Orphan; Matthias Outten Toadvine (of Outten)
F. 421   Guardian; James Toadvine
Sureties; Robert Nairne, Shepherd Johnson

Apprentice; George Harrison (of William), 14 on 16 instant
Bound to; Jeremiah Messick
Trade; chaise maker
Sureties; Thomas Milbourn, George S. Gunby

F. 422   Apprentice; George Claywell (of Thomas), 17 last Sept.
Bound to; Belitha Hook
Trade; shoe making
F. 423   Sureties; Littleton R. Purnell, Eli Hudson

F. 424
F. 425
Josiah Bratten & Joseph J. Gilliss to view estate of John H. & William Bishop, in care of Patrick Waters, guardian: report; dower of Mrs. Truitt, their mother; 1/2 of garden is property of Miss Mary Spence; 40 acres called 'Dover'; part called 'Devorixs Adventure'

Edward Stevenson & James Tilghman to settle dispute between Bennett H. Clarvoe & John Stevenson, adm. cwa of Samuel Gillett

F. 426
Apprentice; Levin [also Charles] Blake, by consent of his mother
Bound to; Purnell Johnson,, Jr., firmer [farmer]
Term; 8 years
Trade; farmer
Signed by Leah Blake [mother?, couldn't write]
Before Benjamin Johnson, Shipherd Johnson

F. 427
Apprentice; Henny Johnson, child of the Poor House
Bound to; Sarah McMaster
Trade; housework; sewing, spinning & c.
Term; till 16, on 30 Mar., 1814
Sureties; John S. Martin, John Selby
By Trustees for the Poor; Samuel Handy, Sen., McKimmey Porter, Ephraim K. Wilson

F. 428 Jeptha Tarr, adm. of Michael Tarr, allowed for fodder fed to stock; list: wit.; Wm. Rownd

Leah Brittingham, adm. of Elijah Brittingham, to sell personal estate (except legacies & wearing apparel)

John Toadvine & George Persons, adms. of Outten Toadvine, to sell personal estate (except negroes & wearing apparel)

F. 429 Christopher Ball, adm. of John Ball, to sell personal estate

William Richards, exe. of John Richards, to sell team, farming utensils, flax, fodder & corn

William Richards, guardian to William Richards (of Jno.), to clear 10 acres down a ditch cut by Col. Gunby, a part of land bought by John Richards of exes. of Col. Gunby

F. 430 Elizabeth Devorix, late adm. of John Devorix, allowed 5% on estate

Frederick Conner, adm. dbn of John Devorix, allowed 5% on estate

Frederick Conner, adm. of Elizabeth Devorix, allowed 10% on estate

William Parker, guardian to Elizabeth Selby (of Levin), to give her 3 months schooling

Kendal Holloway, adm. of Joshua Holloway, to sell personal estate (except wearing apparel)

Eben Christopher & Joshua Morris to view property of Matthias O. Toadvine, in care of James Toadvine, guardian

James Toadvine, guardian to Matthias O. Toadvine, to repair buildings on farm bought by Matthias' father from John Ingersol & to
F. 431   repair saw mill held in partnership between orphan & Samuel Pollett

Sarah Covington, adm. of William Covington, to sell personal estate (except wearing apparel)

Levin Long, exe. of Jesse Long, to sell personal estate (except legacies & negroes)

Peter Riley, adm. of Thomas Riley, to sell personal estate

Anthony Bacon & George S. Gunby, exes. of John Gunby, to sell negro Ebben

F. 432   Ambrose White, adm. of Joshua Matthews, allowed full time to settle estate, as it is insufficient to cover debts

Sally Fleming, adm. of Joshua Fleming, Jun., to advertise in Poulson's paper at Philadelphia & the Federal Gazette at Baltimore for creditors to exhibit claims

New warrant to Anthony Bacon & John T. Taylor to appraise property of Joshua Fleming, Jun.

Thomas Barnes & Henry Dickerson, adms. of Thomas Barnes, to sell property

Littleton R. Purnell, exe. of Dennis Hudson, allowed 7% on sale of real estate sold by direction of will

F. 433   Received Dec. 4, 1811, of Rachell Bassett, guardian, all my part on the movable property on John Bassett

Test.; William Handcock   hir
                                      Rachell X Bassett
                                              mark

Received Dec. 2, 1811, of Nancy Davis, exe. of Joshua Davis, my part of his estate

Test.; Daniel Handcock   Henny Davis

F. 434   [blank]

F. 435   Littleton Robins, Sen., John Bishop & Zadok Sturgis appointed
          Justices

Robt. Bowie   W. Kilty, Chanc.

Wit.; The Honorable William Kilty, Esq., Chancellor

Tues., Feb. 11, 1812   All Justices present

          Joseph Henderson & Thomas Merrill, bond from Henry Adams (of Somerset
              Co.), guardian to John, Susan & Sarah Adams: sureties; John
F. 436   Stevens, John R. Slocomb

          Orphan; Jesse Long (of Jesse)
F. 437   Guardian; Rebecca Long
          Sureties; William Mills, Levin Long (of Jesse)

          Orphan; Josiah Long (of Jesse)
          Guardian; Rebecca Long
F. 438   Sureties; William Mills, Levin Long (of Jesse)

Orphan; John Long (of Jesse)
Guardian; Rebecca Long
Sureties; William Mills, Levin Long (of Jesse)

F. 439   Orphan; Rebecca Long (of Jesse)
          Guardian; Rebecca Long
          Sureties; William Mills, Levin Long (of Jesse)

          Orphan; James Long (of Jesse)
F. 440   Guardian; Rebecca Long
          Sureties; William Mills, Levin Long (of Jesse)

          Orphan; John Ball (of John)
          Guardian; Christopher Ball
F. 441   Sureties; Samuel Ball [couldn't write], Thomas Collins

Orphan; Luther Ball (of John)
Guardian; Christopher Ball
Sureties; Samuel Ball, Thomas Collins

          Orphan; Delia Ball (of John)
F. 442   Guardian; Christopher Ball
          Sureties; Samuel Ball, Thomas Collins

          Orphan; Peter Lindsey (of Major)
          Guardian; William Aydelott
F. 443   Sureties; Severn Pruitt [couldn't write], Henry Mitchell

Orphan; James Lindsey (of Major)
Guardian; William Aydelott
Sureties; Severn Pruitt, Henry Mitchell

F. 444   Orphan; Zadok Lindsey (of Major)
Guardian; William Aydelott
Sureties; Severn Pruitt, Henry Mitchell

John A. Townsend discharged from guardianship to Hezekiah Dorman; Ephraim K. Wilson, Esq., new guardian

F. 445   Orphan; Hezekiah Dorman (of Nehemiah)
Guardian; Ephraim K. Wilson
Sureties; John C. Handy, John Townsend (Indiantown)

John A. Townsend discharged from guardianship to Anne S. Dorman; Ephraim K. Wilson, Esq., new guardian

F. 446   Orphan; Anne S. Dorman (of Nehemiah)
Guardian; Ephraim K. Wilson
Sureties; John C. Handy, John Townsend (Indiantown)

Apprentice; Shepherd W. D. Porter, 9, illegitimate child of Anne
Bound to; Laban Hudson
Trade; farming
Sureties; Handy Mills, John Selby, Jun.

F. 447   Apprentice; Kendal Crapper, 12 on 8 Mar. last
Bound to; Peter Truitt
Trade; farmer
F. 448   Sureties; Lemuel P. Spence, Isaac Long

Apprentice; Josiah Armstrong (of Sarah), 11
Bound to; Stephen Rownd, black man
Trade; coopper
F. 449   Sureties; Kendal Crapper, Samuel Long

BOOK 13, MH17, 1812 - 1816

MICROFILM: WK 740-742-1

MSA No.: CM 1123-13

Worcester County Orphans Court Proceedings, MH-17, 1812-16

F. 1   Tues., Feb. 11, 1812(cont.)   All Justices present

Apprentice; Philip Turner (of Henry), 15
Bound to; Daniel Patrick
Trade; boot & shoe maker
Sureties; Samuel Truitt, Jeremiah Messick

F. 2   Apprentice; Elisha Davis (of Matthias), 17 last Nov.
        Bound to; Jeremiah Messick
        Trade; chaise maker
        Sureties; Daniel Patrick, John P. Slemaker

F. 3   Apprentice; John Purnell (of Isaac, Queponco), 15 on 29 July
        last
        Bound to; Thomas Purnell
        Trade; boot & shoe maker
        Sureties; Thomas Jones (Queponco), Major Evans

Thomas Franklin & Isaac Ayres to view estate of Lambert Collier (of
        Kendal), in care of George Davis, guardian; before Peter C.
F. 4   Evans: report; land where Joseph Jons [Jones?] now lives in
        Synepuxon Neck, on east side of road leading from Alexander
Massey's down said neck

F. 5   Edward Stevenson & Esau Boston to view estate of Levi,
        Littleton, Samuel [also has Sally], Peggy & Susanna [also
        Susan] Long, in care of Samuel Tull, guardian; before James
F. 6   Tilghman: report; manner place; place bought of James Merrel;
        place bought of Edward Lambden; land bought of Floyd &
Blades; total 400 acres; widow's dower

        Apprentice; John Graham, 10, child of the Poor House, by
        consent of his parents
F. 7   Bound to; West Watson [couldn't write]
        Trade; farmer
        Sureties; Levin Payne, William Ellis (of Wm.) [neither could
        write]
        By Trustees for the Poor; Samuel Handy, Sen., McKimmy Porter,
        George Hayward

        Apprentice; John Ridley, 11, child of the Poor House, son of
        Wm.
F. 8   Bound to; William Ellis
        Trade; farming
        Sureties; Levin Payne, West Watson
        By Trustees for the Poor; Samuel Handy, McKimmey Porter,
        George Hayward

F. 9   Apprentice; Josiah Linch, 9 on 6 Apr. next, by consent of his
        mother Polly, widow of Belitha Linch [she couldn't write]
                                (cont.)

Bound to; William W. Taylor (of Charles)
Trade; farming
In presence of James Law, Goldsbury Blades

F. 10　Apprentice; Henry Cottingham, 13 this day, by consent of his mother
Bound to; Thomas Brittingham, shoe maker
Trade; boot & shoe making
Before William Schoolfield, James Tilghman

Apprentice; William Cord, by consent of his mother Tabitha [couldn't write]
Bound to; Henry Watts, ship carpenter
Trade; ship carpenter
Term; 3 years, 8 months
F. 11　Before Wm. McGrigor, Wm. Dale

Apprentice; William Benson, 18 on 13 Jan. last, illegitimate, by consent of his mother
Bound to; James Tilghman, shoe maker
Trade; shoe & boot making
F. 12　Before John Williams, Wm. Schoolfield

Apprentice; William Price, 11 on 10 June, 1812
Bound to; Joshua Shockley, farmer
Trade; farming
Before Shipherd Johnson, William Sturgis

F. 13　Jacob Teague & Josiah Bratten's account of application of proceeds of negroes mortgaged to them by John Ayres; cash paid Thomas P. Rackliffe on judgement recovered by George Hall against us in Worcester County Court as survivors [sureties?] for said Ayres on bill dated 22 Jan., 1808; cash paid Levin Dirickson on Purnell Porter's judgement against us in Worcester County Court & affirmed in Court of Appeals; to Samuel Porter on his judgement; to Ephraim K. Wilson, to W. Whittington, Esqs.; negroes sold, men George & Abraham, woman Comfort, girls Lotty & Nancy; John C. Handy, clk.,
F. 14　Worcester Co. Court; Jacob Teague, adm. of John Ayres

Thos. N. Williams, exe. of Elizabeth Smack, exhibits account; mentions Jacob White, slave Jake, Mrs. Isabiah Crapper, slave boy Handy (dead), Isaac Collins, Molly Mitchell, Josiah Hill, slave woman Patt & children, Dr. Wm. Selby, Josiah Davis, John J. Williams, Josiah Mitchell's heirs; before Wm. McGrigor

F. 15　Jacob Teague, adm. of John Ayres, allowed &8.95 for articles consumed in family

On application of James Fleming, adm. of James Devorix, Ambrose White & Thomas Milbourn appointed to adjust accounts of partnership which lately existed between Fleming & Devorix

Alexander Franklin, adm. dbn of William Wright, to advertise in the Star at Easton for creditors to exhibit claims

'255'

John Stevenson & James Tilghman to view property of Jesse & Josiah Long, in care of Rebecca Long, guardian

John Holland & Isaac S. Johnson to view property of Peter, James & Zadok Lindsey, in care of William Aydelott, guardian

George Parsons, exe. of Matthew Jones, allowed 10% on estate

William Lister & wife, exex. of David Johnson, allowed 10% on estate

Thomas N. Williams, exe. of Elizabeth Smack, allowed 10% on estate

Thomas N. Williams, adm. of John Taylor, allowed 10% on estate

James Tilghman, adm. of John Patterson, to sell personal estate

F. 16   James H. Rowley, adm. of Coventon Rowley, allowed 10% on estate

William Adams & wife, adms. of Thomas Milbourn, allowed 10% on estate

John S. Martin, surviving exe. of Col. James Martin, allowed 10% on estate

William Parker, adm. of Col. James Houston, states that a suit has been instituted against Major Claywell for recovery of purchase money of lands sold him by deceased; Claywell claims a deficiency in land & has applied to equity side of County Court for relief

Major Evans, exe. of Zeno Evans, to sell personal estate (except legacies)

Ambrose White, adm. of Joshua Matthews, to advertise in Thomas P. Smith's paper at easton for creditors to exhibit claims

Received Oct. 23, 1811, of Major Dorman, a negro boy Stephen & $34.24, his hire, in full of my claims

Test.; John Rider   Samuel Carey

F. 17   [blank]

F. 18   Tues., Apr. 14, 1812   All Justices present

Orphan; Robert H. Davis (of John)
Guardian; James A. Collins
Sureties; Thomas N. Williams, William Richards

Matthias Lindsey discharged from guardianship to Arthur Price; John Price new guardian

F. 19   Orphan; Arthur Price (of Arthur)
        Guardian; John M. Price
        Sureties; Jesse Sturgis, William Vesey [signed Vezey, couldn't write]

Orphan; Selby Lewis (of James, of James)
Guardian; Mary Lewis [couldn't write]
Sureties; Thomas Dennis, Barzilla Adkins

F. 20   Orphan; John B. Ward (of James)
        Guardian; Thomas Curren
        Sureties; Levin Dirickson, William Quinton

Apprentice; William Morris (of James), 16 last fall
Bound to; Jesse Simpson
Trade; farmer
Sureties; Barzilla Parker, Stephen Adams

F. 21   Apprentice; John, negro, 4 last Sept., son of Tabitha (late slave of Nathaniel Bratten)
        Bound to; George Richardson
        Trade; farmer
        Sureties; Purnell Johnson, John Holston

F. 22   Apprentice; James Davis (of Philip), 14 on 8 Mar. last
        Bound to; Whittington Bowen
        Trade; farmer
        Sureties; Robert J. H. Handy, Peter Parker

F. 23   Littleton R. Purnell, exe. of Dennis Hudson, exhibits account of sale of land by direction of will; bought of Sewell Turpin, Esq., 286 3/4 acres; widow's dower

F. 24   Eben Christopher & Joshua Morris to view estate of Matthias O. Toadvine, in care of James Toadvine, guardian; before George Maddux: report; one plantation bought of John
F. 25   Ingersol, 160 acres called 'Summerfield'; other plantation left to deceased by his father, 100 acres; plantation bought of Benjamin Fooks, 267 acres called 'Fort Neck'; 1/2 of saw mill bot of Benjamin Fookes; 3/4 of saw mill bought of Stephen Roach; 100 acres bot of David Brown; 17 acres bought of Joshua Stanford

F. 26   John Stevenson & James Tilghman to view estate of Josiah Long, in care of Rebecca Long, guardian; before William Schoolfield: report; negro Arnold 45 or 50; 100 acres

F. 27   John Stevenson & James Tilghman to view estate of Jesse Long, in care of Rebecca Long, guardian; before William Schoolfield: report

F. 28   Thomas P. Rackliffe & Benjamin Purnell to view estate of Sally Hudson, in care of William Jones, guardian; before James Givan, Sewell Turpin: report; widow's dower; 9 or 10 acres, part of 'Edward Lott'

'257'

	Thomas P. Rackliffe & Benjamin Purnell to view estate of
F. 29	Littleton R. P. Hudson, in care of William Jones, guardian; before James Givan, Sewell Turpin: report; 120 acres, called
F. 30	'The Head of St. Lawrence'; 21 acres called 'Green Briar'; widow's dower

John Holland & Isaac S. Johnson to view estate of Peter, James & Zadok Lindsey (of Major), in care of William Aydelott, guardian;
F. 31   before Wm. Riley: report; mother's dower; 250 acres called 'Mill Branch' & 'Lock'; negroes Harry 56, Ells 16, Linda 21, 2 children, one Leah 4

F. 32   Abishai Davis & Lemuel Showell to view estate of Joseph & George Harrison, in care of Levin Derickson, guardian: report; largest clearing lately occupied by Mrs. Linch; other by David Linch

F. 33   Apprentice; William Mears, by consent of his parents
Bound to; Robert M. Baker, cart wheel right
Trade; cart wheel right
Term; till 21, on 5 Jan., 1822
Signed by Sarah Latchum [mother?, couldn't write]
Before Lemuel Showell

F. 34   Apprentice; David Welbourn, 16 on 14 instant, by consent of his father William Welbern [signed Welburn], of Accomack Co., VA
Bound to; Samuel McMaster, tanner
Trade; tanning & currying
In presence of James Tilghman, Robert Duer

F. 35   Apprentice; Thomas Pollett, 14 on 7 May last, by consent of his father Joshua
Bound to; Levin Hitch
Trade; boot & shoe maker
In presents of Jesse Townsend, Salathiel Griffith

F. 36   Apprentice; Noah Summers, 17 on 17 Jan. next, by consent of his father Obediah [Obed], of Somerset Co.
Bound to; Bennett H. Clavoe [signed Clarvoe]
Trade; shoe & boot making
In presence of Jesse Sturgis, Jas. Tilghman

F. 37   Apprentice; Samuel Ingersol, 16 on 28 June next, by consent of his father John Ingersoll, of Somerset Co.
Bound to; Ebenezer Leonard
Trade; tanner & currier
In presence of George Maddux, Henry Trayder

Apprentice; John Davis (of Daniel), 12 on 11 Dec. next
Bound to; William Brittingham, farmer [couldn't write]
Trade; Farming
Sureties; Purnell Smith, George Brittingham [couldn't write]
Before Nixon Davis, Thos. D. Purnell

F. 38 Thomas N. Williams, adm. of John Taylor, exhibits account; mentions Jacob White, Josiah Davis; before William Dale

F. 39 William Richards, exe. of John Richards, exhibits account; mentions [crossed out;] Charles Davis; James A. Collins; before Thos. N. Williams

William Richards, exe. of John Richards, allowed $37.75 for maintenance of deceased's mother Leah Truitt, until her death

F. 40 Littleton R. Purnell, exe. of Dennis Hudson, exhibits account; mentions Eli Hudson, slaves Levin & Hannah, Major Mariner

Thomas M. Tull & Anne [Anna] Long, adms. of Littleton Long, exhibit account; mentions Ely Cammel, Edward Sevnson [Stevenson?], John Hall Book?

F. 41 Joseph Young, exe. of Zepheniah Benson, exhibits account; mentions Stephen [negro?], Molly Horsey, Alce Roberts, James Henderson, Stephen Perkins, James Roberts, Molly Erickson

John J. White, adm. of George Dykes, to sell personal estate (except negroes)

Mitchell Gray, exe. of Joshua Gray, to sell personal estate (except corn, wheat, 4 horses, yoke of oxen, farm utensils)

F. 42 Christopher Ball, guardian to John & Luther Ball, to give each 2 months schooling

Order for William McGrigor & Abisha Davis to view property of Eliza White, in care of Seth Whaley, guardian, rescinded; William McGrigor & Mitchell Gray to act

John Stevenson, adm. of Samuel Gillett, allowed 10% on estate

Aaron Mezick, exe. of Daniel Wailes, to sell personal estate (except legacies & negro Sam)

James Bevans, adm. of Nathaniel Bevans, to sell personal estate

Eben Christopher, exe. of John Cathell, Esq., to sell personal estate (except legacies & negroes)

Edward Stevenson & Rebecca Hall, adms. of John Hall, allowed 10% on estate

F. 43 James Bevans & Levin Sturgis to view property of Arthur Price, in care of John Price, guardian

William Parsons, adm. of Samuel Parsons, allowed 7 1/2% on estate

Thomas M. Tull & Anne Long, adms. of Littleton Long, allowed 7 1/2% on estate

John Richards, late adm. of William Wright, allowed 5% on estate

Susanna Townsend, adm. Pendentelite of Elijah Townsend, to advertise in Thomas P. Smith's paper at Easton for creditors to exhibit claims

Peter C. Evans, adm. of George W. Evans, allowed 10% on estate

Joseph Young, exe. of Zepheniah Benson, allowed 10% on estate

1812, Mar. 30, received of John A. Townsend, late guardian to Hezekiah & S. Dorman, $564.66, principle of their property in his hands

Wit.; Matthew Hopkins   E. K. Wilson, guardian

Received Mar. 4, 1812, of Samuel Ennis, my late guardian, $422.10, balance due me from my father's estate

Test.; James Selby, Sen.   Mary Ennis

F. 44   [blank]

F. 45   Tues. June 9, 1812   All Justices present

Orphan; John Patterson (of Anderson)
Guardian; Levin Mills
Sureties; James Dickerson, William M. Bevans

F. 46   Orphan; Levin Patterson (of Anderson)
        Guardian; Levin Mills
        Sureties; James Dickinson, William M. Bevans

Orphan; John Robins Purnell (of Dr. John)
Guardian; Henrietta Purnell
Sureties; Thomas R. P. Spence, Matthew Hopkins

F. 47   Orphan; John Timmons (of Benjamin)
        Guardian; McKimmey Timmons
        Sureties; Lemuel Timmons [couldn't write], Thomas Timmons

Apprentice; Josiah Price, mulatto, 14 last Mar., son of Leah
Bound to; Adam Price
Trade; farmer
Sureties; Joshua Morris, Milby Holland

F. 48   Apprentice; John Melvin (of Isaac), 14 on 6 Feb. last
        Bound to; John Hudson
        Trade; boot & shoe maker
        Sureties; Luke Townsend, Joshua Bevans

F. 49   Purnell Toadvine, by Joshua Morris, his attorney in fact, vs.
        George Parsons & John Toadvine, adms. of Outten Toadvine;
Peter Dashiell & Eben Christopher to adjust accounts between claimant
& deceased, relative to their joint adm. of estate of William Toadvine

        Apprentice; Harriot Brittingham (of Elisha), 8, child of the
        Poor House
        Bound to; Abraham Gibbs
        Trade; house work & family occupations
F. 50   Sureties; Jesse Sturgis, William Taylor
        By Trustees for the Poor; E. K. Wilson, Saml. Handy, Sen.,
        McKimmey Porter

        Apprentice; John Ball, 16 on 9 Jan. last, by consent of his
        guardian
        Bound to; Thomas Brittingham, shoe maker
        Trade; boot & shoe making
F. 51   Before Wm. Schoolfield, Jas. Tilghman

        Apprentice; Littleton Collick, 13 on 19 Feb. next, by consent
        of his mother Nancy [couldn't write]
        Bound to; Abel Harmon [couldn't write]
        Trade; farming
F. 52   Sureties; Edward Scarborough, Jno. Selby, Jr.
        In presence of William Rownd, Kendall S. Cropper

Ebenezer Powell, exe. of Zadok Powell, Sen., exhibits account;
mentions A. Holloway, insolvent; before Thos. N. Williams

McKimmey, Lemuel & Thomas Timmons, adms. of Benjamin Timmons, exhibit
account; before Thos. N. Williams

F. 53   Henry Dickeson & Thomas Barns, Jun., adms. of Thomas Barns,
        Sen., exhibit account

Levin Mills & John Logan, adms. of John Mills, to sell personal estate
(except team, farm utensils & provisions for family)

Christopher Ball, guardian to Delia Ball, to give her 2 months
schooling

F. 54   Coventon Rowley, deceased, received for use of heirs of Henry
        Scarborough, to whom there is no guardian, rent of $142;
James H. Rowley, adm. of Coventon, to retain sum untill claims proved

William Rowley, deceased, was indebted to heirs of Henry Scarborough,
to whom there is no guardian, for $50 for rent of land in 1804; James
H. Rowley & Thomas Collins, adms. of William, to retain sum untill
claims proved

Hetty Rowley, guardian to Polly Rowley, excused from rendering
accounts until ward reaches 8

Thomas Collins, guardian to John Collins, excused from rendering accounts untill ward reaches 8

Sally Hammond, adm. of Edward Hammond, to sell personal estate (except wearing apparel)

Ebenezer Powell, exe. of Zadok Powell, allowed 8% on estate

William Jones, exe. of Eli Bowen, allowed 10% on estate

Thomas M. Williams & Jacob Dale to view property of John Timmons, in care of McKimmey Timmons, guardian

F. 55   McKimmey, Lemuel & Thomas Timmons, adms. of Benjamin Timmons, allowed 7% on estate

Henry Bennett, guardian to Isaac Houston, to rent real estate, giving notice at Lane's(?) mill, Poplar Town, Snow Hill, New Town & Salisbury

John Teackle, adm. of Abel Teackle, allowed 6 1/2% on estate

List of estate of Margaret Fassitt (of Rouse), given her by Thomas S. Fassitt, late guardian; list

Received June 10, 1812, of Dr. Thomas S. Fassitt, my late guardian, several negroes allotted to me by distribution made 22 Dec., 1800, & 8 young negroes, the increase; also several obligations for
F. 56   sale of stock; $73.23, my share of my father's estate; profits on my estate from 1 Jan., 1799, to 1 Jan., 1811

Wit.; Littleton Robins, John Bishop   Margaret S. Fassitt

Received of Christopher Ball, $387.54, my part of estate of Levi Ball, Sen.
                                                her
Test.; Gillett Mills, Wm. Hargis   Elesebeh X Ball
                                              mark

Received Sept. 14, 1809, of Christopher Ball, adm. of Levi Ball, $129.16, in full of my demands

Test.; David Baker, William W. Benson   Levi Ball

Received June 13, 1809, of Christopher Ball, adm. of Levi Ball, $129.16, in full of my demands
                                              his
Test.; John Mills   John X Ball
                                              mark

Received Feb. 2, 1809, of Christopher Ball, adm. of Levi Ball, $129.16, in full of my demands
                    (cont.)

Test.; David Baker, John X Henderson   William Ball
                      mark

Received Nov. 28, 1811, of Christopher Ball, adm. of Levi Ball, $129.16, in full of my demands

Test.; David K. Baker   his
                          Samuel X Ball
                           mark

F. 57   Received Aug. 14, 1809, of Christopher Ball, adm. of Levi Ball, $129.16, in full of my demands

Test.; David Baker, Nathaniel Benson   Ralph Richardson

Feb. 17, 1812, received of Mrs. Leah Crapper & Josiah Bowin, $8.65, in full of my wife Rachel's part of William Cropper's estate, for a total of $287.47

Test.; Thos. N. Williams   Jesse Jones

Feb. 17, 1812, received of Josiah Bowin, joint adm. of William Cropper, with myself, $8.65, my due from estate, for a total of $296.13

Test.; Thos. N. Williams   Leah Crapper

Feb. 17, 1812, received of Leah Cropper, joint adm. of Wm. Cropper, with myself, $8.65, my part of Wm. Cropper's estate, for a total of $296.13

Test.; Thos. N. Williams   Josiah Boin [Bowen]

F. 58   [blank]

F. 59   Tues., Aug. 11, 1812   All Justices present

Orphan; Betsey G. Houston (of Caleb)
Guardian; Gillett Mills
Sureties; Levin Mills, Bayly Young [couldn't write]

F. 60   Orphan; Milly Houston (of Caleb)
        Guardian; Gillett Mills
        Sureties; Levin Mills, Bayly Young

Orphan; George Cathell (of John)
Guardian; Eben Christopher
Sureties; George Parsons, Aaron Mezick

F. 61   Orphan; David Cathell (of John)
        Guardian; Eben Christopher
        Sureties; George Parsons, Aaron Mezick

'263'

William Aydelott discharged from guardianship to Zadok Lindsey; Matthias Lindsey new guardian

F. 62
Orphan; Zadok Lindsey (of Major)
Guardian; Matthias Lindsey
Sureties; James Givan, William Guthery

William Aydelott discharged from guardianship to Peter Lindsey; Matthias Lindsey new guardian

Orphan; Peter Lindsey (of Major)
Guardian; Matthias Lindsey
Sureties; James Givan, William Guthery

William Aydelott discharged from guardianship to James Lindsey; Matthias Lindsey new guardian

F. 63
Orphan; James Lindsey (of Major)
Guardian; Matthias Lindsey
Sureties; James Givan, William Guthery

James Laird discharged from guardianship to Rider Rackliffe; James Murray new guardian

F. 64
Orphan; Rider Rackliffe (of John)
Guardian; James Murray
Sureties; John H. Rackliffe, William Whittington

Apprentice; Charles Davis (of Baynum), 17 next Sept.
Bound to; William P. Crapper
Trade; house carpenter
Sureties; Edmond Crapper, Kendal S. Crapper

F. 65
Apprentice; Nehemiah Allen, born Whitsunday, 1803, son of Comfort
Bound to; James Holland
Trade; house servant & waiter
Sureties; Robert J. H. Handy, Jeremiah Messick

F. 66
Apprentice; Tubman Gray (of Johnson), 10 on 10 Feb. last
Bound to; Kendal S. Crapper
Trade; blacksmith
Sureties; William E. Sturgis, Lemuel Purnell

F. 67
Apprentice; Samuel Kollick (of Levin), 12 on 15 Oct. next
Bound to; James Knox
Trade; house servant & waiter
Sureties; Rackliffe Pointer, David Truitt

F. 68
F. 69
William McGrigor & Mitchell Gray to view estate of Eliza White, in care of Seth Whaley, guardian; before Jacob Dale: report; land on Manklens(?) Creek; widow's dower; 410 acres; land adjoining John Laws where Thomas Gray, Sen., formerly
(cont.)

lived, 70 acres; negroes Luke 38, Sam(?) 38, Henry 35 (infirm), James 13, Abner 10, Jude 45 (infirm)

F. 70 Joshua Prideaux & William McGrigor to settle dispute between Major Evans, exe. of Zeno Evans, & William Hickman & George Crippen, representatives; account; mentions coffin for Angelo Evans; John B. Williams, Agnes Evans, James Dale, Moses Freeman, John Lindel, John Jones

Account of sale of real estate of James Ward, by James Tilghman, exe., according to will; Thomas P. Rackliffe, Esq., bought land; crop bought by Parker Collins

F. 71 George Parsons & Peter Dashiell to settle dispute between Levi Cathell & Eben Christopher, adm. cwa of John Cathell

George Parsons & Peter Dashiell to settle dispute between Levi Cathell & Aaron Mezick, exe. of Daniel Wails

Apprentice; Asbery [also Ayresbury] Conner, born 27 Jan., 1802, by consent of his parents
Bound to; Elisha Jones
Signed Elisha Conner [father?, couldn't write]
Before Saml. A. Harper

F. 72 Apprentice; Isaac Gray, 14, by consent of his father Benjamin [couldn't write]
Bound to; Micajah Bowen
Trade; boot & shoe maker
In presence of James Givan

Major Evans, exe. of Zeno Evans, exhibits account; list

F. 73 Major Evans, exe. of Zeno Evans, allowed $20 for keeping stock

Patty Wheeler & James Dickeson, exes. of Zadok Wheeler, Sen., exhibit account; support of negro Rose (superannuated) for 19 months after testator's death; before Jas. Tilghman

Sarah Tracey, adm. of Arthur Tracy, to sell personal estate (except wearing apparel)

Edward Stevenson & Benjamin Aydelott to view property of Betsey & Milly Houston, in care of Gillett Mills, guardian

Aaron Mezick, exe. of Daniel Wailes, to advertise in paper at Easton for creditors to exhibit claims

Edward Stevenson & Benjamin Aydelott to view property of John & Levin Patterson, in care of Levin Mills, guardian

F. 74 John Dashiell & Thomas Fooks to view property of George & David Cathell, in care of Eben Christopher, guardian

'265'

Court orders John Logan, one adm. of John Mills, to strike horse & carriage from inventory, since they are his & only loaned to deceased

John Holland & Isaac S. Johnson to view property of Zadok, Peter & James Lindsey, in care of Matthias Lindsey, guardian

Register to state account for Joshua Holloway, late adm. of Joseph Holloway, charging him with inventory, sales & debts

Matthias Lindsey, guardian to Zadok, Peter & James Lindsey, to dispose of right of minors in certain negroes from estate of their father Major

James Toadvine, guardian to Matthias O. Toadvine, to repair saw mill called Roach's Mill

Stephen Townsend, adm. of Josiah Henderson, to sell personal estate

F. 75 Handy Davis, adm. of Nehemiah Burbage, to sell personal estate

Eben Christopher, guardian to George Cathell, to repair house & mills

Joseph J. Gillis & Benjamin Richardson to view property of William P. Spence, in care of Lemuel P. Spence, guardian

William Holland, adm. of John Williams (blacksmith), to sell personal estate

Patty Wheeler & James Dickeson, exes. of Zadok Wheeler, Sen., allowed 7% on estate

Eben Christopher, exe. of John Cathell, to advertise in paper at Easton for creditors to exhibit claims

Mar. 5, 1811, received of Benjamin Purnell, my former guardian, L.5/12/6, in full of my claims

Test.; John S. Martin   J__?__ Enniss

F. 76 [blank]

F. 77 Tues, Oct. 13, 1812 All Justices present

Orphan; James W. L. Sturgis (of Littleton)
Guardian; Jane Sturgis
Sureties; Zadok Sturgis, John Sturgis (Bognetonorton)

F. 78 Orphan; William Townsend (of Lemuel)
   Guardian; Mary Townsend
   Sureties; John Corban, Isaac Brittingham

Orphan; Fanny [also Fannay] Holloway (of Joseph)
Guardian; John Riley
Sureties; Littleton Riley, Lemuel Purnell

F. 79   Orphan; Joseph Holloway (of Joseph)
        Guardian; John Riley
        Sureties; Littleton Riley, Lemuel Purnell

        Orphan; Elijah Long (of David)
        Guardian; Bennett H. Clarvoe
F. 80   Sureties; James Tilghman, Michael Murray

Orphan; Ebenezer Holloway (of Joseph)
Guardian; Esther Holloway [couldn't write]
Sureties; Lemuel Showell, Lemuel Holloway

George Davis discharged from guardianship to Lambert Collier;
Nathaniel R. Cannon new guardian

        Orphan; Lambert Collier (of Kendal)
F. 81   Guardian; Nathaniel R. Cannon
        Sureties; James Riley, Lemuel Purnell

Apprentice; Purnell Booth Carey, 17 on 28 Sept. last
Bound to; Jeremiah Messick
Trade; wheel making & turning in carriage or chaise making business
Sureties; James Givan, Littleton Quinton

F. 82   Apprentice; James Blake, mulatto, 8 on 1 Nov. instant, son of
        Leah
        Bound to; Stephen Ruark
        Trade; common laborer
        Sureties; Jackson Turner, James Wonnell, Jun.

F. 83   Apprentice; Thomas Purnell (of Milby), [blank] on 24 Dec.
        last
        Bound to; Major Tarr
        Trade; shoe & boot making
        Sureties; David K. Hopkins, John Allen (of Joshua)

F. 84   Apprentice; Israel Collick, mulatto, 10 on 9 Sept. last, son
        of Nancy
        Bound to; Frederick Conner, Sen.
        Trade; farmer
        Sureties; Levin Conner, Kendal S. Crapper

        Apprentice; Henry Davis, mulatto, 17 on 21 Mar. last, son of
        Nancy Collick
        Bound to; Edward Broughton
F. 85   Trade; common laborer
        Sureties; John C. Bacon, William E. Sturgis

John H. Townsend, by Ephraim K. Wilson, his attorney, files petition; states Elijah Townsend died 17 Mar. last, his will left all lands to me; asks that will be admitted to probate

F. 86   Joshua Townsend (of Elijah), under 21, by Susanna Townsend, his next friend, by William Whittington, Esq., his counsel, answers petition; states that after writing of will, Elijah married Susanna Pilchard on 15 Feb., 1808, & on 3 Jan., 1810, had a son, Joshua, who is only & natural heir; Elijah said & wrote that his property should go to his wife & son; asks that will be rejected

F. 87   Will of Elijah Townsend, Dec. 10, 1803;
1) to John H. Townsend, all lands
2) brother Levin Townsend appointed exe.

Wit.; John Thornton, Parker Hickman   Elijah Townsend
Polly Hargis

Deposition of John Thornton & Polly Buchannan (late Polly Hargis); Elijah of sound mind

F. 88   Mem.; defendant presents proof of marriage after writing of will, & of his birth; Elijah's personal estate will not cover debts

Court declares Elijah's remarriage, & birth of son, are in point of law a revocation of will & it is therefore null & void; adm.
F. 89   granted to Susanna Townsend, widow

Benjamin Richardson & Joseph J. Gillis to view estate of William P. Spence, in care of Lemuel P. Spence, guardian; before Nixon
F. 90   Davis: report; negro woman Zilpah; part of tracts called 'Dover'(?) & 'Chance'

John Dashiell & Thomas Fookes to view estate of David
F. 91   Cathell, in care of Eben Christopher, guardian; before
F. 92   Shipherd Johnson: report; 320 acres, part of 'Safeguard' & 'Dover'; negroes Bill 21 (verry sickley), Ester 19, boy Tite(?) 13

John Dashiell & Thomas Fookes to view estate of George
F. 93   Cathell, in care of Eben Christopher, guardian; before Shipherd Johnson: report; land in Somerset Co., 215 acres, called 'Little Neck' & 'Green Briar'; plantation in Worcester
F. 94   Co., 465 acres, called 'Summerfield', 'Good Luck' & 'Hunger & Thirst'; negroes George 45, Jacob 40, Harry 15

Thomas N. Williams & Jacob Dale, Esqs., to view estate of
F. 95   John Timmons, in care of McKimmey Timmons, guardian: report; 120 acres now occupied by Lemuel Timmons; 78 acres occupied by McKimmey Timmons; 160 acres on west side of Pocomoke River; lot at Liberty Town; widow's dower; mentions balance to McKimmey Timmons, Lemuel Timmons, Thomas Timmons, Andesiah Timmons, John Timmons

F. 96   John Cottingham & John C. Bacon to view estate of William
        Townsend, in care of Mary Townsend, guardian; before John
F. 97   Williams: report; 85 acres

        Edward Stevenson & Benjamin Aydelott to view estate of John
F. 98   & Levin Patterson, in care of Levin Mills, guardian; before
        Jas. Tilghman: report; plantations on both sides of County
road leading to VA

F. 99   Apprentice; Richard Samples, back [black?], illegitimate, 6
        last summer, by consent of his mother
        Bound to; John Whittington, farmer
        Trade; farmer
        Before Jas. Tilghman, William Schoolfield

Mrs. Sarah Covington, adm. of William Covington, exhibits account;
list; before Thos. N. Williams

        James Tilghman, exe. of James Ward, allowed $16.67 for claims
F. 100 of George Bennett, John Smock, Isaac Hodge & Charles Kelly

Purnell Porter & wife, admx, of Edward Hammond, Jun., to sell negroes

Thomas P. Rackliffe & Kendal S. Crapper to view property of James W.
L. Sturgis, in care of Jane Sturgis, guardian

John Cottingham & John C. Bacon to view property of William Townsend,
in care of Mary Townsend, guardian

Kendal Jones, adm. of Annanias Bradford, to sell personal estate
(except negroes)

Mitchell Gray & Adam Bravard to view property of Fanny & Joseph
Holloway, in care of John Riley, guardian

Purnell Porter & wife, admx. of Edward Hammond, Jr., allowed for negro
man who died

        Mary Davis, adm. of Edward Davis, to sell personal estate
F. 101 (except corn)

Bennett H. Clarvoe, guardian to Elijah Long (of David), to sell
perishable estate (except negro Comfort)

Sarah Covington, adm. of William Covington, allowed 7% on estate

James Fleming, adm. of James Devorix, allowed 10% on estate

Mitchell Gray, exe. of Joshua Gray, to sell property reserved by order
of Apr. last

Lemuel Showell & John Tull to revalue property of Theodore Gray, in
care of Samuel Gray, guardian

William Parsons, adm. of Samuel Parsons, allowed for deficiency in corn caused by wrong estimation

F. 102   Joshua Prideaux & William Fassitt to view property of Lambert Collier, in care of Nathanial R. Cannon, guardian

John Selby, adm. of Henry Sturgis, to sell personal estate (including his right to certain negroes, if representatives of age & guardians of those underage agree)

Daniel G. Robins, granted adm. of estate of Anthony Bacon, to receive estate from George S. Gunby, late collector

William Jones, exe. of Eli Bowen, allowed for negro Stephen, recovered by Whittington Bowen in Worcester Co. Court

Elijah Vinson, adm. of Isaac Vinson, to sell personal estate (except legacies)

McKimmey Porter & George Hayward to divide negroes from estate of John Gunby, in hands of George S. Gunby, surviving exe.

F. 103   John Stevens, adm. of George Richardson, allowed for so much of proceeds of negroes from estate of Robert M. Richardson, which were sold under order of June term, 1811, as will cover debts, & cost of judgement against Nancy Richardson, adm. of Robert M., in Worcester Co. Court, in Nov., 1806

Polly Mitchell, adm. of Levin Mitchell, allowed $72.53 for county levy paid Robert Nairne, late sheriff, due in 1804 on his property, & property of heirs of Joshua Mitchell

Polly Mitchell, adm. of Levin Mitchell, allowed $779.45 paid Elizabeth Smock, adm. dbn of Joshua Mitchell, balance due from deceased as late exe. of Joshua, & $169, a debt due Joshua from John Postly

Polly Mitchell, adm. of Levin Mitchell, allowed 8% on estate; order of Apr. term, 1809, rescinded

Evans Hudson & wife, admx. of Robert M. Richardson, allowed for negroes Shadrach & Zadok, since dead

Betsey Long & Thomas Tull, guardians to Levi, Littleton, Sally, Peggy, Susan, Betsey & Thomas Long (of Littleton), to rent real estate

F. 104   Polly Truitt, adm. of James Truitt (of Jas.), to sell personal estate

Daniel G. Robins, adm. of Anthony Bacon, to sell personal estate

William Dixon, exe. of Nathaniel Dixon, to sell personal estate

Lemuel Purnell, exe. of Esther Purnell, to sell personal estate (except wearing apparel, negroes & corn)

'270'

John Bishop, surviving exe. of Robert Hudson, allowed 7 1/2% on estate

Matthias Lindsey, guardian to Zadok, Peter & James Lindsey, states that orphans are entitled to 2/3 of negroes from estate of their
        father Major, & William Aydelott, who married widow, is due
F. 105   1/3; John Holland & William Holland to divide negroes

Nancy Duer & Robert Duer, adms. of James Duer, to sell personal estate (except wearing apparel, negroes, corn & bank stock)

John O. Selby & Benjamin Gunby, adms. of Jonathan Garrison, to sell personal estate (except negroes)

F. 106   [blank]

F. 107   Tues., Dec. 8, 1812   All Justices present

George Hayward, Esq., Sheriff

John Laws discharged from guardianship to John Henderson; Robert Givans new guardian

Orphan; John Henderson (of Curtis)
Guardian; Robert Givan, Sen.
Sureties; Robert Givan, Jun., John Harris

F. 108
       Orphan; Mordecai Davis (of John, blacksmith)
       Guardian; John Jones (of McClemmy)
       Sureties; Robert Nairne, Barzilla Parker

Orphan; Peter Campbell Davis (of John, blacksmith)
Guardian; John Jones (of McClemmy)
Sureties; Robert Nairne, Barzilla Parker

F. 109   Orphan; Louisa Atkinson Bevans (of Nathaniel)
       Guardian; Eleanor Bevans
       Sureties; James Bennett, John Bradford

       Orphan; Nathaniel Bevans (of Nathaniel)
       Guardian; Eleanor Bevans
F. 110   Sureties; James Bennett, John Bradford

Apprentice; Thomas Devorix, 15 on 9 Sept. last, son of Samuel
Bound to; Peter Richardson
Trade; farmer
Sureties; Peter Truitt, Jethro Richardson

F. 111   Apprentice; John Price (of Amey), mulatto, 10
       Bound to; Joshua Morris
       Trade; farmer
       Sureties; William Dixon, Nathaniel Dixon (of Ambrose)

F. 112   McKimmey Porter & George Hayward to distribute negroes from
         estate of Col. John Gunby, in hands of George S. Gunby,
surviving exe., according to will; before Thomas Milbourne: inventory;
         Malacha, Stephen, Calob, Abner & Dinah dead; Ebben sold;
F. 113   1) to Ann; negroes Bob 42, Cosmose 18, George 51, Stephen 16,
         Lydia 50, Peggy 43, Sarah [also Sally] 6 months (increase),
Ann 6 months (increase), Hetty 11
2) To Sally White; Frank 38, Jack 43, Jim 17, Comfort 12, Esther 43,
Kendal 9, Sarah 4 (increase)
3) to John; Lott 50, Will 22, Ned 45, Belitha 15, Joice 53, Handy 8,
Sue 7, Lambert 3 (increase)

F. 114   Edward Stevenson & John Stevenson to divide negroes from
         estate of Jesse Long; before James Tilghman;
F. 115   1) to widow; negroes Stephen, Phylis, Mary
         2) to Jesse Long; Leah
3) to Nancy Long; York
4) to John Long; Arnold
5) to Rebecca Long; Saml.
6) to Harriott J. Long; Robert

John Stevenson & Bayly Young to settle dispute between Susanna
Townsend, adm. Pendentelite of Elijah Townsend, & Levin Townsend

George Hayward & Robert J. H. Handy, Esqs., to settle dispute between
William Bacon & Daniel G. Robins, adm. of Anthony Bacon

         Apprentice; Major Hutt (19 on last of Mar. next), Jonathan
F. 116   Hutt (17 on last of May next), Henry Hutt (13 on last of May
         next), Moses Hutt, Jun. (11 on last of June next), by consent
         of their father Moses [couldn't write]
         Bound to; John Williams
         Trade; farming
         In presence of John Cottingham, Jackson Turner

         Apprentice; John Dunnaway, 12 on 24 Dec., 1812, illegitimate,
         by consent of his mother
         Bound to; Jesse [also has Elijah] Dale, farmer
F. 117   Trade; farming
         Before Josiah Mitchell, Robert Mitchell

Apprentice; James Redden, 16 on 29 Nov. last, by consent of his father
Shadrach [couldn't write]
Bound to; Luke Townsend
Trade; blacksmith
In presence of James Tilghman, Moses U. Jones

         Littleton R. Purnell, on adm. of William Davis (blacksmith),
F. 118   exhibits account; list; mentions negroes Ruben, Lige, Isaac,
         George, Charles, Moses; McKimmey Pennewell, Purnell
Pennewell, Thomas Pennewell, Stephen [negro?]; slave girl Rhoda

William Crapper, adm. of Anne Crapper, to sell personal estate

Kendal Holloway, adm. of Joshua Holloway, allowed 8% on estate

Kendal Holloway, adm. dbn of Joseph Holloway, allowed 4% on estate

F. 119   John Dashiell & George Parsons to view property of George N. Fooks, in care of Joshua Johnson, guardian

Cord Hazzard & Kendal S. Crapper to appraise property of Nehemiah Burbage not in inventory

Edward Stevenson & John Stevenson to divide negroes from estate of Jesse Long, in hands of Levin Long, exe.

Selby Parker & Thomas D. Purnell to view property of John Henderson, in care of Robert Givan, Sen., guardian

Zadok Sturgis, adm. of Littleton Sturgis, allowed 7 1/2% on estate

Alexander McAllen & Betty, his wife, admx. of Joseph Kellam, allowed 8% on estate

Alexander McAllen & Betty, his wife, admx. of Joseph Kellam, to sell negroes

Register, as trustee for heirs of Robert M. Richardson, to pay William Whittington, Esq., $15, & Josiah Bayly, Esq., $10, their trial fees on suit brought by John Thompson against admx., & monies as proceeds of certain negroes

F. 120   John Stevenson, adm. of Betsey Jones, to sell negro Esther

John Stevenson, adm. of Josiah Long, to sell personal estate

Order appointing Selby Parker & Thomas D. Purnell to view estate of John Henderson, in care of Robert Givan, guardian, rescinded; Selby Parker & William Parker to act

Mary Ann Rice, adm. dbn of John S. Bratten, to advertise in paper at Easton for creditors to exhibit claims

Daniel G. Robins, adm. of Anthony Bacon, allowed full time to settle estate, as it is insufficient to cover debts

Sally Fleming, adm. of Joshua Fleming, Jun., states that Anthony Bacon, one person appointed to appraise property not in inventory, is dead; John T. Taylor & Thomas Milbourn to act

F. 121   [blank]

F. 122   Tues., Feb. 9, 1813   All Justices present

F. 123   Orphan; Thomas May Purnell (of John, of Wm.)
Guardian; Thomas Purnell (of William)
Guardian; Joshua Prideaux, William Riley

Lemuel P. Spence discharged from guardianship to Irving Spence; John
S. Spence new guardian

Orphan; Irving Spence (of George)
Guardian; John S. Spence
Sureties; Lemuel P. Spence, Joshua Prideaux

F. 124   Apprentice; Levin Johnson (of Micajah), 12 next May
Bound to; John Bowen
Trade; boot & shoe maker
Sureties; Barnabas Henderson, Purnell Porter

F. 125   Apprentice; Joshua Burbage (of Nehemiah), 15 on 14 Jan. last
Bound to; Josiah Hickman
Trade; coasting
Sureties; Barnabas Henderson, George Davis

F. 126   Apprentice; James Burbage (of Nehemiah), 17 on 7 June next
Bound to; James Gray
Trade; tanner & currier
Sureties; William Holland (of Levin), Levin Crapper

F. 127   John Dashiell & George Parsons to view estate of George Noble
Fookes, in care of Joshua Johnson, guardian; before Shipherd
F. 128   Johnson: report; 356 acres called 'Driskells Industry' &
'Sarahs Choice'

       Selby Parker & William Parker to view estate of John
F. 129   Henderson, in care of Robert Givan, Sen., guardian; before
William Townsend: report; 320 acres called 'Adventure'

       Joshua Prideaux & William Fassitt to view estate of Lambert
F. 130   Collier, in care of Nathaniel R. Cannon, guardian; before Wm.
F. 131   McGrigor: report; 350 acres

       Thomas P. Rackliffe & Kendal S. Crapper, Esqs., to view
F. 132   estate of James W. L. Sturgis, in care of Jane Sturgis,
guardian; before Edwd. Broughton: report; widow's dower; land
called 'York', 190 acres

Purnell Toadvine, by Joshua Morris, his attorney, vs. George Parsons &
John Toadvine, adms. of Outten Toadvine; Peter Dashiell & Eben
       Christopher to adjust accounts between claimant & estate of
F. 133   deceased relative to their joint adm. of estate of William
Toadvine; adms. of Outten to pay Purnell $435.45

       Apprentice; John Covington, 16 on 22 Mar. next, by consent of
his father Thomas, of Somerset Co.
Bound to; Henry Hayman
Trade; House carpenter & joiner
F. 134   In presence of Levin Jones, Sen., John H. Bell

'274'

	Apprentice; John Henderson, 8 this month
	Bound to; Isaac Benson, copper [cooper]
F. 135	Trade; copper, as far as the branch of a cedar copper
	Surety; William Benson
	Before Jas. Tilghman, James Patterson

```
           Apprentice; John Henderson, 8 this month
           Bound to; Isaac Benson, copper [cooper]
F. 135     Trade; copper, as far as the branch of a cedar copper
           Surety; William Benson
           Before Jas. Tilghman, James Patterson

           Apprentice; Parker Selby, 17 next Oct., by consent of his
           mother Comfort [couldn't write]
           Bound to; Goldsborough [also Goldsbury] Blades
F. 136     Trade; blacksmith
           In presence of James Law, James W. Taylor

           Apprentice; William Handy Wailes, by consent of his father
           Benjamin, of Somerset Co.
           Bound to; Ebenezer Leonard
           Term; 9 years from 7 Apr. next
           Trade; tanner & currier
F. 137     Wit.; George Maddux

           List of property of Littleton Sturgis, deceased, appraised &
F. 138     not sold; mentions Dr. Stephen White, Kendal S. Cropper,
           Josiah Cropper, Cornelius Cropper, Dr. Rownd, Jesse Dear (for
making coffin for negro boy Bob), Leml. Bowin, Josiah Collins; Zadok
Sturgis, Esq., adm.
```

Edward Robins & William Johnson to view property of Thomas May Purnell, in care of Thomas Purnell (of Wm.), guardian

Nancy Miller, exe. of Joseph Miller, to sell personal estate (except legacies)

Sally Fleming, adm. of Joshua Fleming, to sell property in additional inventory (except wearing apparel & negro Hetty)

Elisha & George Davis, exes. of Jesse Davis, to sell personal estate (except negroes)

F. 139   Samuel Tarr, guardian to Patty Taylor, excused from rendering accounts

James Tilghman, exe. of James Ward, allowed 7% on estate

Benjamin Richardson, adm. of Samuel Bishop, to sell personal estate

Zadok Sturgis, adm. of Littleton Sturgis, allowed for negro Bob, dead

Purnell Toadvine, exe. of Priscilla Toadvine, allowed 10% on estate

Purnell Toadvine, exe. of Priscilla Toadvine, allowed for corn & pork

John Bishop, surviving exe. of Robert Hudson, allowed for fodder & hogsheads

F. 140 John Bishop, surviving exe. of Robert Hudson, to retain $40 to meet claim due from deceased as security on Nehemiah Davis' guardianship to William Hudson

George Parsons, acting exe. of Matthew Jones, allowed for corn, pork & c., overestimated in inventory

Received 5 Dec., 1812, of Dr. John S. Martin, surviving exe. & trustee under will of Col. James Martin, negro man Peter & woman Patience, & $285.59, my third of proceeds of land sold by direction of will

           Mary Martin

Received Baltimore, [blank] 5, 1812, of Dr. Jno. S. Martin, $285.59, my part of estate of Col. James Martin

Test.; James Dawes   Mary Wise

Snow Hill, Nov. 21, 1812, received of John S. Martin, surviving exe. of Col. James Martin, cow & $53, a legacy left me in will

           Betsy Wise

Snow Hill, Mar. 1, 1813, received of John S. Martin, surviving exe. & trustee under will of Col. James Martin, $200, my part of proceeds of land sold by direction of will

Wit.; Samuel Trehearn   James P. Martin

Snow Hill, Oct. 23, 1812, received of Dr. John S. Martin, surviving exe. & trustee under will of Col. James Martin, $200, my part
F. 141 of proceeds of land sold by direction of will

Wit.; Leml. Purnell   Thos. L. Martin

Baltimore, Dec. 5, 1812, received of Dr. Jno. S. Martin, $285.59, my part of estate of Col. James Martin

           James Dawes
F. 142 [blank]

F. 143 Tues., Apr. 13, 1813 All Justices present

Hannah Campbell, by Leah Ball, her guardian & next friend, vs. Christopher Ball, adm. of John Ball; property in list marked 'A' came to hands of deceased by his marriage with Leah Campbell, widow of John Campbell, father of Hannah, & it belongs, by right & justice, to his representatives; defendant to pay Hannah, only child of John, $38.25, being 2/3 of what he sold it for; list

F. 144 Foregoing is true list of property we appraised at Benjamin Davis'
           Benj. Aydelott
           Benjamin Cluff

1812, Sept. 5, Warner Davis swears that above articles were removed from house of John Cambel, Accomack Co., VA, to house of Benj. Davis, by Wm. Davis & myself after death of said Campbell

Wit.; Jas. Tilghman

F. 145
 Orphan; Nancy M. McNeill (of Robert)
 Guardian; James A. Collins
 Sureties; Alexander Franklin, Stephen Purnell

Orphan; Nathaniel M. McNeill (of Robert)
Guardian; James A. Collins
Sureties; Alexander Franklin, Stephen Purnell

F. 146
 Orphan; Henry Bishop (of Samuel)
 Guardian; John Richardson (of Thos.)
 Sureties; Josiah Bratten, Benjamin Thomas Richardson

Orphan; Hannah Davis Campbell (of John)
Guardian; Leah Ball [couldn't write]
Sureties; William M. Bevans, Joshua Brittingham

F. 147
 Orphan; James Ayres Gillett (of Ayres)
 Guardian; John Gillett
 Sureties; Samuel McMaster, John Buchannan [signed Bowhanan]

F. 148
 Apprentice; James Sturgis (of John), 15 [blank] instant
 Bound to; John Spencer
 Trade; boot & shoe making
 Sureties; Levin Hill, William Walton

F. 149
 Apprentice; Littleton Burbage (of Nehemiah), 11 on 12 Aug. last
 Bound to; Levin Crapper
 Trade; farming
 Sureties; William Richardson (of Whittington), Lemuel Purnell

F. 150
 Apprentice; James Taylor (of Teackle), 11
 Bound to; Stephen Jones
 Trade; farmer
 Sureties; John Allen, John Selby

F. 151
 Apprentice; Richard Tilghman, 16 on 14 Dec. last
 Bound to; Stephen Ennis
 Trade; house carpenter & joiner
 Sureties; John J.(?) White, Cord Hazzard

F. 152
 Apprentice; Henry Bishop (of Samuel), 16 next Aug.
 Bound to; Stephen Ennis
 Trade; house carpenter & joiner
 Sureties; Cord Hazzard, John J. White
 John Richardson, guardian

Apprentice; Thomas Dukes (of Robert), 16
Bound to; McKimmy Lecount
Trade; ladies shoe making
F. 153 Sureties; Jeremiah Messick, Isaac Brittingham

Apprentice; John Dukes (of Robert)
Bound to; James Wonnell
Trade; farming
Sureties; John Powell, Loudy Riggin

F. 154   Edward Robins & William Johnson to view estate of Thomas May
F. 155   Purnell, in care of Thomas Purnell (of Wm.), guardian; before
Thos. N. Williams: report; 300 acres called 'Genezar' in Synepuxent Neck

         Thomas N. Williams & Cord Hazzard, Esqs., to view estate of
F. 156   Nancy M. McNeill, in care of James A. Collins, guardian;
         before Peter C. Evans: report; lot in Buckingham Hundred,
F. 157   part of 'Unity', 8 1/2 acres; plantation in Acquango Hundred,
         where William Hosier lives, 150 acres; widow's dower

         Thomas N. Williams & Cord Hazzard, Esqs., to view estate of
F. 158   Nathaniel M. McNeill, in care of James A. Collins, guardian;
         before Peter C. Evans: report; land, saw & grist mill in
F. 159   Aquongo Hundred, where Joseph Miller lately lived, 375 acres;
         widow's dower

George Hayward & William Quinton to distribute personal estate of
         William Smullen, Sen., in hands of Peter Smullen, adm.;
F. 160   1) to Scarborough Smullen, widow; list
         2) to Scarborough Smullen, daughter; list
3) to Comfort Smullen, daughter; list
4) to Peter Smullen, son; list
5) to Randle Smullen, son; list
6) to Sally Smullen, daughter; list

F. 161   On application of James Fleming, adm. of James Devorix,
         surviving partner of Fleming & Devorix, Ambrose White &
Thomas Milbourn to adjust accounts; debts due to William Cannon,
merch., Baltimore, & Jackson Turner; mentions Wm. Devorix, Wm. E.
         Brittingham;
F. 162   Share due James Fleming; mentions Micajah Selby, Wm. Cutler,
         Zepheniah Hosier, Milby Holland, John Jones, John Dryden,
Jeremiah Messick, Wm. Tingle, Wm. Richardson, John Barrett, Isaac
Collins, Wm. Dryden, Isaac Pewsey, Asa Bell, Jessee Mumford, Wm.
Stanford, Joseph Furrow
Share due estate of James Devorix; mentions John Johnson (of Leonard),
John P. Slemaker, Joshua Brittingham, Patrick Waters, Wm. E.
Brittingham, Wm. Rownd, James Ward, Robt. Henry, Wm. Savage, McKimmy
Lecompt, John Lockerman, William Lecompt, Joshua Fleming, Esq.,
         Timothy Irons, Parker Purnell, Moses Greer, James Holland,
F. 163   Edwd. H. Rownd, Parker Dukes, James Driden, Abraham Enos
         [Ennis?], Danl. Patrick, Thos. Cottingham, Wm. Tingle, Robert
                              (cont.)

Moore, Milby Atkinson, Saml. Pettitt, Thos. Milbourn, Littleton Riley, Hugh McGan, Wm. Smith, George McNeill, Hannah Webb, James Ellis, E. K. Wilson, Esq., Peter Parker, Saml. Marshall, Elias Paynter, Thos. Shockley, Saml. Johnson, John Pettit, Dr. John Neill, Parker Bowen, Jackson Turner, Sally Murphey, Laben Hudson, Jas. Brown, Jesse Ennis, Thos. Jones, Jas. Dennis (of Valentine), Isaac Pewsey, Isaac Quinton, Benj. Adams, Valentine Dennis, Turner Davis, Peter White, John Bell, James Bennett, Saml. Handy, Jr., Wm. Gaston(?), Jas. Truitt (of Betty), Saml. Truitt, Jas. Conner, Jas. Ishom, Wm. Truitt, Elijah Turpin, Betsey Taylor

Dr. John Stevenson & James Tilghman, Esq., to settle dispute between William Warrington, adm. of Joshua Townsend, & Susanna Townsend, adm. of Elijah Townsend

Alexander Franklin & George W. Purnell to settle dispute between Thomas S. Fassitt & Sarah Tracey, adm. of Arthur Tracey

F. 164 Apprentice; James Adams, 15, by consent of his mother
Bound to; James Tilghman, shoe maker
Trade; boot & shoe making
Surety; Moses Jones
Before William Schoolfield, James Patterson

Apprentice; Peter Davis, 17 on 4 Sept. last, by consent of his father Nixon
Bound to Henry White
Trade; blacksmith
F. 165 In presence of Richard Beathard, James Holland [neither could write]

Apprentice; William Allegood [also Alligood], 11 on 27 Jan., 1813, by consent of his grandfather Adam Price
Bound to; William Bigland [also Biglen]
F. 166 Before Nathan Gordy, George Maddux

Apprentice; James Christopher, 13 on 1 Mar. last
Bound to; William Gordy, farmer
Trade; farming
Before George Maddux, Nathan Gordy

Apprentice; Samuel Smith (17 on 4 Sept. next), Jacob Smith (14 on 2nd of present month), George Smith (11 on 2 Sept. next), by consent of their mother Celia [couldn't write], in consideration of pork & corn paid by Littleton Dennis, Sr.
Bound to; Littleton Dennis
Trade; farming
F. 167 N.B.- Samuel free 4 Sept., 1817; Jacob free 2 Apr., 1820; George free 2 Sept., 1823
In presence of John Cottingham, Wm. Schoolfield

Apprentice; William Dryden, 17 on 7 Feb. last, by consent of his father William
(cont.)

F. 168   Bound to; Robert Smith
         Trade; coach & carriage making
         In presence of Danl. G. Robins, William S. Corbin

Elisha Baynum, adm. of William Baynum, exhibits account; mentions John
         Davis, Eli Powell, Levin Blake, Nancy Baynum, Isaac Bredell,
F. 169   negro girl hired of Dr. Stephen White, Armwell Holloway,
         Isaac Long

Loudy & Pierce Riggen, exes. of John Riggen, exhibit account; mentions
negro Harry hired of Betsey Atkinson; John F. Atkinson, one appraiser

F. 170   Christopher Ball, adm. of John Ball, exhibits account;
         mentions Thomas Ball, Levi Ball, Luther Ball, Wm. Davis, B.
Davis, Susey Outten, Dr. E. H. James

F. 171   James Davis, guardian to Wesley & Patsey Melvin, to give each
         1 month schooling

Dr. John Stevenson, adm. of Samuel Gillett, allowed $10.75 for stear
[steer] sold, but lost

Rebecca Sears, adm. of John Sears, to sell personal estate (except
negro boy Milby)

James Melvin, adm. of Spencer Davis, to sell personal estate

Thomas N. Williams & Cord Hazzard to view property of Nancy M. &
Nathaniel M. McNeill, in care of James A. Collins, guardian

Levin Long, exe. of Jesse Long, allowed 6% on estate

New commission to Nehemiah Holland & James Bevans to view property of
James [John crossed out] Sturgis, in care of John Allen, guardian

         William Handy & George Hayward, exes. of Bowdoin Robins,
F. 172   allowed 8% on estate

Daniel G. Robins, adm. of Anthony Bacon, to advertise in the American
at Baltimore & a paper at Easton for creditors to exhibit claims

Alice Perdue, adm. of Elizabeth W. Perdue, to sel personal estate

Kendal Holloway, adm. of Joshua Holloway, to retain amount of claim of
Edward Dingle

Kendal Holloway, adm. of Joshua Holloway, to retain, as adm. dbn of
Joseph Holloway, amount due from Joshua as late adm. of Joseph

Thomas Rackliffe & Jacob Teague to distribute negroes from estate of
Joshua Bowen, in hands of Barnabas Henderson & Elizabeth, his wife,
guardians to Sally Bowen, if representatives of Joshua, who are of
age, consent

F. 173   John Stevenson, adm. of Josiah Long, allowed full time to
           settle estate, as it is insufficient to cover debts

John Stevenson, adm. of Josiah Long, to advertise in paper at Easton
for creditors to exhibit claims

Levin Long, exe. of Jesse Long, allowed $9.33 for debt returned as
collected from James Tilghman

John Allen, guardian to James Dukes, excused from rendering accounts
untill he reaches 14

Christopher Ball, adm. of John Ball, allowed 10% on estate

F. 174   [blank]

F. 175   Tues., June 8, 1813   All Justices present

Apprentice; James Brittingham (of Isaac), 16 on 13 Oct. next
Bound to; Thomas Dorman
Trade; taylor
Sureties; James Cottingham, Isaac Brittingham

F. 176   Apprentice; John Ames (of Caleb), 14 on 16 July instant
           Bound to; Levin Watson
           Trade; boot & shoe maker
           Sureties; William Holland, John Selby (of Daniel)

F. 177   Nehemiah Holland & James Bevans to view estate of James
F. 178   Sturgis, in care of John Allen, guardian; before Wm. Riley:
           report; 10 acres

John Holland & Isaac S. Johnson to view estate of James, Peter & Zadok
           Lindsey, in care of Matthias Lindsey, guardian; before Wm.
F. 179   Riley: report; negro Harry 50, boy Ells(?) 18, Leah 6; 250
           acres called 'Mill Branch' & 'The Lock'

John Holland & William Holland to distribute negroes from estate of
Major Lindsey (died intestate, leaving a widow & sons Peter, Zadok &
James), in hands of Matthias Lindsey, guardian; 1/3 of negroes to be
           allotted to William Aydelott, who married the widow; before
F. 180   Wm. Riley;
                1) to William Aydelott; Linda 20, girl 18 months
      2) to 3 sons in common; Harry 50, Ells 18, Leah 6

Thomas P. Rackliffe & Jacob Teague to distribute negroes from estate
of Joshua Bowen; Barnaby Henderson & Elizabeth, his wife (late widow
           of Joshua & guardian to Sally Bowen), state that negroes fell
F. 181   to widow & 5 children, John, Hetty, Caty, Joshua & Sally;
           Caty (Catherine) & Joshua are since dead & several negroes
           have been born; ask new distribution; dead since appraisal,
F. 182   women Sarah & Hannah; increase, Lydia 10, Leah 8, Rachel 7,
           Samuel 5, Thamar 18 months;
                              (cont.)

'281'

1) to Barnaby Henderson & wife; Sarah, Rachel, Samuel
2) to John Bowen; Hannah
3) to Hetty, now married to William Beachboard; Leah, Tamar
4) to Sarah Bowen; Lydia

F. 183   Apprentice; James Oliphant, 17 this month, by consent of his father Hugh, of Somerset Co. [couldn't write]
Bound to; Levin Hitch
Trade; boot & shoe maker
Term; till 1 Mar., 1815
In presence of Purnell Trader, Jesse Townsend

F. 184   Apprentice; Henrietta [also Henny] West, 13 on 29 Apr. next, by consent of her stepfather, Francis Rosse
Bound to; Euphemia [also Euphamy] Brittingham [couldn't write]
Trade; weaving, spinning, sewing & nitting
In presence of Levin Dirickson

F. 185   Apprentice; Burton Cannon, 16 on 9 Apr. next, by consent of his father Burton, of Somerset Co.
Bound to; Isaac Porter
Trade; tanner & currier
In presence of Robt. Smith, Thomas Milbourn

F. 186   Apprentice; George B. R. Coston, 16 on 11 Mar. next, by consent of his stepfather, Burton Cannon, of Somerset Co.
Bound to; William B. S. Riley
Trade; currier & tanner
In presence of Robt. Smith, Thomas Milbourne

John Logan & Levin Mills, adms. of John Mills, exhibit account; mentions Handy Mills, John P. Patterson

F. 187   Levin Mills & John Logan, adms. of John Mills, allowed 7 1/2% on estate

George Hayward, adm. of Rev. David Ball, to sell personal estate (except negroes & wearing apparel)

Matthias Anderson, of White Co., Tenn., gives power of attorney to Robert W. Roberts to conduct his business in MD

14 May, 1813   Jno. Jett, John Bryan
                                         Justices of the Peace

F. 188   Jacob A. Lane, clerk of Court of Pleas & Quarter Sessions for said county swears that above are Justices of said county

John Bryan, Chairman Protem for Court of Pleas & Quarter Sessions

July 12, 1813, received of William Tingle & wife, Elizabeth Tingle (alias Rankin), $195.81 & negroes, man George, woman Janny; bond on
                                    (cont.)

John Dale (Tennessee) for boy Charles for $81.50, in said Dale's hands, in full of claims due Matthias Anderson & wife, Molly Anderson (alias Green), from said Tingle & wife, as guardians to Molly

Test.; Thos. N. Williams   Robt. W. Roberts

F. 189-90 [blank]

F. 191   Tues., Aug. 10, 1813   All Justices present

Orphan; Mary Elizabeth Dennis (of Benjamin)
Guardian; William Townsend (of Solomon)
Sureties; John J. White, Henry Dickerson

F. 192   Orphan; Jesse Gray (of Joshua)
           Guardian; Mitchell Gray
           Sureties; William McGregor, Asher Burroughs

F. 193   James Bevan & Levin Sturgis to view estate of Arthur Price, in care of John Price, guardian; before Nehemiah Holland: report

Dr. John Stevenson & James Tilghman, Esq., to settle dispute between William Warrington, adm. of Joshua Townsend, & Susanna Townsend, adm. of Elijah Townsend; Susanna to pay William $84, being 5/6 of
F. 194 $100.81, the distributive share of Joshua's father's estate

Account of sale of real estate of John Riggen, deceased, according to will, by Pierce & Loudy Riggen, exes. & trustees, 15 Dec., 1811; bought by John Riggen, Jun.

           Littleton R. Purnell & William Parker to pay to Hetty Bowen,
F. 195   widow of Riley, her thirds according to will; before Thos. D.
F. 196   Purnell: list

Charles Bennett, Sen., & George Hayward to settle dispute between Nancy & Robert Duer, adms. of James Duer, & John J. White, adm. of George Dykes

Apprentice; Stephen, negro, 8 on 15 Sept. next, by consent of his mother
Bound to; William S. White, copper
Trade; cypress cooper
Surety; Edwd. Lambden
Before Jas. Tilghman, Wm. Schoolfield

F. 198   Apprentice; Eliza Tarr, 7 next Nov., child of the Poor House, daughter of Betsy Turnell [Tunnell?]
           Bound to; Levin Watson
           Trade; spinning, nitting & other housework
           Sureties; Jesse Sturgis, Daniel Handcock
F. 199   By Trustees for the Poor; Samuel Handy, Joshua Duer, George Hayward

F. 200
Apprentice; McKimmy Smock, 17 on 30 Oct. next, by consent of his father Henry
Bound to; McKimmy Lecompt
Trade; shoe making
In presence of John McDaniel, William H. Carey

F. 201
Apprentice; Samuel Peacock, child of the Poor House
Bound to; Benjamin Polk
Trade; farmer
Term; till 21, on 27 Jan., 1821
Sureties; Wm. Harper, Major Tarr
By Trustees for the Poor; Joshua Duer, George Hayward, Ephraim King Wilson

F. 202
Apprentice; James Beezy, 13 on 20 May last, by consent of his mother Sally Bezzy
Bound to; George Conner
Trade; farmer
Before Levin Dirickson, Thomas Milbourn

John Laws, exe. of Curtis Henderson, exhibits account; family has 11 members

Josiah Nelson, adm. of William Willis, to sell personal estate

Michael Murray, exe. of Joseph Young, to sell personal estate (except legacies, cypress ware & timber)

F. 203
Dr. John Stevenson, exe. of Betsey Jones, allowed 10% on estate

John Dashiell & Eben Christopher to distribute negroes from estate of Matthew Jones, in care of George Parsons, acting exe.

William Bowen, adm. of Micajah Bowen, to sell personal estate (except corn & property in Philadelphia)

Luke Townsend, guardian to Lydia & Milcha Bevans, to give each 2 months schooling

Elijah Vinson, adm. of Isaac Vinson, allowed 10% on estate

James Tilghman, adm. of John Patterson, to advertise in paper at easton for creditors to exhibit claims

James Tilghman, adm. of John Patterson, allowed 10% on estate

F. 204
Rebecca Hall & Edward Stevenson, adms. of John Hall, to advertise in paper at Easton for creditors to exhibit claims

John Laws, exe. of Curtis Henderson, allowed 8% on estate

William McGregor, exe. of Jesse Gray, Sen., to sell personal estate (except legacies)

Thomas N. Williams & Edward Bredell to view property of Jesse Gray, in care of Mitchell Gray, guardian

James A. Collins, guardian to Nathaniel M. McNeill, to rent real estate

Hetty Bowen, exe. of Riley Bowen, to sell personal estate, as directed by will

Littleton R. Purnell & William Parker, Esqs., to pay 1/3 of estate of Riley Bowen to Hetty Bowen, widow

F. 205 Stephen Pilchard, adm. of Pompey Jones, to sell personal estate

Received 27 Feb., 1810, of William Watts & Zipporah, his wife, my guardians, $383, my estate, & $37.50, the profits of lands from the death of my father, John S. Purnell, until now

James Bowin, Riley Bowin   Sarah Purnell

Received Mar. 25, 1812, of Robert Cluff, who married my mother Joanna Sturgis, my late guardian, $499.07, in full of my estate; also specifics from estate of my father Joshua Sturgis, equalling L.169/1; also negro man Daniel left me by will of my uncle Major Guy

Present; Joseph C. Oliver   Nancy Sturgis

Stephen Purnell, exe. of Thomas Gray, Sen., vs. Francis Lane, by John Lane, his guardian; gives petition filed at Apr. term, 1813; Stephen, in Sept., 1808, administered estate of Thomas Gray, Sen., & there was order to sell personal estate, supposing proceeds from sale
F. 206 would cover claims; William McGrigor & Edward Bridle were to divide negroes; as there is a deficiency, asks that Francis pay his share; court finds deficiency to be $268.73; Francis
F. 207 to pay Stephen $99.40

F. 208 Tues., Oct. 12, 1813   Littleton Robins, John Bishop present

Orphan; George Sturgis (of John)
Guardian; John Allen (of John)
Sureties; John Aydelott, John Costin

Christopher Ball discharged from guardianship to Luther Ball; David K. Baker new guardian

         Orphan; Luther Ball (of John)
F. 209   Guardian; David K. Baker (of Accomack Co., VA)
         Sureties; Christopher P. Ball, John Aydelott

Christopher Ball discharged from guardianship to Delia Ball; David K. Baker new guardian

         Orphan; Delia Ball (of John)
         Guardian; David K. Baker (of Accomack Co., VA)
F. 210   Sureties; Christopher P. Ball, John Aydelott

Orphan; Ebenezer Gray (of Rouse)
Guardian; Joseph Robinson
Sureties; Thomas Franklin, Elijah Fookes

         Orphan; James Baynum (of William)
         Guardian; Elisha Baynum
F. 211   Sureties; John Walter [couldn't write], Barzilla Parker

Orphan; Hetty Baynum (of William)
Guardian; Elisha Baynum
Sureties; John Walter, Barzilla Parker

         Orphan; Dixon Q. Henderson (of John L.)
F. 212   Guardian; Sally Long
         Sureties; William Houston, Levi Henderson

         Orphan; Sally L. Henderson (of John L.)
         Guardian; Sally Long
F. 213   Sureties; William Houston, Levi Henderson

Orphan; Isaac Covington (of William)
Guardian; Sarah Covington
Sureties; Daniel Tingle, William Tingle [signed William Bishop]

         Orphan; Elizabeth Anne Covington (of William)
F. 214   Guardian; Sarah Covington
         Sureties; Daniel Tingle, William Tingle

Apprentice; Thomas Prideaux (of Thomas), 17 on 31 Jan. last
Bound to; Thomas P. Rackliffe
Trade; coasting business
Sureties; James A. Collins, Ambrose White

F. 215   Apprentice; Molly Purnell (of Robert), 10 on 5 Feb. next
         Bound to; Kellam Lankford
         Trade; spin, weave, sew & knit
         Sureties; John Selby (of Daniel), William Veasey

F. 216   Apprentice; William Bishop (of Samuel), 16 on 20th of present
         month
         Bound to; Edward Dymock
         Trade; taylor
         Sureties; Lemuel P. Spence, John Stevens

F. 217   Thomas N. Williams & Edward Briddell to view estate of Jesse
F. 218   Gray, in care of Mitchell Gray, guardian; before Wm.
         McGrigor: report; land devised by his grandfather Jesse Gray,
150 acres

Charles Bennett, Sen., & George Hayward to settle dispute between
Nancy & Robert Duer, adms. of James Duer, & John J. White, adm. of
George Dykes; estate of James indebted to estate of George for $96.60

F. 219   Account of sale of property (except negro Comfort) of Elijah
         Long (of David), left him by Elijah Burnett, as sold by
Bennett H. Clarvoe, guardian; sold to Benjamin Cotman, Robert Lambdon,
Levi Powell, B. H. Clarvoe, Sally Long

F. 220   William McGrigor & Thomas N. Williams, Esqs., to settle
         dispute between Jesse Dale, & Elisha & George Davis, exes. of
Jesse Davis

Apprentice; Stephen Redden, 16 on 2 Apr. next, by consent of his
mother
Bound to; James Tilghman, shoe maker
Trade; boot & shoe making
Before Nehemiah Holland, Wm. Schoolfield

           Apprentice; Skinner Taylor, 14 on 17 Aug. last, by consent of
F. 221   his sister
           Bound to; Samuel Tarr, farmer
           Trade; farming
           Sureties; Stephen Jones, Henry Jones
           In presence of Wm. Riley, N. Holland

           Apprentice; William Lewis, 13 on 1 Apr. last
           Bound to; Jacob Downs, farmer
F. 222   Trade; farming
           Before Robert Mitchell, Billy Fookes

Apprentice; John Parker, 14
Bound to; Samuel Melson
Trade; farmer
Before Isaac Hearn, Nathan Gordy

           Apprentice; John Morris, 17 on 16 Feb. next
           Bound to; John Walter, farmer [couldn't write]
           Trade; farming
F. 223   Surety; Nathaniel R. Cannon
           Before Wm. McGrigor, Thos. N. Williams

Stephen Purnell, exe. of Thomas Gray, vs. Francis Lane, by John Lane,
guardian; Fieri Facias issued against property of defendant for
failing to comply with decree

Wheetly Dennis, adm. of Benjamin Dennis, to sell personal estate

F. 224   William Jones, adm. of Isaac Selby, to sell personal estate

Nancy Pollett, adm. of Samuel Pollett, allowed 7% on estate

Mary Truitt, exe. of John K. Truitt, to sell personal estate, as
directed by will

William Jones, guardian to John & Priscilla Hudson, to apply $10 of principle for their support, as they are too young to work

James Knox, guardian to George & Leah Hudson, to give each 6 months schooling

Adam Bravard & Edward Briddle to view property of Ebenezer Gray, in care of Joseph Robinson, guardian

John Stevenson, adm. of Molly Long, to sell personal estate

F. 225 Sarah Taylor, adm. of William H. Taylor, to sell personal estate (except negroes & wearing apparel)

Anne Long & Thomas M. Tull, adms. of Littleton Long, to sell negroes

William Holland & Thomas Taylor to view property of Dixon Q. Henderson, in care of Sally [no surname given], guardian

William Holland & Thomas Taylor to view property of Sally L. Henderson, in care of Sally Long, guardian

Isaac Marshall, guardian to Samuel Gibbons, allowed to get 1000 rails from timber to make a road on land

Thomas N. Williams & Kendal Williams to view property of Isaac & Elizabeth Covington, in care of Sarah Covington, guardian

William Riley & Kellam Lankford to view property of Matilda Selby, in care of John Selby, guardian

William Riley & Kellam Lankford to view anew property of George Selby, ward

F. 226 Thomas Curren & Lydia, his wife, vs. James Tilghman, exe. of James Ward; farm in Talbot Co. belonging to Lydia, formerly wife of James Ward, was rented in 1811, the year James died, which rent has since be paid to James Tilghman; rent to be paid to Lydia

Hugh Gemmill(?), adm. of David W. Morris, allowed 7% on estate

Hugh Gemmill(?), adm. of David W. Morris, allowed for saddle in appraisal, but never found

Col. Thomas Martin, exe. of Thomas Martin, Sen., allowed expense of carrying negroes Flora, Dinah & Adah to Baltimore to be sold, & for money paid William Tarr

Col. Thomas Martin, exe. of Thomas Martin, Sen., allowed for negro Augusta, run away

F. 227 Col. Thomas Martin, exe. of Thomas Martin, Sen., allowed for money paid Daniel Ruark for surveying lands sold per will

'288'

Received Mar. 11, 1813, of Mary Aydelott, $200, negro boy Whittington & girl Ginney, & list, legacies given me by William Aydelott

Test.; David K. Baker
     John Aydelott

               her
Sarah X Aydelott
              mark

In consideration of $100, I appoint James B. Robins, my attorney, to collect my claims on estate of Samuel Cowley, [exe?] of my father

In presence of William Dryden

           her
Charlotte X Newton
           mark

2 Apr., 1813, received of Samuel Cowley, $96.24, in full of claims of Charlotte Newton

Mary H. Moore   James B. Robins

Received 20 Nov., 1813, of Col. Thomas Martin, adm. dbn of Rosanna Martin, $1,111.48, balance of estate due Rosanna's representatives, James Upshur & Susanna, his wife, & Sarah S. Martin

Test.; Matthew Hopkins   John S. Martin

F. 228-29 [blank]

F. 230   Tues., Dec. 14, 1813   All Justices present

Apprentice; Peter Fisher, negro, 19 on 9 Aug. last, son of Patience
Bound to; William Riley
Trade; common labor
Sureties; William Quinton, William Parker

F. 231   Stephen Purnell, exe. of Thomas Gray, Sen., vs. Francis Lane,
         a representative, by John Lane, guardian; decree of 11 Aug. last, for Francis to pay Stephen $99.40, not being complied with, sheriff to seize that amount of Francis' property; George Hayward, sheriff, seized negro man Briston, which he sold to John Lane for $250

F. 232   Received Dec. 6, 1813, of John J. Williams, $109.74

                                 Stephen Purnell

Apprentice; Bayly Young, 14 on   25 May last, by consent of his mother
Bound to; Joseph Scott, farmer
Trade; farming
Surety; James Tull
Before James Patterson, Jas. Tilghman

          Apprentice; James Henderson (of Saml.) [couldn't write]
F. 233   Bound to; John Marchant
          Term; 3 years, 6 months
              (cont.)

```
          Trade; ship carpenter
          Before James Tilghman, Edwd. U. Blake

          Apprentice; Henry Dulany, 11 on 15 Apr. last, by consent of
          his mother
          Bound to; Ebenezer Leonard, tanner
F. 234    Trade; tanning & currying
          Before George Maddux, Thomas Hooper
```

Apprentice; Benjamin Jones Dashiell, 15 on 22 Nov. last
Bound to; Ebenezer Leonard
Trade; tanner & currier
Before Booz Walston, Billy Fookes

```
          Apprentice; Maria [also Mariah] Powell, 11 on 12 July next,
F. 235    child of the Poor House
          Bound to; David L. Truitt
          Trade; nitting, sewing, spinning & weaving
          Sureties; Barzilla Parker, James Knox
          By Trustees for the Poor; Col. Samuel Handy, McKimmy Porter,
          Joshua Duer

F. 236    Apprentice; Jacob Ginn, free born black, 12 this day
          Bound to; Ralph Henman, ship carpenter
          Trade; ship carpenter
          Sureties; Bennett H. Clarvoe, William Wheeler
          Before Jas. Tilghman, James Patterson

          Apprentice; Littleton Price, free born black, 18 on 15 Mar.
F. 237    next
          Bound to; Isaiah Smith
          Trade; common labour
          Surety; Billy F. Farlow
          Before Booz Walston, Billy Fookes
```

Nelly Shockley, adm. of Stuart Shockley, to sell personal estate
(except wearing apparel)

F. 238   William Richards, exe. of John Richards, to sell negro Beck
          & her youngest child

Mary Burroughs, adm. of Henry Burroughs, to sell personal estate

Register to state account for Mary & Nehemiah Burbage, late adms. of
Edward Burbage, allowing them for delivering 350 bushels of corn to
Mason's Landing

Register to state account for Nehemiah Burbage, late adm. of Mary
Burbage, [same as above]

Cord Hazzard, adm. of Robert Johnson, to sell personal estate

F. 239   On 5 Nov., 1813, I sold negro man Frank, from estate of
         Benjamin Dennis, who was levied by me as constable of Snow
Hill Hundred, to satisfy a fieri facias of John Bishop, exe. of Robert
Hudson, against said Dennis & Peter Shockley; balance from sale paid
to Wheetly Dennis, adm. of Benjamin
                                        Patrick Waters

Mary R. Slocomb, adm. of John R. Slocomb, to sell personal estate
(except wearing apparel)

James A. Collins, adm. of Luke Teeling, to sell personal estate

F. 240   Samuel Stevenson, adm. cwa of John Stevenson, Sen., allowed
         10% on estate

Whereas Henny Hughs was bound on 16 Mar., 1811, to John Floyd, Jun.,
to learn to spin, weave & c., & John is now dead, Elizabeth Floyd, the
widow, not wishing to retain apprentice, delivers her to Court

I, Rider Rackliffe, of Somerset Co., one heir of John Rackliffe, of
Worcester Co., release James Murray, of Somerset Co., my guardian,
from all claims against him on my lands & estate in Worcester Co.

         Test.; Wm. E.(?) Sturgis   Rider H. Rackliffe
                Wm. Whittington
                John W. Rackliffe

F. 241   [blank]

F. 242   Littleton Robins, Sen., Zadok Sturgis & John Bishop appointed
         Justices

Lev. Winder   W. Kilty, Chanc.

Wit.; The Honourable William Kilty, Esq., Chancellor

Tues., Feb. 8, 1814   All Justices present

                 Orphan; Jethro Bowen (of Riley)
F. 243   Guardian; Hetty Bowen
         Sureties; James Bowen, Littleton Bowen

Orphan; Zadok Wright Bowen (of Riley)
Guardian; Hetty Bowen
Sureties; James Bowen, Littleton Bowen

                 Orphan; Mary Purnell Bowen (of Riley)
F. 244   Guardian; Hetty Bowen
         Sureties; James Bowen, Littleton Bowen

Orphan; Elizabeth Bowen (of Riley)
Guardian; Hetty Bowen
Sureties; James Bowen, Littleton Bowen

F. 245   Orphan; Sarah Outten Bowen (of Riley)
         Guardian; Hetty Bowen
         Sureties; James Bowen, Littleton Bowen

         Orphan; Riley Bowen (of Riley)
         Guardian; Hetty Bowen
F. 246   Sureties; James Bowen, Littleton Bowen

Orphan; Henry Toadvine (of Henry)
Guardian; Isaac Toadvine
Sureties; James Toadvine, William Toadvine (of Jesse) [signed Wm. Jones]

         Orphan; William Collins
F. 247   Guardian; Thomas Collins, father
         Sureties; Barney Davis, Solomon Tull [couldn't write]

Orphan; James H. R. Collins
Guardian; Thomas Collins, father
Sureties; Barney Davis, Solomon Tull

F. 247b Apprentice; Peter Smith Hudson (of John), 17
         Bound to; Joshua Donohoe
         Trade; shoe making
         Sureties; James Cottingham, Joshua Bevans

F. 248   Apprentice; Peter Ennis (of Lemuel), 18 on 8 Dec. last
         Bound to; John Blair
         Trade; house carpenter
         Sureties; Josiah Bratten, John Richardson (of Thomas)

F. 249   Thomas N. Williams & Kendal Williams to view estate of Isaac
         & Elizabeth Covington, in care of Sally [also Sarah]
F. 250   Covington, guardian; before Peter C. Evans: report; 250
         acres; widow's dower

         Apprentice; Levi Davis, 10 on 10 May next, by consent of his
         mother
         Bound to; Milbourn Lewis
F. 251   Trade; farming
         Before William Parker, William Townsend

         Apprentice; William Pollett, 14 on 3 Oct. next, by consent of
         his father Joshua
         Bound to; Levin Hitch
         Trade; boot & shoe maker
F. 252   In presence of Isaac Denson, Jesse Townsend

Apprentice; Jeptha Kinningin, 18
Bound to; Moses Benson, farmer
Trade; farming
Surety; Bennett H. Clarvoe
Before Jas. Tilghman, Jas. Patterson

F. 253 James Davis & James A. Collins, exes. of John Davis, exhibit
        account; mentions cash allowed Thos. N. Williams for hire of
negro Stephen; before Wm. Rownd

Rebecca Parsons (alias Sears), adm. of John Sears, exhibits account;
mentions fodder bought of Isaac Franklin; before Thos. N. Williams

Joseph Scott, adm. of James Gunby, exhibits account; list

F. 254 John Lane, guardian to Francis Lane, received of George
        Hayward, Esq., sheriff, $135.63, balance of sale of negro
Bristor, sold to satisfy claim of Stephen Purnell, Esq.

Samuel McMaster, exe. of Rev. Samuel McMaster, allowed 7 1/2% on
estate

Thomas N. Williams, adm. of Isaac Hill, to sell personal estate

Nixon Davis & William Parker to view property of Jethro, Zadok & Riley
Bowen, in care of Hetty Bowen, guardian

Eleanor Bevans, guardian to Nathaniel & Louisa Bevans, excused from
rendering accounts untill they reach 14

John Allen, guardian to George Milbourn, to give him 3 months
schooling

James Baynum, guardian to William Baynum, to give him 2 months
schooling

F. 255 Barny Davis, adm. of Matthias Davis, allowed 10% on estate

Order of 8 instant, for sale of part of personal estate of Isaac Hill,
rescinded; Thomas N. Williams, exe., to sell whole personal estate
(except negroes that are legacied)

Peter Collier, adm. of William Collier, to sell personal estate
(except legacies)

John Selby, adm. of Henry Selby, allowed 8% on estate

James Davis & James A. Collins, exes. of John Davis, allowed 7 1/2% on
estate

Martha Timmons, adm. of Stephen Timmons, to sell personal estate

F. 256 Justice Pointer, adm. of John Pointer, to sell personal
        estate

William Purnell, exe. of Thomas Dixon Purnell, to sell personal estate
(except legacies, negroes & wearing apparel)

Register to state account for John Davis, & Schoolfield Bradford &
Elizabeth, his wife, late adms. of Benjamin Davis

Alexander McAllen & Betty, his wife, admx. of Joseph Kellam, to retain $240 to meet judgements recovered against them in Worcester Co. Court, & other claims for which deceased is liable as security for Polly Marchment, adm. of Riley Marchment

Handy Jones, adm. dbn of Charles Hammond, allowed 6% on estate

Received Jan. 29, 1808, of Thomas Collings, adm. of John Collins, $81.84, the dowery of my husband's estate

Test.; James Ball, Thomas R. Ball Nancy X Collings, wife
             her / mark

F. 257 Received 29 [blank], 1812, of Thomas Collings, adm. of John Collings, $38.77, my child Hetty Collings' part of my husband John Collings' estate, entered in Accomack Co., VA, Court

Test.; James Ball, Thomas R. Ball her Nancy X Collings, guardian mark

Feb. 8, 1813, received of Thomas Collings, adm. of John Collings & guardian to Elebeth Collins, daughter of John, $30.87, her share of hir father's estate

Test.; Isaac Ayres   X Elebeth Collings

F. 258 [blank]

F. 259 Special Court, Apr. 14, 1814, at instance of James Davis & James A. Collins; all Justices present

Jesse Sturgis, adm. of William Vernetson, to sell personal estate (except wearing apparel)

William McGregor, exe. of Jesse Gray, Sen., to advertise in a paper at Easton for creditors to exhibit claims

James Davis & James A. Collins, exes. of John Davis, to retain balance due by him to estate of Benjamin Davis, of which he was one adm.

F. 260 Tues., Apr. 17, 1814 All Justices present

Orphan; John Handy Sears (of John)
Guardian; Zepheniah Parsons
Sureties; Elisha Davis, John Parsons (of Zepheniah)

   Orphan; David Gault (of Archibald)
F. 261 Guardian; Rachel Gault [couldn't write]
   Sureties; George Davis [couldn't write], Jesse Dale

Fisher Richardson discharged from guardianship to Ann Holland; William Holland new guardian

Orphan; Ann Holland (of Thomas)
Guardian; William Holland
Sureties; Benjamin Gunby, Benjamin Polk

F. 262   Apprentice; Harry Blake, mulatto, 7 on 27 Oct. last, son of Hannah
Bound to; John Allen (of Stephen)
Trade; farming
Sureties; Stephen Allen, George Selby

F. 263   Apprentice; Edmund Bayly Shrieves, mulatto, 8, son of Nancy Shries
Bound to; Patrick Waters
Trade; common labourer
Sureties; Samuel Handy, Jun., James Holland

F. 263   Apprentice; Lemuel Truitt (of George), 16 on 15 July next
Bound to; Luke Townsend
Trade; blacksmith
Sureties; Jacob Richards, John C. Bacon

F. 265   Apprentice; John Wright (of Hezekiah), 14 on 11 Oct. last
Bound to; Major Tarr
Trade; shoe & boot making
Sureties; Timothy Irons, Edward Knock [Knox?]

F. 266   William Holland & Thomas Taylor to view estate of Dixon Q. Henderson, in care of Sally Long, guardian; before Nehemiah Holland: report; land called 'Parramores Double Purchase', 200 acres, held jointly with Sally L. Henderson

F. 267   William Holland & Thomas Taylor to view estate of Sally L. Henderson, in care of Sally Long, guardian; [same as above]

F. 268   William Parker & Nixon Davis, Esqs., to view estate of Riley Bowen, in care of Hetty Bowen, guardian; before Robert Smith: report; widow's dower; 101 acres

F. 269
F. 270   Nixon Davis & William Parker, Esqs., to view estate of Jethro Bowen, in care of Hetty Bowen, guardian; before Robt. Smith: report; widow's dower; 125-30 acres

F. 271   Nixon Davis & William Parker, Esqs., to view property of Zadok Bowen, in care of Hetty Bowen, guardian; before Robt. Smith: report; widow's dower; 40 acres cleared

F. 272   John Dashiell & Eben Christopher to divide negroes from estate of Matthew Jones, in hands of George Parsons, exe.; before Nathan Gordy;
1) to Purnell J. & Nancy Jones; negro man Mitchell
2) to Nancy Jones, widow; woman Lindy

F. 273   McKimmy Porter & George Hayward to settle dispute between
         George S. Gunby, surviving exe. of Col. John Gunby, & Daniel
G. Robins, adm. of Anthony Bacon

George W. Purnell & Thomas N. Williams to settle dispute between Sarah
Tracey, adm. of Arthur Tracey, & Henry Watts

Dr. John Stevenson, James Patterson & James Tilghman, Esqs., to settle
dispute between Michael Murray, exe. of Joseph Young, & Stephen
Townsend, adm. dbn of Zepheniah Benson, regarding 2 notes of hand from
Zepheniah to Joseph

Peter Dashiell, Eben Christopher & Joshua Morris to settle dispute
between Isaac Toadvine, & John Toadvine & George Parsons, adms. of
Outten Toadvine

F. 274   Apprentice; James P. Hudson, 15
         Bound to; Ephraim Townsend, blacksmith
         Trade; blacksmith
         Before Nehemiah Holland, Wm. Riley

F. 275   Apprentice; James Cherix, 16 on 14 Dec. last, by consent of
         his mother
         Bound to; Levin Conner, former
         Trade; farming
         Sureties; John Coston, Jehu Watson
         Before Jas. Tilghman, Jas. Patterson

F. 276   Apprentice; John Reed (of Elijah), 18 on 1 Sept. next, by
         consent of his mother Jannetta
         Bound to; Samuel Tindell [also Tindle, Tindel]
         Trade; house carpenter
         Sureties; John Walter, William Watts
         In presence of Thos. N. Williams, Wm. McGrigor

F. 277   Barney Davis, adm. of Matthias Davis, exhibits account;
         mentions Wm. Holland; Matthias, son of deceased

James Melvin, adm. of Spencer Davis, allowed for expense with property

Allexander McAllen & wife, adms. of Joseph Kellam, allowed $30 for
expenses with 2 young negroes born since appraisal, which were sold

F. 278   Littleton R. Purnell, exe. of Dennis Hudson, allowed $59.37
         for 3 1/2 acres sold to Sewell Turpin, & taken away by an
         Elder survey; map & bounds given, showing 'Pointers Gift to
Purnell', 'Hudsons Bail' & 'Friends Exchange'

Kendal Powell, exe. of William Powell (of Gabrel), to sell personal
estate (except legacies)

Thomas N. Williams & Joseph Truitt to view property of John H. Sears,
in care of Zepheniah Parsons, guardian

Stephen White, exe. of William White, allowed 5% on estate

John Stevenson, adm. of Josiah Long, allowed for negro Stephen, sold by sheriff

F. 279   John Stevenson, adm. of Josiah Long, allowed 10% on estate

John Stevenson, adm. of Molly Long, allowed 10% on estate

William Richardson, adm. of John Mumford, to sell personal estate

Ishmael Baker, adm. of Isaiah Baker, to sell personal estate (except wearing apparel)

William Davis, adm. of John Bradford, to sell personal estate

William Crapper, adm. of Nancy Crapper, allowed 10% on estate

F. 280   William Riley & William Walton to view property of Anne Holland, in care of William Holland, guardian

Thomas Franklin, adm. of Jenethan Powell, allowed 10% on estate

James Fookes & [blank] Fookes, exes. of Thomas Fookes, to sell personal estate (except negroes & wearing apparel)

William Franklin & Thomas Franklin, exes. of John Franklin, allowed 7% on estate

Thomas White & wife, admx. of David S. Walston, allowed 7% on estate

James Davis, guardian to Patsey Melvin, to give her 1 month schooling

F. 281   [blank]

F. 282   Tues., June 14, 1814   All Justices present

Orphan; Thomas Fookes (of Thomas)
Guardian; Leah Fookes [couldn't write]
Sureties; Eben Christopher, James Fookes

F. 283   Orphan; Daniel Fookes (of Thomas)
          Guardian; Leah Fookes
          Sureties; Eben Christopher, James Fookes

Orphan; Laticia Fookes (of Thomas)
Guardian; Leah Fookes
Sureties; Eben Christopher, James Fookes

F. 284   Apprentice; Littleton Ginn, negro, 8 on 3 Apr. last, son of Elijah
          Bound to; William Mills
          Trade; common labour
          Sureties; James Burnett, James Davis

	Apprentice; Wesley Melvin (of William), 15 next Aug. Bound to; John Spencer, Jun.
F. 285	Trade; boot & shoe maker Sureties; Ephraim K. Wilson, William Allen

	Thomas N. Williams & Joseph Truitt to view estate of John H.
F. 286	Sears (of John), in care of Zepheniah Parsons, Jun.,
F. 287	guardian; before Peter C. Evans: report; 60 acres; widow's dower

	Mitchell Gray & Robert Mitchell to view estate of David
F. 288	Gault, in care of Rachel Gault, guardian; before Isaac Mitchell: report; 130 acres, part of 'Duncans Delight Enlarged' & 'Jarmon Chance'

George Hayward, Robert J. H. Handy & Ambrose White to settle dispute between Rowland Bevans, Jun., adm. of William Bacon, & Daniel G. Robins, adm. of Anthony Bacon

	Apprentice; Henry Jacobs [also has Henry Isaacs], black, 9 on 24 Dec. next, by consent of his mother Bound to; Stephen Dryden, farmer
F. 289	Trade; farming Surety; Noble Dryden Before Jas. Tilghman, Jas. Patterson

	Apprentice; Jane Cammeron, 10 on 15 Mar. next, a child of the Poor House Bound to; James Jones
F. 290	Trade; house keeper Sureties; Ralph Henman, Robert J. H. Handy By Trustees for the Poor; Samuel Handy, McKimmy Porter, Geo. Hayward

	McKimmey Porter appointed trustee for sale of 2 lotts in town of Snow Hill, property of William & Eleanor Fleming (of Joshua), at
F. 291	request of Sally Fleming, their mother: surety; Ephraim K. Wilson; in presence of John C.(?) Duffield

Henry White, adm. of Stephen White, allowed 7% on estate

F. 292	Sarah Sturgis, adm. of William Sturgis, to sell personal estate (except negroes & wearing apparel)

Thomas N. Williams, adm. of Zedekiah Bradford, to sell personal estate

William McGrigor & Isaac Marshall to appraise residue of estate of William H. Taylor, in hands of Sarah Taylor, adm.; personal estate to be sold

F. 293	[blank]
F. 294	Tues., Aug. 9, 1814 All Justices present

Orphan; Ann Elizabeth Gray (of Joshua)
Guardian; Comfort Gray
Sureties; Joseph Ennis, Mitchell Gray

F. 295
Orphan; Levin Gray (of Joshua)
Guardian; Joseph Ennis
Sureties; Mitchell Gray, James A. Collins

Orphan; Henry Gray (of Joshua)
Guardian; Joseph Ennis
Sureties; Mitchell Gray, James Gray

F. 296
Orphan; Walton Gray (of Joshua)
Guardian; Joseph Ennis
Sureties; Mitchell Gray, James A. Collins

F. 297
Orphan; John Stevens Dennis (of Wheetly)
Guardian; Nancy F. Dennis
Sureties; Robert Truitt, Henry Bennett, George Hayward

Orphan; James Wheetly Dennis (of Wheetly)
Guardian; Nancy F. Dennis
Sureties; Robert Truitt, Henry Bennett, George Hayward

F. 298
Orphan; Joseph Kellam (of Joseph)
Guardian; Alexander McAllen
Sureties; Robert J. H. Handy, Littleton Quinton

Orphan; James Kellam (of Joseph)
Guardian; Alexander McAllen
Sureties; Robert J. H. Handy, Littleton Quinton

F. 299
Orphan; Rebecca Kellam (of Joseph)
Guardian; Alexander McAllen
Sureties; Robert J. H. Handy, Littleton Quinton

Orphan; Milby Hudson (of Robert)
Guardian; Stephen D. Ruark
Sureties; Elget Ruark, John J. White

F. 300
Apprentice; Handy Blake, mulatto, 9 on 27 July last
Bound to; James Scott
Trade; common laborer
Sureties; Patrick Waters, Edward Scarborough

F. 301
Apprentice; Henry Ginn, negro, 3 on 2 May last, son of Elijah
Bound to; James Davis
Trade; common laborer
Sureties; Levin Mills, Thomas Collins

F. 302
Apprentice; William Tier (of Comfort), 15 on 20 Nov. next
Bound to; William Tier
Trade; farming
Sureties; John Tier, John Smith

	Apprentice; James Grooms, 8, son of Amelia
	Bound to; William Schoolfield
F. 303	Trade; common laborer
	Sureties; John Bevans, John Dorman

	William Riley, Esq., & Killiam Lankford to view estate of Matilda Selby, in care of John Selby & Mary, his wife, guardians;
F. 304	before N. Holland: report; 500 acres; grist mill on 3 1/2 acres; slaves Thomas 21, Eade 25, Lear 23, Charles 7, Litt 6,
F. 305	Rose 4, Noah 1

	William Riley & Kellam Lankford to view estate of George Selby, in care of John Selby & Mary, his wife, guardians; [same as
F. 306	above]

F. 307	William Riley, Esq., & William Walton to view estate of Anne Holland, in care of William Holland, guardian; before Nehemiah Holland: report; 200 acres; negro Ned 30

	Apprentice; Price Collins (of John), 12 on 17 Jan. last, by consent of his mother Elizabeth
	Bound to; Ebenezer Powell, Jun.
	Trade; shoe & boot making
F. 308	Sureties; John Scott, Jun., Isaac Henderson
	In presence of Thos. N. Williams, Wm. McGrigor

	Apprentice; Robert Bowen, by consent of his father James
	Bound to; Joshua D. Truitt, carpenter
	Trade; carpenter
F. 309	Term; till 21, on 15 Dec., 1818
	Before Thos. N. Williams, Purnell Porter

	Apprentice; Henry George, 6 on 13 July last, illegitimate, by consent of his mother
	Bound to; John Spencer, Jun.
F. 310	Trade; farmer
	Before Wm. Riley, Nehemiah Holland

John Richardson qualifies as Deputy Register of Wills

Saml. R. Smith

Polly Lamberson & Joshua Holloway, adms. of John Lamberson, to sell personal estate (except wearing apparel & crop)

F. 311	Henry Franklin, exe. of Isaac Franklin, to sell personal estate (except negroes, wearing apparel & bank stock)

Elijah Laws, Jun., adm. of Elijah Laws, Sen., to sell personal estate (except wearing apparel)

Thomas N. Williams & William Richards to view property of Ann Elizabeth Gray, in care of Comfort Gray, guardian

Thomas N. Williams & William Richards to view property of Levin, Henry
& Walton Gray, in care of Joseph Ennis, guardian

Order at June term for John Dashiell & John Johnson to view property
of Thomas Fookes, in care of Leah Fookes, guardian, rescinded; Aaron
Mezick & John Johnson to act

Order at June term for John Dashiell, Sen., & John Johnson to view
property of Daniel Fookes, in care of Leah Fookes, guardian,
rescinded; Aaron Mezick & John Johnson to act

John Crapper & wife, admx. of Elijah Reed, allowed 10% on estate

F. 312 Catherine Crapper, adm. of Levin Crapper, to sell personal estate

Mary Burroughs, adm. of Henry Burroughs, to advertise in a paper at
Easton for creditors to exhibit claims

Sewell Turpin & Thomas P. Rackliffe to view property of Milby Hudson,
in care of Stephen D. Ruark, guardian

June 12, 1814, received of Thomas Collings, adm. of John Collings, &
gardend [guardian] to Mary Collings, $32.77, my part of my father's
estate

Test.; Jonathan Cluff

          her
         Mary X Collings
          mark

F. 313-14 [blank]

F. 315 Tues., Oct. 11, 1814 All Justices present

Orphan; Joshua Gray (of Rouse)
Guardian; Joseph Robinson
Sureties; James Powell, John Cathell

F. 316 Orphan; Rebecca Porter (of McKimmy)
    Guardian; Isaac Porter
    Sureties; Robert J. H. Handy, John T. Taylor

Orphan; William Porter (of McKimmy)
Guardian; Isaac Porter
Sureties; Robert J. H. Handy, John T. Taylor

F. 317 Orphan; James Porter (of McKimmy)
    Guardian; Isaac Porter
    Sureties; Robert J. H. Handy, John T. Taylor

    Orphan; Matthew Porter (of McKimmy)
    Guardian; Isaac Porter
F. 318 Sureties; Robert J. H. Handy, John T. Taylor

Orphan; William W. Duer (of James)
Guardian; Nancy Duer
Sureties; Robert Duer, Levin Cottingham

F. 319 Orphan; Margaret Duer (of James)
Guardian; Robert Duer
Sureties; Nancy Duer, Levin Cottingham

Eben Christopher discharged from guardianship to David Cathell; John Cathell new guardian

Orphan; David Cathell (of John)
Guardian; John Cathell
Sureties; Jonathan Fookes (of J.), Tubman Christopher

F. 320 Orphan; James Martin Cathell (of John)
Guardian; John Cathell
Sureties; Jonathan Fookes (of J.), Tubman Christopher

Orphan; William Chandler Truitt (of George)
Guardian; John Truitt
F. 321 Sureties; Thomas Parker, Lemuel Hozier [also Hoshier]

Apprentice; Anthony West Brittingham, 7 on 1 Mar. last, son of Tabitha
Bound to; William Schoolfield
Trade; common labourer
Sureties; Teague Donoho, William Townsend

F. 322 Adam Bravard & Edward Briddle to view estate of Ebenezer Gray, in care of Joseph Robinson, guardian; before Mitchell Gray: report; estate of Ebenezer & Joshua Gray, which Biddy
F. 323 Robinson, their mother, has a life estate in; 44 acres called 'Grays Lot Enlarged'

Apprentice; Isaac Eshom [also Eashom], 21 on 7 Nov., 1821, son of Solomon
Bound to; Thomas Maddux
Trade; shoe & boot maker
F. 324 In presence of James Dennis, John Corbin

Apprentice; James Arbuckle, black, 10 on 1 Dec. next
Bound to; James Tilghman (of New Town)
Trade; farming & taning
Surety; Edwd. Lambden
F. 325 Before Wm. Schoolfield, Jas. Patterson

Mary Parker, exe. of James Parker, exhibits account; mentions George Parker

William McGrigor, exe. of Jesse Gray, exhibits account; list

F. 326 Mitchell Gray, exe. of Joshua Gray, exhibit account; mentions John Davis, Burroughs & Gray, John Fassitt, Isaac Riley, Burton Gray; before Thos. N. Williams

F. 327   Mary Parker, adm. of James Parker, allowed 10% on estate

John Selby (of Daniel), adm. of Henry Selby, allowed 8% on estate

Adam Bravard & Edward Bredell to view property of Joshua Gray, in care of Joseph Robinson, guardian

George Hayward & William Quinton to view property of James W. Dennis, in care of Nancy F. Dennis, guardian

George Hayward & William Quinton to view property of John S. Dennis, in care of Nancy F. Dennis, guardian

Caleb Morris, adm. of Esme Purnell, to sell personal estate (except negroes)

Zipporah Bowen & Josiah Collins, adms. of William Bowen, to sell personal estate (except negroes & corn)

Polly Lamberson & Joshua Holloway, adms. of John Lamberson, to sell corn & fodder excepted by order of 9 Aug. last

F. 328   Stephen Purnell, adm. of Benjamin Purnell, to sell personal estate (except negroes & wearing apparel)

William McGrigor, adm. of Jesse Gray, allowed 8% on estate

Polly Hudson & William Richardson, adms. of Joshua Hudson, allowed 10% on estate

George Hayward & Samuel Handy to view property of Rebecca, William, James & Matthew Porter, in care of Isaac Porter, guardian

Hugh Gemmill, adm. of David W. Morris, to retain money to meet claim of John Bishop, on note of Littleton Riley, to which note deceased is security

Thomas N. Williams, adm. of Zedekiah Bradford, to advertise in the Maryland Gazette at Annapolis for creditors to exhibit claims

F. 329   George Hayward & Col. Samuel Handy to view property of William W. Duer, in care of Nancy Duer, guardian

George Hayward & Col. Samuel Handy to view property of Margaret Duer, in care of Robert Duer, guardian

John Dashiell & George Maddux to view property of David & James M. Cathell, in care of John Cathell, guardian

John Dashiell & George Maddux to distribute negroes from estate of John Cathell, in hands of Eben Christopher, exe.

'303'

Isaac Porter, adm. of McKimmy Porter, to sell personal estate (except leather, tanyard materials, negroes & wearing apparel)

Received Oct. 11, 1814, of William Handcock, my late guardian, $164.68 & list, willed me by my father John Jones

Test.; Thomas Snead   Leah Jones

F. 330   [blank]

F. 331   Special Court, Dec. 2, 1814, at instance of Isaac Porter; all Justices present

Order of 18 Nov. last, for sale of personal estate of McKimmy Porter, rescinded; Isaac Porter, adm., to sell estate (except wearing apparel, leather & tanyard materials)

William Allen, adm. of Job Allen, to sell personal estate

F. 332   Tues., Dec. 13, 1814   All Justices present

Orphan; Patty Purnell (of Esme)
Guardian; Caleb Morris
Sureties; Turner Davis, Josiah Coulbourn

          Orphan; Julian Purnell (of Esme)
F. 333   Guardian; Caleb Morris
          Sureties; Turner Davis, Josiah Coulbourn

Order at Apr. term last for George Hayward & McKimmy Porter to settle dispute between George S. Gunby & Daniel G. Robins, adm. of Anthony Bacon, rescinded; George Hayward, Samuel R. Smith & James Givan to adjust accounts relative to Bacon & Gunby's joint adm. on estate of John Gunby

          Apprentice; Peter Selby, negro, 7 on 18 July next, son of
          Rachel [couldn't write]
          Bound to; John Collins
          Trade; farming
F. 334   In presence of James Law, Goldsbury Blades

Henry Watts, adm. of Thomas Mitchell, to sell personal estate (except wearing apparel)

Joshua Prideaux & Cord Hazzard to appraise property of Isaac Franklin, in hands of Henry Franklin, exe.

Sally Smullen, adm. of Peter Smullen, to sell personal estate

          Zipporah Bowen & Josiah Collins, adms. of William Bowen, to
F. 335   sell corn

Rachel Selby, exe. of Thomas Selby, to sell personal estate (except wearing apparel, legacies & negroes)

Caleb Morris, adm. dbn of Esme Purnell, allowed 5% on estate

Register to state account for Dolly Purnell, late exe. of Esme Purnell, allowing her $200 for negro Jacob, freed by will under particular limitations, which he complied with

George S. Gunby, surviving exe. of Col. John Gunby, allowed 6% on sale of real estate as directed by will

Christopher Ball, adm. of Isaac Ayres, to sell personal estate

F. 336 John Stevenson, adm. of Stephen Townsend, to sell personal estate (except legacies)

Snow Hill, Feb. 13, 1815, received Polly Smith's notes for $387.66, out share of our father's estate

Saml. R. Smith, Jane G.(?) Smith, Isaac P. Smith, William Walea

I promise to pay William Cannon $187.21, balance due on his wife's dividend of her father's estate

Wit.; Henry Parker   Pollay Smith

In consideration of $187.21, I assign to Saml. R. Smith said sum against Mrs. Polly Smith; 13 Mar., 1813

Wit.; Henry Parker   W. Cannon

Received July 28, 1813, of Matthew Hopkins, a draft on Levin Dirickson, Esq., for $191.41, which when paid, will be in
F. 337 full of said note, which I transfer to said Hopkins

Test.; Levin Dirickson   Samuel R. Smith

July 28, 1813, received of a credit on my account on books of Mrs. Polly Smith for amount of this note

                                             M. Hopkins

Received Aug., 1811, of Polly Smith, adm. of Walter Smith, L.74, balance due Robert Smith, his share of his father's estate

                                    Isaac P. Smith, adm. of Robert
F. 338   [blank]

F. 339   Tues., Feb. 14, 1815   All Justices present

Orphan; Elizabeth Wailes [also Wales] (of Daniel)
Guardian; Betsey Wailes
Sureties; James Powell, John Cathell

F. 340 Orphan; Eliza Cathell (of David)
Guardian; Reuben Davis
Sureties; Eben Christopher, John Cathell

F. 341 Aaron Messick [also Mezick] & John Jonson to view estate of
Thomas Fookes, in care of Leah Fookes, guardian; before Billy
Fookes: report; 130 acres

F. 342 Apprentice; David Truitt (of George), 15 on 25 Jan. last
Bound to; Edward Stevenson
Trade; boot & shoe making
Sureties; Major Tarr, Edward Dymock

F. 343 Apprentice; Henry Ginn, mulatto, 7, son of Sarah
Bound to; Ralph Henman
Trade; ship carpenter
Sureties; Smith Horsey, John McFaddon

F. 344 Aaron Mezick & John Johnson to view estate of Daniel Fookes,
F. 345 in care of Leah Fookes, guardian; before Billy Fookes:
report; 133 acres; widow's dower

F. 346 John Dashiell & George Maddux to view estate of James M.
Cathell, in care of John Cathell, guardian; before Nathan
Gordy: report; 1/3 of land formerly property of George
Cathell, now in hands of John Cathell, guardian to James, which land
lies part in Somerset Co. & part in Worcester Co.; land in Somerset
Co. part of 'Little Neck' & 'Green Briar', 215 acres; land in
Worcester Co. part of 'Summerfield', 'Good Luck' & 'Hunger &
F. 347 Thirst', 260 acres; negroes Sandy 10, Peter 12, Levin 27,
Henny 23

F. 348 John Dashiell & George Maddux to view estate of David
Cathell, in care of John Cathell, guardian; before Nathan
Gordy: report; land in Worcester Co., 320 acres, part of
'Safe Guard' & 'Dover'; land in Somerset Co., formerly
F. 349 property of George Cathell, 215 acres, part of 'Little Neck'
& 'Green Briar'; 250 acres in Worcester Co., part of
F. 350 'Summerfield', 'Good Luck' & 'Hunger & Thirst'; negroes Noah
15, Saul 8, Titus 15, Esther 21, Bill 23

F. 351 John Dashiell & George Maddux to distribute negroes from
estate of John Cathell, in hands of Eben Christopher,, exe.;
before Nathan Gordy;
1) to John Cathell; negroes York 62, Bathsheba 67, Silvey 52 & child,
Elijah 14
2) to David Cathell; Noah 15, Saul 8
3) to James Cathell; Sandy 10, Peter 12
4) to George Cathell; Mariah 11, Peggy 20, Tamer 64

F. 352 Apprentice; Polly Gould Hobbs (of Joseph), 9 on 10 June last
Bound to; Rebecca Lamberson, widow [couldn't write]
Trade; sew, spin & weave

(cont.)

Surety; Thomas Lambertson
Before Booz Walston, Billy Fookes

F. 353 Apprentice; John M. Rock, by consent of his father John
Bound to; John S. Martin & John P. Duffield, trading under the firm of Martin & Duffield
Term; till 25 Feb., 1819
Trade; clerk in the mercantile business
In presence of Joseph Hutcheson, Matthew S. Dorman

F. 354 Apprentice; Justice [also Justus] Morris Bratten [also Broughton], by consent of his father George
Bound to; John T. Taylor
Trade; boot & shoe maker
Term; till 21, on 10 Sept., 1818
In presence of Jacob Teague

F. 355 Apprentice; Noah Bruington, 16 on 7 June last, by consent of his father John [couldn't write]
Bound to; Riley Truitt
Trade; house carpenter & joiner
Wit.; Booz Walston, Billy Fookes

F. 356 Apprentice; John Calhoon, by consent of Cord Hazzard (who was authorized by Benjamin Butler, of Sussex Co. DE, guardian to John)
Bound to; Peter Lister
Trade; blacksmith
Term; 4 years, 3 months, from 25 Dec. next

F. 357 In presence of Thos. N. Williams, Wm. McGrigor

Mitchell Gray, exe. of Rouse Gray, exhibits account; mentions James Rownds, John Lane, Littleton Gray, William McGrigor, Esq., Isaac Bredell, Peter C. Evans, Esq., Lemuel Purnell, Esq., Littleton Robins, Esq., Stephen Roach (for serving warrant on Elisha Holland &

F. 358 John MacNeal, & summons on John C. Mumford), James Law

Rowland E. Bevans, adm. of John Cutler, allowed $136.52, paid on a judgement obtained by the U.S. against him as adm.

Whereas Zadok Wheeler, in his will, left horse & saddle to his daughter Margaret, & it appears there is no saddle, ordered that Patty Wheeler & James Dickerson, exes., buy a saddle

William Holland, adm. of George T. Greer, to sell personal estate

John J. White, adm. of George Dykes, allowed 10% on estate

F. 359 Benjamin Melson, adm. of Joseph Melson, allowed 10% on estate

Susanna Pilchard, adm. of Elijah Townsend, allowed $2.95 for judgements of George Justices, Thomas Woldridge, James Melvin, Drumond Welbourn & James W. Melvin, & $.50 for warrant against Henry Thornton, which was not sustained

Nancy Jones, exe. of Daniel Jones, to sell personal estate (except wearing apparel & legacies)

James H. Rowley, adm. of George C. Evans, to sell personal estate

Henry Franklin, exe. of Isaac Franklin, to sell personal estate (except negroes & bank stock)

F. 360 Purnell Taylor, exe. of Thomas Taylor, to sell personal estate (except legacies & wearing apparel)

John Corbin, adm. of James W. Riggen, to sell personal estate

John Cathell, adm. of George Cathell, to sell personal estate (except wearing apparel)

Peter Collier, adm. of William Collier, allowed 10% on estate

James A. Collins, adm. of Luke Teeling, allowed 10% on estate

Thomas Franklin, adm. of Jenethan Powell, to retain $23.70 to meet claim of Isaac Bowdon & wife, the deceased being security for Jesse Crapper for maintenance of illegitimate child, & said Crapper being dead & insolvent

F. 361 Feb. 14, 1815, received of Polly Smith, exe. of Walter Smith, on 23 Dec., $387.66, my share of deceased's estate

                                                 Mary Anne Rice

F. 362 [blank]

F. 363 Littleton Robins, Zadok Sturgis & John Bishop appointed Justices

Lev. Winder, Gov.   W. Kilty, Chanc.

Wit.; The Honourable William Kilty, Esq., Chancellor

Tues., Apr. 11, 1815   All Justices present

F. 364 Orphan; Maria Scarborough Smullen (of Peter)
Guardian; Sally Smullen [also Smulling]
Sureties; William Fookes, Ephraim Smullen

Orphan; William Quinton Smullen (of Peter)
Guardian; Sally Smullen
Sureties; William Fookes, Ephraim Smullen

F. 365 Orphan; James Edward Smullen (of Peter)
Guardian; Sally Smullen
Sureties; William Fookes, Ephraim Smullen

'308'

         Orphan; James Bowin (of John)
         Guardian; Josiah Collins
F. 366   Sureties; Nathaniel R. Cannon, Parker Collins

Orphan; John Sturgis Shockley (of Stuart)
Guardian; Nelly Shockley
Sureties; Ebben Christopher, John Richardson (of Jno.)

         Orphan; Polly Richardson Shockley (of Stuart)
F. 367   Guardian; Nelly Shockley
         Sureties; Eben Christopher, John Richardson (of Jno.)

         Orphan; Sally Shockley (of Stuart)
         Guardian; Nelly Shockley
F. 368   Sureties; Eben Christopher, John Richardson (of Jno.)

Orphan; Daniel Benston Shockley (of Stuart)
Guardian; Nelly Shockley
Sureties; Eben Christopher, John Richardson (of Jno.)

         Orphan; Matty Shockley (of Stuart)
F. 369   Guardian; Nelly Shockley
         Sureties; Eben Christopher, John Richardson (of Jno.)

         Orphan; Madison Shockley (of Stuart)
         Guardian; Nelly Shockley
F. 370   Sureties; Eben Christopher, John Richardson (of John)

Orphan; Tubman Willis (of William)
Guardian; Elijah Williss
Sureties; Zadok Townsend [couldn't write], John F. Atkinson

         Orphan; Joshua Riley (of Thomas)
F. 371   Guardian; Peter Riley
         Sureties; Thomas Franklin, William Franklin

Orphan; Anna Riley (of Thomas)
Guardian; Peter Riley
Sureties; Thomas Franklin, William Franklin

F. 372   Upon application of Lemuel Purnell to be released from
         securityship to John Riley, on guardianship of Francis &
Joseph Holloway, ordered that guardian give new security: security; Er
Truitt, Peter Riley

Orphan; Frances Holloway (of Joseph)
Guardian; John Riley
Sureties; Peter Riley, Er Truitt

         Orphan; Joseph Holloway (of Joseph)
F. 373   Guardian; John Riley
         Sureties; Peter Riley, Er Truitt

Orphan; John Black (of Cornelius)
Guardian; James Roach [couldn't write]
Sureties; Charles Roach [couldn't write], Elijah Fookes

F. 374   Orphan; Woodman Black (of Cornelius)
         Guardian; James Roach
         Sureties; Charles Roach, Elijah Fookes

         Orphan; Frances Black (of Cornelius)
         Guardian; James Roach
F. 375   Sureties; Charles Roach, Elijah Fookes

Orphan; Sarah Purnell (of John)
Guardian; Thomas Purnell (of Wm.)
Sureties; Joshua Prideaux, Edward Robins

         Orphan; William Purnell (of John)
F. 376   Guardian; Thomas Purnell (of Wm.)
         Sureties; Joshua Prideaux, Edward Robins

         Orphan; Mary Anne Garrison (of Jonathan)
         Guardian; John O. Selby
F. 377   Sureties; Charles Parker, Selby Parker

Apprentice; Joseph Crapper (of Joseph), 18 on 4 Aug. last
Bound to; Levin Hitch
Trade; boot & shoe maker
Sureties; James Knox, Ebenezer Hearn

F. 378   Apprentice; Littleton Ginn, mulatto, 7 on 15 this month, son
         of Barsheba
         Bound to; Elijah Burnett
         Trade; farmer
         Sureties; James Tilghman, James H. Rowley

         Apprentice; Moses Richards (of Matthias), 14 on 25 Jan. last
         Bound to; James Q. Johnson
F. 379   Trade; saddle & harness maker
         Sureties; Rowland Bevans, Robert Johnson

         Apprentice; Sally Porter (of John), 12 on 23 Nov. last
         Bound to; Purnell Porter
F. 380   Trade; spin, weave & knit
         Sureties; Kendal S. Crapper, William Richardson

         Apprentice; Peter Lindsey (of Major), 13
         Bound to; Benjamin Spencer
F. 381   Trade; boot & shoe maker
         Sureties; John Spencer, Jun., James Maddux

         William Quinton & George Hayward to view estate of James W.
F. 381b Dennis, in care of Nancy F. Dennis, guardian; before Sam. R.
[no 382] Smith: report; 1/2 of land in Indian Town belonging to heirs
                              (cont.)

F. 383   of Wheetly Dennis, 542 1/4 acres; land occupied by Mrs.
            Comfort Floyd; negro Sam 7, given to James by his grandmother
Schoolfield; widow's dower

            William Quinton & George Hayward to view estate of John S.
F. 384   Dennis, in care of Nancy F. Dennis, guardian; [same as above,
            but no slaves]

F. 385   Samuel Handy & George Hayward to view estate of James Porter,
F. 386   in care of Isaac Porter, guardian; before Saml. R. Smith:
            report; 1/8 on land belonging to heirs of McKimmy Porter, 472
1/2 acres; 3 1/2 lots in Snow Hill Town; lot occupied by Mrs. Sarah
            Fleming; lot occupied by Jno. Dashiell; lot occupied by
F. 387   guardian; 1/2 of tanyard lot occupied by guardian

            Samuel Handy & George Hayward to view estate of Matthew
F. 388-9   Porter, in care of Isaac Porter, guardian; [same as above]

            Samuel Handy & George Hayward to view estate of William
F. 390-1   Porter, in care of Isaac Porter, guardian; [same as above]

            Samuel Handy & George Hayward to view estate of Rebecca
F. 392-4   Porter, in care of Isaac Porter, guardian; [same as above]

William McGrigor & Thomas N. Williams, Esqs., to settle dispute
between Jesse Dale, & Elisha & George Davis, exes. of Jesse Davis;
Jesse Dale to pay estate of Jesse Davis L.56/17/9 [also has that he is
due this amount]

F. 395   Peter Dashiell, Eben Christopher & Joshua Morris, Esqs., to
            settle dispute between Isaac Toadvine, & John Toadvine &
            George Parsons, adms. of Outten Toadvine; estate of Outten
F. 396   owes Isaac $520; Outten died Jan., 1812

Dr. George W. Purnell & Thomas N. Williams, Esq., to settle dispute
            between Sarah Tracey, adm. of Arthur Tracey, & Henry Watts;
F. 397   Sarah to pay Henry L.8/14/8

Received Nov. 10, 1815, of Sarah Tracey, adm. of Arthur Tracy, by the
hand of Cord Hazzard, L.8/14/8, award against estate of Arthur

                              Henry Watts

Order at Apr. term, 1814, for John Stevenson, James Tilghman & James
Patterson to settle dispute between Michael Murray, acting exe. of
Joseph Young, & Stephen Townsend, late adm. dbn of Zepheniah Benson,
relative to 2 notes of hand from Benson to Young, rescinded; Edward
Stevenson, James Tilghman & James Benson to act, as John Stevenson is
now adm. dbn cwa of Zepheniah

F. 398   George Hayward, Esq., & Dr. Thomas R. P. Spence to settle
            dispute between Timothy Irons & Isaac Porter, adm. of Mckimmy
Porter

Apprentice; Joshua Hambling, 14 on 27 Jan. last, by consent of his
father Marshall [couldn't write]
Bound to; Jonathan Fookes (of D.)
Trade; farming
Before Billy Fooks, Robert Mitchell

F. 399 Apprentice; Thomas Handcock, 12 on 27 Dec. last,
illegitimate, by consent of his mother
Bound to; John Givan, mill rite
Trade; building mills
Before Billy Fookes, Milby Adkins

Apprentice; Peter Davis [couldn't write], by consent of his
parents
Bound to; Robert M. Baker, cart wheale right
Trade; cart wheale right
Term; from 3 June last till 3 June, 1818
F. 400 Before Peter C. Evans, James Law

Apprentice; Ezekiel Maddux, 15
Bound to; Riley Truitt, carpenter & joiner
F. 401 Trade; carpenter & joiner
Before Booz Walston, Billy Fookes

John Stevenson, adm. of Josiah Long, exhibits account; mentions Edwd.
Lambden, W. Houston, Jno. Peden

Ambrose White, adm. of Joshua Matthews, exhibits account; list

F. 402 Joshua Holloway, adm. of John Lamberson, exhibits account;
mentions Thomas Gouty(?), Belitha Willis, Jonathan Carey,
Kendal Lowe, Daniel Carey, Wm. White

John Powell, adm. of Jesse Davis, to sell personal estate (except
wearing apparel & negroes)

F. 403 Samuel Tubbs, adm. of William Tubbs, to sell personal estate

William Quinton & Patrick Causey to view property of Maria, William &
James Smullen, in care of Sally Smullen, guardian

Thomas S. Fassitt & Kendal S. Crapper to view property of James Bowen,
in care of Josiah Collins, guardian

Mary Truitt, adm. of John K. Truitt, allowed 8% on estate

William Dirickson, adm. of Joseph Miller, to sell personal estate

Zadok Sturgis, adm. of Littleton Sturgis, to retain $10 to meet claim
of Irvine & Barnes, late editors of the Whig at Baltimore

F. 404 Luke Townsend & wife, guardian to Lydia & Milcha Bevans, to
build addition on house

Zepheniah Parsons, guardian to John H. Sears, to work up down & waisting timber

William Franklin, adm. of Robert Kerby, to sell personal estate

Lemuel Purnell Spence, adm. of Samuel Marrett, to sell personal estate

Billy Fookes & Eben Christopher to view property of John, Woodman & Frances Black, in care of James Roach, guardian

Mitchell Gray, exe. of Joshua Gray, allowed 10% on estate

Mitchell Gray, exe. of Rouse Gray, allowed 10% on estate

Thomas Timmons & Nancy, his wife, exex. of Joseph Miller, allowed 8% on estate

F. 405   Nancy Richardson, adm. of Joseph Richardson, to sell personal estate

John O. Selby & Benjamin Gunby, adms. of Jonathan Garrison, to sell negroes Caleb, Leah & Wise

Leah Mills, exe. of Levin Mills, to sell personal estate (except wearing apparel & legacies)

George Maddux & James Fookes to view property of John, Polly, Sally, Daniel, Matty & Madison Shockley, in care of Nelly Shockley, guardian

F. 406-7 [blank]

F. 408   Tues., June 13, 1815   All Justices present

Orphan; John Patterson (of Anderson)
Guardian; James Patterson
Sureties; William Houston, Samuel McMaster

F. 409   Orphan; Levin Patterson (of Anderson)
          Guardian; James Patterson
          Sureties; William Houston, Samuel McMaster

Orphan; Frederick Hill (of Levin)
Guardian; Catharine Hill [couldn't write]
Sureties; John Selby, Sen., John Holland

F. 410   Orphan; Molly Hill (of Levin)
          Guardian; Catharine Hill
          Sureties; John Selby, Sen., John Holland

          Orphan; Betsey Hill (of Levin)
          Guardian; Catharine Hill
F. 411   Sureties; John Selby, Sen., John Holland

'313'

Orphan; Rachel Hill (of Levin)
Guardian; Catharine Hill
Sureties; John Selby, Sen., John Holland

F. 412
Orphan; James Gibbs (of Elisha)
Guardian; Abraham Gibbs [couldn't write]
Sureties; George Taylor, Henry L. White, Johnson Hill

Orphan; Robert Gibbs (of Elisha)
Guardian; George Taylor
Sureties; Abraham Gibbs, Henry L. White, Johnson Hill

F. 413
Orphan; Hetty Gibbs (of Elisha)
Guardian; George Taylor
Sureties; Abraham Gibbs, Henry L. White, Johnson Hill

Lydia Hargis discharged from guardianship to Hugh M. Stevenson; George Nelson new guardian

F. 414
Orphan; Hugh M. Stevenson (of Jonathan)
Guardian; George Nelson
Sureties; Levin Townsend, Ralph Milbourn

Apprentice; James Grooms, 8, son of Amelia
Bound to; John Bevans
Trade; coasting business
Sureties; Joshua Bevans, John Bowland

F. 415
Apprentice; Docia Blake, 7 on 12 Mar., daughter of Polly
Bound to; James Knox
Trade; common house work
Sureties; William Allen, George Parsons

F. 416
F. 417
F. 418
George Maddux & James Fookes to view estate of John Sturgis, Polly Richards, Sally, Daniel Benson, Matty & Madison Shockley, in care of Nelly Shockley, guardian; before Billy Fookes: report; land called 'Long Acre' & 'Nevens Addition', 183 acres; Nelly's right of dower; tract called 'Outlet', 50 acres; tract called 'Liberty', 46 acres

Apprentice; William Venables, 14 on 15 Apr. last, by consent of his mother
Bound to; David Mills, planter
Trade; common labour
Before Booz Walston, Billy Fookes

F. 419
Thomas N. Williams, adm. of Zedekiah Bradford, exhibits account; mentions James A. Collins, W. Taylor, W. Collins; before Peter C. Evans

F. 420
Nancy Timmons, exe. of Joseph Miller, exhibits account; mentions James Fausit, Samson Adkins, Wm. Jones; before Saml. R. Smith

Josiah Collins, adm. dbn of Micajah Bowen, & one adm. of William Bowen, late adm. of Micajah, exhibits account; mentions Mr. Williamson

F. 421   Thomas N. Williams, adm. of Zedekiah Bradford, allowed 10% on estate

Matty Cathell & Aaron Mezick, adms. of David Cathell, allowed 6% on estate

William Brown, adm. of Andrew Brown, to sell personal estate (except legacies & wearing apparel)

Sarah Toadvine, exe. of John Toadvine, to sell personal estate

James Patterson, adm. of Anderson Patterson, allowed 8 1/2% on estate

David Smith & Thomas Hargis to view property of John & Levin Patterson, in care of James Patterson, guardian

William Williamson, exe. of Stuart Williamson, to advertise in the United States Gazette at Philadelphia for creditors to exhibit claims

F. 422   William Holland & John Spencer, Jun., to view property of Frederick, Molly, Betsey & Rachel Hill, in care of Catharine Hill, guardian

Estate of Samuel Gunn consists of tools & materials for carriage making, which would not sell well at public sale; Tabitha Wise, adm., to sell in private sale

Register to state account for William Bowen, late adm. of Micajah Bowen, allowing him 7% on estate

Josiah Collins, adm. dbn of Micajah Bowen, allowed commission on estate

Leah Sturgis, adm. of John O. Sturgis, allowed 10% on estate

John Selby, Sen., & George Hayward to view property of Hugh M. Stevenson, in care of George Nelson, guardian

F. 423   Turner Davis, adm. of Henry Davis, having made oath that he paid Elijah Read L.12/3/7, for which he didn't get receipt & Read is now dead, allowed for same

Apr. 4, 1815, received of Matthias Warren, by hands of Henry Franklin & William Richards, $176.23, balance due on administration of Robert Mitchell's estate, & in full as guardian to my wife Julianna

Test.; Thos. N. Williams   John R. Pitts

Apr. 4, 1815, Dr. John Pitts acknowledges above received in full of what was due his wife Julianna from Matthias Warren & wife, on her father Robert Mitchell's estate

              Thos. N. Williams

We, Hugh McVea [couldn't write], Arthur McCann & Ally, his wife, Catharine McVea [couldn't write], Patrick McVea & Ellen McVea [couldn't write], of the Kingdom of Ireland & county of Armagh, give Edward McVea, of Worcester Co., MD, U.S., power of attorney, to receive of exe., adm. or trustee of Edward McGee [also Magee] all monies or legacies due us; 21 Mar., 1808

F. 424 In presence of Wm. Browlow, Henry McCagh(?)

County of Armagh; I certify above power of attorney was duly acknowledged before Wm. Brownlow & Henry McCragh, Esqs., two of his Majesties Justices of the Peace at a General Sessions of the Peace, this 25th of Apr., 1808

              Robt. McKinstry, clk.

Nov. 2, 1808, received of Caleb Williams, exe. of Edward McGee, $800, in part of L.750 bequeathed to Hugh McVea, Arthur McCann & wife, Catharine McVea, Patrick McVea & Ellen McVea, by Edward McGee

Test.; Thos. N. Williams   Edward McVeay

   I, Edward McVea, acknowledge that I received Nov. 11, 1809,
F. 425 $400, & this day $708.16, in full of the bequest willed to my
   brothers & sisters named in this power of attorney, received
by me of Caleb Williams; Mar. 9, 1811

Test.; Thos. N. Williams   Edward McVea

9 Mar., 1811, Edward McVea acknowledges receipt of above in full for legacy of L.750 willed to above named persons & their mother

I, Bernard McGee, of Butler Co., PA, give my son Edward McGee, of Philadelphia, power of attorney to collect sums in hands of Caleb Williams, exe. of Edward McGee, late of Poplar Town, Worcester Co., MD; 23 Oct., 1810

In presence of Wm. Ayres, Reuben Ayres

F. 426 I, Jacob Mechling, Prothonotary of Court of Common Pleas,
   certify that Reuben Ayres, Esq., is a duly qualified Justice of the Peace

July 12, 1811, received of Caleb Williams, exe. of Edward Mcgee, by hand of Thos. N. Williams, $908.16, for use of Barnard McGee, & L.750 willed to him by his brother Edwd. McGee

Test.; Arthur Tracy   E. McGee, Jun.

12 July, 1811, Edward McGee, Jun., acknowledges receipt of above as final discharge to Caleb Williams, exe. of Edward McGee, Sen., to a legacy of L.750 willed to Barnard McGee

                                                      Thos. N. Williams

F. 427-8 [blank]

F. 429   Tues, Aug. 8, 1815   All Justices present

Orphan; Henry Franklin (of Isaac)
Guardian; Henry Franklin (of Henry)
Sureties; Alexander Franklin, Robert J. Henry, Jr.

F. 430   Orphan; Amelia Franklin (of Isaac)
         Guardian; Henry Franklin
         Sureties; Alexander Franklin, Robert J. Henry, Jr.

Orphan; Milcah [also Milcha] E. Franklin (of Isaac)
Guardian; Henry Franklin
Sureties; Alexander Franklin, Robt. J. Henry, Jr.

F. 431   Orphan; Louisa Franklin (of Isaac)
         Guardian; Henry Franklin
         Sureties; Alexander Franklin, Robert J. Henry

         Orphan; Mary Franklin (of Isaac)
         Guardian; Henry Franklin
F. 432   Sureties; Alexander Franklin, Robert J. Henry, Jr.

Orphan; William H. Tilghman (of Caleb)
Guardian; James Tilghman
Sureties; Bennett H. Clarvoe, Thomas T. Dorman

F. 433   Orphan; Julianna Cluff (of Darius)
         Guardian; John R. Pitts
         Sureties; Mitchell Gray, Hillary Pitts

         Orphan; John Savage (of John)
         Guardian; Comfort Savage [couldn't write]
F. 434   Sureties; Littleton Quinton, Thomas Martin

Orphan; Elizabeth K. Savage (of John)
Guardian; Comfort Savage
Sureties; Littleton Quinton, Thomas Martin

Thomas R. P. Spence discharged from guardianship to George R. Richardson; Henry Richardson new guardian

         Orphan; George R. Richardson (of Robert M.)
F. 435   Guardian; Henry Richardson
         Sureties; Thomas R. P. Spence, Lemuel P. Spence

'317'

F. 436	Orphan; Maryanne Vernetson (of William) Guardian; Jesse Sturgis Sureties; John Selby, Jun. (of Parker), John Hutcheson

Orphan; Elias Vernetson (of William)
Guardian; Jesse Sturgis
Sureties; John Selby, Jun. (of Parker), John Hutcheson

F. 437 Orphan; Sally Vernetson (of William)
Guardian; Jesse Sturgis
Sureties; John Selby, Jun. (of Parker), John Hutcheson

F. 438 Orphan; William Vernetson (of William)
Guardian; Jesse Sturgis
Sureties; John Selby, Jun. (of Parker), John Hutcheson

Apprentice; Henry Waggamon, 15
Bound to; Henry Watts
Trade; ship carpenter
Sureties; Kendal S. Cropper, James Knox

F. 439 Apprentice; Major Claywell (of Thomas), 11
Bound to; Henry Watts
Trade; ship carpenter
Sureties; James Knox, Kendal S. Crapper

F. 440 Apprentice; Teackle Townsend (of Levin), 15 on 27 June last
Bound to; William Walea
Trade; coach & carriage making
Sureties; Isaac P. Smith, Robert Smith

F. 441 Thomas S. Fassitt & Kendal S. Cropper to view estate of James
F. 442 Bowen, in care of Josiah Collins, guardian; before Saml. R.
Smith: report; 90 acres

F. 443 Apprentice; John Ridley, 14 last Mar., child of the Poor
House, son of James
Bound to; David L. Truitt
Trade; farming
Sureties; William Truitt, Peter Truitt
F. 444 By Trustees for the Poor; Samuel Handy, Joshua Duer, Geo. Hayward

F. 445 Apprentice; John Long, 15 on 24 Nov. last, by consent of his mother
Bound to; Jesse Long, shoe & boot maker
Trade; shoe & boot making
Surety; Levin Long
Before Jas. Patterson, Wm. Schoolfield

Apprentice; John Watson, black, 7, by consent of Sally Stockly
[couldn't write]
Bound to; Samuel Tarr, farmer
(cont.)

Trade; farmer
Surety; William Townsend
In presence of N. Holland, Jonathan Cluff

F. 446 Nancy Timmons, late wife & exe. of Joseph Miller, exhibits account; mentions Wm. Hancock, Thomas Sneed, Zadok Townsend, Robert Givans, slave Dinah (old & helpless)

F. 447 Amount of property belonging to estate of Rouse Gray, kept by widow, under direction of will, for use of family & legacies; list

1812, June 4, received of Mitchell Gray, exe. of Rouse Gray, above articles

Test.; Joseph Robinson   Biddy Gray

Cord Hazzard & Joshua Prideaux to view property of Henry, Amelia, Milcha, Louisa & Mary Franklin, in care of Henry Franklin, guardian

Edward Stevenson & Dr. John Stevenson to view property of William H. Tilghman, in care of James Tilghman, guardian

Mary Burroughs, adm. of Henry Burroughs, allowed 10% on estate

F. 448 Polly Lamberson & Joshua Holloway, adms. of John Lamberson, allowed 8% on estate

Edward Briddle, guardian to Mary Bell, to repair barn

Thomas Timmons & Nancy, his wife, exex. of Joseph Miller, allowed for negro Bob, manumitted by will

Martha Timmons, adm. of Stephen Timmons, allowed 10% on estate

Robert J. H. Handy, adm. of John Stevens, to sell personal estate (except wearing apparel)

Dolly Purnell, late exe. of Esme Purnell, allowed $105.36 paid to Edward Hammond, Jun., 5 May, 1808, on deceased's note assigned from Thomas D. Purnell; Caleb Morris, adm. dbn, swears that he paid the sum for late exex. after his marriage to her & did not, nor can he get, a receipt, Edward Hammond having died

F. 449 Daniel G. Robins, adm. of Anthony Bacon, to retain $10.33, the cost of suit of Frederick Ball, adm. of William (use of Samuel Talbot), against him, now pending in Worcester Co. Court; also $420, amount of sale of estate of Col. Peter Chaille by deceased, as collector of said Peter

Daniel G. Robins, adm. of Anthony Bacon, allowed 10% on estate

Josiah Collins, guardian to James Bowen, to repair barn

'319'

Elizabeth Brittingham, adm. of Isaac Brittingham, to sell personal estate (except negroes & wearing apparel)

John Williams, adm. of James Furniss, to sell personal estate (except wearing apparel)

F. 450   Littleton R. Purnell & Jacob Teague to distribute specifics from estate of Jesse Bennett, according to will, in hands of Henry Bennett, exe.

Ishmael Baker, adm. of Isaiah Baker, allowed 10% on estate

Ishmael Baker, adm. of Isaiah Baker, to retain money to meet claim of Selathiel Baker, minor, for his share of estate of his father Archibald Baker, which estate this deceased administered

James Bevans, adm. of Zachariah Pepper, to sell personal estate

John J. Williams, adm. of John Postly, to sell property as directed by will

Sarah Bradford, adm. of William Bradford, in account with John Truitt & Henny, his wife

F. 451   Received Jan. 13, 1814, of Sarah Bradford, adm. of Wm. Bradford, full amount of above, $477.75, in full of Wm. Bradford's estate

Test.; John Bishop   John Truitt

F. 452   [blank]

F. 453   Tues. Oct. 10, 1815   John Bishop, Zadok Sturgis present

Orphan; Elizabeth Truitt (of John K.)
Guardian; Mary Truitt
Sureties; Jacob Teague, Henry Richardson

F. 454   Orphan; John K. Truitt (of John K.)
Guardian; Mary Truitt
Sureties; Jacob Teague, Henry Richardson

Orphan; Mary Truitt (of John K.)
Guardian; Mary Truitt
Sureties; Jacob Teague, Henry Richardson

F. 455   Orphan; Henrietta Truitt (of John K.)
Guardian; Mary Truitt
Sureties; Jacob Teague, Henry Richardson

F. 456   Orphan; Edward Stevens (of John)
Guardian; David Richardson
Sureties; Ephraim K. Wilson, John W. B. Parsons

Orphan; John Stevens (of John)
Guardian; David Richardson
Sureties; Ephraim K. Wilson, John W. B. Parsons

F. 457   Orphan; William Stevens (of John)
Guardian; David Richardson
Sureties; Ephriam K. Wilson, John W. B. Parsons

F. 458   Orphan; John Smith Mills (of Levin)
Guardian; Leah Mills
Sureties; Samuel Boston, Jacob Boston

Orphan; Ebenezer Brevard Davis (of Abisha)
Guardian; Martha Davis
Sureties; Edward Briddle [also Bredell], John Fassitt (of Elijah)

F. 459   Orphan; Abisha Davis (of Abishai)
Guardian; Martha Davis
Sureties; Edward Briddle, John Fassitt (of Elijah)

F. 460   Orphan; Leonard Morris (of Jethro)
Guardian; Rackliffe Morris
Sureties; Jethro Morris, Shipherd Johnson

Orphan; Martha Truitt (of James)
Guardian; David Taylor
Sureties; Whittington Bowen, John Scott (of Joshua)[neither could write]

F. 461   Orphan; Lemuel Truitt (of James)
Guardian; David Taylor
Sureties; Whittington Bowen, John Scott

F. 462   Orphan; Molly Truitt (of James)
Guardian; David Taylor
Sureties; Whittington Bowen, John Scott

Apprentice; Harry Selby, 13 on 14 Nov. last, son of Nancy
Bound to; John G. Purnell
Trade; druggist
Sureties; Henry Richardson, William E. Sturgis

F. 463   Apprentice; Parker Allen, 9 next Dec., son of Comfort
Bound to; John Bowen
Trade; shoe maker
Sureties; William Jones, Barnabas Henderson

F. 464   Apprentice; Hesekiah Dorman (of Nehemiah), 17 next Feb.
Bound to; David Richardson
Trade; coasting business
Sureties; Henry Richardson, Thomas Milbourne

F. 465   David Smith & Thomas Hargis to view estate of John Patterson,
F. 466   in care of James Patterson, guardian; before William
Schoolfield: report; estate of John & Levin Patterson; 110 acres, part of 'Chery Stones'

F. 467   David Smith & Thomas Hargis to view estate of Levin Patterson, in care of James Patterson, guardian; [same as above]

F. 468   Thomas N. Williams & William Richards to view estate of Henry Gray, in care of Joseph Ennis, guardian; before Thomas Jones:
F. 469   report; 140 acres; widow's dower

F. 470   Thomas N. Williams & William Richards to view estate of Walton Gray, in care of Joseph Ennis, guardian; before Thomas Jones: report; 122 acres; widow's dower

F. 471   Thomas N. Williams & William Richards to view estate of Levin Gray, in care of Joseph Ennis, guardian; before Thomas Jones: report; 100 acres; widow's dower

F. 472   Thomas N. Williams, Esq., & William Richards to view estate of Anne Elizabeth Gray, in care of Comfort Gray, guardian;
F. 473   before Thomas Jones: report; 1/2 of 275 acres; widow's dower; 1/3 of land belongs to Joseph Ennis

F. 474   Thomas N. Williams & Cord Hazzard to divide negroes from estate of Isaac Franklin, in hands of Henry Franklin, Jun., exe.; before Peter C. Evans: increase since Isaac's death,
F. 475   boy Isaac; Robin & Stephen freed by will; reappraisal; shares to widow & 6 children;
1) to widow, Martha Franklin; Spry, Worcester, Betty, Comfort, Sall
2) to Dr. Robert Purnell & wife; Marcus
3) to Henry; Ceasor, Primas, Arnold
4) to Millia; Littleton, Levin
5) to Milky; Lewis, Joshua, Lavina
6) to Louisa; Rachel, Handy, Isaac
7) to Mary; Ned, Hulda

F. 476   Order at Apr. term, for George Hayward & McKimmy Porter to settle dispute between George S. Gunby & Daniel G. Robins, adm. of Anthony Bacon, rescinded; George Hayward, Samuel R. Smith & James Givan to adjust accounts relative to Bacon & Gunby's joint adm. of estate of Col. John Gunby; long account; mentions Ann D.
F. 477-8 Gunby, Sally W. Gunby, John Gunby, Major Henry, slave Ebben, J. C. Handy, E. K. Wilson, R. J. H. Handy, Martin & Hayward;
F. 479   Daniel to pay George $10,508.55

Ambrose White & John Thompson exhibit final settlement of estate of Mary Perkins; mentions Nixon Davis, John Williams, John Richards, Wm. Houston, Eli Tar, Matthew Hopkins, Major Marinder, Frances
F. 480   Brown, John Orr, Joshua Duer, John C. Handy, Wm. Whittington,
(cont.)

Ezekiel Wise; cash collected by Nixon Davis, Esq., from;
Elisha Hadder, Levin Holland, Matthias Davis, Wm. Richards, Terbet
Wright, John Knox, slave Sarey, Wm. Bassett (for negro James);
mentions Wm. Parker, John Walter, Joseph Miller, Littleton
F. 481   Purnell, Saml. Smith, Isaac Franklin, John Thompson, Joshua
Duer (on Nancy Richardson's note), Jas. Trippe, Evans Hudson
(balance of Nancy Richardson's note), John Williams, Rich. Sturgis,
Joseph Miller, Isaac Franklin, W. Brown, John Richason, Major Mariner,
Saml. Smith, Thomas Williams (on John Rankin's note), Elijah Reed,
Kendal Jones, Thomas Cooper, White P. Fassitt

F. 482   Ambrose White, John Thompson

Joseph J. Gillis & Josiah Bratten to adjust accounts between Henry
Watts, adm. of Thomas Mitchell, & Edward Scarborough

           Apprentice; Littleton Stevens, black, 7 on 18 Dec. last
           Bound to; William Watson (of Jehu), planter
           Trade; farming
F. 483   Sureties; James Jones (of Elisha)
           Before Jas. Patterson, Jas. Payne

           Apprentice; James B. Selby, 16 on 22 Feb. next, by consent of
           his father Lemuel
           Bound to; Ambrose White
           Trade; clerk in a retail store
F. 484   In presence of Thomas Robins

           Apprentice; Eliza Stevens, black, 8 last June
           Bound to; James Jones (of Elisha), or wife
           Trade; common housework; spinning, weaving & c.
           Before Jas. Patterson, Jas. Payne
F. 485   Surety; William Watson (of Jehu)

Mitchell Gray, exe. of Abishai Davis, to sell personal estate (except
wearing apparel & legacies)

John J. Williams, adm. of Thomas Franklin, to sell personal estate

New warrant to Col. Samuel Handy & George Hayward to appraise effects
of McKimmy Porter

Isaac Porter, adm. of McKimmy Porter, to sell property in additional
inventory

F. 486   Thomas N. Williams & Cord Hazzard to distribute negroes from
           estate of Isaac Franklin, in hands of Henry Franklin, Jun.,
exe.

Daniel Handcock, adm. of John Bonnewell, to sell personal estate
(except corn & fodder)

James Watson, exe. of Jehu Watson, to sell personal estate (except
legacies & corn)

Nehemiah Burbage, late adm. of Mary Burbage, allowed $4.58 for clothes furnished negro Ben belonging to Mary Purnell, who was hired by deceased for 1811

Thomas Morris, adm. of Jethro Morris, to sell personal estate

F. 487   John Stevenson, adm. of Josiah Long, to retain the proportion on the claims of Levi Powell & Isaac Atkinson, which are in dispute, & on the claims of George S. Gunby

Dr. John Stevenson & Joshua Sturgis to view property of John S. Mills, in care of Leah Mills, guardian

Holland Smith, exe. of Elsea Smith, to sell personal estate (except wearing apparel & negroes)

William Franklin, adm. of Robert Kerby, to advertise in the Maryland Gazette at Annapolis for creditors to exhibit claims

New warrant for Dr. John Stevenson & Joshua Sturgis to appraise effects of Levin R.(?) Mills; Leah Mills, exe., to sell same

William Quinton & Jackson Turner to view estate of Edward Stevens, in care of David Richardson, guardian

F. 489   William Quinton & Jackson Turner to view property of John & William Stevens, in care of David Richardson, guardian

John Powell, adm. of Esther Powell, allowed 10% on estate

Cord Hazzard & David Gray to view property of Ebenezer B. & Abishai Davis, in care of Martha Davis, guardian

Sarah Tracey, adm. of Arthur Tracey, to advertise in the Democratic Press at Philadelphia for creditors to exhibit claims

Hannah Ball, exe. of Levi Ball, to sell personal estate (except legacies)

Received 21 Mar., 1815, of Thomas Collins, my guardian, $272.63, my part of my father William Rowley's estate

Test.; Peter Holland   Susanna X Rowley
                                          her
                                         mark

Received Sept. 21, 1815, of Rachel Parsons, the full of my part of personal estate of my father

Test.; Billy Fooks   Isaac Parsons

F. 489-90 [blank]

F. 491   Tues., Dec. 12, 1815   All Justices present

George Parsons, Esq., sheriff

Apprentice; Patrick Hall, negro, 6 on 25 Dec. last, son of Rachel
Bound to; Thomas Milbourn
Trade; common laborer
Sureties; Ralph Milbourn, Joshua Brittingham

F. 492 Joshua Prideaux & Cord Hazzard to view estate of Henry
        Franklin (of Isaac), in care of Henry Franklin (of Henry),
F. 493 guardian; before Thomas N. Williams: report; manner
        plantation; widow's dower; negroes Primus 13, Cezar 78,
        Arnold 3; fence between Jacob White & W. Warren; 210 acres,
F. 494 part of 'Ratcliffs Discovery'; land where wind mill stands,
        40 acres, called 'Mount Pleasant'; land in Berlin, 1/4(?)
acre, part of 'Burlin'; land where Annanias Jarman lives, subject to
division among six representatives; 1/2 of fence to be kept up by Cap.
Daniel Tingle & 1/2 by Littleton Davis; 150 acres, part of 'Content'

F. 495 Joshua Prideaux & Cord Hazzard to view estate of Milcha
        [also Milka] Franklin, in care of Henry Franklin, guardian;
F. 496 before Thos. N. Williams: report; widow's dower; negroes
        Lewis 10, Levina 7, Joshua 1 1/2; fence to be kept up by
Capt. Daniel Tingle & Littleton Davis; 150 acres called 'Content'

        Joshua Prideaux & Cord Hazzard to view estate of Amelia
F. 497 Franklin, in care of Henry Franklin, guardian; before Thos.
        N. Williams: report; widow's dower; negroes Littleton 7,
F. 498 Levin 7; [fence & land as above]

        Joshua Prideaux & Cord Hazzard to view estate of Mary
F. 499 Franklin, in care of Henry Franklin, guardian; before Thos.
        N. Williams: report; widow's dower; negroes Ned, Hulda;
[fence & land as above]

F. 500 Joshua Prideaux & Cord Hazzard to view estate of Louisa
        Franklin, in care of Henry Franklin, guardian; before Thos.
        N. Williams: report; widow's dower; negroes Rachel 30 & two
F. 501 children, Handy 4, Isaac 6 months; [fence & land as above]

        Apprentice; Levin Handcock, 13, son of James, a child of the
        Poor House
        Bound to; Thomas T. Dorman
F. 502 Trade; taylor
        Sureties; James Sturgis, Robert Smith
        By Trustees for the Poor; Samuel Handy, Joshua Duer, Geo.
        Hayward

F. 503 Apprentice; John Graham, 14, child of the Poor House
        Bound to; Asa Bell
        Trade; farmer
        Sureties; Peter Truitt, David Truitt
        By Trustees for the Poor; Joshua Duer, John S. Martin, Geo.
        Hayward

F. 504 Apprentice; Sally Conner, 10 on 10 Mar., daughter of Elisha, child of the Poor House
Bound to; James Q. Johnson [also has James Q. Selby]
Trade; housework
F. 505 Sureties; William Walea, Robert Smith
By Trustees for the Poor; Samuel Handy, Joshua Duer, John S. Martin

James Patterson, exe. of Anderson Patterson, exhibits account; mentions Lemuel Henderson, Robert Lambden

F. 506 John Aydelott, adm. of John G. Taylor, to sell personal estate (except wearing apparel)

James H. Rowley, adm. of George C. Evans, allowed 10% on estate

William Davis, adm. of John Bradford, allowed 10% on estate

Christopher Ball, adm. of Isaac Ayres, allowed 10% on estate

New warrant to Nehemiah Holland & John Holland to appraise effects of John Bonnewell not in inventory; Daniel Handcock, adm., to sell same

Zipporah Bowen & Josiah Collins, adms. of William Bowen, to sell negroes

Joseph Carey, adm. of Jonathan Carey, to sell personal estate

F. 507 Johnson Gray, adm. of William Gray, to sell personal estate

Rebecca Hall & Edward Stevenson, adms. of John Hall, allowed 7 1/2% on estate

George Hayward & John S. Martin to distribute negroes from estate of James Duer, in hands of Nancy & Robert Duer, adms.

James Patterson, guardian to John & Levin Patterson, to build house

Powell Patey, exe. of John Bradford, allowed 8% on estate

William Holland, adm. of John B. Williams, allowed 10% on estate

F. 508 John Bishop, exe. of Edward Hammond, Sen., to sell personal estate (except legacies)

Samuel R. Smith, adm. of Sarah Smith, to sell personal estate (except wearing apparel)

F. 509 [blank]

F. 510 Special Court, Dec. 29, 1915, at instance of William Allen; Zadok Sturgis, John Bishop present

Orphan; Edward Hammond (of Charles)
Guardian; Littleton Bowen
Sureties; Isaac P. Davis, Lemuel Purnell

Whereas Abisha Davis, Sen., bequeathed articles to his widow, which
articles were excepted in order for sale of estate, & widow
F. 511   has renounced will, articles becoming part of residue;
Mitchell Gray, exe., to sell same; exe. to dispose of house
on land of John Mitchell

Isaac P. Davis, exe. of Nixon Davis, to sell personal estate (except wearing apparel, legacies & wheat)

William Allen, exe. of John Allen, Sen., to sell personal estate (except wearing apparel & legacies)

F. 512   Special Court, Feb. 2, 1816, at instance of John Sturgis; all Justices present

Orphan; Stephen Hammond (of Edward, Jun.)
Guardian; Purnell Porter
Sureties; Selby Parker, William W. Porter

Orphan; Charles Hammond (of Edward, Jun.)
F. 513   Guardian; Purnell Porter
Sureties; Selby Parker, William W. Porter

Orphan; Nancy Hammond (of Edward, Jun.)
Guardian; Purnell Porter
F. 514   Sureties; Selby Parker, William W. Porter

Orphan; Deligent Mumford (of John)
Guardian; Caleb Morris
Sureties; Levin Holland, John J. White

John Sturgis, exe. of Major Mumford, to sell personal estate (except legacies, corn & wearing apparel)

F. 515   William Jones & James Bowen [Hammond crossed out] to view
property of Stephen, Charles & Nancy Hammond, in care of
Purnell Porter, guardian

William Allen, adm. of Joseph Callahan, to sell personal estate

Caleb Morris, guardian to Deligent Mumford, to sell negro Eben

James Morris, exe. of William Pollett, to sell personal estate

F. 516   Littleton Robins, Zadok Sturgis & John Bishop appointed Justices

C. Ridgely of Hampt.   W. Kilty, Chanc.

Wit.; The Honourable William Kilty, Esq., Chancellor

Tues., Feb. 13, 1816   Zadok Sturgis, John Bishop present

F. 517
Orphan; Maryanne Dennis Stevens (of John)
Guardian; Mary D. Stevens
Sureties; Robert J. H. Handy, Charles Parker

Orphan; Wealthy Taylor Greer (of George T.)
Guardian; Purnell Taylor
Sureties; John Selby, Sen., John Selby, Jun. (of Parker)

F. 518   Apprentice; William Hopkins (of Jacob), 12
Bound to; Philip Morris
Trade; coasting business
Sureties; Henry Richardson, John Bowen

F. 519   Apprentice; John Blake, mulatto, 11
Bound to; Risdon McDaniel
Trade; farmer
Sureties; William Dryden, Littleton Quinton

F. 520   Dr. John Stevenson & Joshua Sturgis to view estate of John S. Mills, in care of Leah Mills, guardian; before Wm.
F. 521   Schoolfield: report; plantation part of 'Cherry Stones', 147 3/4 acres; lot at New Town

Thomas Duncan & Moses Purnell to view estate of Edward
F. 522   Hammond (of Charles), in care of Littleton Bowen, guardian; before Thos. Jones: report; plantation formerly property of William J. Houston, 132 acres, part of 'Fair Meadow', 'Chance' & 'Discovery'; land formerly property of John Chaille, 200
F. 523   acres, part of 'Purnell Security' & 'Sherbourn'; land formerly property of John Morris, 45 acres, part of 'High Fields'; life time right of Sarah Smack, an aged woman, in land called 'Partnership'; land formerly property of John Rownd, 240 acres, part of 'Johns Inheritance' & 'Bleachinghurst'

William Quinton & Patrick Causey to view estate of Maria,
F. 524   William & James Smullen, in care of Sally Smullen, guardian; before Saml. R. Smith: report; real estate in the Forrest belonging to heirs of Petter Smullen, called 'Indian Ridge',
F. 525   'Desert' & 'Branch Lot', 164 acres, occupied by guardian; thirds of widow of old William Smullen; thirds of widow of Petter Smullen; 'Addition to Desert', 104 acres, occupied by Levi Riggen

Apprentice; Thomas Greer, by consent of his mother Lotty
Bound to; Ebenezer Powell, Sen., shoe maker
F. 526   Trade; shoe maker
Term; 8 years from 11 May next
Surety; Moses Freeman
F. 527   Before Thos. N. Williams, Thos. Jones

I, Lotty Greer, agree to within articles

Wit.; Jas. Riley

                                                her
                                        Lotty X Greer
                                             mark

        Apprentice; Isaac Armstrong, 6 on 4 Apr., 1816, by consent of his father Abel
        Bound to; John Selby, Sen.
        Trade; farmer
F. 528   In presence of Purnell Taylor, Edmd. J.(?) Bennett

I agree to pay Abel Armstrong $20/year of above indenture, & if I die, Isaac will be at disposal of said Abel

Wit.; Edmd J. Bennett   John Selby, Sen.

        Apprentice; James Blake, son of John (of George) [couldn't write]
        Bound to; John Holland, farmer
        Trade; farmer
F. 529   In presence of Nehemiah Holland

Apprentice; John Pruitt [also Prewitt], aged 14 years, 17 days, by consent of his mother [indenture dated 9 Mar., 1816]
Bound to; Isaac Townsend, blacksmith
Trade; blacksmith
Before N. Holland, James Payne

F. 530   Apprentice; Ezekiel Henderson, 11 on 13 Sept. last, by consent of his mother
        Bound to; Annanias Timmons, farmer
        Trade; farming
        Sureties; Jesse Timmons, Kendal Truitt
F. 531   Before Wm. McGrigor, Peter Whaley

Kendal Truitt, adm. of Nehemiah Truitt, to sell personal estate

Levi Cathell & John Cathell, exes. of Levi Cathell, to sell personal estate (except legacies)

William Hill, exe. of Elizabeth Hill, to sell personal estate (except negroes, wearing apparel & legacies)

Thomas N. Williams, adm. of Belitha Burbage, to sell personal estate

F. 532   James Morris, exe. of William Pollitt, to sell personal estate (except wearing apparel, legacies & negroes)

Thomas N. Williams & James A. Collins to view property of William Richards, in care of William Richards, guardian

George W. Purnell, adm. of Thomas M. Purnell, to sell enough personal estate to cover debts

Charles Parker, adm. of William Parker, to sell personal estate
(except legacies)

James Sturgis, exe. of John O. Sturgis, to sell personal estate
(except legacies)

F. 533   Nancy Coston & William Rowley, adms. of John Coston, to sell
          personal estate (except wearing apparel)

Charlotte Dale, adm. of Jacob Dale, to sell personal estate (except
wearing apparel)

Whereas by account settled on estate of Mary Burbage, 11 Oct. last,
there is a balance in hands of Nehemiah Burbage, late adm., of
$512.22, & whereas by account settled on estate of Edward Burbage, 25
Feb., 1814, on which estate Mary & Nehemiah were joint adms., there is
a balance of $677.18 including widow's thirds, which deducted leaves
$451.46, ordered that Handy Davis, adm. of Nehemiah, to retain half
for representatives of Edward Burbage, & pay half to Samuel Porter,
adm. dbn of said Mary

F. 534   Handy Davis, adm. of Nehemiah Burbage, to retain, as adm. dbn
          of Edward Burbage, $451.46, the balance due representatives
of Edward from Nehemiah & Mary Burbage, late adms.

Robert & Nancy Duer, adms. of James Duer, allowed 7 1/2 on estate

Robert & Nancy Duer, adms. of James Duer, having accounted for profit
on sale of estate & dividends received on bank stock, allowed interest
on debts

It being represented by Robert & Nancy Duer, adms. of James Duer, that
deceased had 100 shares in Farmers Bank of Somerset & Worcester, they
to deduct shares sold

F. 535   Robert J. H. Handy, adm. of John Stevens, to advertise in
          paper at Easton for creditors to exhibit claims

James G. Townsend, adm. of Levin Townsend, to sell personal estate
(except wearing apparel)

Josiah Collins, & Risdon Mumford & Zipporah, his wife, adms. of
William Bowen, allowed 7% on estate

Received Oct. 24, 1814, of Severn Pruitt, $127.44, the same on account
of William Aydelott's guardianship to heirs of Major Lindsey

Test.; Jas. Bevans   Matthias Lindsey

Patrick Waters, guardian to John H. Bishop (of Charles, of Wm.),
exhibits account; mentions cash received of John Bishop, Esq., balance
due orphan from George Truitt & wife, late guardian

F. 536   Feb. 27, 1816, received of Patrick Waters, my late guardian, $78.78, balance due me agreeable to above account, which sum was settled by his acceptance of order drawn by me on him in favor of John Richardson for $79.90

                              his
                         John X Bishop
                              mark

F. 537   [blank]

F. 538   Special Court, Mar. 8, 1816, at instance of Daniel G. Robins & William Corbin; Zadok Sturgis, John Bishop present

Thomas N. Williams, adm. of Isaac Hill, exhibits account; mentions Peter Parker, young slaves Molly & Lanta, Molly Hill; before Thos. Jones

F. 539   Daniel G. Robins, adm. dbn cwa of Daniel Robins, Sen., vs. William Corbin, surviving exe. of Peter S. Corbin; Thomas N. Williams & George Hayward to settle dispute respecting estate of Daniel Robins, Sen, which came to hands of Peter S. Corbin, by his marriage to Comfort Robins, exe. of Daniel, or as adm. dbn of said Daniel, after death of Comfort

Wit.; Ann D. Wilson

F. 540   John C. Handy, adm. of William W. Gray, to sell personal estate

Thomas N. Williams, adm. of Isaac Hill, allowed 10% on estate

F. 541   Tues., Apr. 9, 1816   All Justices present

Orphan; Wise Allen (of John)
Guardian; Peter Allen
Sureties; William Allen, John O. Selby

F. 542   Orphan; Eleanor Townsend (of Levin)
         Guardian; Levin Townsend
         Sureties; John C. Handy, William Quinton

F. 543   Orphan; Henry Jones (of Daniel)
         Guardian; Nancy Jones
         Sureties; William Jones, Obed Jones

Orphan; Elizabeth Jones (of Daniel)
Guardian; Nancy Jones
Sureties; William Jones, Obed Jones

F. 544   Orphan; Gertrude Davis (of Jesse)
         Guardian; George Gray
         Sureties; Mitchell Gray, Isaac Mitchell

F. 545
Orphan; Rachel Davis (of Jesse)
Guardian; George Gray
Sureties; Mitchell Gray, Isaac Mitchell

Orphan; Julianna Davis (of Jesse)
Guardian; George Gray
Sureties; Mitchell Gray, Isaac Mitchell

F. 546
Orphan; John Davis (of Jesse)
Guardian; George Gray
Sureties; Mitchell Gray, Isaac Mitchell

F. 547
Orphan; Lemuel Dale (of Ebenezer)
Guardian; Elizabeth Dale [couldn't write]
Sureties; Seth Whaley, John Bratten

Orphan; Burton Dale (of Ebenezer)
Guardian; Elizabeth Dale
Sureties; Seth Whaley [also Waley], John Bratten

F. 548
Orphan; Solomon Carey (of Jonathan)
Guardian; Levin Carey
Sureties; Stephen Roach, Elijah Carey

F. 549
Orphan; Zadok Hall (of John)
Guardian; Edward Stevenson
Sureties; John Stevenson, Arthur Powell [couldn't write]

Orphan; Elizabeth Hall
Guardian; Edward Stevenson
Sureties; John Stevenson, Arthur Powell

F. 550
Orphan; Sally Hall (of John)
Guardian; Edward Stevenson
Sureties; John Stevenson, Arthur Powell

F. 551
Orphan; Elgate Ruark (of Elgate)
Guardian; Thomas Ruark
Sureties; Jackson Turner, Robert Nairne

Orphan; Mary Ruark (of Elgate)
Guardian; Thomas Ruark
Sureties; Jackson Turner, Robert Nairne

F. 552
Apprentice; Ned Riggen, negro, 16 on 10 Dec. last
Bound to; John Hozier
Trade; farmer
Sureties; Barney Davis, Charles Parker

F. 553
Apprentice; Major Armstrong, mulatto, 13 last Sept., son of Peggy
Bound to; Edward Dymock
Trade; house servant & waiter
Sureties; John J. White, James Holland

'332'

F. 554   Apprentice; Tubman Willis (of William), 17 last Aug.
          Bound to; Major Tarr
          Trade; boot & shoe maker
          Sureties; Levin Holland, Samuel Dorman

F. 555   Thomas N. Williams & James A. Collins to view estate of
F. 556   William Richards, in care of William Richards, guardian;
          before Thos. Jones: report; 80 acres devised to minor by his
          grandfather Edwd. Hammond; widow's dower; 350 acres where
F. 557   father of minor lived; negroes Isaac, James, Amos, Lanta

          William Quinton & Jackson Turner to view estate of Edward
F. 558   Stevens (of John), in care of David Richardson, guardian;
          before Charles Parker: report; 1/4 of land in Indian Town
F. 559   Forrest called 'Broad Neck', 217 acres; tract called
          'Aquitico(?) Savana', 50 acres; tract called 'Deffyance
          Inlarged' & 'Mill' or 'Naswango Mill', 1100 acres; widow's
F. 560   right of dower; lot in New Town, 1/2 acre, claimed by negro
          woman Meriar, left her by will of Wm. Stevens; lot in New
Town, 1/8 acre; tract called 'Cowley', adjacent to New Town, 108
          acres; land in Somerset Co. near Steven's Ferry, occupied by
F. 561   James Broadwater; land occupied by Benjamin Maddux, former
          residence of William Stevens; land occupied by Thomas Hargis

          William Quinton & Jackson Turner to view estate of William
F. 562   Stevens (of John), in care of David Richardson, guardian;
F. 563-5 [same as above]

          William Quinton & Jackson Turner to view estate of John
F. 566   Stevens (of John), in care of David Richardson, guardian;
F. 567-9 [same as above]

F. 570   Eben Christopher & Billy Fookes to view estate of John,
          Woodman & Francis Black, in care of James Roach, guardian;
F. 571   before Booz Walston: report; 160 acres

          William Holland & John Spencer, Jun., to view estate of
F. 572   Frederick Hill, in care of Catharine Hill, guardian; before
          N. Holland: report; land called 'Robersons Inheritance' &
'Willets Outlet'

Michael Murray, acting exe. of Joseph Young, vs. Dr. John Stevenson,
adm. dbn cwa of Zepheniah Benston; order at Apr. term, 1814, for John
Stevenson, James Tilghman & James Patterson to settle dispute between
plaintiff & Stephen Townsend, late adm. dbn of Zepheniah, relative to
          2 notes of hand from Zepheniah to Young, rescinded; Edward
F. 573   Stevenson, James Tilghman & James Patterson to act; one note
          dated 2 Nov.. 1809, for $399.55, ought to be retained by
Young out of estate of Benson; other note dated 22 July, 1809, for
$255, is null & void

'333'

F. 574 Daniel G. Robins, adm. dbn of Daniel Robins, Sen., vs.
William Corbin, surviving exe. of Peter S. Corbin; Thomas N.
Williams & George Hayward to ascertain estate of Daniel Robins which
came to hands of Peter by his marriage to Comfort, late exe. of
Daniel; account; profit of negroes from death of Comfort to
F. 575 death of Peter, being 6 1/2 years; negroes Abel, Stephen,
Adam, Peter, Jenny, Betty; support of young negroes James
1 1/2, Leah 3 1/2, Jesse 6 1/2, Rachel 3 1/2; also Abner;
F. 576 widow's dower

F. 577 Littleton R. Purnell & George Hayward to settle dispute
between John Bishop, exe. of Edward Hammond, Sen., & Purnell
Porter & Nancy, his wife, admx. of Edward Hammond, Jun.

Littleton R. Purnell & George Hayward to settle dispute between
Purnell Porter & Nancy, his wife, & John Bishop, exe. of Edward
Hammond, Sen.

John Dale & William McGrigor to settle dispute between Jacob Postly,
free negro, & John J. Williams, adm. cwa of Col. John Postly,
respecting building done on property of deceased during his life by
plaintiff

William McGrigor & Edward Briddle to settle dispute between Levin
Dirickson & Mitchell Gray, exe. of Abishai Davis

William McGrigor & John J. Williams to settle dispute between Mitchell
Gray, exe. of Abishai Davis, & William Dirickson

John Dale & William McGrigor to settle dispute between Job Postly,
free negro, & John J. Williams, adm. cwa of John Postly,
F. 578 respecting building done on property of deceased during his
lifetime by plaintiff

Littleton R. Purnell & George Hayward to settle dispute between John
Bishop, exe. of Edward Hammond, & William Richards

Apprentice; Benjamin Williams, negro, 8 on 15 Apr. next, by
consent of his mother
Bound to; Israel Townsend, Sen., farmer
Trade; farming
F. 579 Surety; Isaac Johnson
Before Wm. McGrigor, Adam Bravard

Apprentice; Littleton Ginn
Bound to; Thomas Landon, farmer
Trade; farming
Surety; Edwd. Lambden
F. 580 Before Jas. Patterson, Wm. Schoolfield

William Brown, adm. of Andrew Brown, exhibits account; list

F. 581 Mary Davis, adm. of Edward Davis, exhibits account; list

'334'

F. 582   Christopher Ball, adm. of Isaac Ayres, exhibits account; mentions Henry Jones, Peter Holland

Peter Collier, exe. of William Collier, Sen., exhibits account; list

Sally Hill, exe. of Laban Hill, to sell personal estate (except negroes)

F. 583   William Dale & William Parker to view property of Henry & Elizabeth Jones, in care of Nancy Jones, guardian

Upon application of William Corbin, exe. of Peter S. Corbin, value of negroes Jane, Stephen, Abel, Abner, Peter, Betty, James, Leah, Jesse & Rachel, in inventory, but awarded to adm. dbn of Daniel Robins, to be deducted

Josiah Nelson, adm. of William Willis, allowed 10% on estate

William Brown, adm. of Andrew Brown, allowed 8% on estate

Jemiah Hall, adm. of Hezekiah Davis, to sell enough personal estate to cover debts

F. 584   Giles Jones, adm. of Henry Jones, to sell personal estate (except a negro girl)

Mary Davis, adm. of Edward Davis, allowed 10% on estate

McKimmy Porter, appointed trustee to sell real estate of Joshua Fleming, deceased, for benefit of widow Sally & children William & Eleanor, is dead; George Hayward appointed trustee to complete sale

F. 585   New warrant to Littleton R. Purnell & Jacob Teague to appraise effects, not in inventory, of Jesse Bennett, in hands of Henry Bennett, exe.

Josiah Nelson, adm. of William Willis, to retain $16 to meet claim of Severn Pruitt (use of Matthias Lindsey)

Levin Henderson, exe. of Sarah Melvin, to sell personal estate (except legacies)

Peter Whaley & John J. Williams to view property of Gertrude, Rachel, Juliann & John Davis, in care of George Gray, guardian

William McGrigor & Peter Whaley to view property of Lemuel & Burton Dale, in care of Elizabeth Dale, guardian

James Davis, guardian to Patsey Melvin, to give her 2 months schooling

F. 586   David Richardson, guardian to Edward, John & William Stevens, to make repairs on farm at Steven's Ferry

William Richardson, adm. of John Mumford, allowed 10% on estate

'335'

Thomas Ruark, exe. of Elgate Ruark, to sell personal estate (except crop)

Whereas by account settled 11 July last for William Bowen, late adm. of Micajah Bowen, there appears to be balance due from estate of William to estate of Micajah of $508.14, ordered that Josiah Collins, one adm. of said William & adm. dbn of Micajah, to retain that sum

George W. Purnell, exe. of Thomas M. Purnell, to prosecute suit commenced by deceased against Peter Johnson

Nelly Shockley, adm. of Stuart Shockley, allowed 10% on estate

F. 587   Mitchell Gray, exe. of Abishai Davis, to advertise in the Philadelphia Gazette for creditors to exhibit claims

Alexander Franklin, exe. of James Franklin, to sell personal estate

Henry Bennett, exe. of Jesse Bennett, allowed 5% on estate

Kendal Porter, adm. of Merrill Smith, to sell personal estate

Edward Stevenson & [blank], adms. of John Hall, allowed for negro Black Peter, accidentally drowned

James Burnett & Levin Long to view property of Zadok, Elizabeth & Sally Hall, in care of Edward Stevenson, guardian

F. 588   James Patterson, guardian to John & Levin Patterson, to receive their estate from Leah Mills, exe. of Levin Mills, late guardian

Thomas Milbourn, adm. of Thomas D. Shockley, to sell personal estate

William Quinton & Thomas R. Handy to view property of Elgate & Mary Ruark, in care of Thomas Ruark, guardian

George Bratten & Nehemiah Holland to settle dispute between Susanna Henderson & William Allen, adm. of Joseph Callahan

F. 589   I, William Smith, of County Handcock, GA, by virtue of letter of attorney from my sister Hetty, & in consideration of $70.36, I release William Daley, Sen., of Worcester Co, MD, guardian to Hetty

In presence of Jesse Townsend,   William Smith,
              Nathan Gordy   attorney for Hetty Smith

F. 590-1 [blank]

F. 592   Tues., June 11, 1816   All Justices present

Orphan; Elizabeth Ayres (of Isaac)
Guardian; Hetty Ayres [couldn't write]
Sureties; John Aydelott (of Ben), Levin Wilkinson

F. 593   Orphan; John L. B. Robins (of Littleton)
         Guardian; James B. Robins
         Sureties; Thomas R. P. Spence, Leonard Johnson

F. 594   Orphan; James B. Robins, Jr. (of Littleton)
         Guardian; James B. Robins
         Sureties; Thomas R. P. Spence, Leonard Johnson

Apprentice; Robert Ginn, negro, 6, son of Sarah
Bound to; John Stevenson
Trade; house servant & waiter
Sureties; Michael Murray, Levin Cottingham

F. 595   Apprentice; Henry Irons (of Timothy), 12 on 11 Oct. next
         Bound to; Isaac Cottingham
         Trade; coach or carriage maker
F. 596   Sureties; George Hayward, Frederick Conner

         Apprentice; Hammond Runnells (of Edmond), 10 on 17 Sept. last
         Bound to; Benjamin Bennett
         Trade; house carpenter & joiner
F. 597   Sureties; Frederick Conner, William Allen

         Apprentice; Sally Grooms, daughter of Milly
         Bound to; David Richardson
F. 598   Trade; house servant & waiter
         Sureties; Benjamin H.(?) Martin, Arthur McAllen

F. 599   Apprentice; Mary Anne Irons (of Timothy), 9 on 2 Nov. next
         Bound to; Nathaniel R. Cannon
         Trade; spin, knit & sew
         Sureties; William B. S. Riley, John P. Ratledge

F. 600   James Burnett & Levin Long to view estate of Zadok, Elizabeth
F. 601   & Sally Hall, in care of Edward Stevenson, guardian; before
F. 602   Wm. Schoolfield: report; 50 acres, part of 'Cowley'; negroes
         Joseph 50, Gedian 16, Peter 12, Easter 20 (to be free when
    25) & child 1

         William McGregor & Peter Whaley to view estate of Lemuel
F. 603   Dale, in care of Elizabeth Dale, guardian: report; entitled
         to 1/2 of lands by will of his father Ebenezer after decease
F. 604   of his mother; mother's thirds, brother's part; 209 acres;
         negro Stephen 14

         William McGrigor & Peter Whaley to view estate of Burton
F. 650-6 Dale, in care of Elizabeth Dale, guardian; [land same as
         above]; negro Jacob 10

'337'

F. 607 William Quinton & Thomas R. Handy to view estate of Elgate Ruark (of Elgate), in care of Thomas Ruark, guardian; before Levin Conner: report; land in the Forrest called 'Turners Choice', 94 acres, occupied by guardian

F. 608 John J. Williams & Peter Whaley to view estate of Gertrude, Julianna, Rachel & John Davis, in care of George Gray,
F. 609 guardian: report; 107 acres; guardian's thirds; negroes Robin 45, Daniel 14, Isaac 10, Comfort 12, Amy 37, Elijah 3, Harry 3, Abram 7, Jacob 5, Sue 7

F. 610 Cord Hazzard & David Gray to view estate of Abishai Davis, in care of Martha Davis, guardian; before Adam Bravard: report; widow's dower; lot called 'Waits Place', 40 acres;
F. 611-2 Annanias Hudson's farm, 114 acres; home place, 300 acres

F. 613 William Dale & William Parker to view estate of Henry Jones, in care of Nancy Jones, guardian; before William Townsend: report; 250 acres; widow's dower; 2 negro men, 28

F. 614 William Dale & William Parker to view estate of Elizabeth Jones, in care of Nancy Jones, guardian; before William Townsend: report; 200 acres called 'Forest Grove' & 'Dear Harbor'; negro Pegg 45

F. 615 Apprentice; Risdon Holland Williams, 17 on 2 mar. last, by consent of his father Eli, who has left state
Bound to; James Holland, blacksmith
Trade; blacksmith
F. 615 Sureties; Robert J. H. Handy, Littleton Quinton
Before Thos. N. Williams, John Bishop

Apprentice; William Turpin, 17 on 7 Dec. last, by consent of his mother
Bound to; Ebenezer Leonard, tanner
Trade; tanning & currying
F. 617 Before Booz Walston, Benjamin Parsons

Benjamin & John Aydelott, exes. of William Aydelott, exhibit account; list

F. 618 Joshua & Mary Rownd, exes. of William Rownd, to sell personal estate (except negroes, crop & wearing apparel)

Michael Murray, exe. of Joseph Young, allowed 10% on estate

Levin Cottingham, exe. of James Tilghman, to sell personal estate (except wearing apparel & legacies)

Register to state account for Joseph Young, late exe. of Zepheniah Benson, allowing sums in orders of Apr. term, 1812, & 17 May last

John Stevenson, adm. of Stephen Townsend, to pay David Smith, adm. dbn
of Josiah Henderson, $192.53, balance due Townsend from
F. 619   estate of Henderson, of which he was adm.

John Powell, adm. of Jesse Davis, allowed 7 1/2% on estate

Littleton Davis, exe. of John Smith, allowed 10% on estate

Aaron Mezick, exe. of Daniel Wailes, to sell negro boy Samuel & as much of legacies as will cover debts

Aaron Mezick, exe. of Daniel Wailes, allowed 10% on property sold by sheriff

Sally Sturgis, adm. of William Sturgis, allowed 10% on estate

Isaac Toadvine, adm. dbn of John Toadvine, to sell personal estate

F. 620   Eben Christopher, exe. of John Cathell, allowed for negro
Sam, recovered by exe. of Daniel Wailes in Worcester Co.
Court at May term, 1815

Isaac Marshall, adm. of Isaac Bowen, to sell personal estate

Samuel R. Smith, adm. of Sarah Smith, to advertise in the American at Baltimore for creditors to exhibit claims

Thomas R. P. Spence & William B. S. Riley, adms. of Timothy Irons, to sell personal estate (except corn & oats)

William Bishop, adm. of Benjamin Bishop, to sell personal estate

F. 621   Luke Townsend & wife, guardians to Milcha Bevans, to get 3000
red oak barrel staves & apply proceeds to cloathing & schooling

F. 622   [blank]

F. 623   Tues., Aug. 13, 1816   Zadok Sturgis, John Bishop present

Orphan; Benjamin Rownds (of William)
Guardian; Mary Rownds [couldn't write]
Sureties; William Brittingham [couldn't write], Robert Givan, Sen.

F. 624   Orphan; Jane Bowen (of William)
Guardian; Josiah Collins
Sureties; Isaac Marshall, Samuel Hozier [also Hosiear]

F. 625   Orphan; Jesse Bowen (of William)
Guardian; Josiah Collins
Sureties; Isaac Marshall, Samuel Hozier

Orphan; Stephen Bowen (of William)
Guardian; Josiah Collins
Sureties; Isaac Marshall, Samuel Hozier

F. 626   Orphan; Charles Bowen (of William)
          Guardian; Josiah Collins
          Sureties; Isaac Marshall, Samuel Hozier

F. 627   Orphan; William Bowen (of William)
          Guardian; Josiah Collins
          Sureties; Isaac Marshall, Samuel Hozier

Orphan; Elizabeth Evans (of George C.)
Guardian; Henry Davis
Sureties; William Aydelott, Benjamin Aydelott

F. 628   Apprentice; John Beauchamp (of Daniel), 17 next Mar.
          Bound to; Levin Watson
          Trade; shoe & boot maker
          Sureties; Cord Hazzard, Stephen Ennis

F. 629   Apprentice; George Price, mulatto, 18, son of Rachel
          Bound to; William Cottingham
          Trade; farming
          Sureties; Peter Townsend, Thomas Ruark

F. 630   Act of the General Assembly passed Dec. session, 1815, to
          appoint trustee to sell Nassaongo Mills & land belonging to
heirs of John Stevens; David Richardson, guardian to Edward, John &
William Stevens, & Mary D. Stevens, guardian to Mary D. H. Stevens,
          children of John, petition court for sale of said mills;
F. 631   George Hayward appointed trustee; notice to be posted at Snow
          Hill & Salisbury: sureties; John C. Handy, John S. Martin

F. 632   William McGrigor & David Gray, Esqs., to settle dispute
          between Er Truitt & Cord Hazzard, adm. of Robert Johnson

Apprentice; Seth Hobbs (of Joseph), 6 on 9 June, 1816, by consent of
his mother
Bound to; James Smith
Trade; common labour
Before Booz Walston, Milby Adkins

F. 633   Apprentice; William B. Truitt, 12 on 17 Aug., 1816, by
          consent of his mother
          Bound to; Joseph Truitt
          Trade; common labour
          Before Booz Walston, Milby Adkins

          Apprentice; Ebenezer Gray [couldn't write], by consent of his
          parents
          Bound to; Tubman Gray, blacksmith
          Trade; blacksmith
                              (cont.)

Term; till 21, on 20 Dec., 1819
F. 634   Before Peter Whaley

F. 635   William Purnell, exe. of Thomas D. Purnell, exhibits account; list

James A. Collins, guardian to Nathaniel M. McNeill, to rent mills & real estate

William Purnell, exe. of Thomas D. Purnell, states that deceased, as trustee for sale of real estate of Milby Purnell, had received $3,959.77, & after paying creditors, had a balance of $1,309.27

William Purnell, exe. of Thomas D. Purnell, to retain $58.45 to meet claim of Levi Purnell

William Purnell, exe. of Thomas D. Purnell, allowed 5% on estate

Sewell Turpin & Jacob Teague to view property of John L. B. Robins, in care of James B. Robins, guardian

F. 636   Sewell Turpin & Jacob Teague to view property of James B. Robins, in care of James B. Robins, guardian

Sarah & Samuel T. Carey, exes. of Dennis Carey, allowed 10% on estate

John Richards, deceased, as adm. of William Wright, was indebted to said Wright for $116.30 by account of 14 May, 1812, which has been paid by William Richards, his exe., to Alexander Franklin, adm. dbn of Wright

William Richards, exe. of John Richards, allowed 7 1/2% on estate

Upon application of William Richards, adm. dbn on Isaac Richards, Register to state account for John Richards, late exe. of Isaac; William is exe. of John

William Richards, exe. of John Richards, allowed interest to Oct. 1, 1812

F. 637   William Richards, exe. of John Richards, allowed $142.50 paid to John R. Pitts & Julianna, his wife, for which deceased was liable as security to Matthias Warren, late guardian to Julianna

Lemuel P. Spence, adm. of Samuel Marrett, allowed 10% on estate

Matthew Hopkins, appointed trustee to sell negroes for benefit of heirs of Robert M. Richardson, to pay them $557.75, remaining proceeds of sale

William Bishop, exe. of Benjamin Bishop (of William), to deduct $177.20 for articles in inventory, but not property of deceased; list

'341'

Henry Franklin, exe. of Isaac Franklin, allowed 5% on estate

Benjamin Dykes, adm. of Ephraim Dykes, to sell personal estate (except wearing apparel & negroes)

F. 638   David Richardson & Mary D. Stevens, guardians to Edward, John, William & Mary Anne D. Stevens, to rent real estate

William Richards, exe. of John Richards, to retain $14 to meet claim of Levin Stuart

Snow Hill, 7 Sept., 1816, received of Henry Richardson, my late guardian, $8.93, balance due me from my estate to 1 Jan., 1815, the whole profits being $93.13, to this time amounting to $484.20; also $44, being 1/5 of $220 received from Matthew Hopkins on sale of negroes Esther & Sarah from estate of my father

Test.; Matthew Hopkins   Jno. Richardson

F. 639   [blank]

F. 640   Special Court, Aug. 30, 1816, at instance of William Williamson; Zadok Sturgis, John Bishop present

Petition of Zipporah P. Williamson; previous to my marriage with Stuart Williamson, I possessed in my own right 1/2 of farm in Synapuxent, the other 1/2 belonging to my sister Margaret Fassitt; in 1814, the year Stuart died, he rented entire farm to John Scott; rent was paid to William Williamson, exe. of Stuart; asks for 1/2 of rent

Stuart Williamson died at Sinyrnod(?), Del., on 17 June, 1814

F. 641   Court orders William Williamson, exe. of Stuart Williamson, to pay $109.37 1/2

Aug. 31, 1816, received of William Williamson, exe., $109.37 1/2, my portion of rent of Synapuxent farm for 1814

                                Zipporah Williamson

William Williamson, exe. of Rev. Stuart Williamson, exhibits account; mentions B. Farrow, R. Patterson, Mrs. McDowell, D. McDowell,
F. 642   Sweany Saxton, Charles Kemmey, Jacob Stout, Dr. J. B. Harris, D. Lockwood, L. P. Williamson, W. Bowin, Jesse Jones, J. J. Williams, John Scott, L. Bowin, P. Collins, negro Ben; total
F. 643 $237.12 for funeral & family expenses

William Williamson, exe. of Rev. Stuart Williamson, allowed 6 1/2% on estate

William Williamson, exe. of Stuart Williamson, to deduct $172.60 for corn from Synepuxent farm in inventory, which was property of Margaret Fassitt

William Williamson, exe. of Stuart Williamson, to retain $60 to meet claim of W. P. Farrand & Co.

F. 644   Special Court, Sept. 27, 1816, at instance of Zadok Purnell, Esq.; Zadok Sturgis, John Bishop present

Charles Bennett, adm. of Charles Bennett, Sen., to sell personal estate (except negroes & wearing apparel)

Zadok Purnell, adm. of John Purnell (seaside), to sell personal estate (except wearing apparel & negroes)

William Holland, adm. of Anne Bowin, to sell personal estate (except wearing apparel & crop)

[on last page of book;]

Liber MH No. 17, commenced & ended by, G. Hudson

GENERAL INDEX

ADAMS;

Benj. 278
Eli 60
Henry 74,88,154,157,168,182,
206,250
James 278
John 154,157,182,250
Kitturah 92,164
Philip 201
Sarah 74,88,250
Sarah D. 154,157,182
Stephen 247,256
Susan 154,157,182,250
William 92,164,255
William F. 4,7,9,65,74,88,154,
157,168,206

ADKINS;

Barzilla 256
John 42
Milby 194,311,339
mrs. 60
Samson 313
William 90

AFRICA; (Free Negro?)

Sarah 59

AITKIN;

Andrew 57

ALEXANDER;

Elizabeth 56
James 56

ALLEGOOD; (Alligood)

William 278

ALLEN;

Comfort 263,320

Job 303
John 14,19,28,30,48,60,75,77,
154,156,159,202,220,247,266,276,
279,280,284,292,294,326,330
John S. 5,15
Joseph 104
Joshua 266
Leah 151,170,206
Nehemiah 263
Parker 320
Peter 330
Stephen 57,151,170,206,294
widow 58
William 16,20,21,22,166,297,303,
313,325,326,330,335,336
Wise 330

ALLIGOOD (See Allegood)

AMERICA; (Free Negro?)

James 59

AMES;

Caleb 280
John 280

AMWOOD;

James 60

ANDERSON;

Charlotte 190
Leah 195
Kellam 202
Matthias 281,282
Molly 282
Reuben 175
Stephen 63,113,178
Thomas 195

ARMSTRONG;

Abel 328
(cont.)

(Armstrong cont.)
Baham 59
Hannah 218
Isaac 328
Jeremiah 59
Jesse 59
Josiah 251
Robert 218
Sarah 251

ARMWOOD;

Daniel 215
Ephraim 215
Major 215
Nancy 215

ATKINSON;

Angello 18,23,49,57,63,86,87,
147,150,237,242
Anne 63
Benjamin 63
Betsy 63,279
George 63
Isaac 63,323
James 57,58,64
John 57,150
John F. 182,279,308
Joshua 63
Milby 57,69,74,171,278
Robert 64,69
Sarah 63
Thomas 18

AYDELOTT;

Benjamin 13,21,23,52,56,57,67,
76,86,100,101,104,105,113,114,
124,127,128,132,133,146,150,151,
152,159,165,170,189,190,194,198,
200,205,206,264,268,275,336,337,
339
Betsy 127,151
Bety 206
Howard 39
James 13,203,204
John 38,185,189,190,194,196,198,
200,203,204,206,213,217,284,285,
288,325,336,337
Leah 127,146
Mary 198,212,288
Peter 150
Polly 206

Sally 212
Sarah 288
Susanna 38
William 13,76,125,132,133,136,
138,141,157,165,189,190,196,198,
200,206,212,217,250,251,255,257
263,270,280,288,329,337,339

AYRES;

Elizabeth 336
Hetty 336
Isaac 3,7,10,12,52,56,57,69,71,
95,108,116,136,171,172,193,200,
237,253,293,304,325,334,336
John 57,70,90,127,144,148,192,
195,254
Micajah 208,209
Reuben 315
Wm. 315

BACON;

A. 51
Anthony 30,35,36,42,49,52,54,75,
79,87,148,151,152,160,164,166,
171,203,249,269,271,272,279,295,
297,303,318,321
James 29,36,38,41,42,43,55,57,
61,79,87
John 79
John C. 63,75,79,87,99,172,195,
216,266,268,294
William 16,79,82,87,89,148,271,
297

BAILEY (See Bayley)

BAKER;

Archibald 226,319
David 261,262
David K. 262,284,285,288
Hancock 10,77
Isaiah 226,296,319
Ishmael 296,319
James 14
John 23
John B. 65,68,77,96
Jonathan 70,84,86,167
Laban 72
Levin 65,68,70,74,84,86,96
Martha 10,77

(cont.)

(Baker cont.)
Mary 96
Robert M. 10,257,311
Selathiel 319
Zadok 72

BALL;

Christopher 172,248,250,258,260,
261,262,275,279,280,284,304,325,
334
Christopher P. 284,285
David 58,59,281
Delia 250,260,284,285
Elizabeth 261
Frederick 318
Hannah 323
Hulda 203
James 293
John 59,203,248,250,258,260,
261,275,279,280,284,285
Leah 275,276
Levi 172,261,262,279,323
Luther 250,258,279,284
Samuel 229,250,262
Thomas 279
Thomas R. 293
William 59,215,262,318

BALLARD;

Betty 61
Job 188

BANKS;

Samuel 58,156
Wilson 156

BANUM (See Baynum)

BARCLAY;

James 160

BARNES; (Barns)

Benjamin 235,243
Parker 235,243
Rosa 243
Sophia 242
Thomas 232,235,237,242,244,249,
260
William 243

BARNETT (See Burnett)

BARNS (See Barnes)

BARRETT; (Barrott)

Caty 78
James 78
John 277

BASSETT; (Bassitt)

John 90,92,95,96,249
Rachel 90,95,96,249
Sophia 95
William 96,322

BATHARD, BATHERD (See Bethard)

BATTS;

Henry 88
James 88

BAYLEY; (Bailey, Bayly)

Esme 16,20
George 57
Josiah 28,272

BAYLIS;

James F. 215

BAYNE;

Walter 86

BAYNUM; (Banum)

Belitha 31,228
Elisha 222,225,279,285
Hetty 225,285
James 225,228,245,285,292
Nancy 279
William 31,222,225,228,279,285,
292

BEACHBOARD;

Hetty 281
Joshua 59,129
Wealthy 129
William 60,281

BEATHARD (See Bethard)

BEAUCHAMP;

Daniel   339
John   339

BEAZY; (Beezy, Bezzy, Beazey)

James   283
John   223
Nathaniel 223
Sally   283
Samuel   60

BELL;

Ann   122,125,129
Asa   46,236,277,324
George 3,6,10,12,15,25,30,48,
53,54,63,74,130,180
Henry 10,16,24,38
Henry G. 24
James 122,125,129,216
John   46,195,200,278
John H. 273
Mary   122,125,129,198,201,318
mr.   72
Robert 46
Ruth   24
William 122,125,208,216
William B. 244

BELTS;

Rebecca 61

BENNETT; (Bennitt)

Anne   123,124
Benjamin 185,336
Charles 3,10,16,21,30,58,69,70,
91,93,105,108,126,148,149,150,
156,167,198,202,213,231,282,286,
342
Edmd J. 328
Elijah   20
George   268
H.   221
Henry   156,166,181,182,184,186,
207,214,261,298,319,334,335
James   57,58,77,100,115,150,161,
211,270,278

Jesse   5,7,9,10,11,14,16,18,26,
30,32,38,42,53,63,73,78,100,105,
123,124,142,147,182,188,199,207,
225,243,319,334,335
Jesse H. 228
M.   60
Peggy   150
Prissy 186
Rebecca 115
Sarah   69,93,126,149,156
William 58,59,77,111,115,123,
124,125,228,236
William O. 111
William P. 163

BENSON; (Benston)

Elias   9,75,133
Esther   77
Isaac   4,7,9,75,88,274
James   310
John   71,77,78,199,200,213,222,
240
Michael 54
Moses   103,156,291
mrs.   78
Nathaniel 262
Thomas   1,7,9,72,74,79
William 4,6,9,86,133,254,274
William W. 261
Zepheniah 51,52,218,258,259,295,
310,332,337

BENTON;

Michael 150
William 150

BETHARD; (Bathard, Beathard)

Abijah   106,107
Benjamin   107
Daniel C. 106,107
Elijah   30
Elizabeth 106,107
Esther   61,107
Henry   38
Isaac   61,106,107
James   61,107
Mary   106,107
Richard   107,278

BEVANS; (Bevan)

Barshaba   89
Benjamin   59,159
Brittingham   89
Eleanor   270,292
James   28,70,72,77,82,189,208,
209,212,213,225,227,235,258,279,
280,282,319,329
Jane   44
John   105,159,299,313
Joshua   259,291,313
Louisa   292
Louisa A.   270
Lydia   89,216,240,283,311
Lydia A.   225
Milcah   89,216,225,240,283,311,
338
Mills   28,32,34,35,89,189,212,
225
mrs.   58,61
Nathaniel   258,270,292
Rowland   28,29,49,53,54,55,57,
58,65,68,77,83,86,97,101,106,
297,309
Rowland E.   20,23,34,48,57,66,
68,94,102,145,146,147,157,165,
180,200,214,240,247,306
Thomas   60
William   58,60,77,86,89,148
William M.   26,45,48,114,259,276

BEZZY (See Beazy)

BIGLAND; (Beglen)

William   19,278

BIRCH (See Burch)

BIRD;

Major   5

BISHOP;

Benjamin   32,37,46,58,79,100,132,
147,154,171,177,205,338,340
Benjamin E.   5,144
Charles   57,58,125,148,153,155,
156,162,166,169,182,200,201,206,
241,329
Charlotte   5
Denny   57

Elizabeth   28,79,100,131
George   182
Hannah   58
Henry   276
James   231
John   8,9,13,18,21,26,32,35,37,
38,42,64,67,69,75,87,89,91,94,
100,102,122,133,137,142,143,152,
153,155,158,162,168,170,171,175,
181,182,183,198,200,201,203,206,
214,219,222,223,227,250,261,270,
274,275,284,290,302,307,319,325,
326,327,329,330,333,337,338,341,
342
John H.   18,200,201,206,241,244,
248,329
Joseph   9,38,141,156,166
Joseph E.   130
Lemuel   57
Levi   26,60
Levin   5,46,131,132,147
Lotty (Lottee)   131,132,144,146,
147
mrs.   57
Purnell   58,171
Samuel   32,37,59,79,90,93,98,
100,274,276,285
William   18,21,26,38,57,69,143,
152,153,162,168,169,170,201,206,
217,241,244,248,285,329,338,340
Wilson   182
Zipporah   125,148,153,155,156,166

BLACK;

Cornelius   309
Frances   309,312,332
John   309,312,332
Levin   156,166
Mary   60
Woodman   309,312,332

BLADES;

Ballard   242
Benjamin   198
Floyd   242
Goldsbury   254,274,303
Henry   35
James   4,35
Samuel   35
Selby   4,238

BLAIR;

John   45,182,208,291
Robert 76

BLAKE;

Charles   248
Docia   313
Edwd. U. 289
George   205,328
Hannah   14
Harmon   104,112
James   328
John   14,328
Leah   48,205,248
Levin   8,104,248,279
Nehemiah 98,122,123
Polly   313
Thomas   57
William   112

BOHANNON (See Buchannan)

BOIN (See Bowen)

BOLDS;

Edward 243

BONNEWELL;

Elizabeth 176
George   176
John   57,322,325

BOOTHAM;

James 167

BOSTON;

Esau   157,182,199,213,226,232,
242,253
Jacob   67,320
James   59
Jesse   56
Samuel 320

BOUNDS;

John 14

BOUSEE;

Joseph 140,142,173
Mary   140

BOWDEN;

Isaac   307
Jacob   135
James M. 67
Jesse   135
William   60

BOWEN; (Bowin, Boin)

Anna (Anne)   105,342
Asa   58,171,198
Catherine (Caty) 43,280
Charles   339
Comfort   105
David   133,195
Eleanor   137
Eli   203,261,269
Elijah   59,137
Elisha   60
Elizabeth   17,36,38,43,280,290
Esme   137
Esther   43,68
George   195
Hetty   17,36,38,280,281,282,284,
290,291,292,294
Isaac   205,338
James   50,117,284,290,291,299,
308,311,317,318,326
Jane   338
Jepthah   56
Jesse   338
Jethro   290,292,294
John   2,17,36,38,43,60,64,68,109,
142,273,280,281,308,320,327
Joshua   11,17,43,101,279,280
Josiah   176,187,198,262
Kitty   17,36,38
L.   341
Lemuel   56,134,274
Littleton   290,291,326,327
Mary P.   290
Micajah   264,283,314,335
Milby   61
Nathaniel   41,62,64,72,142,168,
209
Parker   28,61,278
Parker S.   80,105,109
                  (cont.)

(Bowen cont.)
Polly 179
Riley (Ryla) 205,282,284,290,
291,292,294
Robert 299
Sally 17,36,38,279,280
Sarah 68,281
Sarah O. 291
Selby 203
Stephen 339
Thomas 61
W. 341
Whittington 256,269,320
William 42,195,198,283,302,303,
314,325,329,335,338,339
Zadok 292,294
Zadok W. 290
Zipporah 302,303,325

BOWHANNAN (See Buchannan)

BOWIE;

Robert 75,102,122,250

BOWIN (See Bowen)

BOWLAND;

John 313

BRADFORD;

Annanias 51,113,114,137,268
Avery 30,213
Burton 15
Elizabeth 198,292
Henny 230,239
Henrietta 223
John 222,270,296,325
Levin 15
Nanny 15
Samuel 4,7,11,115,124,224,240
Sarah 222,223,227,230,231,232,
319
Schoolfield 198,233,292
Solomon 59
Sophia 213
William 30,98,222,227,230,231,
232,319
Zadekiah (Zed) 2,59,191,297,
302,313,314

BRADSHAW;

Betsy 45,46,51,190,225
John 45,46,51
Margaret 45,46,51
Morgan 21,27,48,51,52,190,225
Polly 45,46,51

BRASHIER (See Brazier)

BRATTEN; (Broughton)

Adam 169
Elizabeth 119
George 26,45,83,94,95,119,145,
146,151,167,168,169,182,226,239,
242,306,335
James 34,145,146,151,168
John 12,171,207,208,238,331
John S. 11,20,21,45,60,272
Josiah 26,57,102,110,127,200,
209,244,248,254,276,291,322
Justice (Justus) M. 306
Margaret 145,146,151,168
Nathaniel 58,256
Sophia 209
William 239

BRAVARD; (Brevard)

Adam 8,12,15,47,48,71,73,82,135,
151,153,161,170,268,287,301,302,
333,337
Anna 47
Ebenezer 151,170
Ebenezer C. 47,135,153,161
James 8,12,15,71
John 47,48,170
R. 170
Sarah 47

BRAZIER; (Brashier)

John 60,171
Levin 236

BREDELL (See Bridell)

BREVARD (See Bravard)

BRIDELL; (Briddle, Bredell)

Anne 198,201,216
(cont.)

(Bridell cont.)
Benjamin 83
David 83
Edward 47,82,177,183,187,198,
201,216,218,230,284,285,287,301,
302,318,320,333
Isaac 169,279,306
Levin 83
Nancy 169

BRIMER;

Levi 86

BRITT;

Severen 14

BRITTINGHAM;

Anthony W. 301
Elijah 16,31,60,70,78,248
Elisha 163,260
Elizabeth 31,37,319
Euphemia 59,281
George 257
Harriot 260
Isaac 7,19,44,47,58,77,209,265,
277,280,319
James 64,280
John 50,52,90,134,139
Joshua 276,277,324
Leah 248
Mary 52
Nancy 59
Nathaniel 19,30,99,100,123,175,
240
Obediah (Obed) 14,60,100,240
Purnell 70,148
Rachel 60
Rowland 41
Solomon 7,44,47
Tabitha 301
Thomas 148,179,183,202,254,260
widow 15
William 41,59,257,338
Wm. W. 277

BROADWATER; (Brodwatters)

capt. 34,35
James 23,33,34,50,78,99,113,
124,129,156,332

BROUGHTON; (See Bratten)

Edward 266,273

BROWLOW (See Brownlow)

BROWN;

Andrew 18,58,77,186,314,333,334
David 256
Frances 321
Jackson 18
Jas. 278
W. 322
William 18,21,27,169,205,314,
333,334

BROWNLOW; (Browlow)

William 315

BRUFF;

James 65
Joseph 65
Thomas 60
Zipporah 65

BRUINGTON;

John 306
Noah 306
William 19

BRUMBLY;

Jabez 61
mrs. 57

BRYAN;

John 281

BUCHANNAN; (Bowhannan)

Esther 211
John 3,6,39,211,276
John M. 153
Polly 267

BUNTING (See Burton)

BURBAGE; (Burbidge, Burbige)

Belitha 2,100,176,177,328
Edward   203,289,329
Elias   231
James   273
John   273
Levin D. 243
Littleton 276
Mary   203,244,289,323,329
Nehemiah 203,244,265,272,273,
276,289,323,329
William 2,54,61,235

BURCH;

George   60
Levina   60

BURNETT; (Barnett)

Elijah   20,286,309
James   166,194,296,335,336

BURROUGHS; (Burrows)

Asher   2,10,151,194,282
Henry   19,100,289,300,318
Mary   289,300,318

BURTON; (Bunting?, Benton?)

Esme   9
James   211
Michael 150
William 150

BUSH;

Silas C. 30

BUTLER;

Benjamin 306
Ezekiel 59
James   78
Joshua   60
Robert   60
Samuel   78
William 16

CALHOON;

John   306

CALLAHAN;

Joseph   51,211,326,335

CAMBEL (See Campbell)

CAMERON; (Cammeron)

Jane   297
John B. 10
William 10

CAMMEL;

Ely   258

CAMMERON (See Cameron)

CAMMOCK;

William 27

CAMPBELL; (Cambel)

Betsey   226
Hannah   275
Hannah D. 276
John   275,276
Leah   275
Peggy   226
William 113

CANNON;

Burton   281
Nathaniel R. 266,269,273,286,
308,336
W.   304
William 277,304

CAREY;

Daniel   311
Dennis   58,340
Elijah   331
Elisha   141
Eliza   59
Handy   141
Jonathan 311,325,331
Joseph   325
Levin   141,331
Levy   141
Moses   64
                    (cont.)

(Carey cont.)
Obediah 76,141
Purnell B. 266
Samuel 255
Samuel T. 340
Sarah 141,340
Shadrach 78
Solomon 331
Thomas 78,125,126,128,131,134, 190
William H. 283

CARTER;

Jesse 73
John 92
Polly 73

CASHABY;

Chloe 60

CATHELL;

David 43,130,135,164,168,172, 175,212,213,228,233,262,264,267, 301,302,305,314
Eliza 305
George 262,264,265,267,305,307
Haste 187
James 305
James M. 301,302,305
James T. 164,168,169,175,212, 213,214,217,228,230,232
John 16,19,26,42,43,51,52,56, 63,74,77,88,91,92,97,108,131,134, 135,138,145,147,168,172,175,230, 233,234,258,262,264,265,300,301, 302,304,305,307,328,338
Joshua 164,168,169,175,212,213, 214,217,228
Levi 187,213,228,264,328
Matty 233,314

CAUDRY; (Caudery, Cordray)

John 28,58,154,179,180
Jonathan 180
Nancy 180
Sarah 105
William 28,60,61,80

CAUPER (See Cowper)

CAUSEY;

Patrick 311,327

CHAILLE; (Challie?)

col. 33
John 60,213
John P. 220
Moses 60
P. 20
Peter 16,20,21,22,49,54,60,318
Stephen 123,125,129,192
William 60

CHALLIE; (Chaille?)

John 187

CHELTON; (Shelton, Chilton)

Fleet (Sleetees) 193,228,230

CHERICKS; (Cherix)

James 60,295

CHILTON (See Chelton)

CHRISTIE;

William 134

CHRISTOPHER;

Belitha 144,145
Ebben 87,140,147,168,169,193, 200,212,214,219,224,230,232,234, 235,238,242,249,256,258,260,262, 264,265,267,273,283,294,295,296, 301,302,305,308,310,312,332,338
Elijah (Eli) 59,144,145
George 205
James 205,278
Lowden 205
Tubman 301
William 205

CLARK;

John 92,132
Levin 210
Rhodes 63,132,145
(cont.)

(Clark cont.)
Sarah 132
Thomas 142,148
William 145

CLARVOE (See Clavoe)

CLAVIL (See Claywell)

CLAVOE; (Clarvoe)

Bennett H. 184,210,217,228,248,
257,266,268,286,289,291,316
B. H. 286
John 228
John C. 217

CLAYWELL; (Clavil)

George 247
Isaac 100
James 241
Major 221,255,317
Moses 5,58,103,182
Peter 5,103
Thomas 58,171,241,247,317
William 58,103
Zadok 60

CLUFF;

Benjamin 238,275
Darius 316
Henry 210
Joanna 51,157,165,284
John 165
Jonathan 215,300,318
Juliana 316
Michael 1,7,9,72,74,79
Robert 51,132,136,138,157,159,
165,284

COE;

William 232

COLBORN (See Coulbourn)

COLLICK; (Kollick)

Anne 171
Esther 171
Levin 203
Littleton 260

Nancy 260
Samuel 263
Sarah 171

COLLIER; (Collyer)

Catherine 169
John 12
Kendal 23,93,106,108,253,266
L. 116
Lambert 12,23,88,95,108,158,216,
253,266,269,273
Layfield 43,158
Lemuel 3,12
Molly 108,158
Nancy 169
Peter 116,169,292,307,334
Sarah 12,23
William 73,292,307,334

COLLINS; (Collings)

Belitha 148
Branson 86
Chambers 174
Eli 174,232
Elizabeth (Elebeth) 151,168,293,
299
Ephraim 59
Hetty 293
Isaac 19,24,115,116,117,143,146,
151,166,194,254,277
James 41,43,76
James A. 12,18,45,64,84,94,95,
101,111,114,155,156,218,224,227,
230,232,233,242,255,258,276,277,
279,284,285,290,292,293,298,307,
313,328,332,340
James H. R. 291
John 113,135,151,152,168,261,
293,299,300,303
Josiah 41,42,103,211,274,302,
303,308,311,314,317,318,325,329,
335,338,339
Mary 151,168,300
mrs. 195
Nancy 293
P. 341
Parker 165,264,308
Price 299
Susanna 152
Tabitha 24,115,116,117,143
(cont.)

(Collins cont.)
Thomas   112,113,135,151,152,168,
170,178,179,181,188,237,250,260,
261,291,293,298,300,323
W.   313
Walter   74
Walton   64,80,170
Watson   2
William   291

COLLYER (See Collier)

CONNELLY;

Hugh   60

CONNER;

Abner   186
Asbery (Ayresbury)   264
Benjamin   73
D.   60
Dennis   60
Elisha   264,325
Frederick   5,30,32,34,37,46,50,
75,79,90,91,94,95,99,100,112,
131,132,134,144,148,155,167,169,
186,218,220,222,223,224,228,229,
247,248,266,336
George   283
James   60,278
Levin   94,95,159,170,266,295,337
Sally   325

COOPER;

Bennett   129
Isaiah   129
Thomas   322

CORBIN; (Corban)

Comfort   148,330,333
Eliza   99
Harris P.   59
John   99,136,137,140,142,148,171,
172,235,244,265,301,307
Molly   128,132,136,137,182,184,
194
mrs.   187
Peter   33

Peter S.   5,9,10,11,12,15,16,18,
19,23,24,25,26,27,33,38,43,44,48,
51,53,54,57,58,63,70,91,94,103,
109,128,131,139,148,182,203,238,
330,333,334
William   1,4,6,7,8,13,14,16,18,
21,23,27,75,79,96,97,99,131,132,
136,137,139,148,182,187,194,203,
238,330,333,334
William S.   128,147,182,184,187,
279

CORDRAY (See Caudry)

COSTON; (Costin)

Abel   208
Ezekiel   77,125,132,208,209,214,
217,219,229
George B. R.   281
John   208,209,214,217,219,229,
284,295,329
Nancy   329
Peter   217,219,229
Sally   60
Shadk.   60

COTMAN;

Benjamin   286
Jane   20

COTTINGHAM;

Daniel   44,58,109
George   54
Grace   57
Henry   58,254
Isaac   20,50,58,132,152,167,169,
199,207,209,239,336
James   16,54,56,57,280,291
John   15,32,33,34,35,36,57,71,72,
79,96,97,99,124,140,142,156,172,
236,237,242,244,268,271,278
Levin   301,336,337
Nathan   57,141
Susannah   54
Thomas   57,277
William   339

COULBOURN; (Coulborn, Colborn)

Charlotte   3
                    (cont.)

(Coulbourn cont.)
Elijah   69
James   3
John   3,60
Josiah   303
Mary   54
Rachel   3
William   54

COVINGTON; (Coventon)

Elizabeth   287,291
Elizabeth A.   285
Isaac   285,287,291
John   273
Sally   291
Sarah   249,268,285,287,291
Thomas   273
William   2,24,116,188,193,249,
268,285

COWLEY;

Hinman   58
Samuel   102,288

COWPER; (Cauper)

Henry   59
Isaac   13

COX;

Elizabeth   108
Noah   108
Whittington   19

CRAPPER; (Cropper)

Abia   2
Anne   271
Catherine   300
Cornelius   243,274
Cyrus   165
Edmond   15,37,46,51,100,123,147,
167,263
Isabiah   114,254
Jesse   2,307
John   37,300
Joseph   309
Josiah   37,221,245,274
Kendal   72,77,205,251

Kendal S.   204,205,211,216,221,
236,260,263,266,268,272,273,274,
309,311,317
Leah   137,139,176,262
Levi   58
Levin   273,276,300
Nancy   296
Noble   165
Reuben   15
Sally   243
Stephen   114
Thomas G.   64
Thomas N.   98,126,159
William   2,37,46,87,137,139,164,
172,176,262,271,296
William P.   204,263

CRIPPEN;

George   163,264

CROCKETT;

Joseph U.   98,101,104

CROPPER   (See Crapper)

CROTHER;

Pruitt   60
Selby   60

CURREN;

Lydia   287
Thomas   256,287

CUTLER;

John   52,59,110,111,180,306
Wm.   277

DAILY; (Dayly, Daley, Dailey)

William   73,144,163,168,206,335

DALE;

Annanias   66,170,190,191
Burton   331,334,336
Charlotte   329
Ebenezer   331,336
Elijah   271
(cont.)

(Dale cont.)
Elizabeth 191,194,331,334,336
Esther 170,190,191,194
Jacob 3,28,30,153,158,162,169,
199,201,211,215,218,225,235,
239,261,263,267,329
James 62,167,264
Jesse 271,286,293,310
John 282,333
John P. 28,80
Lemuel 331,334,336
Margaret 190,194
Martha 191,194
Mary 167
Molly 191,194
Thomas 18,43,61
William 10,38,44,52,56,63,108,
114,165,188,254,258,334,337

DALEY (See Daily)

DANIEL;

Rachel 124
Thomas 124

DASHIELL;

Benjamin J. 289
George 59
Isaac 1
John 1,88,108,124,146,149,167,
168,172,175,178,186,195,198,201,
214,219,233,242,264,267,272,273,
283,294,300,302,305,310
Peter 260,264,273,295,310

DAUGHERTY;

Josiah 226
Nathaniel 226

DAVIS;

Abijah 143,154,164,167
Abisha 47,48,53,60,63,66,68,73,
74,77,96,104,130,147,153,155,174,
176,182,184,191,192,194,199,201,
202,210,211,212,221,257,258,320,
322,323,326,333,335,337
B. 279
Barney 244,291,292,295,331
Baynum 263

Benjamin 4,6,9,30,143,144,145,
146,149,150,151,153,154,155,162,
177,198,233,275,276,292,293
Betty 160
Charles 38,258,263
Comfort 62
Daniel 58,211,218,257
Ebenezer B. 320,323
Edward 8,12,37,42,59,215,219,
221,231,268,333,334
Elijah 191,192,199,201
Elisha 253,274,286,293,310
Elizabeth 42,153,154,162.177
Elsea 194,199,201,203
Ezekiel 42,62,233
George 52,88,93,95,106,108,158,
190,216,231,253,266,273,274,286,
293,310
Gertrude 330,334,337
Handy 67,216,231,243,265,329
Henny 249
Henry 100,112,113,124,140,151,
152,172,177,180,191,192,194,203,
244,314,339
Hezekiah 41,334
Hulda 144,151,155
Hulda P. 155
Isaac 143,149,150,154
Isaac P. 326
James 37,60,76,81,83,101,104,
112,122,123,176,208,218,232,233,
256,279,292,293,296,298,334
Jesse 129,130,140,158,274,286,
310,311,330,331,338
John 4,5,18,29,42,51,60,78,86,
101,111,122,123,149,150,153,154,
162,163,166,169,177,198,216,218,
224,225,231,232,233,255,257,270,
279,292,293,301,331,334,337
Joshua 8,12,194,199,201,224,225,
227,230,249
Josiah 92,95,99,100,254,258
Julianna 331,334,337
Keziah 211,218
Leah 62,144,145,151,155,219,233
Levi 59,144,145,155,291
Levin 62
Lewis 62
Littleton 76,113,114,122,143,
149,150,154,164,167,181,184,187,
191,198,199,208,324,338
Lydia 59
Major 112

(cont.)

(Davis cont.)
Margaret 155
Martha 47,48,74,130,194,199,
201,320,323,337
Mary 22,24,268,333,334
Matthias 57,91,105,114,134,141,
143,145,148,164,186,193,199,201,
205,209,215,224,231,236,244,253,
292,295,322
Molly 130,194,199,201
Mordecai 225,270
mrs. 63
Nancy 38,151,155,249
Nathaniel 53,54,64
Nehemiah 275
Nixon 30,31,38,55,74,78,80,91,
109,111,112,114,123,132,134,148,
149,150,155,158,166,169,177,186,
187,199,201,211,218,231,232,239,
243,257,267,278,292,294,321,322,
326
Peggy 145,151,155,224,227
Peter 278,311
Peter C. 270
Philip 256
Polly 129
Rachel 331,334,337
Reuben 305
Robert H. 255
Sally 93,231
Sampson 60,194
Samuel 30
Sarah 88,95,108,158,218
Sinah 243
Solomon 190
Sophia 59
Spencer 279,295
Stephen 45
Thomas 112,172,177,192,216,231,
243
Tressey 194,199,201
Truitt 42
Turner 57,75,77,180,191,194,199,
201,224,243,244,278,303,314
Warner 276
Warrington 114
William 22,24,58,59,76,110,148,
155,188,211,219,221,243,271,276,
279,296,325
William D. 112,113,124
Zepheniah 206
Zipporah 225

DAWES;
James 275
DAYLY (See Daily)
DEAN; (Deen)
Jesse 221
DEAR; (Duer?)
Jesse 274
DECKERSON (See Dickerson)
DELASTATIUS;
Joseph 33,43,51,53,55,57,63
Peter 21

DENNIS;
Benjamin 3,5,10,16,21,30,35,45,
49,51,72,140,142,180,182,184,186,
282,286,290
Henry 193
J. 20
James 41,46,49,53,59,88,166,188,
278,301
James W. 298,302,309,310
John 52,58,97,114,193
John S. 298,302,310
Johnson 193
L. 20
Littleton 46,49,53,72,79,119,
184,210,278
Mary 73
Mary E. 282
Nancy F. 298,302,309,310
Polly 59
Sally B. 180
Sally C. 180
Shalmz. 58
Thomas 73,256
Valentine 8,41,57,110,134,193,
214,278
Wheetly 286,290,298,310
William 58
Zedekiah 73

DENSON; (Denston)

Addams 23
Isaac 291

DERICKSON; (Dirickson)

Levin 19,21,77,98,117,143,151,
170,176,181,182,191,192,194,200,
202,203,208,212,220,225,227,241,
242,254,256
Milby 236
Mitchell 236
Samuel 225
William 311,333

DEVORIX;

Comfort 235
Elizabeth 115,222,248
Henrietta 115
James 226,228,237,254,268,277
John 115,218,220,222,224,228,
235,247,248
Littleton 224,247
Samuel 60,270
Thomas 270
William 60,218,277

DICKERSON; (Deckerson, Dickeson)

Betty 8,106,124
Charles 19
Cornelius 94,126,235
Edmond 12
Henry 232,235,237,242,249,260,
282
James 50,72,80,190,193,200,202,
220,222,259,264,265,306
Jesse 4,19
John 7,11,18,66,242
Josiah 59
Levin 12
Nancy 242
Parker 126
Peter 14,50
Samuel 4
William 7,8,14,50,106,124,132,
150

DIKES (See Dykes)

DINGLE;

Chas. 104
Edward 279

DIRICKSON (See Derickson)

DISHAROON;

Obediah 245
Rebecca 233
Stephen 24
Tempy 246

DIXON;

Ambrose 270
Nathaniel 221,269,270
Thomas 12,14,16,18,19,139
Thomas Q. 138
Thomas W. 11
William 269,270
William Q. 11,86,138

DONE;

John 58
Wm. 238

DONOHOE; (Donoho)

Joshua 291
Teague 301

DORMAN;

Anne S. 147,185,251
Betsy 31
Hezekiah 146,186,251,259,320
James 155
John 16,21,58,65,299
Joshua 142,157
Littleton 16,21
Major 14,235,238,255
Martha 142,157
Mary 146,147
Matthew 32
Matthew S. 306
Matthias 7,72
Nehemiah 5,32,146,147,185,186,
251,320
Peter 113,155
S. 259

(cont.)

(Dorman cont.)
Samuel   18,22,65,91,95,332
Tabitha   113
Thomas   16,21,280
Thomas T.   316,324
William   16,31,65,95

DOUGAL;

Charles   45
James H.   45

DOWNS;

Jacob   286
William   60

DRAPER;

Ralph B.   163,165

DREADON (See Dryden)

DRIDEN (See Dryden)

DRUMMOND;

Ann R.   97
William S.   97

DRYDEN; (Dreadon, Driden)

David   55,60,72
Isaac   19,89,93,174
James   55,61,72,75,77,174,205,277
John   23,59,277
Joshua   39
Martha   80
Nancy   89,93,174
Noble   16,297
Samuel   55,59,61,75,77
Sewell   58,80,91
Stephen   297
Thomas   5,7,8,19,46,58,89,92,93,155,174
William   38,55,59,174,217,277,278,288,327

DUANE;

William   139

DUBBERLY;

John   138
Peter   138

DUER;

James   22,164,180,215,233,270,282,286,301,325,329
Joshua   2,4,24,30,48,56,87,93,136,178,189,282,283,289,317,321,322,324,325
Margaret   301,302
Nancy   270,282,286,301,302,325,329
Peter   60
Robert   257,270,282,286,301,302,325,329
Samuel M.   56,100
William W.   301,302

DUFFIELD;

John C.   297
John P.   306

DUFFY;

Daniel   57
John   235

DUKES;

Henrietta   247
James   247,280
John   162,202,231,232,247,277
Parker   58,226,277
Robert   277
Thomas   202,221,231,232,277

DULANY;

Henry   289

DUNBAR;

James   31
John   31
Joseph   61

DUNCAN; (Dunkin)

Charles   42
(cont.)

(Duncan cont.)
James 42
Jesse 42,62,132
John 29,42,62,97,114,125,142,
157
Levi 195,216,217,218,230
Levin 42,96
Lucy 42
Martha 125
Thomas 42,109,114,123,177,186,
187,195,327
William 15,100

DUNNAWAY;

John 271

William 36

DYKES; (Dikes)

Benjamin 341
Daniel 38
Ephraim 341
George 14,258,282,286.306
John 60
Sarah 38
William 60

DYMOCK;

Edward 58,155,203,247,285,305,
331

EASHOM (See Eshom)

EASTE;

James 244

EDGAR;

Thomas 91

ELLIOTT;

Samuel 215

ELLIS;

James 278
Levi 208
William 253

ELZEY;

Morris 231

ENNIS; (Enos, Enniss)

Abraham 277
Boaz 66,94,175,213,214
Cornelius 4,20,22,29,32,33,35,
36,61,66,97,102,111,112
Elijah 224,226,230
J. 265
Jesse 4,22,29,33,35,36,278
Joseph 11,28,32,34,37,44,58,68,
94,97,145,169,183,222,223,298,
300,321
Lemuel 291
Mary 28,32,35,68,259
Milby 183
Nancy 58
Nelly 22,35
Peter 291
Polly 103
Rachel 20,22,32,33,61,66,97,102,
111,112
Samuel 11,28,29,32,35,36,37,38,
57,68,94,100,145,148,151,152,167,
169,175,183,222,223,259
Stephen 28,32,35,94,183,222,223,
276,339
William 103

ERICKSON;

Molly 258

ESHOM; (Esham, Ishum, Eashom)

Isaac 301
Jas. 278
Jonathan 58,176
Solomon 58,176,301
William 17,18,57

EVANS;

Angelo 264
Agnes 264
Elizabeth 339
George C. 307,325,339
George W. 259
Isaac 47,63,111
Isaac I. 2,38
(cont.)

(Evans cont.)
Jacob 240
John 14,57,240
Joseph 60
Joshua 14,23,66,76,103,132,152,
183
Major 253,255,264
mrs. 57
Nancy 14
Peter 23,58,59,89,189,192
Peter C. 89,114,188,194,199,200,
203,215,216,230,233,253,259,277,
291,297,306,311,313,321
Sally 14
William R. 68
Zeno 255,264

FALLERTON;

Eleanor 11
William 11

FAREWELL;

John 161

FARLOW;

Billy F. 289

FARRAND;

W. P. 342

FARRINGTON;

Lee 126

FARROW;

B. 341

FASSITT; (Fausit)

Eleanor 222
Elijah 15,31,93,320
Elizabeth 43,82,149
James 11,31,39,48,53,63,74,78,
82,116,130,149,313
James M. 43
John 8,11,31,32,47,58,76,78,79,
82,222,301,320
Margaret 4,6,15,44,46,47,67,83,
86,109,150,261,341

Margaret S. 261
mr. 169
Nancy 149
Peggy 10,21,92,119
Rouse 3,6,10,15,32,39,44,47,83,
86,261
Sally 82
Sarah 3,6,32,39
Thomas 3,10,31,32,82,109,119,
170,213,216,239
Thomas S. 4,6,10,11,15,20,21,32,
39,44,46,47,67,83,86,92,109,116,
150,158,163,166,183,184,261,278,
311,317
White P. 322
William 11,78,79,82,88,108,160,
269,273
Zipporah 10,47,83,119

FEDDERMAN;

Henry 52
Josiah 52
William 52

FINDLEY;

Samuel 100

FINNEY;

Betsy U. 247
John 247
William 247

FISHER;

Jacob 218
John 108
Moses 133
Patience 133,218

FLEMING; (Flemming)

Eleanor 297,334
James 14,126,152,178,226,237,
244,254,268,277
John 14,72,126,166
Joshua 14,49,57,77,105,126,129,
138,142,148,149,152,153,156,162,
163,165,171,180,187,189,210,218,
228,230,236,243,244,249,272,274,
277,297,334
(cont.)

(Fleming cont.)
Sally 244,249,272,274,297,334
Sarah 310
William 29,297,334

FLOWERS;

Jeremiah 124,133
Julius A. 133
Ritta 133

FLOYD;

Comfort 310
Elizabeth 290
John 61,226,231,290
William 129

FOOKS; (Fookes)

Benjamin 256
Billy 88,91,286,289,305,306,
311,312,313,323,332
Charles 159
D. 311
Daniel 296.300,305
Eleanor 229
Elijah 87,285,309
Gatty 128,131
George N. 193,198,201,272,273
J. 301
James 88,153,159,161,296,312,
313
Jesse 88,153,161
John 202,207,222
Jonathan 88,91,229,301,311
Joseph 128,131
Laticia 296
Leah 296,300,305
Seth 159
Thomas 92,131,134,140,147,161,
168,169,172,175,198,201,206,214,
264,267,296,300,305
William 307

FOREST; (may not be name)

Jones 60

FOUNTAIN;

Andesiah 119
Levin 119

FRANKLIN;

Alexander 37,38,43,67,73,88,108,
109,139,142,167,169,245,254,276,
278,316,335,340
Amelia 316,318,324
Amutual 32
Catherine 119
Charlotte 114,134,137
Ebenezer 21,32,59
Francis 134
Henry 299,303,307,314,316,318,
321,322,324,341
Isaac 75,76,89,108,116,188,191,
292,299,303,307,316,321,322,324,
341
James 21,24,32,100,114,245,335
John 6,9,37,59,215,243,296
Lemuel 134
Louisa 316,318,321,324
Martha 321
Mary 316,318,321,324
Milcah E. 316
Milcha 318,324
Milky 321
Millia 321
Nathaniel 80
Sally 116
Sarah 21,131
Thomas 53,61,66,86,88,95,108,
114,125,134,137,176,215,216,243,
253,285,296,307,308,322
William 21,80,117,131,215,243,
245,296,308,312,323

FREEMAN;

John 233
Moses 264,327
Rebecca 233

FURMINGTON;

Charles 215
William 215

FURNESS; (Furniss)

Amey 179,184,207,209,210,211,
212,245
Delia 207,209,210,212,245
Ephraim 20,41,101,115
George 207,209,210,212,245
(cont.)

(Furness cont.)
Isaac   207,209,210,212,245
James   319
Littleton   111,127,146,179,184,
207,210,211,212

FURROW;

Joseph   59,277

GARRISON;

Jonathan   270,309,312
Mary A.   309

GASTON;

Wm.   278

GAULT;

Archibald   52,126,293
David   293,297
Obed   202
Rachel   126,293,297

GELLETT (See Gillett)

GEMMILL;

Hugh   287,302

GENKINS (See Jenkins)

GEORGE;

Elizabeth   52
Henny   77
Henry   299
Parker   52
Peter   16

GERMAN; (Jarman?)

Ann   46
Annanias   47
Benjamin   61
mrs.   59

GIBB; (Gibbs)

Abraham   83,147,260,313
Elisha   313
Hetty   313

James   313
John   66,147
Levin   83
Robert   60,313
William   119

GIBBONS;

James   97
Jonathan   136,147,166
Mary   140
Samuel   136,140,147,166,287
William   140

GIBBS (See Gibb)

GILCHRIST;

Andrew   211

GILLETT; (Gullett, Gellett)

Anne   22,24
Ayres   94,276
Elizabeth   19
James A.   276
Jarman   228,232,239,240
John   276
Joseph   26
Polly   26
Samuel   232,248,258,279
Southey W.   94
Wealthy   89,114
William   19,53,114

GILLIS; (Gilliss)

Joseph   119
Joseph J.   204,227,230,244,248,
265,267,322
Mary   119

GINN; (Free Negro?)

Littleton   333

GIVAN; (Givans)

George   245
Isaac   134,136,162
James   58,70,103,165,169,192,204,
207,208,209,224,243,256,257,263,
264,266,303,321
                (cont.)

(Givan cont.)
John   96,140,141,150,194,235,311
mrs.   60
Robert   150,194,210,212,213,270,
272,273,318,338
Round   136,162
Sam   60

GLASGOW;

Patrick   177

GODFREY;

Charles   60
Levin   58

GOODMAN;

James   61

GOOTE; (Gouty)

John   76
Thomas   76,311
William   76

GORDY;

Betsy   109,157
Leonard   109,157
Nathan   134,138,145,162,167,169,
201,205,243,278,286,294,305,335
Noah   109,157
Samuel   112
Thomas   112
William   108,109,112,146,201,278

GORE;

Thomas   135

GORNWELL;

Henry   59,211,216
Major   36,173
Mary   36
Outten   36
Sally   36,173
Sarah   173

GOUTY (See Goote)

GRAHAM;

John   253,324
Robert   57

GRANT;

Paul   59

GRAY;

Ann E.   298,299,321
Benjamin   264
Biddy   301,318
Burton   301
Comfort   298,299,321
David   190,191,236,323,337,339
Ebenezer   285,287,301,339
Eleanor   158
Elizabeth   183,187
George   330,331,334,337
George H.   136,140,147,166
Henry   298,300,321
Isaac   264
James   47,48,53,63,74,201,273,298
Jesse   190,191,192,282,283,284,
285,293,301,302
Johnson   47,48,63,74,130,199,201,
263,325
Joseph   77,88,130,187
Joshua   100,160,258,268,282,298,
300,301,302,312
Levin   298,300,321
Littleton   306
Martha   63,74,201
Martha J.   48
Mitchell   171,172,174,199,201,
218,258,263,268,282,284,285,297,
298,301,306,312,316,318,322,326,
330,331,333,335
mrs.   221
Rouse   285,300,306,312,318
Sally   130
Samuel   16,187,190,191,192,268
Theodore   190,191,192,268
Thomas   74,158,173,177,183,187,
205,210,211,216,221,244,263,284,
286,288
Thomas S.   48,63,201
Tubman   48,63,74,201,263,339
Walton   298,300,321
William   48,63,74,201,325
William W.   330
Zebulon   210,211

GREEN;

John   60
Joseph   89,92,95,99,100
Mary   95
Molly   89,95,99,100,282
Nancy   89,95,99,100

GREER;

George T.   306,327
Jenny   59
Lotty   327,328
Moses   60,277
Thomas   327
Wealthy T.   327

GRIFFITH;

Belitha   112,113,114
Milby   61
Salathiel   257

GROOMS;

Amelia   236,299,313
James   299,313
Milly   336
Sally   336
William   236

GULLETT (See Gillett)

GUNBY; (Gundy)

Ann   271
Ann D.   321
Benjamin   21,23,25,26,31,48,70,
127,164,166,208,209,217,270,294,
312
col.   248
David   60
Elisha   58,65
George S.   151,160,164,166,203,
247,249,269,271,295,303,304,321,
323
James   190,218,292
John   7,10,26,70,151,160,164,166,
202,203,242,249,269,271,295,303,
304,321
Kirk   99,160,175,240
Nancy D.   164
Sally W.   164,321
Saul   61

Susannah   20

GUNN;

Betsy   17,58,79,131
George   12,59,83,131,138
Henry   7,12,33
Mary   7,12,33
Samuel   17,24,25,41,44,52,59,83,
131,138,165,314

GUTHREY; (Guttry, Guthery)

Eleanor   83
James   42
mrs.   59
Nancy   83
Nelly   58
Severn   83
William   42,59,83,263

GUY;

Major   51,55,57,135,136,138,284

HADDER;

Catherine   51
Elisha   322
John   51
Patty   69
Thomas   51

HAINS;

John   151

HALES;

Belitha   60
Jeremiah   58
Leah   59
mrs.   59

HALL;

Ebenezer   19
Elizabeth   331,335,336
George   148,169,226,232,254
Jemiah   334
Jesse   9

(cont.)

(Hall cont.)
John 9,56,61,77,109,115,127,135,
157,209,210,212,222,230,258,283,
325,331,335
Joshua H. 167
Martha T. S. 210
Rebecca 230,258,283,325
Richard 29
Robert 9
Sally 20,331,335,336
Thomas 11,12,57,101,179,204,
206,210,226,232
Zadok 331,335,336

HAMAN (See Hayman)

HAMBLING;

Joshua 311
Marshall 311

HAMMOND; (Hammon)

Bowdoin 60
Charles 2,4,6,31,38,43,44,55,
72,74,97,105,114,133,161,164,173,
177,192,206,237,241,293,326,327
Charlotte 173,177,186,192,213,
241
Edward 23,65,74,96,126,139,142,
149,151,153,161,164,166,167,172,
173,177,179,186,187,192,206,213,
231,237,239,241,243,261,268,318,
325,326,327,332,333
George W. 213
Jonathan 60
Joshua 3,15
Leah 126
Mary 80,96
mrs. 58,96
Nancy 206,231,239,243,326
Rachel 126
Sally 261
Stephen 326
William 50,60,74,80,165,219
Wilson 58

HANCOCK; (Handcock)

Caleb 100
Daniel 62,64,68,78,92,95,96,103,
134,138,204,218,249,282,322,325
Eli 83
Elizabeth 92

James 188,189,324
John 92,122,218
Levin 324
Leah 138
Rachel 59
Thomas 311
William 83,103,134,140,141,184,
186,204,228,249,303,318

HANDY;

col. 68,171
Comfort 49
Esther 128
George 70,72
James 2,41,60,69,70,105,111
John 31,36,59,61
J. C. 321
John C. 9,22,26,81,110,111,116,
135,138,168,171,181,182,251,254,
321,330,339
Levin 45,56,57,70,92,97,116,128,
199
Mary 138
Matthias 70
mrs. 61
Nancy 31,58,69,70,111,128
Peggy 69
Richard 236
Richard H. 64,238
R. J. H. 321
Robert J. H. 46,70,91,124,129,
153,159,164,171,182,189,195,203,
215,224,228,231,247,256,263,271,
297,298,300,318,327,329,337
Sally 128
Samuel 7,10,19,26,30,36,42,44,
46,51,52,63,72,92,104,105,108,
109,113,116,130,132,137,139,141,
142,148,153,158,159,160,166,167,
170,184,187,188,190,195,198,210,
221,223,226,231,235,236,248,253,
260,278,282,289,294,297,302,310,
317,322,324,325
Thomas 2
Thomas R. 2,7,18,63,71,72,81,
128,155,156,166,204,216,230,243,
335,337
William 2,20,32,33,34,35,44,49,
63,81,105,138,185,202,230,232,
243,279

HANSON;

Alexander C. 1,27,49,75,102,122

HARDNETT; (Hardnitt, Hartnett)

Daniel 112,179,181,231
Elizabeth 181
Nancy 181
Sarah 179,181,231
William 181

HARGIS;

Lydia 313
Polly 267
Thomas 194,196,198,314,321,332
William 185,261

HARMAN; (Harmen, Harmon)

Abel 195,260
Anna 154
Charles 159
Harry 46
Hes 156
Jenny 29
Jeremiah 61
Joshua 29
Lazarus 60,67
Leah 46,60
Lloyd 67
Nimrod 159
Sophia 29

HARMONSON;

Edward 31

HARNETT (See Hardnett)

HARPER;

Samuel A. 56,68,70,73,78,96,122,
124,129,146,159,169,171,186,204,
213,218,225,226,235,239,264
William 58,70,125,150,283

HARRIS;

Charles 92
J. B. 341
John 103,223,270

HARRISON;

George 98,101,104,208,212,247,
257
John 98,104,208
Joseph 98,101,104,208,212,257
Rouse 179,181,198
William 247

HARTNETT (See Hardnett)

HAYMAN; (Haman)

Cornelius 234
Elizabeth 233,234
Henry 273
Hezekiah 233
Isaac 160,188,189,233,234,235,
238
James D. 234
John 233,234
Johnson 58,105,144
Martha 160
Mary 233,234
Matty 233,234
Nehemiah 45
Rachel 160,188,189,233,234,235,
238
Talby 234

HAYWARD;

George 1,2,8,11,18,19,21,23,30,
42,46,57,59,64,72,81,86,92,94,95,
96,104,105,108,113,123,124,128,
130,135,136,138,139,140,141,145,
148,153,156,158,159,160,166,167,
169,170,171,176,177,178,182,185,
187,188,190,195,202,204,212,220,
221,225,226,228,230,231,235,243,
253,269,270,271,277,279,281,282,
283,286,288,292,295,297,298,302,
303,309,310,314,317,321,322,324,
325,330,333,334,336,339
mrs. 57

HAZZARD; (Hazard)

Cord 213,216,239,272,276,277,
279,289,303,306,310,318,321,322,
323,324,337,339

HEARN; (Hearne)

Betty 171,229
Ebenezer 229,230
George 230
Isaac 16,19,23,51,67,73,83,97,
124,130,142,162,167,187,188,201,
205,232,286
John 19,171
Saml. 215

HELMAN;

Samuel 90,109

HENDERSON;

Ann 52
Arey 28,31,38,65,67,72
Barnaby (Barnabas) 31,39,43,58,
68,72,80,109,156,159,273,279,
280,281,320

Benjamin 86.127,131,138,179
Benjamin D. 105
Bishop 2,38,55,91
Caty 171
Curtis 7,41,61,62,64,65,68,73,
92,95,99,136,152,194,198,200,
270,283
David 131
David D. 105,127,138
David Q. 285,287,294
Dixon Q. 103,199,204
Elizabeth 68,279,280
Ephraim 68,101
Ezekial 328
Harriet 127,131,138
Isaac 18,29,34,299
Jacob 35,46,72
James 10,28,75,131,258,288
James M. 127,138
Jenkins 56
Jesse 103,113,220
John 46,59,60,78,103,194,198,
199,205,262,270,272,273,274
John L. 285
John T. 136
Joseph 2,154,250
Josiah 265,338
Leah 52
Lemuel 2,38,50,55,91,239,325
Levi 9,10,20,24,35,38,65,67,72,
157,182,188,285

Levin 59,67,75,78,88,98,138,145,
220,334
Lydia 62,64,68,194,199,200,207,
209
Mitchell 34
Nancy 26,29,52,59,78,136,140
Noah 52,136,140
Outten 38,65,72
Parker 145
Peter H. 56
Purnell 12,18,29,46,47,78
Robert 26
Sally 35,131,198,204
Sally H. 199,204
Sally L. 103,285,287,294
Sally Q. 127,138
Samuel 60,98,220,288
Sarah 136,140
Susanna 10,335
Thomas 47,148
William 41,43,46,52,54,80,89,
131,132,139,223
William H. 127,138,179
Zacheus 86,127,131,138

HENMAN (See Hindman)

HENRY;

E. 86
Edward 3,6,8,9,28,29,31,42,43,
47,64,67,71,73,74,83,84,86,88,92,
95,99,100,102,113,114,122,123,
136,137,141,142,161,175,177,178,
181,191,192
Major (may be rank) 321
Robt. 277
Robert J. 316

HICKMAN;

Able 10
Josiah 273
Parker 267
William 264

HILL;

Betsey 312,314
Catherine 312,313,314,332
Elizabeth 328
Frederick 312.314,332
Isaac 111,148,161,292,330
(cont.)

(Hill cont.)
Jesse 169
John H. 226,234,235
Johnson 313
Josiah 245,254
Laban 62,70,84,172,193,334
Levin 58,75,199,276,312,313
Micah 111
Micajah 128
Molly 312,314,330
Purnell 58,144,167,186,202,220,223
Rachel 313,314
Rebecca 111
Robert 161
Sally 334
Stephen 111
William 117,328
William S. 58

HILMAN;

Samuel 136

HINDMAN; (Henman, Hinman)

James 115,127,131,134,139
Nancy 127,131,134
Ralph 228,289,297,305
Sarah 115,127,131,134,139

HITCH;

Levin 205,208,257,281,291,309

HOBBS;

Joseph 305,339
Polly G. 305
Seth 339

HODGE;

Isaac 61,218,268

HODGSON;

Mary 115
Sally 115

HOFFMAN;

George 171
J. 171
Peter 171

HOGSHIER; (Hogshiare, Hogshare)

William 41,75,76,239,243

HOLBROOK; (Hoolbrook)

John 60

HOLLAND;

Ann 293,294,296,299
Betsy 5,135
Elisha 306
James 135,145,229,263,277,278,
294,331,337
John 4,7,15,16,17,18,19,23,27,
33,39,41,42,53,55,57,63,70,71,
115,124,127,132,145,147,152,159,
184,187,199,204,219,225,227,228,
229,255,257,265,270,280,312,313,
325,328
Levi 33,52,139
Levin 151,155,273,322,326,332
Mary 33
Milby 183,259,277
N. 286,299,318,328,332
Nancy 98,101
Nehemiah 24,30,50,57,146,152,
156,159,179,185,186,189,279,280,
282,286,294,295,299,325,328,335
Peter 169,323,334
Polly 33
Samuel 24,86
Thomas 5,98,101,294
W. 56,72,100,124,186,187
William 24,25,26,36,49,51,55,58,
63,78,87,96,97,103,106,109,111,
124,132,133,139,140,141,146,147,
152,156,157,159,165,167,168,178,
179,184,186,187,189,199,200,202,
204,265,270,273,280,287,293,294,
295,296,299,306,314,325,332,342

HOLLOWAY;

A. 260
Armwell 61,279
Betsy 33,61,62,78
Ebenezer 36,266
Esther 266
Fanny 266,268
Francis 308
Hannah 33,61,62
(cont.)

(Holloway cont.)
Jedidah (Giddia)   33,36,61,62
Jesse   2
John   210
Joseph   33,237,265,266,268,272,
279,308
Joshua   237,238,249,265,272,279,
299,302,311,318
Kendal   249,272,279
Lemuel   266
Levi   210
Thomas   33,61,62

HOLSTON (See Houston)

HOOK;

Belitha   174,247
Betsy   60
James   223
John   78
Mary   78

HOOLBROOK (See Holbrook)

HOOPER;

Thomas   135,136,140,147,177,289

HOPE;

Charles   113,122,124,177

HOPKINS;

David K.   266
Edmund   204
Jacob   37,111,204,327
Josiah   204
Luke   59,174
M.   304
Matthew   36,43,50,55,57,62,65,67,
69,70,75,76,78,83,86,87,89,90,91,
94,98,103,109,110,112,122,135,
136,138,203,259,288,304,321,340,
341
mrs.   59
Sally   58
Samuel   41,44,55,60,138,165
Solomon   57
William   174,327
William K.   201

HORNES;

Betty   60

HORSEY;

Edward   26,27
Hetty   25,27
Lambert   26,27
Molly   258
Outterbridge   67
Revel   25,27
Sally   26.27
Smith   153,244,305
Stephen   25,26,27

HOSIER (See Hozier)

HOUSE;

Charles   60

HOUSTON; (Holston, Holstone)

Betsey   264
Betsey G.   262
Caleb   262
George   5,8,50,55,60,76,91,103,
231
George S.   136
Gertrude   207
Isaac   38,58,100,181,182,184,186,
207,214,261
James   57,58,59,69,96,181,182,
184,199,202,207,210,215,221,222,
255
John   1,5,38,55,58,60,76,186,200,
218,221,223,256
Joseph   3,4,7,9,12,31,38,49,55,
66,68,75,77,78,83,86,129,177,209
Levi   10,17,18,28,41,43,46,65,80,
91,136
Levin   60
Milly   262,264
Prissy   186
R.   58
Ralph   59
W.   311
William   59,285,312,321
William J.   46,55,154,186,213,
237,327

HOWARD;

Charlotte 1,3
John 1,3
Martha 1,3
Samuel 1,3
Stephen 1

HOZIER; (Hoshier, Hosiear)

Betty 172,193
Eli 29
Henry 172,193
John 331
Lemuel 301
Samuel 338,339
William 58,277
Zepheniah 277

HUBBELL;

J. 100,125,141,147,159,176,194,
204,210,225
Josiah 35,70,111,137,138,142,
159,163,169,207,209

HUDSON; (Hutson)

Aaron 60,173
Annanias 337
Comfort 106,148,149
Dennis 50,164,189,218,219,220,
230,243,247,249,256,258,295
Edward 50
Eli 11,12,26,37,42,44,68,97,183,
243,247,258
Evans 220,237,269,322
G. 342
George 182,287
Gertrude 219
Henry 66,68,77
Hetty 219
James 169
James H. 36,50,169
James P. 295
John 3,18,23,24,44,57,58,60,108,
147,171,259,287,291
John C. H. 220
Jonathan 5,8,14
Joshua 243,302
Laban 17,58,129,251,278
Leah 182,287
Levi 59
Littleton 222

Littleton R. 171
Littleton R. P. 219,257
Major 18,57,171
Margaret 227
Mary 44,103,171
Micajah 60
Milby 298,300
Mitchell 23
Moses 60,81
Nancy 97,183,220,237
Peter 103
Peter S. 291
Polly 219,302
Priscilla 71,80,112,219,287
Robert 17,36,57,74,227,270,274,
275,290,298
Sally 2,66,77,219,222,256
Samuel 171
Sarah 68,86
Selby 62
Sterling 60,129
widow 59
William 3,60,69,70,71,73,79,80,
106,108,112,148,149,172,182,184,
232,275
Zipporah 243

HUGHES; (Hughs)

Henny 226,290
Jesse 60
William 60,226

HUTCHESON;

John 187,317
Jonathan 17,58,59,71,228
Joseph 228,306
Sally 37

HUTSON (See Hudson)

HUTT;

Henry 271
Jonathan 59,271
Major 271
Moses 271

INGERSOL; (Ingersoll)

John 249,256,257
Samuel 257

IRONS;

Henry 336
Mary A. 336
Thomas 60
Timothy 16,23,31,50,59,65,66,77,
94,214,236,277,294,310,336,338

IRONSHIRE;

Esther 24

ISSACS;

Shadrach 208

ISHUM (See Eshom)

JACKSON;

Thomas 231

JACOBS;

Nimrod 101
Thomas 102

JAMES;

E. H. 279
Thomas 59

JARMAN; (German?)

Annanias 12,30,324
Belitha 65
Benjamin 2,220
Henry 136,140,141,162,182,184,
186
James 29,65,79,97,114,134,139,
199,201
John 134,136,139,141,162,182
Leah 134
William 97,114
William W. 65

JARVIS;

Severn 148,173,245

JENKINS; (Genkins, Jenckins)

Curtis 122,125,150
Ralph 104

JESTER;

John 213
Southy 213

JETT;

Jno. 281

JOHN; (Johnson?)

David 153
William 149

JOHNSON; (Jonson, John?)

Affradoze 188
Amelia 33
Benjamin 51,104,114,130,138,167,
179,180,187,188,208,212,214,216,
231,242,248
David 61,66,77,88,101,104,155,
216,255
Eleazer 133,144
Eliakim 4,6,15,57,133,208
Elisha 60
Elizabeth 113,127,131,140,165
George 58,75
Henny 248
Hezekiah 2,3,34,46,51,58,64,74,
93,125,129,222,223
Isaac 88,333
Isaac S. 222,223,224,255,257,
265,280
James 10,16,53,54,60,77,226,239
James Q. 309,325
Jesse 150
John 45,51,52,58,112,226,240,
277,300,305
John C. 63
Joseph 88,238
Joshua 51,52,193,198,201,202,
207,222,245,272,273
Laban 3,4,6,10,15,21,47,53,61,
62,70,83,84,86,92,93,99,106,111,
113,117,127,140,165
Leonard 45,58,112,148,155,179,
206,210,277,336
Levi 63
Levin 273
Martha 10,77
Micajah 273
Moses 127,131,165
(cont.)

(Johnson cont.)
mrs. 58
Nancy 149,151,153,155
Patience W. A. 151,153,155
Peggy 153
Peter 335
Purnell 33,53,79,83,167,176,
221,233,248,256
Robert 73,225,289,309,339
Sally 144
Samuel 57,171,239,278
Sarah 60
Selby 75,199
Severn 240
Shepherd 144,194,217,230,247,
248,254,267,273,320
Smith 88
Tabitha 60
Thomas 26
William 127,131,151,165,240,274,
277

JONES; (Jons)

Abraham 188
Agor (Major?) L. 183
Annanias (Anias) 185,191,235
Betsy 173,177,209,232,272,283
Caleb 211
Comfort 186
Daniel 41,163,186,189,237,307,
330
Effe 11
Eliakim 184,185,211,227,228,247
Elisha 51,58,76,125,129,209,264,
322
Elizabeth 330,334,337
Elsea 239
Esme 210
Esther 161,163
Giles 57,58,195,209,215,228,334
Handy 88,97,192,206,208,213,219,
220,241,293
Hannah 209
Henry 227,286,330,334,337
Hezekiah 227
Hory 188
James 11,48,60,86,100,162,173,
192,195,209,212,227,297,322
Jemima 11
Jesse 59,97,103,109,236,262,341
John 11,58,60,184,185,191,204,
211,215,225,227,228,229,235,264,
270,277,303

Joseph 185,191,235,253
Kendal 268,322
Leah 11,185,204,228,303
Leonard 11,43
Levi 59,195
Levin 191,235,273
Majer L. 183
Major 163,186,189,228,232,239,
240
Marge 60
Mary 97
Matthew 5,212,214,219,222,243,
255,275,283,294
Milby 147
Milly 147
Moses 278
Moses U. 186,271
mrs. 60,165
McClemmy 270
Nancy 55,96,136,138,177,209,212,
214,232,242,294,307,330,334,337
Nancy M. 173,209
Obediah (Obed) 58,210,330
Peggy 209
Peter 58
Polly 209
Pompey 284
Purnell 147
Purnell J. 212,214,242,294
Rachel 237,262
Riley 169
Sally 177,186,209,228,232
Sally J. 173
Sarah 185
Stephen 169,173,177,185,203,205,
209,276,286
Sterling 3,30,31,50,92,112,153,
162,179,235
Tabitha 177,209
Tabitha Q. 173,209
Thomas 57,86,103,123,134,151,
154,155,158,161,163,166,186,201,
253,278,321,327,330,332
Whittington 162,203,209,212,227,
228,232,239
William 75,76,80,96,103,109,136,
138,156,159,167,173,177,189,203,
204,209,219,220,222,229,230,236,
256,257,261,269,286,287,291,313,
320,326,330
Zipporah 225

JONSON (See Johnson)

JUSTICE; (Justices)

George 306
Jesse 108,123
John 36
Mary 36,105
Nancy 105
Polly 36
Solomon 123

KELLAM;

Betty 71,131
Hannah 2
James 298
John 2
Joseph 1,71,131,233,272,293,
295,298
Rebecca 2,298
Sally 59
William 12

KELLY;

Charles 268

KEMMEY;

Charles 341

KENAN;

Thomas H. 233

KENDALL;

George 135

KENNEY; (Keney)

Joseph 138

KERBY (See Kirby)

KERSY;

James 187

KILTY;

William 122,142,162,181,203,
223,250,290,307,326

KING;

James 12,15

KINNINGIN;

Jeptha 291

KIRBY; (Kerby)

Charlotte 134,137
John 114,125,134,137
Milby 21,53,61,66,134
Molly 134
Nancy 41,45,47,53,61,150
Robert 21,53,61,66,114,115,134,
137,202,312,323
Sarah 63

KNOX; (Knock)

Edward 162,294
Elijah 162
Ezekiel 31,38,39,60
Isaac 123
James 34,145,147,172,182,184,
186,189,204,217,242,263,287,289,
309,313,317
Jens. 61
John 322
John M. 38,41,44,55,123
Martha 38,41,44,55
Mary 41,44,55
Nancy 106,148,149
Nehemiah 148
Priscilla 172
Solomon 3

KOLLICK (See Collick)

LAIRD;

James 170,172,175,176,185,240,
263

LAKE; (See Westlake)

Ann 193
Benjamin 193

LAMBDEN; (Lambdon, Lamden)

Edward 36,41,46,71,77,88,95,111,
113,127,131,137,146,149,162,217,
226,229,242,253,282,301,311,333
James 9,127,131
Mary 9
Robert 127,131,149,286,325
Thomas 127

LAMBERSON; (Lambertson)

John 245,299,302,311,318
John S. 56
Polly 299,302,318
Rebecca 305
Robertson 76
Smith 56
Thomas 306
Thurrowgood S. 198

LANDON;

Thomas 333

LANE;

Francis 150,158,159,178,284,
286,288,292
Jacob A. 281
John 58,177,178,183,238,244,
284,286,288,292,306
Nancy 133
Sally 183
Shadrach 103,133,171
Thomas 183
William 208

LANKFORD;

Joseph 150
Kellam (Killiam) 58,145,146,
159,178,285,287,299
Leah 23
Sabastin 59

LARRIMORE;

John 160

LATCHUM;

Obediah (Obed) 73
Sarah 257

LAW (See Laws)

LAWRENCE;

Mary 21

LAWS; (Law)

Annanias 61,114
Comfort 43
Elijah 59,299
Isaac 224
James 77,136,163,170,171,183,
191,192,236,254,274,303,306,311
John 162,194,198,199,200,205,
221,263,270,283
Major 224
Nancy 38
Stephen 38

LAYFIELD;

Esther 3,5,6,7,12,17,24,36,37
George 9,78
Isaac 1,3,5,6,7,9,12,24,36,37,
71,77,78
Levin 58
Nancy 78
Thomas 17,71,73,78

LAYTON;

Caty 171
David 236
Jonathan 236

LECOMPT; (Lecount)

James 60,153
McKimmy 277,283
William 176,224,277

LEMMON;

Robt. 238

LEONARD;

Ebenezer (Eben) 161,187,216,231,
257,274,289,337
Isaac 231

LEVERING;

E. 164
J. 164

LEWIS; (Lewes)

Isaac   15,157,193
James   23,157,193,199,201,256
John   50
Mary   256
Milbourn   291
Rebecka 23
Scarbrough 50
Selby   256
Thomas 19,231
William 286
Zadok   16

LINCH; (Lynch)

Belitha 253
David   171,257
Elisha 29
John   29
Josiah 253
mrs.   257
Polly   253

LINDEL;

John   264

LINDSEY;

Hetty   214,240
James   250,255,257,263,265,270,
280
Major   58,214,240,250,251,257,
263,265,270,280,309,329
Matthias 56,57,70,72,74,75,227,
235,255,263,265,270,280,329,334
Peter   250,255,257,263,265,270,
280,309
Zadok   251,255,257,263,265,270,
280

LISTER; (Lyster)

Peter   15,56,78,176,182,306
William 2,78,95,97,116,190,216,
255

LITTLETON;

Thomas 231
William 19,23,231

LIVERMORE;

Thomas 150
William 150

LLOYD;

Edw.   203,223

LOCKWOOD;

D. 341

LOGAN;

John   53,260,265,281

LOKEY;

Samuel 78
Thomas 23

LONG;

Anne (Anna) 223,226,242,258,259,
287
Betsey 223,226,242,269
Coulbourn (Colevern) 4,8,11,12,
60,184,215,217,221,225
David   113,266,268,286
Elijah 266,268,286
Hampton 8
Harriott J. 271
Isaac   61,100,245,251,279
James   250
Jesse   200,223,249,250,255,256,
271,272,279,280,317
John   76,250,271,317
Josiah 103,138,199,204,250,255,
256,272,280,296,311,323
Katy   223
Levi   229,232,253,269
Levin   5,30,57,76,243,249,250,
272,279,280,317,335,336
Littleton   43,46,67,72,218,223,
229,232,243,253,258,259,269,287
Molly   287,296
mrs.   58

(cont.)

(Long cont.)
Nancy 200,218,223,271
Peggy 229,232,253,269
Rebecca 250,255,256,271
Sally 223,229,253,269,285,286,
287,294
Samuel 29,79,100,174,184,215,
221,225,232,251,253
Susanna (Susan) 229,232,253,269
Thomas 223,226,242,269
William 5,30,58,200,223

LOWE; (Lowes)

Kendal 311
Tubman 92,97

LUDS;

Stephen 211

LYNCH (See Linch)

LYSTER (See Lister)

MADDUX;

Anny 124
Benjamin 332
Charlotte 28,32,34,35,82
Daniel 29,32,34
Ebben 124
Elsey 24,44
Ezekiel 311
G. 168
George 168,231,238,243,256,257,
274,278,289,302,305,312,313
Hezekiah 113
James 89,90,309
Lazarus 24,44
Marcey 29,31,32,33,34,35,68
Rachel 224
Sally 34,68
Samuel H. 104
Sarah 31
Thomas 44,224,301
William 24,29,32,34,44
Wilson 113,190

MAGAR;

Milly 70
William 70

MAGEE (See McGee)

MALLANY;

Thomas 59

MALLITT; (Mallott, Mallet)

Betsy 59
James 57
John 57
Samuel 58

MARCHMENT; (Marchant)

Charlotte 204
Jesse 60
John 217,288
Levin R. 132,133
Polly 293
Riley 59,132,204
Stephen 204

MARINER; (Marinder)

Major 258,321,322

MARRETT; (Mallitt?, Merritt?)

Samuel 153,312,340

MARSH;

Philip 58

MARSHALL;

Elizabeth 12,60,74,149
Elizabeth P. P. 119
Isaac 27,53,59,116,136,140,147,
166,287,297,338,339
James 23,26,57,116
John 12,27
John P. 27,30,53,54,58,74,79,91,
100,119,120,137,149,160,166,175
Jorge 188
Polly 39
Sally 39
Saml. 278
Sarah 54,59
Thomas 175,202
Thomas P. 119
William 26,45
(cont.)

(Marshall cont.)
William A. 39,58,65,110,148,
155,218
William P. 100,175
Zadok 175

MARTIN;

Benjamin H. 336
Betsy 60
Betty 171
George 57,58,95,105
James 37,58,211,255,275
James P. 275
John S. 125,147,181,208,211,248,
255,265,275,288,306,324,325,339
Leah 59,125
Levin 25,60
Mary 58,105,171,275
Rosanna 25,58,59,143,288
Sarah S. 288
Thomas 25,37,58,81,87,96,115,
125,126,143,171,237,287,288,316
Thomas L. 275
W. B. 171

MASON;

Daniel 195
Hessey 59
Samuel 209

MASSEY;

Alexander 77,100,253
Betsey 163
Daniel 241,242
John 13,15,24,116,216,242
John A. 241
Kendal 216,241,242
Louisa 241,242
Priscilla 161,163,167,172,193
Rachel 242
Rachel I. 241
Sarah 24,216,241,242
William 24

MATTHEWS;

George 239
Henry 242
Joshua 226,239,244,249,255,311
Levi 239
Levin 35,46,60

Stephen M. 124
William 124

MEARS;

William 257

MECHLING;

Jacob 315

MELSON;

Benjamin 176,190,215,216,240,306
Elijah 190,215,216,240
Joseph 176,190,215,306
Polly 190,215,216,240
Samuel 240,286
Samuel U. 215,216
Samuel W. 190

MELVIN;

Avery (Avra, Ava) 24,98,122,123
Isaac 259
James 83,87,91,130,279,295,306
James T. 194
James W. 306
John 24,83,86,91,194,259
Jonathan 122,190,227
Meshach 230
Patsey 98,123,176,232,279,296,
334
Samuel 83
Sarah 227,334
Thomas 83
W. 4
Westly (Wesley) 98,122,176,232,
279,297
William 11,14,86,95,98,122,123,
194,202,297

MERCER;

John F. 27,49

MERRILL;

Eleanor 177
George 205
James 19,167,242,253
Kendal 78,100
(cont.)

(Merrill cont.)
Levi 58,87,88,91,95,102,103,110,
112,113,132,133,137,139,145,171,
177,195,198
Levin 6,20,52,87,88,95,112
Robert 142
Robert M. 124,138,177
Sally 95
Samuel J. 205
Thomas 68,77,154,250
William R. 112,113,137,198

MEZICK; (Messick)

Aaron 258,262,264,300,305,314,
338
Anna 11,24
George 11,24
Jeremiah 247,253,263,266,277

MIFFLIN;

Warner 20

MILBOURN; (Milbourne)

Elijah 220
George 220,292
John 46,60
Kitturah 61,70,71,72,88
Ralph 131,132,146,147,162,215,
231,313,324
Samuel A. 70,71,72
Thomas 22,35,36,46,50,58,61,88,
92,104,125,164,247,254,255,271,
272,277,278,281,283,320,324,335
William 59

MILES;

George 75,94,96,97,99,132,136,
137,140,142,148
Southey 60

MILLER;

Isabbella 116,117
Joseph 37,100,108,116,155,156,
199,201,274,277,311,312,313,318,
322
Nancy 93,274,318

MILLICHES;

James 5

MILLS;

David 313
Gillett 261,262,264
Handy 57,101,109,110,124,125,
234,235,251,281
Henry 188
John 260,261,265,281
John S. 320,323,327
Leah 312,320,323,327,335
Levi 78,100,116
Levin 163,167,201,202,259,260,
262,264,268,281,298,312,320,335
Levin R. 323
Nancy 116,117
Samuel 58
William 250,296

MITCHELL;

Elizabeth 171
Eloise G. P. 217,246,247
Henry 250,251
Isaac 217,246,297,330,331
John 217,246,326
John P. 2,13,23,36,65,68,72,74,
96,157,214,215,216,217,218,239,
246,247
Joshua 13,68,69,89,97,105,106,
112,116,117,123,155,163,164,175,
181,269
Josiah 1,42,66,116,175,191,254,
271
Julianna 97,104,113,171,172,174,
315
Levin 6,9,25,30,32,43,47,54,65,
67,68,69,71,73,74,83,86,88,95,
106,112,163,188,269
Mary 71,73,89,92,123,155,157,
161,175,181,191,206,245
Mary M. 245
Mary P. 217
Molly 254
mrs. 129,191
Polly 95,163,188,214,218,230,
246,247,269
Polly P. 214,218,230,246
(cont.)

(Mitchell cont.)
Robert 74,95,97,104,113,129,
171,172,174,191,192,214,215,217,
218,230,239,246,247,271,286,297,
311,314,315
Rufus 215,217,218
Rufus K. 246
Stephen 109
Thomas 5,8,90,110,146,148,149,
153,168,174,209,214,231,303,322

MONIS;

Caleb 172
Dolly 172

MOORE;

Adam 144,163,168,184,206
Ann 27
James 146,162
John 27,146,162,205
Joseph 146,162
Mary H. 288
mrs. 59
Robert 277,278
Samuel 161
Sarah 146,162
Thomas 59
William 27,240

MORRIS;

Amelia 75,76,88
Caleb 302,303,304,318,326
Charles 75,88,154,156,159
Cornelius 60
David W. 287,302
Dolly 318
Edward R. 216
James 256,326,328
James T. 103
Jethro 173,320,323
John 187,213,215,286,327
Joshua 226,230,235,249,256,259,
260,270,273,295,310
Leonard 320
Molly 62
Nancy 12,37
Peter 76,88
Philip 8,75,76,88,103,159,176,
177,327
Rackliff 16,320
Thomas 323

widow 60
William 12,39,59,256

MOSLY; (Mosley)

George 56

MUMFORD;

Deligent 326
James 143,170
Jesse 59,192,277
John 296,326,334
John C. 306
Joseph 239
Major 326
mrs. 59
Risdon 329
Sally 143
Zipporah 329

MURPHY; (Murphey)

Hessey 67
Sally 60,278

MURRAY;

Charlotte 240
George 59
James 240,263,290
Michael 87,127,207,266,283,295,
310,332,336,337

MacNEAL (See McNeill)

McALLEN; (McKallen)

Alexander 1,17,18,21,22,23,45,
59,81,94,126,233,272,293,295,298
Arthur 21,27,52,145,225,336
Betsy 233
Betty 272,293
Robert 220

McCAGH (See McCragh)

McCANN;

Ally 315
Arthur 315

McCAULEY; (McCalley, McCally)

Amelia 154,156,159,176,177
John 59,78,154,156,159,176,177

McCORMACK;

Benjamin 173,182
James 173,176,182
John 173,176,182

McCRAGH; (McCagh)

Henry 315

McDANIEL;

John 103,133,160,283
Risdon 327
William 103

McDONALD;

John 60

McDOWELL;

D. 241
mrs. 241

McFADDEN;

James 21,60
John 305
Tabitha 59

McGAN;

Hugh 278
Martha 59

McGEE;

Bernard 315,316
Edward 38,64,131,139,155,156,
166,315,316

McGIVAN; (McGiveran)

John 3,6,39

McGREGOR; (McGrigor)

William 38,95,97,99,104,106,107,
111,113,115,123,125,129,130,134,
137,140,147,153,155,157,162,163,
164,166,170,172,174,175,176,177,
178,181,183,187,190,191,192,194,
198,201,202,203,210,211,212,215,
216,217,219,221,225,230,239,242,
244,254,258,263,264,273,282,283,
284,285,286,293,295,297,299,301,
302,306,310,328,333,334,336,339

McHENRY;

John 31
William 198

McIVER;

John 60,61

McKALLEN (See McAllen)

McKERN;

L. 164
R. 164

McKINSTRY;

Robt. 315

McLEAN;

John 217
Joseph 217

McMASTERS; (McMaster)

James 237
Samuel 6,12,22,24,31,38,49,57,
66,83,114,177,209,216,237,257,
276,292,312

McNEILL; (MacNeal)

George 278
John 306
Nancy M. 276,277,279
Nathaniel M. 276,277,279,284,340
Robert 100,276

McVEA; (McVeay)

Catherine   315
Edward   315
Ellen   315
Hugh   315
John   166
Patrick   315

NAIRN; (Nairne)

James   58
Robert   14,19,64,72,87,114,122,
164,171,207,209,212,219,220,231,
247,269,270,331

NEILL;

John   43,55,57,58,278

NELSON; (Nilson)

Elijah   19,86,98,130
George   14,58,94,95,97,150,224,
229,242,313,314
Joel   57,97
John   98,101,104,145
Jonah   58
Josiah   283,334
Margaret   145
Sophia   98,101,104
Susanna   98,101,104,145
William   150

NEWBOLD;

Mary   63
Polly   47
Thomas   41,45,47,53,61,63,150

NEWTON;

Charlotte   17,50,57,102,288
Comfort   53,54,57
Esther   59
Job   205,219
Josiah   57
Levin   16,47,54,55,57,102
Mary   205,219
mrs.   57
Nancy   17,20,23,50,54,55,57,102
Polly   54,57
Sally   17,50,54,57,188
Sarah   16,17,20,23,53,54

Selby   57,60

NICHOLS; (Nicholson?)

Joshua   189

NICHOLSON;

Belitha   189
Isaac   49,59,67,92,105,124,132,
139,185
Joseph   7,11,18,58,105,132,178,
185
Matthias   60
mrs.   58
Nancy   8,71,106,124,132
Polly   60
Samuel   1,11,49,58,67,71,92,139
Thomas   178,185

NIEMBER; (Nimber)

Hugh   137
Rachel   60
William   137

NILSON (See Nelson)

NIMBER (See Niember)

NOBLE;

George   19
Isaac   42
James   138
Jonathan   16,144
Leah   124,144
Mary   19,42
Milly   104,108
Sally   124
Sarah   104,108

NOX (See Knox)

NUTTER;

Charles   160
William   233

NUTTS;

Harriot   138
Henry   138

OGLE;

Ben 1

OLIPHANT;

Hugh 281
James 281

OLIVER;

Joseph C. 284

ORR;

John 321

OTWELL;

mrs. 57

OUTTEN;

Levi 58,171
Susey 279
Thomas 58

OWENS;

John 159,161,206
Peter 168
Thomas 159

PAIN (See Payne)

PARKER;

Anderson 59
Ayres 42
Barzilla 41,203,204,221,229,
256,270,285,289
Charles 57,58,61,309,327,329,
331,332
David 233
Elisha 188
George 108,301
H. 61
Henry 53,60,98,128,131,144,153,
179,304
James 11,20,86,108,110,123,244,
301,302
John 22,24,144,213,286
Lemuel 41,45,71,144,146,147
Mary 244,301,302

Milby 86
Moses 61
mrs. 57,58
Peter 22,43,47,52,63,86,92,130,
164,212,213,256,278,330
Rebeckah 149
Sacker 41,45,71
Sally 24,124
Samson 179
Samuel 58,98
Sarah 20,86,104,108,110,112,123
Schoolfield 53,128,131
Selby 1,7,22,38,49,55,66,69,87,
88,90,91,109,132,174,182,185,199,
205,210,219,227,242,272,273,309,
326
Thomas 301
William 111,130,184,202,204,207,
210,215,219,221,222,248,255,272,
273,282,284,288,291,292,294,322,
329,334,337
William A. 149,245

PARRAMORE;

John 43,69,102
Margaret 102
Mary 69
mrs. 59
Thomas 43,68,69,101,102

PARSONS; (Persons)

Benjamin 228,337
Elijah 63,180,205,245,246
George 96,136,180,205,212,214,
217,222,228,230,232,243,245,246,
248,255,260,262,264,272,273,275,
283,294,295,310,313,324
Henry 245,246
Isaac 323
Jehu 245
John 221,293
John W. B. 228,319,320
Jonathan 63,115,124,205
Jonathan S. 205,228,233,245,246
Jordan 246
Levin 59,205,228,232
Nelly 246
Rachel 115,323
Rebecca 292
Samuel 226,228,258,269
Sarah 232,233
(cont.)

(Parramore cont.)
Sophia 95
Temperance 246
William 171,226,228,258,269
Zechariah 245,246
Zepheniah 293,295,297,312

PATEY; (See Patty)

PATRICK;

Daniel 55,72,104,108,137,162,
201,220,253,277
John 5,43
Sally 5
Sarah 43
Thomas 76

PATTERSON;

Anderson 1,3,4,9,10,20,24,35,51,
67,71,72,78,114,127,222,239,259,
312,314,325
James 153,222,239,274,278,288,
289,291,295,297,301,310,312,314,
317,321,322,325,332,333,335
John 255,259,264,268,283,312,
314,321,325,335
John P. 281
John W. 153,211
Levin 259,264,268,312,314,321,
325,335
Mary 78
R. 341

PATTY; (Pattey, Patey)

Kendall 23,148
Powell 222,325

PAYNE; (Pain)

Elizabeth 53,90,91,93
Jacob 53,90,91,176
James 90,91,322,328
Jeptha 123,129
John 22,24,30,58,90,93,123,176
Levin 253
Moses 123,125
Moses C. 129
Samuel 60
Sarah 93
Wealthy 129
Wrixham 195

PAYNTER (See Pointer)

PEACOCK;

Comfort 231
Samuel 231,283

PEDEN;

John 52,311

PENNEWELL; (Penewell)

John 16,37
McKimmey 271
Powell 63
Purnell 271
Thomas 217

PEPPER;

Eli 60
Lanty 59
Omey 59
Sacker 57
Solomon 4
Zachariah 319

PERDUE;

Alice 279
Arcady 181
Bayley 180
Elijah C. W. 50,53,79,83,182
Elijah S. 180
Elijah S. W. 182
Elizabeth 180
Elizabeth E. Y. 180
Elizabeth W. 279
James 83,176,180,181
James W. B. 50,53,79,83,176,180,
181
John K. H. 50,182
Louden 180,181
Polly K. 180

PERKINS;

John 140
Joseph 179
Mary 140,321
mrs. 59
Stephen 258
William 66,77

'385'

PERSONS (See Parsons)

PETERS;

Ephraim 19

PETTITT;

Absalom 128
Esther 60,87
John 128,278
Samuel 148,278

PEWSEY (See Puzey)

PHILLIPS;

Joshua 65

PILCHARD;

Esau 61,192
Levin 211
Stephen 86,238,284
Susanna 267,306

PITTS;

Hillary 2,8,21,48,53,63,74,97,
102,104,111,117,130,140,147,166,
172,174,316
James 245
John 315
John R. 314,316,340
Julianna 314,315,340

POINTER; (Paynter)

Elias 35,278
John 292
Justice 292
Nancy 59
Rackliff 57,102,111,112,263
Sally 59

POLK;

Benjamin 283,294
James 119
Pompey 58
William 28,32,58,160

POLLITT; (Pollett)

Anna 59
Betsy 68,97
George 24
John 97
Joshua 257,291
Levin 7,36,41,69,77,79,87,92,
116,138,140,142,173
Nancy 286
Sally 39
Samuel 68,97,249,286
Thomas 257
William 68,226,230,291,326,328

PORTER;

Anne 251
David 163,200,208,214
Isaac 235,281,300,302,303,310,
322
James 221,300,302,310
John 309
John S. 166
Kendal 335
Matthew 300,302,310
McKimmy 7,10,22,26,30,36,42,51,
52,63,64,70,74,92,104,105,108,
114,115,116,123,130,147,148,153,
166,170,179,187,188,190,198,200,
202,208,210,221,223,235,236,248,
253,260,269,271,289,295,297,300,
303,310,321,322,334
Nancy 333
Naomi 221
Polly 130
Purnell 36,38,50,51,62,132,134,
164,168,209,219,233,254,268,273,
299,309,326,333
Rebecca 300,302,310
Sally 309
Samuel 37,46,53,78,108,155,254,
329
Seth 162
Shepherd W. D. 251
Solomon 162
Solomon C. 61
Thomas 208
William 58,59,60,219,300,302,310
William W. 326

POSTLY;

John 1,2,3,4,10,13,15,16,19,21,
24,26,27,30,37,38,41,42,43,47,49,
61,62,63,64,67,69,71,73,106,107,
108,116,129,130,139,172,193,269,
319,333

POTTER;

Elijah 60

POWDERS;

Revel 171,173

POWELL;

Annanias 4,6,9,28,44,68,77,198
Arthur 331
Belitha 32,44,68,106,129,130
Caleb 2,61,62,107,179,235
Catherine 2,61
Ebenezer 50,231,260,261,299,327
Eli 279
Esther 129,130,323
Gabrel 295
George H. 61
Handy 26,50,91,100,101
Henry 61
James 208,245,300,304
Jehu 26,225
Jenethan 296,307
Jesse 26,27,32,44,68,73,98,102,
106,130,225
John 23,50,61,68,75,76,77,100,
102,106,129,130,277,311,323,338
Jonathan 199
Kendal 295
Keziah 102,106,129,130
Levi 286,323
Levin 100,228
Maria 289
Milby 2,21,50,61,62
Molly 129
Mordicai 26
Polly 129
Thomas 13,27,76,170,199
William 58,100,295
Zadok 231,240,241,260,261
Zeno 190,199

PRENTISS;

mr. 133

PREWITT (See Pruitt)

PRICE;

Adam 243,259,278
Arthur 3,4,6,15,17,64,68,70,72,
74,224,255,256,258,282
Daniel 58,59
David 57
Drucilla 240
Grace 155
John 4,6,15,224,255,258,282
John C. J. 155
John M. 256
Peter 240
Priscilla 74
Sarah 3,4,6,15,64
Solomon K. 144
William 4,6,7,11,15,58,115,124,
224,227,235,240,254

PRIDEAUX;

James 55
John 2,41,42,43,76
Joshua 2,4,5,10,12,18,32,33,36,
37,41,43,52,59,65,69,88,92,100,
106,111,119,120,131,139,140,158,
160,165,166,175,176,183,184,188,
194,219,227,230,232,239,264,269,
272,273,303,309,318,324
maj. 240
Thomas 55,285

PRUITT; (Prewitt)

Betty 92
Charles 63
Elijah 26,154,223
John 26,160,328
Rebecca 104
Selby 30,31
Severn 30,31,224,227,235,240,
250,251,329,334
Walter 104
William 59,60

PURNELL;

Anne 119,133
Azariah 149,171
Benjamin 29,33,35,36,57,58,59,
64,69,74,93,102,105,109,114,126,
149,150,184,186,213,222,256,257,
265,302
Betsy 59,174
Comfort 59
Dolly 154,156,304,318
dr. 68
Elisha 7,10,11,18,29,30,38,46,
59,149
Elizabeth 89,95,99,100,110,111,
113,114,119,129,149
Esme 2,20,44,51,55,83,86,88,112,
115,123,132,149,156,166,172,302,
303,304,318
Esther 83,100,120,138,269
Euphemia 119
George 17,24,25,44,59,161,240
George W. 4,29,38,57,59,64,84,
100,114,119,157,158,175,183,188,
190,278,295,310,328,335
Gertrude 119
Henrietta 4,259
Hetty 100
Isaac 60,123,154,161,163,166,253
John 4,43,58,59,72,86,88,100,
103,110,113,114,125,126,129,131,
139,145,146,150,151,154,157,158,
159,161,166,174,175,177,178,179,
183,186,191,192,253,259,272,309,
342
John F. 154
John G. 320
John J. 152,154
John R. 259
John S. 15,25,39,42,55,57,59,67,
87,91,284
Julian 303
Lanta 25,39,42,58,100,171
Lemuel 263,266,269,275,276,306,
308,326
Levi 110,340
Littleton 322
Littleton R. 11,20,28,32,33,35,
37,59,87,90,98,128,156,166,173,
183,218,219,220,223,230,243,247,
249,256,258,271,282,284,295,319,
333,334
Margaret 158,161
Martha 158,161
Mary 7,10,59,100,129,151,158,
161,175,323
Mary D. 114
Mary O. 177,183
Milby 11,20,45,46,51,62,69,86,
112,113,115,123,125,132,133,134,
136,139,142,148,149,151,152,153,
155,164,166,167,172,187,236,266,
340
Milby S. 133
Milly 110,112
Molly 110,111,114,115,129,174,
285
Molly O. 174,191
Molly R. 119
Moses 327
Nancy 58,155
Parker 277
Patty 303
Peggy 150
Robert 145,146,147,149,153,178,
187,209,214,285,321
Robert J. H. 119,215
Sally 110,111,113,114,129,174,
178,183,192
Sarah 5,15,46,59,114,129,149,
236,284,309
Stephen 58,173,177,187,205,210,
211,214,215,216,244,276,284,286,
288,292,302
Thomas 54,58,59,93,100,110,111,
114,119,123,129,154,158,161,166,
174,175,178,183,191,253,266,272,
274,277,309
Thomas D. 112,113,114,115,125,
132,134,136,137,139,142,148,149,
151,152,153,155,164,166,167,172,
186,187,199,205,209,211,218,221,
257,272,282,292,318,340
Thomas M. 42,89,157,158,160,183,
188,272,274,277,328,335
Walton 119
William 28,42,47,58,59,100,110,
119,155,157,175,236,272,274,277,
292,309,340
Z. 116
Zadok 8,18,21,42,59,100,106,110,
111,113,114,119,120,129,131,140,
157,158,165,167,174,175,176,177,
183,184,188,191,227,236,342
Zipporah 5,15,100

PUZEY; (Pewsey, Pusey)

George   44,58
Isaac   4,6,13,14,27,31,150,277,
278
John   13,44
Levi   23
Mary   23,44
Purnell   23
Sophia   44

QUILLEN;

Benjamin   3
Moses   3

QUINTON;

Charlotte   172,193
Elizabeth   172,193
Isaac   278
James   161
Littleton (Litt)   152,178,193,
215,266,298,316,327,337
Moses   172,193
Obed   161
P.   115,122
Peter   161
Philip   2,58
Samuel   161,163,167,172,193
William   11,49,59,67,71,82,83,96,
123,124,135,137,147,178,185,207,
224,235,256,277,288,302,309,310,
311,323,327,330,332,335,337

RACKLIFF; (Rackliffe)

Charles   62,87,160
Charlotte   22,25,30,54,93,99,106,
119,140,160,175,240
John   6,22,25,30,31,32,42,43,53,
54,67,73,93,99,119,140,153,160,
161,170,172,175,176,185,240,263,
290
John H.   263
John W.   290
Kitturah   54,99,140,153,160,170,
172,175,176,185,240
Kitty   93,106,119
Kitty H.   22,25,30
Rider   54,93,99,119,140,153,160,
170,172,175,176,185,240,263,290
Rider H.   22,25,30,290

Sarah   6,25,53,54,93,139,157,160,
161,185
Thomas   76,79,279
Thomas P.   17,29,33,35,42,54,82,
91,98,149,168,209,215,221,222,
223,225,230,254,256,257,264,268,
273,280,285,300

RAIN;

Caleb   60

RANKIN;

Betsy   174,203
Elizabeth   177,178,244,281
George   5,6,9
James   5,6,9
John   112,116,126,203,244,322
John M.   157,174,177,178
Molly   4,6,9
mrs.   191,192
Sarah   6
Sarah A.   5,9

RATLEDGE;

John P.   336

READ (See Reed)

REAN;

Comfort   15
John   15
William P.   15

RECORDS;

Elijah   36

REDDEN; (Reddin, Reden)

James   193,271
John   60,64,68
Nehemiah   22,24,30
Peter   60
Sarah   41,62,68
Shadrach   193,271
Stephen   62,64,68,286

REED; (Read)

Elijah 3,76,143,146,169,190,
191,194,201,226,295,300,314,322
James 59,134
Janet 226
Jannetta 295
John 57,59,63,143,145,151,214,
295
Joshua 204
Littleton 60
Major 58,223
Mary 143,145,151
Molly 236
Walter 223
William 204,236

REYLEY (See Riley)

REYNOLDS; (Ronnells, Runnells)

Edmund 61,211,226
Hammond 336

RICE;

George 11,20,21,32,38,42,58,
170,171
Mary 171
Mary A. 32,38,42,45,115,171,
238,272,307

RICH;

John 38

RICHARDS;

Barshaba 57
Elijah 173
Isaac 61,108,157,158,214,340
Jacob 29,31,32,34,57,68,82,89,
91,110,294
John 61,65,67,100,108,109,123,
137,192,214,228,231,240,242,244,
248,258,259,289,321,340,341
Joseph 157
Leah 258
Littleton 108,109,123
Mary B. 228
Matthias 309
Moses 309
Nathaniel 74
Polly 108,109,123

Sally 157
William 61,86,100,157,158,227,
228,230,231,232,240,242,244,248,
255,258,289,299,300,314,321,322,
328,332,333,340,341

RICHARDSON; (Richason)

Alexander 60
Benjamin 265,267,274
Benjamin T. 276
Besty (Betsy?) 101
Charles 59,60
David 80,81,82,86,91,95,319,320,
323,332,334,336,339,341
Elizabeth 81
Esme 80,81,82,86,91,95
Fisher 51,52,91,97,98,101,103,
106,109,110,111,141,165,171,185,
293
George 58,59,64,80,81,91,93,105,
135,171,188,221,242,256,269
George R. 235,316
Henry 115,220,222,226,229,232,
237,244,316,319,320,327,341
Jethro 270
John 60,96,113,141,142,204,220,
222,226,229,232,244,276,291,299,
308,322,330,341
Joseph 8,9,11,312
Levi 8,9,11
Mary 96,220,222,229
Molly 80,81,83,86,91,95,113,141,
142,226,232,244
Nancy 71,80,81,83,86,91,93,95,
96,113,115,141,142,161,171,269,
312,322
Peter 270
Polly 93
Ralph 262
Robert 59,235
Robert M. 5,22,39,42,58,71,93,
141,142,161,171,177,204,220,226,
229,237,269,272,316,340
Samuel 80,81,82,86,91,95,242
Sarah 59
Thomas 276,291
Whittington 9,59,186,276
William 9,67,276,277,296,302,
309,334

RICKETTS;

Elijah   58
John   59

RIDER;

John   255

RIDGELY;

C.   326

RIDLEY;

James   317
John   253,317
Wm.   253

RIGGEN; (Riggin, Rygen)

Henry   8
Isaac   59,171
James   4,5,129
James W.   307
Jesse   58,76
John   4,6,8,13,14,23,27,31,58,
129,222,243,244,279,282
Joseph   60
Kellam   224
Levi   27,327
Levin   60
Lowden (Loudy)   23,222,243,244,
277,279,282
mrs.   59
Noah   60
Pierce   23,213,222,243,244,279,
282
Sally   19
Sena   27

RIGHT (See Wright)

RIGSBY; (Rygsby)

Betsy   45,46,51,110,115,132
James   45,46,51,87,137,164,168,
209
Thomas   42,46,51,58,69,87,110,
125,136,137,149,164

RILEY; (Reyley)

Anna   308

Isaac   59,301
James   266,328
John   266,268,308
Joshua   308
Levin   43,67,73,88,108
Littleton   57,129,130,132,142,
158,159,162,165,167,169,182,212,
217,266,278,302
mrs.   73
Peter   249,308
Stephen   219
Thomas   249,308
William   78,98,101,102,145,168,
214,216,257,272,280,286,287,288,
295,296,299
William B. S.   281,336,338
William F.   108,109,139,142,167,
169

ROACH;

Charles   309
James   309,312,332
Lydia   146
Mary   9,146
Rachel   146
Stephen   11,24,125,146,256,306,
331

ROBERTS;

Allice (Alce)   51,258
Betty   192
Esther   51,52,192
James   52,258
Robert M.   281,282
Sarah   51

ROBERTSON;

John   76
Levi   76
Rhoda   100
Thomas   11,14

ROBINS;

Ann   59
Bowdoin   114,128,131,132,136,137,
139,147,148,184,185,189,230,238,
243,279
Comfort   148,330
                    (cont.)

(Robins cont.)
Daniel 12,139,148,189,202,238,
330,333,334
Daniel G. 2,7,11,18,189,202,238,
269,271,272,279,295,297,303,318,
321,330,333
Edward 59,93,120,127,175,274,
277,309
Isabella 59
James B. 1,27,41,58,119,120,122,
158,175,205,206,211,237,288,336,
340
John 245
John L. B. 336,340
L. 221
Littleton 3,18,28,38,42,47,49,
58,59,64,71,75,83,100,102,106,
111,114,119,120,122,126,136,139,
141,142,143,148,155,158,162,167,
175,176,181,188,198,203,205,206,
209,211,216,223,227,250,261,284,
290,306,307,326,336
Nehemiah S. 2,7,18,189
Thomas 245,322
William M. 60

ROBINSON;

Biddy 301
James 60
Joseph 285,287,300,301,302,318
Thomas 60

ROCK;

John 11,18,81,82,83,91,111,306
John M. 306
Severn 60

RODGERS;

Catherine 38
Joseph 179,181
Mitchell 38,179,181,198

RONNELLS (See Reynolds)

ROSSE; (Ross)

Elizabeth 58,59,202,226
Francis 60,180,189,190,195,202,
224,226,239,281
George 13,32,49,60,138

ROUND (See Rownd)

ROWLEY;

Arthur 162,188,189
Covington (Coventon) 170,211,
255,260
Henry 151,152,178,179,206
Hetty 229,260
James H. 170,178,179,181,185,
188,189,190,198,206,211,255,260,
307,309,325
John 160,185
Nathan 157
Polly 229,260
Richard 157,188,189
Susanna 178,179,237,323
William 170,178,179,185,188,229,
260,323,329

ROWND; (Round, Rownds)

Anne 87
Benjamin 338
Charlotte 64
Charlotte H. 238
dr. 274
Edward 20
Edward H. 22,277
Henry 87
Hetty W. 238
Jacob 134,184,186
James 306
John 87,187,213,327
John W. 236,238
Joshua 337
Martha 87
Mary 337,338
Peggy W. 236,238
Samuel H. 87
William 145,147,169,187,189,192,
200,217,221,238,241,243,248,260,
277,292,337,338

ROWEN; (Bowen?)

Robert 60

ROYAL; (Royals)

Hesse 30
Milby 30

RUARK; (Ruke)

Daniel 154,189,287
Elgate 57,298,331,335,337
James 16
Mary 331,335
Priscilla 16
Stephen 266
Stephen D. 298,300
Stouton 164
Thomas 331,335,337,339

RUNNELLS (See Reynolds)

RYGSBY (See Rigsby)

SAMPSON;

George 190,216,239,240
Julianna R. 207
Mary 185,190,206,207
Richard 23,62,63,73,77,88,163,
185,190,206,207,213,225

SAVAGE;

Comfort 161,316
dr. 81
Elizabeth K. 316
John 58,161,316
William 104,277

SAXTON;

Sweany 341

SCARBOROUGH; (Scarbrough)

Edward 58,192,260,298,322
Henry 57,260
John 32,53,58
Kendal 127,134
McKimmey 57
Samuel 59
Sarah 134

SCHOCKLEY; (Shockley, Shockly)

Banjamin (Ben) 27,178,245
Betty (Betsy) 27
Daniel 312
Daniel B. 308,313
Elijah 178,245
Hezekiah 145

John 58,74,88,312
John S. 308,313
Jonathan 167
Joshua 254
Madison 308,312,313
Matty 308,312,313
mrs. 58,59
Nelly 289,308,312,313,335
Peter 290
Polly 312
Polly R. 308,313
Richard 88,178
Sally 308,312,313
Samuel 57
Solomon 105
Stuart 298,308,335
Thomas 58,278
Thomas D. 58,335
William 57,58,60

SCHOOLFIELD;

Benjamin 67
grandmother 310
Harrison A. 71
Henry 61
Isaac B. 41
Joseph 4,220
Leah 67
Stephen 67
William 3,6,9,95,111,115,123,
135,137,138,209,213,226,239,254,
256,260,268,278,282,286,299,301,
317,321,327,333,336

SCOTT;

Benjamin 59
George 90
Henry 90
James 298
John 23,89,90,299,320,341
John E. 89,90,150
Joseph 29,57,89,90,140,150,156,
158,176,218,288,292
Joshua 320
Levin 90
Mary 213,225,239
Milly 91
Peter 213,225,239,240
Polly 90
Sarah 89,90,150
Susan 90

(cont.)

(Scott cont.)
Thomas 91,101
William 89,183

SEARS;

John 51,279,292,293,297
John H. 293,295,297,312
Rebecca 279,292

SELBY;

Anne 6
Betsy 86,160
Catherine 66
Comfort 274
Daniel 22,24,25,26,27,33,49,55,
57,70,87,91,94,103,109,110,140,
141,185,189,247,280,285,302
Elizabeth 52,65,66,69,84,92,97,
108,128,130,132,159,202,212,219,
230,232,239,240,248
Esther 65
Ezekiel 4,28,62,67,90,91
George 49,55,58,87,97,109,110,
111,146,152,167,168,173,185,186,
189,287,294,299
Glippery 74,89,133
Harry 320
Henry 26,49,55,86,87,97,109,
110,111,292,302
Isaac 6,72,74,114,133,286
James 4,5,6,9,22,24,28,33,37,39,
47,48,49,55,58,59,61,62,64,65,66,
67,68,74,77,80,83,86,90,91,100,
108,109,112,114,116,126,128,132,
157,159,166,170,200,230,240,259
James B. 5,15,22,26,322
James Q. 325
John 22,24,25,26,33,51,52,57,59,
64,70,74,80,87,91,97,102,103,104,
106,108,109,111,128,132,133,140,
141,146,147,152,159,165,168,173,
185,189,204,212,220,230,247,248,
251,260,269,276,280,285,287,292,
299,302,312,313,314,317,327,328
John O. 270,309,312,330
Kendal 66,230
Kitty 230,239
Lemuel 58,322
Levin 49,57,65,69,100,109,169,
185,219,227,248
Martha 66

Mary 112,126,128,132,152,159,299
Math. 59
Matilda 152,167,186,287,299
Micajah 33,53,55,57,63,100,277
Milly 128,132,159
mrs. 57
Nancy 6,48,49,66,68,72,74,77,84,
86,97,114,133,159,160,200,320
Parker 33,34,57,59,74,89,103,
130,132,133,159,204,274,317,327
Patty 230,239
Peggy 66,230,239
Polly 91,97,141,167,186
Rachel 303
Sarah 230
Tabitha 48,49,57,66,68,77,84,86,
97,222,240
Thomas 23,52,66,69,92,108,130,
199,200,202,212,219,230,232,239,
303
William 11,19,22,26,30,33,34,36,
37,39,44,46,47,48,49,54,59,60,61,
63,64,65,66,67,71,72,86,92,95,
130,133,204,240,254
William A. 58,59
Zadok 34,47,48,57,130,154,238

SHARPLY;

William 156

SHELTON (See Chelton)

SHEPHERD;

Elijah 92
Sally 35

SHOCKLY, SHOCKLEY (See Schockley)

SHORT;

Philip 143
Polly 143

SHOWELL;

Hannah 145
Lemuel 53,61,66,77,106,129,130,
184,191,192,194,210,212,257,266,
268
Rachel 145

SILVERTHORN;

William 104

SIMPSON;

Jesse 60,256
Zipporah 42

SLATTERY; (Slaughtery)

John 221

SLEMAKER;

John P. 217,242,253,277

SLOAN;

John 79
Saml. 39

SLOCOMB;

John A. 171
John R. 89,94,132,211,215,228,
250,290
Mary R. 290
Sinah 52,54,139
Thomas 6,11,15,17
William 59

SMACK (See Smock)

SMASHY; (Smashey)

Ezekiel 2,139,243
James 2
William 100

SMITH; (Smyth)

Ann 13
Archibald 205,243
Betsy 139,142
Betty 144
Celia 278
David 314,321,338
Elsey 61,107,143,323
George 112,278
Handy 3
Harry 163
Henry 25,26,142,144,168
Hetty 144,163,168,184,206,335

Holland 323
Isaac P. 169,182,227,304,317
Isaiah 26,289
Jacob 278
James 14,35,60,90,93,135,339
Jane G. 304
John 30,61,84,90,92,108,123,181,
184,187,298,338
Levi 3,112
Levin 108,205
Levin H. 115,135,163
Merrill 335
Mordecai 181,184,187,191
mrs. 157
Polly 58,105,171,304,307
Purnell 59,257
Purnell F. 38,64,69,84,114
Robert 109,110,137,142,148,152,
155,163,166,171,192,211,227,279,
281,294,304,317,324,325
Rosa 142
Samuel 58,72,278,322
Samuel R. 45,96,98,103,110,132,
137,139,142,147,155,171,184,194,
204,215,220,299,303,304,309,310,
313,317,321,325,327,338
Sarah 35,325,338
Solomon 67
Thomas 54,108,181,184,187
Thomas P. 111,125,126,131,135,
151,153,177,211,255,259
Walter 105,171,304,307
William 3,30,42,67,112,135,144,
163,168,184,206,278,335
Wingate 3,30,112,113,114
Zachariah 135

SMOCK; (Smack)

Andasia 53
Elizabeth 89,92,97,105,123,155,
157,161,163,164,175,179,191,254,
255,269
Henry 57,123,168,283
Holland 30
John 268
Kendall 117,171,189
Kerby 245
Levi 50,53,98
McKimmy 283
Sally 98,126
Sarah 213,327
Thomas 50
Zad. 160

SMULLEN; (Smulling);

Comfort 277
Ephraim 57,307
James 311,327
James E. 307
Lowder 60
Maria 311,327
Maria S. 307
Peter 135,168,277,303,307,327
Randle 277
Sally 277,303,307,311,327
Scarborough 277
William 135,168,277,311,327
William Q. 307

SMYLEY;

Samuel 164

SMYTH (See Smith)

SNEED; (Snead)

Robert 4,6,9,78,224
Thomas 303,318
Tully 202,224

SPENCE;

Adam 119
Ara 207
George 59,101,146,207,224,273
Irving 224,273
John S. 114,207,224,273
Lemuel P. 143,147,170,182,207,
217,223,224,235,241,247,251,265,
267,273,285,312,316,340
Mary 248
Nancy 101,146
Polly 59,116
Sally 59
Thomas R. P. 119,207,224,235,
259,310,316,336,338
William 224
William P. 265,267

SPENCER;

Benjamin 309
John 77,215,276,297,299,309,
314,332

SPIERS;

Peter 211

STANFORD;

Joshua 256
Wm. 277

STAPLEFORD;

John 63
William 63

STEEL; (Steele)

Alexander 149
James 15,61
Jesse 59
John 60
Samuel S. 233
widow 60

STEVENS;

Edward 319,323,332,334,339,341
Eleanor 13,32,49
Elizabeth 80,81
Elizabeth M. 95
John 12,39,80,81,82,83,86,91,93,
95,105,109,135,137,140,145,156,
158,171,176,184,186,188,192,194,
215,225,228,250,269,285,318,319,
320,323,327,329,332,334,339,341
Maryanne D. 327,341
Mary D. 327,339,341
Mary D. H. 339
William 320,323,332,334,339,341

STEVENSON;

Adam 60
David 21,54
Edward 36,43,46,51,52,56,57,58,
67,71,72,77,86,88,95,100,104,105,
111,113,115,117,123,135,137,138,
143,145,146,148,151,156,161,162,
163,179,182,183,184,187,188,192,
194,196,198,202,209,210,219,222,
226,229,230,232,239,242,248,253,
258,264,268,271,272,283,305,310,
318,325,331,332,335,336
Elijah 28,31,38,65,177
(cont.)

(Stevenson cont.)
Hugh 60
Hugh M. 62,68,73,194,199,200,
207,209,229,313,314
Jabez 57
James 21,58
John 55,57,89,113,115,116,117,
123,166,184,194,199,200,203,208,
209,210,211,212,215,216,227,230,
232,233,235,248,255,256,258,271,
272,278,279,280,282,283,287,290,
295,296,304,310,311,318,323,327,
331,332,336,338
Jonathan 57,62,64,194,229,239,
313
Joseph 34,58,188,206,239
Mary 243
mrs. 58,60
Polly 117,143
Sally 117,143,239
Samuel 2,23,55,57,91,241,290
Tabitha 116,117
Thomas 57
William 23,24,41,42,74,88,91,
115,116,117,143,146,151,166,177
William I. 200,203,215
William J. 194

STEWART; (Stuart, Steward)

John 115,135,163
Levin 100,137,139,149,341
Mary 149
Thomas 151,172

STOCKLEY;

Sally 317

STOUT;

Jacob 341

STRAN;

Sally 102

STUART (See Stewart)

STURGIS;

Catherine 235
Daniel 59
Elijah 69

Esther 90,92,112,135,177
George 284
Handy M. 234
Henry 145,234,269
Henry P. 34
Jacob 92
James 100,153,154,156,159,195,
276,279,280,324,329
James W. L. 265,268,273
Jane 265,268,273
Jenny 148
Jesse 50,53,54,55,57,104,143,
145,147,151,168,170,202,214,256,
257,260,282,293,317
Joanna 43,51,284
John 54,59,60,61,62,87,154,159,
162,165,169,173,174,186,195,212,
241,243,265,276,279,284,326
John O. 68,73,211,234,235,314,
329
Joshua 34,39,41,57,90,92,94,95,
103,112,136,140,147,157,159,165,
284,323,327
Joshua P. 90,92
Leah 165,211,234,235,314
Levi 20,195,229
Levin 60,70,72,258,282
Littleton 173,193,203,244,265,
272,274,311
Mary 62
mrs. 57
Nancy 43,51,165,284
Peter 236
Priscilla 34,145
Richard 46,51,58,322
Sally 51,165,338
Sarah 43,235,297
Shadrach 17,58,123
Stephen 58,63,96,247
William 60,87,203,217,231,235,
238,254,297,338
William E. 263,266,290,320
Zadok 1,2,11,20,22,24,27,33,34,
36,38,39,41,42,46,47,49,58,59,61,
62,64,69,76,87,88,90,105,106,108,
111,120,124,125,128,131,132,134,
136,137,138,146,147,153,162,171,
173,181,187,198,200,203,207,214,
216,222,223,244,250,265,272,274,
290,307,311,319,325,326,327,330,
338,341,342

SUMMERS;

Noah 257
Obediah (Obed) 257

TACEY (See Tracy)

TALBOT;

Samuel 318

TARR;

Betsy 75,79,94,96
Catrin 46
Elijah (Eli) 46,60,104,178,183,
200,321
Eliza 282
George 34
Hannah 42
Jeptha 248
John 59,104,178,247
Joshua 4
Major 46,55,167,169,183,191,
192,241,266,283,294,305,332
Michael 4,6,15,17,50,58,70,74,
75,133,151,154,248
Nancy 60
Nehemiah 60
Peter 58,75,79,94,96,132,183
Polly 206
Samuel 74,151,185,203,204,206,
227,274,286,317
Sarah 227
Tesa 60
William 59,200,287

TAYLOR;

Abraham 242
Ayres 60
Betsy 34,101,135,167,278
Betty 115
Charles 2,254
Daniel 55
David 59,320
Elias 115
Fisher 180
George 63,100,114,313
Hannah 2
Hezekiah 53
Hope 19
Isaac 113,179
James 20,78,115,147,242,276

James W. 2,274
Jeremiah 60,195
John 6,11,15,16,17,30,31,34,38,
57,58,63,71,87,88,96,105,115,124,
128,129,133,138,147,176,255,258
John F. 105,198
John G. 325
John K. 47,63
John T. 100,210,221,224,242,243,
249,272,300,306
Joseph 20,52,137
Kendal 60
Laban 161,163,167,172,193
Leah 63
Levin 23,145,221
Littleton 19
Lizy 60
Major 56
Mary 63
Milly 167
Nevitt 205
Obed 215
Parsha 167
Patty (Patsey) 34,101,135,203,
227,274
Polly K. 180
Purnell 192,307,327,328
Rebecca 32,34,101
Robert 60
Sacker 61
Sally 34,101,135
Samuel 45
Sarah 287,297
Severin 55
Skinner 286
Stephen 195
Teackle 60,276
Thomas 20,23,26,32,54,55,135,
203,287,294,307
W. 313
William 56,57,221,260
William H. 242,287,297
William W. 254

TEACKLE;

Abel 261
Elizabeth 20
John 261

TEAGUE;

Jacob 9,11,29,58,88,102,110,142,
147,166,169,200,202,209,211,222,
227,229,230,236,254,279,280,306,
319,334,340

TEELING;

Luke 45,290,307

THOMAS;

George 162

THOMPSON;

John 171,272,321,322

THORNS;

Stephen W. 163,203
William 201

THORNTON;

Henry 306
John 267

TIER; (Tyer)

Comfort 298
George 210
John 298
William 298

TIGNAL;

Peter 163

TILGHMAN;

Caleb 86,109,157,316
Ephraim 58,70,133
James 44,86,100,135,145,148,156,
161,162,163,179,183,184,188,192,
194,196,198,199,200,202,207,209,
210,211,213,226,229,230,232,237,
239,242,243,248,253,254,255,256,
257,260,264,266,268,271,274,276,
278,280,282,283,286,287,288,289,
291,295,297,301,309,310,316,318,
332,337
John 105

Joseph 59,86
Richard 276
Sally 109,123
William H. 109,123,316,318

TIMMONS;

Andesiah 267
Annanias 220,328
Bassitt 36,44
Benjamin 29,51,237,259,260,261
Elijah 220,244
Esau 244
Esme 201
Isaac 244
Jesse 2,61,220,328
John 60,259,261,267
Lemuel 208,237,259,260,261,267
Martha 292,318
McKimmey 237,259,260,261,267
Nancy 312,313,318
Nehemiah 220,235
Stephen 36,292,318
Thomas 36,44,201,235,237,259,
260,261,267,312,318

TINDALL; (Tindell,Tindle,Tindel)

Isaac 14
John 98
Samuel 245.295

TINGLE;

Caleb 101,102
Caty 139
Daniel 11,12,89,95,99,100,110,
143,149,164,174,177,191,285,324
Elizabeth 281
Ezekiel 11,12
James 139
John 4,26,101,102,240
William 9,11,49,83,147,277,281,
285

TOADVINE;

Henry 224,291
Hetty 128,131,134
Isaac 224,226,230,291,295,310,
338
Isaiah 125,126,128,131,134
James 247,249,256,265,291
(cont.)

(Toadvine cont.)
Jesse 291
John 233,248,260,273,295,310, 314,338
Matthias O. 256,265
Nancy R. 229
Nelly 134,247,249
Outten 101,111,125,153,229,247, 248,260,273,295,310
Priscilla 211,274
Purnell 101,111,125,153,211, 260,273,274
Rhoda 229
Sarah 314
Stephen 125,126,128,131,134
William 101,111,125,153,260, 273,291

TOWNSEND;

Anna 6
Barclay 59,210,228
Betsy 99
Charles 22,58
Covington (Coventon) 124,198,211
Denwood 58
Eleanor 36,75,79,99,330
Elias 91,104
Elijah (Eli) 217,231,259,267, 271,278,282,306
Eliza 36
Elizabeth 7,32,36,43,49,87
Ephraim 295
Euphemia 70
Gilbert 60
Henry 65
Isaac 328
Israel 333
James 60,102,185,186,199,202
James G. 329
Jane 75,79,94,96,99,132,136, 140,142,148,172
Jenny 36
Jesse 205,245,257,281,291,335
John 8,29,45,57,92,171,185,186, 195,233,251
John A. 25,54,55,67,96,102,110, 185,186,238,251,259
John H. 267
Joshua 42,102,199,267,278,282
Lazarus 59,60,61
Leah 25,54,79,80,110,112
Lemuel 265
Levi 4,57,236

Levin 6,7,13,32,36,43,49,55,58, 59,60,70,71,75,79,80,87,94,95,96, 97,99,112,136,137,142,148,170, 267,271,313,317,329,330
Luke 20,143,155,199,209,216,225, 240,259,271,283,294,311,338
Major 57,102
Maria 36,75,79,94,96,99,132,136, 140,142,148,172
Mary 58,265,268
Matilda 36,75,79,94,96,99,132, 136,137,140,142,148,172
Milby 104
mrs. 57,58,59
Nancy 91
P. 93
Peter 60,339
Rives R. 59
Sally 3,6,75,79,94,96,99,132, 136,137,140,142,148,172
Sarah 36,61
Solomon 50,57,77,282
Stephen 189,193,265,295,304,310, 332,338
Susanna 231,259,267,271,278,282
Teackle 317
Thomas 217
William 3,6,13,41,59,60,79,210, 228,236,238,265,268,273,282,291, 301,318,337
William B. 143
Zadok 18,57,112,308,318

TRACY; (Tracey, Tacey)

Arthur 30,42,127,166,190,239, 264,278,295,310,315,323
Sarah 264,278,295,310,323

TRADER; (Trayder)

Henry 257
James 76
John 76
Jonathan 76
Joshua 26,33
Purnell 33,281
Sarah 33

TREHERN; (Trahearn, Trayhearn)

James 42,57,220,221
Samuel 275
William 60,78

TRIPPE;

James 57,125,126,131,150,151,
154,156,157,158,159,322

TRUITT;

Anne 23,25,27
Belitha 73
Betty 60,88,214,278
David 263,305,324
David L. 289,317
Denny 58
Edward 27
Elizabeth 23,25,27,319
Er 199,298,237,238,308,339
George 18,19,21,28,37,38,58,69,
71,80,91,115,206,218,241,294,
301,305,329
Henrietta (Henny) 319
James 100,214,269,278,320
John 162,301,319
John K. 108,145,155,286,311,319
John P. 60
Joseph 295,297,339
Joshua 5
Joshua D. 299
Kellam 58
Kendal 328
Leah 258
Lemuel 294,320
Levinia 25,27
Littleton 87,88,91
Margaret 58
Martha 320
Mary 44,68,286,311,319
Matthias 87,88,91
Molly 320
mrs. 60,248
Nehemiah 108,328
Outten 91
P. 28
Patey 18,208
Peter 23,46,58,224,229,230,251,
270,317,324
Polly 269
Riley 208,306,311
Robert 162,200,298
Rownds 25,27
Sally 69
Samuel 155,253,278
Sarah 206,237
Tabitha 5
Thomas 87,88,91

William 58,60,73,107,108,208,
278,317
William B. 339
William C. 301

TUBBS;

James 10,173,176,182
John 10
Joseph 2,66,68,77
Kendal 2
Littleton D. 163
Moses 10
Sally 2,66,77
Samuel 170,311
William 311

TULL;

Andrew 38,55,103
Benjamin 59,77
Hannah 25
Isaac 56
James 105,187,288
John 19,25,56,100,166,187,199,
201,268
Peter 60
Samuel 187,229,232,253
Solomon 189,291
Thomas 269
Thomas M. 218,258,259,287

TUNNELL;

Charles 9
John 29,37,39,44,47,57,66,101,
240
Mary 47,66

TURNELL; (Tunnell?, Turner?)

Betsy 282

TURNER;

George 126
Henry 58,138,253
Jackson 15,57,61,96,123,124,160,
210,266,271,277,278,323,331,332
Philip 253
Polly 17,21,23
Sally 18,21,23,126
Samuel 16

(cont.)

(Turner cont.)
Sarah   126
Shadrack M.   16
Thomas   4
Walter   138
William   58

TURNWELL;

John   18
Thomas   18

TURPIN;

Anne (Anny)   3,61,69,73,93,111,
122,125,150
Elijah   278
John   3,12,20,24,48,61,62,65,67,
69,73,93,98,101,111,122,125,150
Sewell   1,3,24,29,54,61,62,65,76,
79,82,87,89,91,98,101,109,111,
122,123,133,148,152,213,215,221,
225,230,256,257,295,300,340
William   65,67,111,125,150,337

TWIGG;

Benjamin   51
Samuel   51
William   51

TWILLEY; (Twilly)

George   167

TYER (See Tier)

TYLER;

Levin   23

UMSTED;

J.   188
John   56

UPSHUR;

James   288
Susanna   288

VALANCE;

William   59

VANCE;

George   180
William   130

VANDOME; (Wandum?)

Edward   116,119

VEASEY; (Vesey, Vezey, Veasy)

William   195,256,285

VENABLES;

William   313

VERNETSON;

Elias   317
Mary A.   317
Sally   317
William   293,317

VESEY, VEZEY (See Veasey)

VICTOR;

James   92,95,199
Thomas   57,81

VINCENT; (Vinson?)

George   87
Gillis P.   87

VINSON; (Vincent?)

Elijah (Eli)   160,269,283
Isaac   269,283

WAGGAMAN;

Henry   317

WAILS; (Wailes, Wales)

Benjamin   12,274
Betsey   304
Daniel   213,258,264,304,338
Elizabeth   304
William H.   274

WAINRIGHT; (Winright)

George 73

WAIT;

Absolom 158

WALEA;

William 304,317,325

WALES (See Wails)

WALEY (See Whaley)

WALKER;

Edward 100
James 180
John 46,51

WALLER;

Esme 12

WALLOP;

John 58

WALSTON;

Boaz (Booz) 19,23,26,27,42,51,
52,53,56,63,67,73,74,79,83,176,
289,306,311,313,332,337,339
Charles 61
David S. 296

WALTER;

Isaac 163
John 2,285,286,295,322

WALTON;

Anne 51,52,62,64,74
Elizabeth 21
Fisher 62
William 276,296,299

WANDUM; (Vandome?)

George 176
John 176

WARD;

David 60
Esther 68
James 146,149,156,165,167,168,
169,187,188,190,192,193,200,214,
237,256,264,268,274,277,287
Jesse 68,103
John 15,23,104,125,138,146,149,
167,168,214
John B. 256
Lilla 68
Lydia 287
Richard 29,57,95,199,208
William 208

WARE;

Attalanta (Lanty) 115
Charles 63
Hugh 115
Polly 58

WARREN;

Elizabeth 97,104,113,171
Isaac 18,43,44,61
John 71
Littleton T. 147
Lydia 71
Mary 18,43,44
Matthias 97,104,113,171,172,314,
315,340
P. 116
Sally 147
Selby 240
W. 324

WARRENTON; (Warrington)

Isaac 63,226,238
John 179
Polly 226,238
William 278,282

WARTERS (See Waters)

WARWICK;

Elinor 14,126
William 14
William R. 126

WATERS; (Warters)

Anne 124
Esther 7,16
Isaac 72
James 192
James B. 210,227
Jesse 123,124,125
John 148,238
Littleton 159
Patrick 7,14,16,58,60,72,132,
153,159,171,174,182,220,221,241,
244,248,277,290,294,298,329,330
Peter 7,16,28,46,153,170,192,221
Polly 124

WATSON;

David 163
James 322
Jehu 295,322
John 122
Jonathan 18,60,167
Jonathan W. 167
Levin 280,282,339
Mary 166
Nancy 156
Rebecca 122,125,132
Sophia 122
West 122,125,132,253
William 155,322

WEATHERLY;

Littleton 245

WEBB;

Esme 50
Hannah 278
John 4,50,161,173
Kendall 76
Thomas 44,68,76

WELBOURN; (Welbern, Welburn)

David 257
Drummond 306
William 257

WEST;

Henrietta (Henny) 281

WESTLAKE; (See Lake)

Anne 172
Benjamin 172

WHALEY; (Waley)

Peter 328,334,336,337,340
Seth 65,72,77,96,171,181,207,
208,212,221,244,258,263,331
Thomas 87

WHEELER; (Whelar)

Elisha 42
Henry 193,199,213
Jacob 193,199,213
Job 193,199,213
John 144,145,155
Major 193,199,213
Margaret 306
Margaret B. 193,199
Mary 193,199
Patty 193,199,200,202,213,222,
264,265,306
William 211,289
Zadok 7,9,139,193,200,202,222,
264,265,306

WHITE;

Ambrose 230,239,243,244,247,249,
254,255,277,285,297,311,321,322
Barcley 3,10,16,71,105,138
dr. 86
Eliza 183,207,212,221,244,258,
263
George 103,141
Henry 1,10,16,21,23,30,33,96,
105,123,138,188,278,297
Henry L. 313
Jacob 41,100,111,114,115,129,
137,164,203,215,245,254,258,324
John 10,14,28,30,58,60,79,100,
236
John J. 258,276,282,286,298,306,
326,331
Joshua 3,10,16,105,138
Major 33,56,87,103,244
Martha 183
Nathaniel 207,244
Peter 8,10,14,16,21,23,30,61,96,
105,124,138,278
(cont.)

(White cont.)
Priscilla 243
S. 58
Sally 271
Sarah 119
Southy 10,30,236
Stephen 31,42,87,100,106,111,
157,188,274,279,296,297
Thomas 296
William 10,16,71,105,138,244,
296,311
William S. 282

WHITTINGHAM;

Heber 23,26
Samuel 23
William 207,225,235

WHITTINGTON;

John 3,6,12,49,94,268
John N. 9,65
Southey 3,61,69,73,93,122
W. 254
William 9,52,57,80,116,119,128,
144,171,263,267,272,290,321

WILKINS;

Leah 134,139
Nathaniel 134,136,139,140,141,
162

WILKINSON;

Levin 336

WILLEY;

Capril 160

WILLIAMS;

Caleb 131,139,155,166,245,315,
316
Edward 245
Eli 188,337
Ezekiel 225
Henrietta 20,45,48,61
Isaac 63,64,69,84,94,95,237
J. J. 341
Jacob 188

John 5,12,20,24,30,55,56,61,63,
74,77,80,86,100,113,124,148,156,
178,236,245,254,265,268,271,319,
321,322
John B. 264,325
John J. 4,5,38,45,48,100,125,
150,174,254,288,319,322,333,334,
337
Joshua D. 188
Joyce 188
Kendal 240,287,291
mrs. 57
Peggy 64,94,95
Presgrave 61
Price 237
Risdon H. 337
Samuel (Sam) 61,245
Sarah 63
Solomon 61
T. N. 245
Thomas 185,322
Thomas N. 2,3,9,10,12,15,18,19,
23,26,30,38,41,43,51,52,56,62,63,
64,71,73,78,84,86,92,93,95,99,
100,104,110,112,113,114,115,120,
123,125,128,129,134,137,139,148,
150,153,154,155,157,160,161,162,
166,172,174,175,178,179,181,183,
187,188,190,191,192,198,201,207,
210,211,212,216,217,227,230,232,
235,239,241,242,243,254,255,258,
260,261,262,267,268,277,279,282,
284,285,286,287,291,292,295,297,
299,300,301,302,306,310,313,314,
315,316,321,322,324,327,328,330,
332,333,337

WILLIAMSON;

L. P. 341
mr. 314
Stuart 181,191,204,206,245,314,
341,342
William 314,341,342
Zipporah 341
Zipporah P. 341

WILLIS; (Williss)

Belitha 311
Betty 207
Elijah 16,239,308
Jabez 59,60
(cont.)

(Willis cont.)
James   51,61,100
John   113
Tubman   308,332
William   60,213,283,308,332,334

WILSON;

Ann D.   330
David   12
E. K.   171,259,260,278,321
Ephraim   58
Ephraim K.   28,44,45,46,65,69,70,
94,98,116,128,144,153,160,166,
168,170,174,182,195,199,207,210,
223,226,235,236,241,248,251,254,
267,283,297,319,320
James   116,164
James P.   13,28

WIMBROUGH;

Richard   97

WINDER;

Lev.   290,307
William   22,25,28,30,31,32,42,43,
53,54,67,73,93,99,106,139,140,
153,157,160,161
William H.   24,25,185

WINRIGHT (See Wainright)

WISE;

Betsy   57,171,275
Ezekiel   22,25,322
George   59
John   24,111
Mary   275
Mitchell   59
Molly   60
Sally   58
Sarah   125
Tabitha   25,58,131,214

WOLDRIDGE;

Thomas   306

WONNELL;

James   64,164,266,277

WORRELAW; (Worrilaw)

John   67,78

WRIGHT;

Abel   60
Attalanta   1,42,89,90,206
Betsy   142
Betty   144,168
Elizabeth   98,101,102,145,168,214
Hezekiah   98,101,102,145,168,214,
294
John   1,13,48,58,59,64,89,90,137,
294
Lanta   13,64
Nancy   1,89,90
Robert   1,89,90,108,142,162,181
Sampson   142,144,168
Turbot   179,206,210,322
William   214,254,259,340

YOUNG;

Bailey (Bayly)   29,36,50,125,223,
228,262,271,288
Daniel   60
John   36,211,216
Joseph   36,50,86,218,258,259,283,
295,310,332,337
Littleton   216
Milby   29,36

INDEX TO SLAVES

Abel   93,95,130,131,133,165,234, 333,334
Abner   80,81,166,183,221,264, 271,333,334
Abraham   72,140,141,160,175,217, 225,254
Abram   97,104,174,337
Adah   287
Adam   34,48,333
Alice (Alse)   159,210
Allen   130,201,217,230
Amanda   161,177
Amilla   166
Amos   20,126,332
Amy   120,230,239,245,337
Ann   271
Arnell   97,104,174
Arnold   256,271,321,324
Attalanta   34
Augusta   287
Ballard   188
Bathsheba   205
Beck   289
Belinda   63
Belitha   271
Benjamin (Ben)   97,120,159,174, 323
Betsy   298
Betty (Bett)   66,84,99,120,130, 160,165,175,217,321,333,334
Bill   160,267,305
Bob   20,71,99,114,116,117,124, 130,133,160,161,166,175,177,201, 202,217,230,245,271,274,318
Bowden   111
Bridgett   5,114,120
Brista (Briston)   183,288,292
Burton   217
Caezar   20,134,159,183,321,324
Caleb   32,73,120,134,137,166,175, 188,191,200,213,230,245,271,312
Capril   130,201
Cartshala   111
Charles   73,99,114,116,117,175, 191,217,230,245,282,299
Charity   78
Charlotte   130

Chloe   97,130,166,210
Clary   201
Clem   242
Comfort   44,73,93,111,124,130, 138,160,161,166,175,177,183,191, 225,230,239,245,254,268,271,286, 321,337
Cook   217
Cool   10
Cosmo (Cosmose)   166,271
Cudge   64
Custis   165
Daniel   10,15,20,120,126,130,201, 230,239,284,337
Dareus   217,230
Darkey   175
David   35,62,134,210,217,239
Davis   230
Dick   20
Dinah (Diner, Dinia)   20,43,66, 73,84,93,95,120,166,183,188,271, 287,318
Doll   166
Dover   44
Draper   157,160,175
Ebben   164,166,217,225,230,239, 249,271,321,326
Ebby   160,175
Edey (Eade)   147,299
Elijah   10,78,97,104,135,160,174, 177,183,230,240,305,337
Elijaham   217
Elisa   174
Ells   257,280
Elsa   239
Elsey   230
Esther   11,14,20,24,38,61,66,93, 99,130,134,137,142,160,166,175, 183,198,201,206,225,233,245,267, 271,272,305,336,341
Euphemia   48
Fanny   97
Flora   27,131,287
Francis   165
Frank   160,175,271,290
Frederick   128
Gatty   114,133,134,139,161,177

(Slaves cont.)
Gedian 336
George 66,73,84,97,99,104,116,
117,120,125,143,150,166,174,175,
183,191,211,234,243,245,254,267,
271,281
Ginny 288
Grace 66,84,114,183
Greg 123
Guy 20
Hagar 73,175,191
Handy 66,84,174,217,254,271,
321,324
Hannah 10,87,123,160,165,183,
196,198,206,225,230,238,239,258,
280,281
Harriott 225
Harry 52,99,112,124,126,147,189,
198,200,217,233,257,267,279,280,
337
Hector 73,88
Henny 93,160,175,183,184,217,305
Henry 3,72,198,221,264
Hess 116,117,230,239
Hester 165
Hetty (Hetta) 10,92,114,133,
175,183,191,243,245,271,274
Honis 217
Hooper 160
Hope 97,104,120,174
Huldah (Huldy) 97,104,174,206,
321,324
Isaac 10,34,47,62,63,73,93,97,
106,148,175,177,183,191,230,234,
245,321,324,332,337
Israel 230,239
Jack 20,66,84,93,95,123,183,271
Jacob 10,27,84,95,120,133,142,
160,165,175,230,238,239,245,267,
304,336,337
Jake 217,254
James 10,20,72,97,99,120,135,
149,160,166,175,199,217,221,230,
242,264,322,332,333,334
Jane (Jany) 10,34,114,123,129,
192,334
Jasper 126
Jenny 64,99,134,230,245,281,333
Jep 130
Jesse (Jess) 116,117,120,160,
166,175,201,230,333,334
Jim 198,271
Jinny 165,186
Job 51,120,165

Joe 34
John 73,159,165,175,191,243,245
Joice 271
Joseph 336
Joshua 130,321,324
Jude 183,221,264
Kate 160
Kendal 271
Keziah 125,150
Kellam (Killiam) 210,212
Lambert 271
Lanta (Lanty, Linty) 10,111,130,
201,245,330,332
Lavina 321,324
Leah 35,62,72,74,87,92,111,120,
165,175,177,183,186,198,230,242,
244,257,271,280,281,312,333,334
Lear 299
Leges (Ledge,Lige) 66,123,124,
135
Leonard 242
Levin 21,34,38,55,66,72,84,106,
111,114,116,117,120,129,133,134,
138,148,160,165,166,175,191,206,
210,217,230,245,258,305,321,324
Lewis 217,321,324
Liddy 20,165
Limon (Limos, Limas) 16,123,124,
217
Linda (Lindy,Leandon) 72,99,143,
160,166,238,257,280,294
Lish 133
Littleton (Litt) 34,47,61,80,
138,183,217,230,239,245,299,321,
324
Lott 166,187,245,271
Lotty 254
Lovey (Love) 34,217,230,243
Loyd 217
Lucy 20,69,73,217
Luke 130,201,221,264
Lydia (Lydda,Lidy) 72,166,208,
230,239,271,280,281
Lynes 166
Major 124,161,217,245
Malacha 271
Manuel 120,183
Marcus 321
Margaret 120
Maria 126,217,225,305
Martha 34
Mary 160,175,225,230,271
Milby 48,99,111,120,133,160,175,
183,191,192,217,225,245,279

(Slaves cont.)
Milcah 175
Milly (Milla,Millia) 66,84,97,
104,117,123,166,174,217,245
Mine 245
Mingo 120,183,191
Minty (Minto,Minta,Minter) 20,
25,73,111,116,117,123,175,191,
217,245
Mitchell 294
Molly 330
Monday 159
Moses 106,124,126,165,175,217,
230
Nancy (Nance) 34,73,120,130,
160,175,191,201,206,245,254
Nanny (Nan) 20,110,120,187
Nasa 210
Nathan 159
Ned (Need) 66,84,99,130,142,
201,217,245,271,299,321,324
Nell 230,239
Nice 159,160
Nimrod 120
Noah 165,299,305
Nocker 183
Omey 245
Orris 49
Parker 183
Patience 159,198,275
Patt 230,254
Paul 10
Peggy (Peg) 128,165,183,217,
237,271,305,337
Peregrine 20
Peter 10,52,99,120,198,210,225,
275,305,333,334,335,336
Phillis (Fillis) 5,20,194,198,
217,230,271
Pleasant 10,120,165,175,183
Plem 73,175,191,245
Pool 120,183,191
Preston 198
Priester 34
Primas 321,324
Prince 217
Priscilla (Priss) 10,120,165,225
Quash 166
Rachel 7,73,83,99,106,120,134,
137,142,148,160,165,175,183,191,
217,238,245,280,281,321,324,333,
334
Ralf 165
Reuben 120

Rhoda (Rody) 5,10,47,97,99,104,
174,177,202,271
Richard (Rich) 47,160
Robert 271
Robin 198,321,337
Rose (Ross) 10,130,165,201,230,
233,264,299
Rummey 134
Sabro 20,93,237
Sacker (Sacre) 99,230,239
Sally (Sall) 10,20,111,112,124,
130,238,271,321
Sambo 20,123
Sampson 97
Samuel (Sam) 35,120,183,210,221,
258,264,271,280,281,310,338
Sandy 43,172,305
Sarah (Sarey) 25,69,73,97,104,
124,126,130,134,135,160,174,175,
183,188,191,198,201,217,230,231,
245,271,280,281,322,341
Satira 230
Saul 160,175,305
Sevron 83
Shadrack 134,137,269
Sinah 20
Sophia 12
Spry 321
Stephen 20,52,68,73,114,120,129,
139,153,160,166,175,183,191,203,
238,243,245,255,269,271,292,296,
321,333,334,336
Susan (Sue) 47,73,165,175,179,
191,245,271,337
Susa 10
Sylvia (Silva,Silviah) 11,99,
143,175,217,230,305
Tabitha (Tab) 34,183,191,217,256
Tally (Tal) 51
Teb 191
Thamer (Tamer) 280,281,305
Thomas (Tom) 20,111,142,186,238,
299
Tite 267
Titus 11,114,129,188,191,305
Tony 10,175,191,245
Usina 130,201
Vinah 210
Whittington 288
William (Will) 35,93,160,175,
225,271
Wise 312
Worcester 321
York 271,305

(Slaves cont.)
Zadok 95,161,177,269

Zeb 73,175,231,245
Zilpah (Zilf) 243,267

INDEX TO FREE NEGROES

NO SURNAME;

Anus 43
Barick 226
Ben 341
Bob 318
Ceazar 60
Charles 271
Comfort 205
Flora 61
George 271
Hope 59
Isaac 271
Jacob 51,231,304
Jesse (Jess) 16,59
Jet 60
John 208,256
Joseph 188
Levin 59,221
Lige 271
Littleton 221
Lydia 208
Meriar 332
Moses 271
Peter 188,205
Planner 211
Rhoda 220,221
Robin 321
Ruben 271
Sampson 41
Sarah 188
Somerset 211
Stephen 231,258,271,282,321
Tabitha 256
Titus 59
William 220

ALLEN;

Dolly 59

AMERICA;

Jacob 169
Leah 169,204
Mandey 204

ARBUCKLE;

James 301

ARMSTRONG;

Benjamin 221
Benjamin L. 88
Betsy 96
Betty 171.221
Esther 150,152
Hannah 88
Harry 96
Jacob 154
Jacob J. 152
James 154,171
Levin 150
Major 331
Peggy 331
Rhoda J. 152
Sarah 154

BALLARD;

Betty 35,152,189
Experience 152
James 152,189
John 152
Peggy 35
Samuel 152

BLAKE;

Handy 298
Hannah 294
Harry 294
James 266
John 327
Levin 266

COLLICK;

Israel 266
Nancy 110,266

(Free Negroes cont.)
COLLINS;

Branson 77
Mary 77

COSTON;

Hagar 208
Sally 208

DAVIS;

Henry 110,266

DICK; (Dicks)

Harry 186
Isaac 182
Jesse 110
Nancy 30,182,186
Nanny 110
Peter 30

DUFFY;

James 165
Levin 238
Zipporah (Zippy) 165,238

FISHER;

Jack 60
John 213
Joshua 59
Patience 288
Peter 288

GINN;

Barsheba 309
Elijah 296,298
Henry 298,305
Jacob 289
Littleton 296,309
Robert 336
Sarah 305,336

HALL;

Patrick 324
Rachel 324

HANDY;

Harry 94
Jenny 94
Susanna 94

HARMON; (Harman)

Betsy 154,195
Betty 195
Daniel 81
Esther 81
George 195
Henry 81
Jacob 186
James H. 189
Leah 186
Mary 154
Polly 189
Samuel H. 189
Stephen 186

HEATH;

Levin 208

HUTT;

George 192
Levin 192

ISAACS;

Amey 192
Bridget 129
Esau 159
Esther 129
George 161
Henry 297
Isaac 158
Middlesex 158,159

ISHMAEL; (Ismael)

Harriot 209
Joshua 208
Samuel 208
Sophia 208,209

JACKSON;

Stephen 45

(Free Negroes cont.)
JACOBS;

Henry 297

JOHNSON; (Jonson)

Esther 77
Harry 104
Isaac 156
Sovereign 156
Stephen 77
Tabitha 110
William 110

JONES;

James 8
Jemima 8
John 8
Leonard 8
Levin 8

LONG;

Barick 226
Milly 226

MARSHALL;

Leah 148

MILLER;

George 243

McGATH;

Milly 56
Nancy 56
Rhoda 56

PARSONS;

Levin 243

PETERS;

George 1
Robert 162

POSTLY;

Jacob 333
Job 333

PRICE;

Amey 270
George 339
John 270
Josiah 259
Leah 259
Littleton 289
Rachel 339

PURNELL;

Azariah 59
Jacob 58

REED;

Peter 91,152
Rachel 91,152

RIGGEN;

Jacob 147
Ned 331
Peter 147

ROACH;

John 208

ROBERTS;

Betty 195
Eli 195
Esther 195
Moses 195

ROWND;

Stephen 251

SAMPLES;

Richard 268

SELBY;

Peter 303
Rachel 303

(Free Negroes cont.)
SHRIEVES; (Shries)

Edmund B. 294
Nancy 294

SPENCE;

Ephraim 60
George 60

STEVENS;

Ayres 238
Eliza 322
Littleton 322
Nancy 238

TAYLOR;

Lina 18
Ned 18

WATSON;

Caleb 51
John 317

WILLIAMS;

Benjamin 333

WILSON;

Tom 58

WRIGHT;

John 204

INDEX TO INDIANS

NO SURNAME;

Sarah 59,60